THE CIRCLE OF THE DANCE

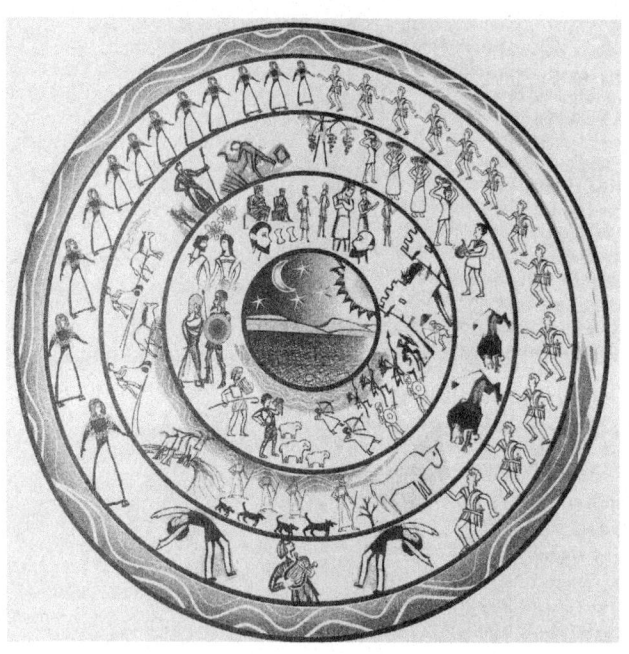

*Achilles' Shield, Odysseus' Oar,
Calypso's Axe, and the New Golden Age*

Alex Homer Jack

AMBER WAVES PRESS

The Circle of the Dance
By Alex Homer Jack

© 2018 by Alex Homer Jack

All rights reserved. Printed in the United States of America.
First Edition.

For further information on special sales, mail-order sales, wholesale distribution, translations, foreign rights, contact the publisher: Amber Waves, PO Box 487, Becket MA 01223 • (413) 623-0012 shenwa26@yahoo.com

ISBN 13 - 978-1722409951
ISBN 10 - 1722409959

10 9 8 7 6 5 4 3 2 1

For Bettina

"To the Fairest"

CONTENTS

Introduction: Mythic Roots	6

The Iliad

1. The Sleep of Bronze	28
2. Achilles' Shield	47
3. The Grain-Giving Earth	67

The Odyssey

4. The Long Way Home	85
5. Plowlands Kind with Grain	109
6. Odysseus's Oar	125

The New Golden Age

7. Calypso's Butterfly Axe	154
8. Return to Paradise	176
9. Gently Down the Stream	197

Appendices

	202
A. The Spiral of History	203
B. Homeric Recipes	213
C. Journey to Atlantis	
	224
Glossary	228
Bibliography	230
Acknowledgments	231
Index	232
About the Author	254

Introduction
MYTHIC ROOTS

Growing up with a father named Homer awakened me to myth, legend, and epic poetry at an early age. Not only did he share the name of the ancient Hellenistic poet, but also my dad was born in Greece, N.Y., just outside of Rochester, and studied at Cornell University in Ithaca, named after the site of Odysseus's homeland. He then even lived and taught in Athens for a year on the eve of World War II. Like the ancient Greek hero, my father liked to wrestle or "roughhouse" with my sister and me. Lucy, born two years later, was fascinated with owls, the totem of Athena, goddess of wisdom, whose fierce devotion to the truth, she embodied.

I did not have a middle name growing up, but on my eighteenth birthday chose Homer as my middle name when I applied for a Social Security card. My father had taken Alexander (his father's name) as a middle name, and I decided to continue the tradition. In the years since, I rarely used it, and only now, while writing this book, did I realize it also resonated with the putative author, or authoress, of the Homeric epics. For the first time in my literary career, it appears on the cover of one of my books.

In the 1950s, as minister of the Unitarian Church in Evanston, Illinois, my father led integration efforts throughout the Chicago area and ultimately the nation. Homer befriended a young Baptist minister in Birmingham, Martin Luther King, Jr., to whom he helped introduce Gandhian principles of nonviolence. Devoted to the highest ideals, my father liked nothing more than triumphing in verbal combat over modern day Scyllas and Charybdises on both the left and right whose monstrous ideologies could give rise to a Stalin or a Hitler. At the Community Church in New York City, where he served as guest minister in the summer of 1953, he preached a famous sermon: "Is McCarthy a Concealed Communist?" Like Homer's wily seafarer, my father was heavy-set, short-tempered, resourceful, and fearless in pursuing his goals. But he treated his elders and senior colleagues kindly—Norman Thomas, Dr. Schweitzer, Prime Minister Nehru, Albert Einstein—as Odysseus revered his father Laertes and his mentor Nestor. Growing up I experienced him more as a warrior, albeit a nonviolent one, than a bard or priest. At the end of his life, as an internationally renowned leader on religion and peace, he completed the circle, leaving his autobiography unfinished, which I completed and published as *Homer's Odyssey: My Quest for Peace and Justice*.

My mother, Esther Williams, also had a given name that hearkened back to the ancient world. Her namesake, Queen Esther, foiled the Persian king and saved the children of Israel, a feat commemorated in Purim. As a Unitarian, my mother taught the Bible as literature in Sunday school, not divine scripture, and the myths, legends, and teachings in the Old and New Testaments formed another major influence in my life. There was also a Greek resonance with my mother. She was fair-haired and glamorous like Esther Williams, the movie star and swimmer, who had an identical first and last name. Because of her striking appearance and graceful nature, as a child I always felt she was the most beautiful woman in the world—a trait I would later identify with Helen of Troy.

My own introduction to the classics began in the third grade. In class, we read a small introduction to the Greek myths and an entirely new world opened up. I was surprised to learn that Alexander—my first name and also Greek in origin—was another name of Paris, the Trojan shepherd and prince who had given the Golden Apple inscribed "To the Fairest" to Aphrodite and eloped with Queen Helen. Until then the only Alexander I knew was Alexander the Great, the conqueror, whose blood-soaked legacy didn't appeal to me.

Passage to the East
Beside Greek mythology, I was attracted to Far Eastern philosophy and culture. On the eve of my twelfth birthday, Homer took me to Japan. While my father attended an international ban-the-bomb conference in Tokyo, I spent days with a Japanese family with children my own age. In Hiroshima and Nagasaki, we visited survivors of the atomic bombing, including a ward of children my own age who still suffered from radiation sickness many years later. Their plight made a lasting impression on me. When I returned home to Evanston, I accompanied my father on a long peace march against nuclear testing in Chicago. A couple years later, our family moved to the New York metropolitan area where Homer served as a founder and executive director of SANE, the peace organization that led the campaign for nuclear disarmament. Thanks to the behind-the-scenes

diplomacy of Norman Cousin's, another founder of SANE, President Kennedy and Chairman Khrushchev concluded the partial nuclear test ban treaty in 1963 and put the first brakes on the escalating Cold War.

In college, I spent a junior year abroad in Benares, India, the holy city of Hinduism, studying religion and philosophy. I became vegetarian, primarily for ethical reasons, and the appalling conditions of modern factory farming only made me more convinced than ever that this was the right choice. My fieldwork project during the year was a study of the *Bhagavad Gita* and its teachings on war and peace. The *Gita*, the most popular Hindu scripture, was part of the *Mahabharata*, a poetic chronicle of the Great Bharata War. It was nearly as old as the *Iliad* and *Odyssey* to which it shared many parallels. Like Achilles, Prince Arjuna, the hero of the *Gita*, throws down his weapons and refuses to fight. Like Odysseus, Yudhisthira, Arjuna's elder brother and leader of the Pandava clan, embarks on a homeward journey in which the virtues of domesticity and peace, including a balanced vegetarian diet, triumph over the warrior's code of conquest and vengeance.

Less than a year after coming home from India, I returned to Asia as a foreign correspondent for the *Oberlin Review*, the student newspaper, and a syndicate of college, university, and small town publications. Because of my peace orientation, I gravitated to the Buddhist community, often visiting the School for Social Work on the outskirts of Saigon founded by Thich Nhat Hanh, who was then living in exile in Paris. A young Buddhist nun who befriended me tragically immolated herself during my stay, leaving me some of her poems. In the heart of Saigon, I also discovered, a secret hospital ward of children severely injured by napalm and white phosphorus dropped by American planes. Such experiences engraved the terror and horror of war on my mind. Like the black death spirits that shrouded the eyes of countless Achaeans and Trojan men, women, and children, including Astyanax, Hector and Andromache's infant son, the furies of the war in Southeast Asia maimed a generation of Vietnamese and Americans.

The highlight of my tour of duty in Vietnam was meeting Thich Tri Quang, a Zen Master and spiritual leader of the nation. Tri Quang was then in his early forties and had already inspired street demonstrations that had brought down several previous regimes. The year before in Hue, the holy city in Central Vietnam, South Vietnamese troops with American air cover, slaughtered four thousand of his followers. He had fled south and sought sanctuary in the An Quang Pagoda in Cholon, Saigon's sister city. As a Pentagon-accredited journalist, I was able to arrange an interview and enter the temple which was surrounded by government tanks.

My first impression when I arrived at the pagoda was that Tri Quang was the most radiant person I had every met. He glowed and seemed to have an aura like the dynamic leaders and holy men in the ancient Indo-European epics. The first half of our interview covered the usual political, social, and cultural aspects of the conflict. At one point, he asked me what I thought would happen in his country. I told him that I had just come back from an aircraft carrier off the coast of North Vietnam that was bombing Hanoi and Haiphong every day, and some of the pilots had confided to me that there were nuclear weapons secretly stored on board. Of course, this was electrifying news because Southeast Asia was nuclear-free. For either of the superpowers to introduce atomic bombs in the region constituted a dangerous provocation. To this report, Tri Quang replied that he had heard through the grapevine from the north that the Soviets had stationed tactical nuclear weapons in North Vietnam.

"Aren't you afraid this will lead to nuclear war and World War III through miscalculation, computer accident, or design?" I inquired.

"Of course, that's a real possibility," Tri Quang nodded in agreement. "But there is something far worse than nuclear war."

When he spoke these words, the room where we were talking and sipping tea seemed to spin and dissolve. Time slowed down and stopped, as I tried to wrap my mind around the notion that there could be something worse than nuclear war. As a child born two weeks after the atomic bombings in August 1945, as a visitor to Hiroshima and Nagasaki on my twelfth birthday, and as an ordinary American who knew that ICBMs—Hercules, Nike Zeus, and others named after the Greek gods and heroes—could destroy the country in a matter of minutes, I was thunderstruck by his remarks.

"I beg your pardon," I finally replied. "What could be worse than World War III?"

"The rice," he replied thoughtfully.

Again, I had no idea what he was talking about. "What about the rice?" I asked.

"Alex, you have to understand that Vietnam is a small, non-industrialized country," he explained. "We have been the target of invaders for thousands of years. China, the Mongols, Japan, France, and now America. We are very good at survival. If the Communist North wins the war, they will unify the country violently, but life will go on, as it does for Buddhists today in the north. Similarly, if the Americans win the war, the multinational corporations will come in, destroy our environment, and continue to support an authoritarian state. But life will continue and eventually things will improve.

"However, because of the bombings, chemicals, and defoliants, Vietnam's rice fields have been destroyed, and we can no longer grow our own food," he said, reaching his peroration. "For the first time in our thousands year history, Vietnam is dependent on food from abroad. The rice we eat today comes from your president's country." By this he meant Texas, President Lyndon Johnson's home state.

"That rice is not alive," he continued, explaining that it was 100% polished white rice. The germ, bran, and other key layers with essential energy and nutrients had been removed, rendering it a lifeless food.

"This will mark the end of my country," he went on. "Food is the foundation of life. It not only quells our hunger and gives us energy, but it also creates our health and well-being. Every level of society, from the family to art, culture, and religion depends on the quality of the food we eat. If nuclear war breaks out, your country, Europe, Russia, Japan, and other industrialized regions of the world will be annihilated. Many Vietnamese will also die from radioactivity, but some will survive, and life will go on. But if the underlying quality of our food and agricultural system is destroyed, that is the end. We will never recover. That is what worries me most about the war in Southeast Asia."

I had never considered such a deep teaching about food and human destiny before. In that era, the basic connection between food and health was widely unrecognized. Everyone thought the modern diet, high in meat, poultry, and other animal food, was the best the world had ever produced and that the only nutritional diseases were those of malnutrition and vitamin deficiency. To most scientists, nutritionists, physicians, and the general public, the idea that a high-protein, high-fat diet could lead to heart disease, cancer, or diabetes was preposterous. For me, becoming vegetarian was not related to health and vitality, but to morality and nonviolence. For the first time, I learned that food—the domain of Demeter, goddess of the harvest—was integral to social destiny and even spiritual development. It was a revelation.

After returning from Vietnam, I settled in Boston, where my parents had moved, and appeared on radio and TV shows talking about my experiences in Vietnam, wrote articles for *Vietnam Summer News* (a publication of the growing peace movement), and founded the New England Resistance with several colleagues. We plastered Harvard, MIT, B.U., Brandeis, Yale, and other New England campuses with posters inviting young men to "Bust the Draft" and organized a rally on Boston Common on October 16, 1967 featuring Howard Zinn and Noam Chomsky. We expected a few hundred people; over five thousand came. We then marched to the nearby Arlington Street Church, where we held a service in which young men were invited to turn in their draft cards to a priest, rabbi, and minister. Others elected to burn their Selective Service cards on the altar over the candlestick of William Ellery Channing, the great nineteenth century abolitionist who was minister of the church. We expected a handful of resisters to come forward since noncooperation carried a stiff penalty: up to 5 years in federal prison and a heavy fine. Again our estimates were woefully low. Nearly 350 young men came down the aisle. The spontaneous display of mass civil disobedience electrified the nation. It energized the peace movement and led to the landmark trial of Dr. Spock and Rev. William Sloane Coffin, our keynote speaker, as the government sought to stifle dissent. As draft resistance spread across the country, active conscription ended, never to be resumed. Achilles and Odysseus, who unsuccessfully tried to avoid being drafted to fight in Troy as young men and later learned the futility of war during ten years of combat and self-reflection in Hades, would have been proud.

That autumn, I enrolled in Boston University School of Theology. I decided to follow in the footsteps of my father and grandfather and become a Unitarian minister. Though most of my time was taken up with peace activities, I majored in biblical studies and wrote a term paper on the *Song of Songs*. I started a seminary newsletter *Up Against the Cross*, investigating the ties of the university to defense research and encouraging the faculty and students to speak out on the war, racial injustice, and other burning issues. Despite widespread draft resistance across the nation, pouring of blood over Selective Service files, and other acts of civil disobedience, the war in Southeast Asia continued to rage.

In our next step to blunt the conflict, my associates and I organized a sanctuary for soldiers who didn't want to go to Vietnam. In my studies of the bible, the classics, and history, I discovered that from ancient times, churches, temples, and mosques were widely regarded as sacred places where the civil law stopped at the front gate or altar. Practically, this meant that fugitives—including escaped or wanted criminals, heretics and infidels, and others who had fallen afoul of established authority—could seek refuge and be immune from arrest. English law recognized the right of sanctuary from the fourth to the seventeenth century. Thich Tri Quang's asylum in the An Quang Pagoda was a contemporary example. In the Trojan War, Ajax the Lesser abducts Cassandra from Athena's temple where she had taken sanctuary, and Priam, the king of Troy, is killed seeking asylum at the temple of Zeus. These violations of *themis*, or divine order, bring swift retribution from the gods. Most of the Greek fleet is destroyed on its return, and Odysseus's homecoming is delayed ten years.

We introduced sanctuary for soldiers who refused to go to Vietnam at

Arlington Street Church, and it quickly spread to Harvard Divinity School, several areas churches, and eventually nationwide. At Boston University, we granted asylum to a young G.I. who had gone AWOL in protest of the war. For a week at Marsh Chapel, thousands of students joined in nonviolent solidarity with the young soldier, sleeping in the pews, playing music, and holding prayer vigils around the clock. The dean and faculty of the divinity school were shell-shocked. From our perspective, they should have been grateful that the chapel had never been so filled with prayer, dance, and holiness. After the FBI sent a SWAT team into the chapel before sunrise (at "rosy-fingered dawn") one Sunday morning to seize the soldier, the dean of the School of Theology suspended me from school as the ringleader of the demonstration. I felt like Socrates who had been forced to drink hemlock for corrupting the youth of Athens. Fortunately, the example we set lived on. Today entire cities have declared themselves sanctuaries to protect refugees from political oppression and climate change and from arrest as illegal immigrants.

Learning from Yahweh and Elijah

In Boston, I gravitated toward macrobiotics, a way of life synthesizing Eastern and Western teachings. I took a seminar with Michio Kushi, the pioneer of the natural, organic foods movement and leading macrobiotic educator, and to my surprise found he was teaching the same thing as Tri Quang, the Vietnamese Zen master. By now, I was ready for a more comprehensive physical, social, and spiritual approach to food and society and joined the staff of the *East West Journal*, the leading magazine of the counterculture.

As a student of history and literature, I quickly discovered that macrobiotics long predated its modern incarnation as a Japanese dietary philosophy and way of life. Its roots went back to ancient Greece. The first appearance of the word *makrobios*, or "long life," appears in the essays of Hippocrates, who lived about four hundred years after Homer. As the father of medicine, Hippocrates introduced a naturalistic approach to healing that attributed health and sickness to our relationship with the natural world, not with the stars or the Homeric gods. His motto "Let food be thy medicine, and thy medicine be food" was incorporated into the Hippocratic Oath that binds physicians to "give dietetic advice to the best of their ability." It prohibits surgery, potentially deadly drugs, and other extreme measures. These injunctions have been taken out of the modern oath because medicine is no longer oriented in a holistic direction. Instead the innocuous phrase "do no harm" was substituted, though it is not found in the original. Hippocrates's macrobiotic approach to health and well-being is the exact opposite of the medical and healthcare profession today.

As my macrobiotic sojourn began, I married Ann Fawcett, a Unitarian seminarian whom I had dated for several years. She was interested in myth, ritual, and theater. One spring she enrolled me in *Moonshadow*, a skit based on Cat Stevens' song of that name. For a performance in front of Boston University's Marsh Chapel, we made a large papermache head for the lead actor. In Marblehead, the picturesque seaport north of Boston where we lived, I had a dream touching on song and dance that was the supreme mystical experience of my life. In the dream, I was watching a dance exhibition in a large tent thronged with people. A Sufi or yogi of radiant disposition was performing a whirling dance, casting off sheathes of his body to display ever more subtle veils of the soul. Many observers were transfixed by this performance, but I found it annoying and I started to leave. Suddenly, everyone fell prostate to the ground, which vexed me all the more. Curious, I looked up to what had interrupted this gathering, and in awe beheld a wizened little old man watching from on high.

He had a long, white beard, a crown on his head, long flowing robes, and was sitting on a bejeweled throne. Gradually, I realized it was God Almighty right out of the Bible, William Blake's engravings, and a thousand and one evangelical broadcasts on the far end of the radio dial. I, too, instinctively fell immobile to the floor, as waves of blissful energy emanated from His presence to fill every corner of the tabernacle. In this hushed setting, God proceeded to narrate a marvelous history of the universe, taking special care to enumerate the plagues and pestilences regularly sent to humanity over the ages as a result of ignoring or disobeying nature's laws.

At each word Yahweh—the Hebrew Zeus or ruler of heaven—spoke in a deep, resounding voice, we were transported in time and space to experience particular scourges. "And I sent sandstorms . . ." and in a flash I was in the desert, sand blowing so thickly around me I couldn't breathe. "And I sent locusts . . ." And instantly I was inundated with a storm cloud of flying insects.

At length Yahweh explained that He was also the God of mercy, compassion, and forgiveness, as well as judgment, and he bid us to get up off our knees, cooperate with one another, and celebrate life. Soon everyone had forgotten his or her earlier individual, highly esoteric pursuits. All linked arms and formed a circle. As we danced, waves of bliss from the throne intensified, and soon we were lost in pure ecstasy, the distinction between self and other melting away in radiant light.

As we danced in a big circle, I awoke and found myself still filled with oceanic feelings of love from head to toe. It took several days for the visionary energy to subside, and I slowly resumed ordinary consciousness.

A couple years later, I had another transformative experience. Ann and I went out to eat one spring evening to a local Israeli restaurant. It served falafel, hummus, baba ganoosh, pita bread, and other Middle Eastern delicacies. To our disappointment, it was closed. A small handwritten note on the front door explained that it was shut for a religious holiday. As we stood there contemplating where to go instead, the door opened. A man came out, ushered us inside, and quickly bolted the door again. To our amazement, the entire restaurant was filled with people in their finest array, and the banquet tables were heaped with platters of food. We were escorted to the head table and seated as guests of honor like Odysseus washed up on the shore of Scheria and feted by the royal court. We had no clue what was going on! Then it was explained to us that tonight was the Sedar, the festival celebrating the beginning of Passover and the deliverance of the Jews from bondage in Egypt.

For thousands of years, midway through the Sedar festivities, the front door of the tabernacle was opened for a moment to allow the Prophet Elijah to enter and partake of a special cup of wine. As in many ancient myths and legends, it was believed the gods and holy prophets traveled in disguise and took the form of ordinary people. In the Homeric epics, for example, Athena frequently appears as an old man or shepherd to protect or test Achilles and Odysseus. Since Ann and I appeared at the exact moment the door was opened, we were welcomed as Elijah! In addition to wine, we were served all of the other Passover dishes, including appetizers, bitter herbs, and most of all matzah, or unleavened bread. This traditional flat whole-grain bread dated back to the Bronze Age and Moses, who led his people from the land of Pharaoh across the Red Sea to the Wilderness and the Promised Land. The festive evening also featured music and dancing (on tables as well as in a circle around the room), and the joyous thanksgiving for deliverance went on late into the evening.

The experience took me back to my father's Jewish forebears who celebrated Passover for untold generations. Since I was working at *East West Journal* at the time, I was particularly interested in matzah and the largely plant-based items in the meal. In the biblical tradition, Elijah is described as meditating in the desert and fed by ravens that bring him bread every day. The wondrous evening connected me with the past, strengthened my feeling that I was on the right path now with macrobiotics, and inscribed a prophetic mission for the future.

Learning from Animal Messengers

In 1977 the *East West Journal* moved to Brookline, and Ann and I relocated from Marblehead to a large, spacious three-bedroom apartment about a half-mile away. From typesetter, I had climbed the editorial ladder to associate editor and was now writing Scroll, a monthly column on literature, philosophy, and religion. The following summer, we drove out west to Montana in our rebuilt '71 Beetle to attend a ten-day seminar with Joseph Campbell, the mythologist and author of *A Hero with a Thousand Faces*. In the cover story I later wrote for the magazine, I described our destination "Helena—Fair Maiden of the Plains":

> Helena—capital of Montana—stepping-stone for Lewis and Clark's expedition, namesake of the most beautiful woman of Greek mythology—is a city constructed of dreams. In 1864 four despondent prospectors stumbled on what they sardonically termed Last Chance Gulch, only to find gold in what is now the main street of town.
>
> Like the fabled treasure of Troy, ancient juncture of East and West, Helena soon attracted swift-footed Achilleses from the Minnesota logging camps; heavy-boned Ajaxes from behind plows in Nebraska; proud Agamemnons from the wharfs of New York, enchanting Circes from New Orleans, and dutiful Penelopes from Boston.
>
> The heroes and heroines of this new Ilium realized their personal dreams in monumental art and architecture. A gothic Cathedral (a meticulous copy of the Dom in Koln) and Moorish mosque of black and white stone towered over the saloons, corrals, and rail depots of Helena, distinguishing Montana's fair maiden from other capitals and cow towns.
>
> Gold, the magic metal of the sun, transformed and transmuted the divergent mythologies of pioneer America into a single frontier myth of destiny made manifest. In the alchemical melting pot of immigrant imagination, natural feelings of reverence for the new land and its traditional stewards turned to basest stone. To keep open the overland route to Helena (and Oregon to the west), General Custer lost the battle with the Sioux and Cheyenne, but the spirit of Western civilization descended from those Greeks of Troy who won the epic war. Valiant native Hectors fell before advancing mineral aspirations, and at Wounded Knee and countless other battlesites, their Andromaches and Astyanaxes were mercilessly slain or enslaved.
>
> Today Our Fair Lady of the Plains has lost some of her noble form and features: Helena's per capita income is no longer the continent's highest. As elsewhere, hot-rod races, shopping malls, and fast-food franchises form the mythic coastline for would-be Ulysseses. The

Cathedral is now mainly a tourist attraction, the mosque a civic center. Still, in secular form, the archetypal symbols persist. In the political labyrinths of state and the electronic ziggurats of the mass media, the regional barons seek oil, gas, and timber leases like wish-fulfilling gems. Family farms are consolidated into corporate lotus-lands, small businesses swallowed up with Cyclopean gusto, the American Dream lost in a whirlpool between the clashing rocks of petroleum and nuclear energy production.

Yet as in Ireland and India, defeated gods and goddesses have a way of returning and ultimately triumphing over their conquerors. Throughout the New West, like clouds filling up the giant sky, the ghosts of the American Indian hover over the horizon. Below, on earth, beneath the interstates, stretch the dusty trails of self-reliant homesteaders, solitary mountain men and women, religious sectaries, and utopian colonists who have lived in harmony, to one degree or another, with their environment.

Joseph Campbell had long been one of our heroes, and Ann and I were thrilled to go to Montana. But the sudden illness of our aging cat Shakespeare just before we left, almost torpedoed our trip. Entrusting her, at last, to a kindly vet, we departed, like Gilgamesh in quest of Utnapishtim, the wise old man of Sumerian legend, to partake of the waters of mythic life. The seminar was held at the Feathered Pipe Ranch, a small environmentally-conscious community and healing center in the mountains west of Helena. Campbell would lecture two or three times a day for several hours to a rapt group of about twenty participants. We slept in a tipi in the forest and took communal meals with vegetarian options in a spacious lodge.

The overall theme was the unification of opposites, and on the first evening Campbell talked about Navajo mythology and explained that the playful accord between heaven and earth, the inner and the outer, nature and the world of humans, is maintained by animal messengers. Every bird, deer, or fish brings a personal message. Over the next week and a half, Campbell astonished us with his command and insight into Hindu and Buddhist teachings, Jesus's parables, Mohammad's revelations, Ovid's tales, and Arthurian romance. In his view, human culture reached a peak with *Parzival*, the Grail epic composed by Wolfram von Eschenbach in the twelfth century. "Parzival," he explained, "means 'piercing the valley,' going through the middle, neither on this side or that, through Scylla and Charybdis, through good and evil, or whatever you want. At birth, Parzival is piebald, or black and white in complexion. Wolfram is saying that there is no deed that does not have a negative reflex, or aspect. But by favoring the white, we achieve what can be achieved."

Contemporary conflicts, Campbell suggested, can be healed by applying a proper mythological formula to the situation. In terms of male/female relationships, the classical authority he turned to was Homer. "In the *Odyssey*, we have a chap who has been ten years in a man's world where women were just booty. For the length of the war, Odysseus has been taking cities, taking women. He's the big thing, macho in spades. Finally he leaves Troy with his twelve ships, symbolic of the Zodiac, with himself as the solar center, to return home to his wife Penelope. But the gods say, 'This is no way for a man to go home to his wife.' So they blow him astray for another ten years. They put him through an ordeal, which involves several gals whom he couldn't push around. The first one was Circe who turns men into swine, but they were swine already. The next is Calypso, with whom he spent seven years, a kind of middle-aged nymph. Finally it was darling Nausicaa. So Odysseus has experienced women in three modes, the modes of Aphrodite, Hera, and Athena, the three goddesses who had been judged by Paris, leading to the start of the Trojan War.

"The male has to experience women, not as something to be put down, but something to match," Campbell continued. "Real manliness consists in matching womanly talents. Homer recognized that there were two orders of male power. One is that of the sheer masculine work of the warrior, which is under the sign of the Sun. His arrows kill. The other is the field of life where sheer masculine violence has to be tempered with the feminine principle, the water and lunar power. Penelope, representative of the waxing and waning force of the Moon, has been weaving and unweaving her web for nineteen years. If the Sun and the Moon are in the same sign of the zodiac, it will be nineteen years before they are together again. Odysseus has been away exactly that long.

"Myths are representatives of archetypal human situations and possibilities," Campbell concluded. "My feeling is that people get stuck because of some wrong idea pushing them. These stories and tales can bring that revelation of where you stand in the picture of humanity. The most important function of my work today is linking the actual psychological problems of people with the lore. People can find it out for themselves, if they can just be given the mythic materials. Odysseus' journey is the typical voyage of visionary discovery and recovery of spiritual balance. Like many people today, he was off balance, way over on the masculine aggression side. He had not come into counterplay with the female principle. He got blown off course and had to acquire a new psychological position."

During our stay at Feathered Pipe Ranch, Ann and I had several memorable experiences. One hearkened back to a dream I had a few months earlier in which I was pursued through the Underworld by some furies. Endless caverns opened up ahead as I raced to outdistance my tormentors. Suddenly, like the Cheshire Cat in *Alice in Wonderland*, our aging cat Shakespeare appeared before me and said in a very clear voice, "Take this leaf. Water it, and your wishes will be granted." I sped off, leaf in hand, but could find no water. At last my assailants trapped me. As a revolver went up to my head, I became aware of the distinct drip of water to one side. I held the leaf out to the faucet and, a moment before the shot went off, ascended into a bright new world.

In the lodge I found a book by Black Elk, the prophet of the nearby Dakotas, and read a few pages. I discovered that his series of remarkable visions, beginning as a child, commended one day after eating with a holy man in his tipi. Reflecting on my own dream this spring, I came to see that the wish-fulfilling leaf that Shakespeare gave me was nature personified, the magic herb *moly* Hermes gives to Odysseus emblematic of the kingdom of grains and vegetables whose order and scope I was increasingly recognizing. Already, I connected the water "faucet" in the dream with Ann Fawcett, my wife. I realized that my activity in the natural world, like Odysseus' in Campbell's interpretation, must continually be refreshed by the feminine element.

The afternoon following Campbell's lecture on the Homeric epics, a small tabby kitten named Woodstock greeted us in our tipi after lunch. It had markings similar to Shakespeare's, and affectionately rubbed up against us. After playing for a while, the kitten proceeded to walk in a full circle between the inner and outer canvas linings of the tipi. After sitting protectively in the entranceway for a few minutes, it disappeared into the sunshine. Ann and I found its mandala like movements curious. Later we learn that our noble bardic cat died back home in Brookline at precisely the day and hour when the frisky young kitten appeared in the tipi. In real life, as in my dream, Shakespeare was extremely psychic and, in her royal manner, often communed directly by sending us mental images. Ann and I wept when we finally heard the news—in sadness for her passing, in joy for her sage way of saying farewell.

Many myths describe the quest for gold or the Golden Age, Campbell concluded. It is a recurrent image: the gold in the psyche, the wealth in the depths of the unconscious, the treasure of an enlightened mind. On the way, Ann and I stopped in Boulder and stayed with my high school friend David Rome, who was secretary to Chogyam Trungpa, a Tibetan lama and founder of Naropa Institute. We spent a delightful evening with poet Alan Ginsberg, a Naropa faculty member, and returned home, to our little Ithaca, refreshed and inspired for the challenges ahead.

As the seventies ended, Michio promoted me to editor-in-chief of *East West Journal,* and Ann and I mingled with poet Robert Bly, singer John Denver, Taoist physicist Fritjof Capra, *Diet for a Small Planet* author Frances Moore Lappé, and other heroes of the counterculture. I went to China on an ecumenical visit with my father Homer as guest of the Buddhist, Christian, and Muslim communities. The highlight was cooking a macrobiotic banquet for our hosts at the ancient Zen Temple in Beijing. It included brown rice and miso from America.

As the eighties unfolded, Ann and I went our separate ways and parted aimably. I turned to writing fulltime and co-authored several books with Michio and Aveline Kushi, including *The Cancer Prevention Diet, Diet for a Strong Heart, Aveline Kushi's Complete Guide to Macrobiotic Cooking,* and *One Peaceful World.* The last, an in depth study of war and peace, included a section on the Homeric epics that introduced the broad themes in this book. In 1986, I moved to Dallas for a couple years with my new wife Gale Beith, a macrobiotic cooking teacher. We eventually came back to New England to direct the Kushi Intitute and related macrobiotic organizations over the next couple decades. Our lives were immeasurably enriched with the adoption of our daughter Mariya, who spent the first seven years of her life in an orphanage in Moscow.

Marlowe and Mozart

Aside from managing, teaching, and writing books with the Kushis, I devoted time in the nineties and early aughts to the Shakespeare authorship question. My grandfather, Rev. David Rhys Williams, the minister of the Unitarian Church of Rochester, N.Y., was a pioneer Marlovian who believed Christopher Marlowe, the poet-spy, wrote the poems and plays attributed to Shakespeare. Marowe was the acclaimed author of *Tamburlaine, Doctor Faustus,* and other sublime plays, when he reportedly died in a tavern brawl in 1593. At the time, he was on bail after being arrested during a heresy investigation instigated by the archbishop of Canterbury in which he could have been burned at the stake. Ten days later, the first work in Shakespeare's name appeared in *Venus and Adonis,* a poem in his characteristic style and diction. In the Marlovian view, the Elizabethan secret service, headed by his superior Lord Burghley, faked his death and spirited him out of the country to Italy. The "tavern" turned out to be a secret service safe house, and the body of a leading Separatist who had just been hung at the order of the archbishop was probably substituted for Marlowe's in the inquest.

As a religious liberal, my grandfather closely identified with Marlowe's radical religious views and championed his cause. I found the conspiracy to save Marlowe compelling, but was primarily interested in the literary and poetic depths of the canon. Both Marlowe and Shakespeare's works are saturated with Homeric imagery and allusions. In *Doctor Faustus*, Kit describes Helen of Troy—who appears in the play—as having "the face that launched a thousand ships." A ghostly experience inspired me to publish an edition of *Hamlet* in Marlowe's name, with a long commentary on its mythic elements, including the scene in the play-within-the-play set at the end of the Trojan War. My book got rave reviews from fellow Marlovians but was ignored by everyone else. Mark Rylance, the artistic director of Shakespeare's New Globe Theatre and a leading Shakespearean actor, invited me to an authorship conference in London where I debuted my book.

Music and dance emerged as another theme during this period of quiet domesticity, parenthood, and teaching. I ghostwrote *The Mozart Effect: Tapping the Power of Music to Heal the Body, Strengthen the Mind, and Unlock the Creative Spirit*, a book on the power of sound and music for Don Campbell, an accomplished musician and holistic lecturer on musical healing traditions around the world. To our surprise, it became an international bestseller.

Christopher Marlowe had won a scholarship to Cambridge on the basis of his musical talents, including the ability to sing plainsong. The tonality of the Marlovian and Shakespearean works further whet my interest. I studied the yin and yang of sound and became a passionate devotee of Apollo, the god of both music and medicine, and the Muses, the daughters of Zeus and the goddess of Memory whose name gave rise to "music," "museum," and my favorite light-hearted attitude "amusing."

As the world of oral culture opened up, I had another remarkable dream. I was floating in space sound asleep when I heard the most beautiful song I ever heard. I awoke in the dream and glided toward the sound. Far below, I approached the earth, a small turquoise ball in the starry firmament. As I continued to follow the entrancing song, I entered the atmosphere and, like a Homeric god, darted swiftly down to a large city that I later realized was Chicago. Down, down, down I sped as the cityscape rose toward me at breathtaking speed, and I passed tall buildings, parks, and other landmarks. The exquisite music took me to a small apartment by the university where my parents lived. My expectant mother, Esther, was singing to her new baby. When I awoke, I realized I had dreamt my own birth! Later, I learned that in many cultures, a couple who wanted children would sing a song before making love and invite the spirit of their new baby into their family.

During this time, I also became friends with Anne Teresa de Keersmacher, a noted contemporary dancer and choreographer, whom I met while teaching in Amsterdam. Anne Teresa had a macrobiotic food service at her dance academy in Brussels and invited me to teach. In addition to diet and health, I gave lectures on sacred dance, the most fundamental art form in ancient cultures and the rhythmical framework for the *Iliad* and *Odyssey*. Like art and architecture, traditional dances employed spirals, circles, and other geometric shapes that mirrored the Golden Ratio. Anne Teresa, who used sacred themes in her compositions, created *Golden Hours*, a rendition of *As You Like it*. She had been inspired by a commentary on its alchemical symbolism in my edition of the play. In Act 5, the action climaxes in a sacred wedding dance in which Rosalind, Orlando, Touchstone, and the other characters form an image of the Philosopher's Stone.

My greatest musical epiphany occurred one summer at the International Macrobiotic Conference in the Netherlands. For two weeks, about 250 individuals and families met a conference center about two hours south of Amsterdam. Participants came from about fifty countries and six continents. On Hiroshima Day, August 6, I gave a prayer after lunch for world peace in the large central hall. At the close of my words, someone asked if we could sing a peace song. Soon, one by one, students from different countries came forward to lead a peace song in their native language. Merry tunes in Spanish, Italian, Russian, Portuguese, French, Japanese, Korean, and many other languages soon wafted through the auditorium. Each group of singers taught the assembled to sing the concluding verse with them in their native tongue. Spontaneous line or circle dancing was added to some of the repertoires. The last two groups to sing came from the Middle East. Throughout the conference, a chilliness, if not hostility, prevailed between Arabs and Israelis. Although united by a common devotion to healthy natural foods and a philosophy of unifying opposites, the macrobiotic Muslims and Jews at the conference conspicuously avoided each other.

In Israel and Palestine that summer the long simmering conflict neared the boiling point, and the tension could be felt in and out of the classroom. Finally, the large Muslim contingent took center stage and taught the group an Arabic peace song and led the participants in a long undulating line dance. When the few Israelis joined in, an audible sigh of relief spread through the auditorium. Then, when it was their turn, the small Jewish contingent taught everyone to sing *Hava Nagila* and led a circle dance in which the Muslims joined in. To everyone's astonishment, several dozen Arabs joined together with the Israelis to sing in Hebrew and dance happily around the room in a large circle. Waves of bliss enveloped the auditorium as everyone was united in deep peace and harmony. All differences and reservations dissolved, and for a moment we were all living the dream of "One Peaceful World." It was the fulfillment of my long ago mystical vision of dancing in a circle as God's grace streamed through our hearts and minds.

The Ages of Humanity

Transmutation also became a passion during these years. In the early 1960s, Michio Kushi and his teacher, George Ohsawa, had experimented with transmuting elements into one another. According to modern science, it was impossible to create new elements except during the Big Bang or under nuclear or stellar conditions such as the birth of supernovae and nuclear reactions. For many years, Ohsawa had taught that elements were constantly created under natural conditions. From the most elementary and peripheral elements—hydrogen, helium, and lithium—they moved inward in a logarithmic spiral to form radium, uranium, and the other heavy radioactive elements in the center. This process could be created, accelerated, or reproduced in a laboratory under ordinary temperatures and pressures. Scientists and skeptics dismissed this as alchemy, but the macrobiotic educators conducted scientific experiments based on the findings of French biochemist Louis Kervran that were confirmed by independent testing and analysis. For example, they produced iron out of carbon and turned sodium into potassium.

For a half century, these pioneer experiments were largely forgotten, ignored, or lived on in fragmented form in cold fusion, a contemporary quest to create excess energy under laboratory conditions. In the early 2000s, my colleagues Edward Esko and Woody Johnson and myself founded Quantum Rabbit LLC to take transmutation to the next level. We took our name from *Alice in Wonderland*, the odyssey of a little girl who encounters the White Rabbit and falls into a rabbit hole and experiences a quantum world that operates beyond the usual laws of physics. Over the next several years, we created minute amounts of about twenty elements in tabletop and vacuum tube experiments in small laboratories in Vermont, New Hampshire, and Maine, including titanium, palladium, scandium, germanium, and other valuable industrial metals.

Kushi and Ohsawa always saw transmutation as the key to humanity's future. By changing cheap, abundant materials like silicon (beach sand) into essential ones like titanium (used today to replace steel in airplane manufacture), humanity would transcend scarcity and be able to play freely in the infinite universe. On an industrial scale, transmutation would end underground mining, the competition for scarce resources, and territoriality—all major causes of war such as the conflict minerals crisis in Central Africa, as well as climate change—and thus usher in a new era of peace and prosperity. In creating minute amounts of gold, silver, copper, tin, and iron in our laboratories, we recreated the Four Ages of classical metallurgy. (Bronze is an alloy of copper and tin.) According to this sequence, humanity enjoyed a Golden Age of bright virtue, abundance, and peace followed by several ages of successive decline. The Silver Age marked the beginning of strife and a decline in the worship of the gods. Bronze Age society was governed by incessant war and moral deterioration. The current Iron Age, or era of vice and misery, is witnessing the triumph of evil. Hesiod, a contemporary of Homer and author of *Theogony* and *Works and Days*, introduces the Ages, and they play a key role in both the *Iliad* and *Odyssey*.

In his seminars, Michio Kushi lectured on the origin and destiny of humanity and cycles of time. His basic model was the 25,800-year cycle of the precession of the equinoxes. Known as the Vega Cycle, it describes how changing electromagnetic energy reaching the earth from the slow, gradual change in pole stars, and the angle of the Milky Way relative to the earth produces four distinct eras. The first is the Age of Paradise, which reached its zenith about 20,000 years ago when the center of the galaxy was directly overhead, showering its highly charged electromagnetic energy on the earth. This energy field created an abundance of crops, enhanced psychic and telepathic abilities among humans, and a worldwide peaceful planet. In antiquity, the precessional cycle was also known as the Platonic Year and the Astrological Ages (Aires, Pisces, Aquarius, etc.) with unique characters and tendencies.

Then about 12,500 years ago, or half way back on the cycle, the star Vega rose overhead and the ancient Spiritual and Scientific World Civilization collapsed as the energy striking the earth diminished. *Vega* is an Arabic word and means "fall" or "decline" pointing to this reversal. A partial axis shift and other earth changes, especially a Great Flood or impact of a giant comet, ushered in an era of hardship that reached its peak with the rise of a star in the constellation of Heracles overhead. The Twelve Labors of Heracles, an earlier hero mentioned in the Homeric epics, symbolized the trials and tribulations of humanity as it strove to survive in the new Wilderness Age, and collective memories of Lost Paradise receded.

Following a warming trend and the retreat of glacial ice, the third of the four precessional eras dawned about 6,500 years ago. It was characterized by domestication of plants and animals, urban civilization, written language, advances in metallurgy, and the rise of territoriality and war. The fourth quadrant of the circle has seen unparalleled advances in technology, transportation, and material development. The age of empires and ideologies arose. The world was explored and circumnavigated, trade connected East and West, and living standards reached new heights. As modern science triumphed, a decline of dietary awareness, the loss of sacred art and architecture, and destruction of the natural environment threatened the future of the species.

The momentum of this last era, which Michio called the Spiral of History, climaxes in about 2030 to 2040, as Polaris, the present North Star, reaches a zenith and begins to fade. As the pace of life accelerates, the world is now splitting into two directions: 1) the artificial, based on agribusiness, consumerism, fossil fuels, modern medicine, genetic engineering, smart bombs, autonomous vehicles, and algorithms and 2) the natural, based on natural food and organic farming, holistic health care, sustainable economic practices, and nonviolence. The end result is a contest between globalization dominated by governments, multinationals, and Big Data and grassroots planetary consciousness led by organic farmers, distributed new energy networks, and social media. An unparalleled material prosperity lies ahead as the Internet, smartphones, and other new technologies transform our lives. At the same time, the threat is growing of global destruction through nuclear war or accident, global warming and other climate change, the spread of artificial electromagnetic radiation, and new viral epidemics. These fire like catastrophes on the horizon are the counterpart to the water destruction half way back on the Vega cycle enshrined in the Great Flood in Genesis and other legends. If we pass safely through the center of the spiral, Michio taught, humanity would create a planetary commonwealth, or truly peaceful, democratic world government, conquer scarcity, and lay the foundation for a new Golden Age.

At Quantum Rabbit, we felt that transmutation—the art sacred to Hephaestus, the god of metallurgy, and Athena, goddess of skilled craftsmanship—held the key to a sustainable future. As Michio often said, the diet and health revolution pioneered by macrobiotics was essentially over. Modern science and medicine are now moving in a holistic direction with the introduction of the Food Guide Pyramid and integrative health care practices. As a practical first step to introducing a new model of the Periodic Table, our top priority became to reverse engineer radioactive elements into stable ones. The nuclear era has spawned millions of tons of deadly waste for which there is no permanent solution. Transmutation offers a simple, safe way to neutralize deadly isotopes of plutonium, uranium, cesium, strontium, and other heavy elements. The Quantum Rabbit research team networked with several green energy companies to make this a reality. Our ultimate goal is also to develop a new paradigm to explain the origin of the universe and replace the Big Bang, the dark, violent creation myth of the atomic era, with a bright, peaceful one.

Learning from Myths and Dreams

"Myth is a collective dream, and dream is a personal myth," Joseph Campbell observed. In this introduction, I have described the intersection of these twin dimensions in my personal life. The function of the artist, writer, or teacher of life is to unify the ephemeral and the everlasting, or as Blake put it: "To see a world in a grain of sand / Heaven in a wild flower / Hold infinity in the palm of your hand / And eternity in an hour." A social maxim pointing to this is "All politics is local." It means that your success as a leader in enacting community values and social justice is a function of your ability to understand and influence the needs of your constituents or neighbors. For many people, Homer's epics are ancient history and have no relevance. For others, they see life through the prism of other myths, legends, and stories. My mother Esther lived in a literary environment shaped by the novels of Dickens, Austen, and Proust. I myself make use of multiple lenses, often drawing on images from the *Bhagavad Gita/Mahabharata, Divine Comedy,* and the Marlovian/Shakespearean canon, as well as the Homeric epics. Friends and colleagues often model their lives on the characters and plotlines of modern epics such as *Star Trek, Star Wars, Lord of the Rings,* or *Harry Potter.*

The Circle of the Dance explores the Homeric epics, the foundation of classical Western culture along with the Bible, and offers fresh insights and perspectives into these beloved tales. I draw on many of the tools of analysis I have used in my earlier books and lectures. These include 1) yin and yang, the complementary opposites that govern all things, 2) the logarithmic spiral (the universal form from galaxies to DNA), 3) the Seven Levels of Consciousness (the natural unfolding of mind, body, and spirit in seven stages), 4) the traditional diet of humanity (centered on whole cereals grains and other predominantly plant-quality foods), 5) the healing power of art, music, and dance, 6) the Four Ages of Humanity (mirroring the 25,800-year Vega Cycle), and 7) the Spiral of History (the last quadrant) which is now drawing to a close, but has the potential of leading to the construction of a new Golden Age. All of these elements, as we shall see, feature in the *Iliad* and the *Odyssey.* They converge to illuminate the way of the immortal heroes and heroines, our own individual spiritual journeys, and the destiny of humanity.

Atlantis Rising

In the early 2000s, I left the One Peaceful World Society that I had been managing since the late 80s and spent the next decade teaching abroad. I lived for a while in rural France, Vienna, and Amsterdam and taught in London, Brussels, Tokyo, Kyoto, and other cities. My marriage was strained, and after our daughter Mariya was grown, Gale and I parted ways. Like Hera, the wife of Zeus and goddess of marriage and the family, she was a devoted mother and homemaker. But we did not always agree on other priorities.

I continued to work with Michio Kushi and brought out a new edition of our most popular book, *The Cancer-Prevention Diet*. In 2012, he asked me to return to the Kushi Institute to teach and give consultations. The following year, Michio asked me once again to manage the school which was facing a major financial crisis. Over the next several years, with Edward Esko, Bettina Zumdick, Sachi Kato, and other teachers and colleagues, we embarked on a successful effort to revive the school. At one Summer Conference, as executive director, I addressed the Gala with lessons drawn from the Homeric manuscript I was writing:

> Managing Kushi Institute is something like navigating a ship through troubled waters. When Michio asked Edward Esko and myself to take the helm a couple years ago, K.I. was in danger of capsizing. The Sirens of fame and fortune tempted us to cut corners by offering popular New Age courses, minimizing the use of 'yin and yang,' and even avoiding the term 'macrobiotics' altogether. Seductive Circes tried to lure us to modify the Standard Macrobiotic Diet by adding richer animal foods, coconut oil, exotic tropical drinks, and highly profitable supplements to attract a wider, more affluent clientele. But we knew that such departures from the mean would only turn our students and program participants, like Odysseus's heedless crew, into swine.

We kept the Institute going for several years after Michio passed away. But after his death, the Kushi family, which owned the land on which the school was located, decided to close the Institute and sell the property. Like Odysseus, the returning Greek sailor, I felt I had lost all my ships and crew and was marooned in stormy seas.

In 2017, Edward, Bettina, and I reorganized macrobiotic education under the aegis of Planetary Health, Inc., nonprofit sponsor of

Amberwaves, a grassroots network we started at the turn of the new millennium to help preserve rice, wheat, and other grains from genetic engineering. Over the last several years, we have been holding macrobiotic conferences and programs at Eastover, a large holistic resort in Lenox, MA.

This past spring, Bettina and I started the *Miso Happy Show*, an online learning and variety webinar, streamed live over the Internet on the first of each month. In May we gave a seminar and counseled in Sussex and continued on to Germany to visit her mother and relatives. After several memorable days in the northern part of the country, I went on to Greece for a week. It was my first visit to the land of Homer and the epic tradition.

The highlight was a trip to the island of Santorini, a principal site of the ancient Minoan civilization and the biggest volcanic eruption in recorded history. In ancient times, it was known as Thera and is probably the source for Plato's description of Atlantis. Walking through the excavated ruins of the 3500-year-old city of Akrotiri and viewing the beautiful frescoes, elegant cookware, and other objects on display in the National Archaeological Museum in Athens was a revelation. The peaceful, harmonious Minoan culture lasted over fifteen hundred years and contrasted sharply with the violent, warlike Mycenaean and Classical Greek eras that followed, including the Homeric Age.

Returning to London, I met Bettina, and we broadcast the *Miso Happy Show* live before returning home to the Berkshires. Several of our colleagues in the UK described their experience successfully treating diabetes, depression, autism, and other chronic modern ills with a balanced macrobiotic diet and lifestyle. Celtic music from the Morning Star Consort was interspersed between the talks. My reflections on this European sojourn, "Journey to Atlantis," appear as an appendix in this book. My odyssey, including a prophecy from a Tiresias like guide in the Underworld, helped put the Homeric epics into a broader and deeper perspective and reaffirm the key insights in this volume.

1
THE SLEEP OF BRONZE

Conventional wisdom holds that the *Iliad* and *Odyssey* glorify war, valor, and the code of the warrior. On the surface, the Homeric epics depict the martial values of the Bronze Age, but at heart they are among the staunchest antiwar poems ever composed. Like Shakespeare's Henriad, the central theme is the folly of war. Like Falstaff, the fat irrepressible knight who does everything possible to avoid combat in Henry V's invasion of France, the participants in the Trojan War would rather melt away or make peace with their enemies than fight. Throughout both epics, the core message is that military victory is hollow and that a quiet, peaceful life is preferable to honor, fame, and battlefield glory.

In *The War That Killed Achilles: The True Story of Homer's Iliad and the Trojan War*, Carolyn Alexander catalogues the epic's consistent anti-

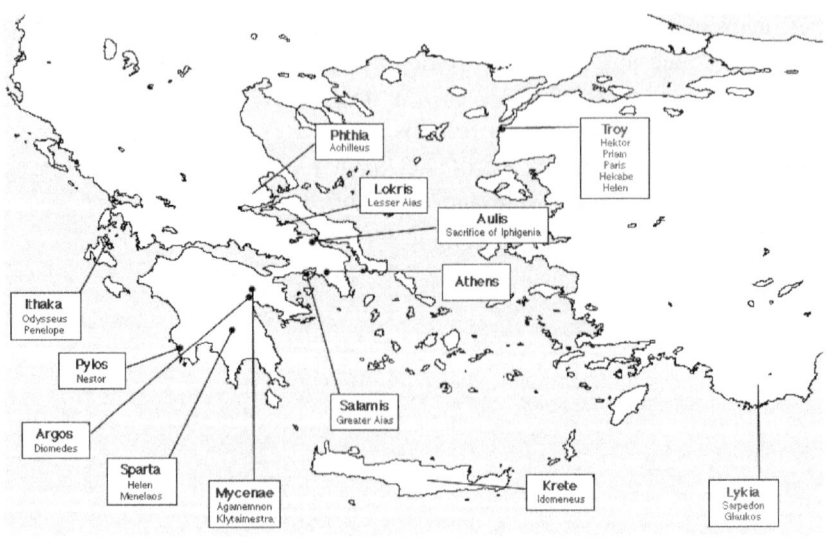

The World of the Iliad

war theme. "Strikingly, no man at Troy prays for his own side to win. The Achaeans and Trojans are indifferent to the outcome—so long as it brings the war to any end.... The war seems to have gathered autonomous momentum, which, as the epic emphasizes, will end in mutual destruction." In the end, Achilles sacrifices his life, not for glory and honor, but for his love for Patroclus. "The *Iliad* recounts the bloody battles, heroic speeches, and the pride of a warrior's *aristeia* [glory] and never betrays its subject war," Alexander observes. "Homer concludes the epic with a series of funerals, inconsolable lamentation, and shattered lives. War makes stark the tragedy of mortality. A hero will have no recompense for death, although he may win glory."

Through the ages, common sense has always been guided by the principle of "live and let live." For endless generations, parents have protected their children from foreign wars in which they have no stake. Like many young men, the heroes of the *Iliad* and *Odyssey* both try to dodge the draft. According to the epic cycle, when a recruiter comes to Ithaca, Odysseus is plowing his field. Feigning insanity, he sows his furrow with salt. But the recruiter outwits him by placing his infant son, Telemachus, in front of the plow. Odysseus swerves around the boy, demonstrating his rationality and fitness to serve.

Achilles also seeks to evade the draft. As the offspring of the immortal nymph Thetis and the elderly human king Peleus, Achilles is mortal. According to prophecy, he is destined to die young heroically in battle or peacefully at home in old age. By dipping her son into the river Styx, Thetis hopes to give him eternal life. However, by holding him by the heel, she leaves him vulnerable. Desperate to save Achilles from a premature death, Thetis then hides her son on remote Skyros Island among the women of King Lykomedes's court. Achilles even disguises himself as a girl. But when Odysseus (newly impressed himself) and Diomedes come to conscript the prophesized hero of the war, they find him dancing in female attire and force him into service. Achilles fulfills his destiny in the final assault on Troy when he is slain by an arrow that lodges in his heel.

Over the next ten years, the Trojan War claims myriads of casualties, including nearly all the inhabitants of the besieged city. Countless young men suffer agonizing deaths, elderly mothers and fathers lose sons, and wives and maidens end bereft of husbands and sweethearts. Indeed, most of the victors never return home. Their ships are wrecked by storms, pirates, or supernatural monsters, as the gods turn against them. As the war unfolds and especially in its aftermath, the men and heroes of the epic constantly ask themselves: What are we here for? What is the point of all this death and destruction? Over and over again, the answer is: We are fighting for the sake of a mere girl. The abduction of Helen, the world's most beautiful woman, sets the war in motion. In the epic cycle, a diverting, but meaningless beauty pageant among three goddesses who decisively influence the outcome of the war, precedes this episode. Zeus's lustful and adulterous proclivities lie even beyond this event. On the battlefield itself, Achilles' refusal to fight—an act of disobedience that would have brought summary execution in most wars—arises when Agamemnon, his commander-in-chief, claims Briseis, his captive "wife." In turn, Agamemnon's refusal to return Chryseis, another comely girl whom he has seized as booty, to her father opens the story.

Like middle school students, the gods and heroes of the Homeric epics decide the destiny of men and nations on the basis of adolescent whims, petty sleights, and raging hormones. The subtext of the classic tales is, There is far more to life than satisfying physical desire. Nor is *kleos*, the Greek ideal of battlefield honor and glory, worth all the grim suffering and consequences of battle, including the premature death of countless men, the widowing and ravishing of wives and orphaning of children, and laying waste of entire regions.

After reaching the pinnacle of glory and slaying Hector, the mightiest of the Trojans, in single combat, Achilles is slain. In Hades, several years after the war has ended, Odysseus addresses the shade of Achilles: "No man before has been more blessed than you, nor ever will be. Before, when you were alive, we Argives honored you as we did the gods, and now in this place you have great authority over the dead. Do not grieve, even in death, Achilles."

The spirit of Achilles rebukes him, "O shining Odysseus, never try to console me for dying. I would rather follow the plow as thrall to another man, one with no land allotted him and not much to live on, than be a king over all the perished dead."

The Trojan War

The Trojan War extends back three thousand years and is commemorated in myths, legends, and other oral accounts known as the Epic Cycle. The Homeric epics constitute the main part of this largely lost oral collection of songs and dances and were codified in final written form about the 8th century BCE According to tradition, the genesis of the Trojan War lay in the decision of Zeus, the ruler of the heavens, to end the Heroic Age and reduce the human population. The supreme deity feared he would be dethroned by one of his many progeny as he had overthrown his father Cronus.

As part of Zeus's plan, the Olympian gods are invited to the marriage of the immortal nymph Thetis and the mortal king Peleus. Angry at being left off the guest list Eris, the goddess of strife and discord, crashes the wedding and tosses a golden apple into the crowd inscribed "To the Fairest." The goddesses Aphrodite, Athena, and Hera all vie for the title. Zeus names Paris, a young Trojan prince, to settle the dispute. Unaware of his heritage, Paris is living peacefully as a shepherd on Mount Ida because of an augury that one day he would bring destruction to Troy. As the bitter quarrel rages, each of the goddesses tries to bribe him. Athena offers Paris wisdom and skill in battle. Hera dangles untold wealth and power, and Aphrodite promises him the most beautiful woman in the world. Paris awards the apple to the goddess of love. This episode is known as the Judgment of Paris.

Later, Paris reunites with his royal family in Troy and embarks on an embassy to visit King Menelaus. In Sparta, he meets the monarch's divine-looking wife Helen, who according to some legends was the daughter of Zeus. Fulfilling her pledge, Aphrodite makes the handsome prince irresistible to Helen, the most beautiful woman in the world. When Menelaus departs for a funeral, the two lovers elope to Troy along with a ship filled with treasure. Before her nuptials, Helen's many suitors swore an oath to come to the aid of her future husband to safeguard the sanctity of the marriage. When Troy rejects Menelaus's entreaties to return Helen to Sparta, his brother Agamemnon, the king of Mycenae and paramount chieftain in Greece, launches an armada to bring Helen back by force of arms. As poet Christopher Marlowe later enthused: "Was this the face that launched a thousand ships/And burnt the topless towers of Ilium?" The enormous invasion force, drawn from across the Greek isles, numbered about 100,000 strong. Historians and archaeologists agree that the Epic Cycle was based on a core of historical truth. In the nineteenth century, Frank Calvert and Heinrich Schliemann excavated the ancient site, known today as Hisarlik. Subsequent investigation has concluded a major war took place about 1270 BCE Hittite records mention King Alaksandu who presided over Wilusa about this time. Alexandros was Paris's alternate name, and Wilusa is linguistically related to Ilium [or Wilium], the formal name for Troy, and hence the *Iliad*.

Ancient Troy was located in Anatolia by the Dardanelles in present-day Turkey. The *Iliad* opens in the last year of the siege. For ten years, the Greeks (known interchangeably in the epic as the Achaeans, Argives, or Danaans) have been fruitlessly seeking to conquer the city. They have looted and sacked the home isles of many Trojan allies during the first nine years, but taking the citadel eludes them. When the action in the epic opens, they are encamped on the sandy beach outside of the walled city.

Troy embodies the highest culture and civilization. King Priam, its venerable head, presides over a peaceful principality, renowned for its mighty horses, textiles, and fair-haired women. He has sired fifty sons, including Hector, a towering, seemingly invincible warrior, who stymies the Greek advance and even manages to turn the tide and set fire to some of their ships. Aeneas, the son of the goddess Aphrodite and Anchises, a mortal, is the second most illustrious Trojan fighter. One of the few survivors of the sack of Troy, his story is continued in the *Aeneid*, the Latin epic composed by Virgil in the 1st century BCE. Aeneas goes on to found Rome, and his nephew Brute or Brutus is the eponymous founder and first king of Britain. The Trojan allies are drawn from across Asia Minor and North Africa and include the Thracians, the Phrygians, the Amazons, and the Ethiopians.

The *Iliad* begins with Chryses, a priest of Apollo, coming to the Achaeans offering ransom for his captive daughter, Chryseis. They are from Thebes in Sicily and allies of the Trojans. Agamemnon, the Greek commander in chief, regards the girl as his personal booty, and arrogantly rebuffs the imploring father. Apollo hears the old man's prayers and visits a plague among the Achaeans. After nine days of death and disease among the army, Achilles asks the prophet Calchas to explain the cause of the scourge. He says that Agamemnon's insolent behavior has angered Apollo, and Chryseis must be returned. The furious Greek leader reluctantly agrees to return the girl but in return demands Breseis, Achilles' trophy combat wife. The enraged warrior sends her back to Agamemnon's tent but vows to withdraw from the war against Troy, and even return home with the Myrmidons, his countrymen, and their fifty warships.

As Achilles sulks in his tent, the battle between the Greeks and Trojans seesaws back and forth through most of the *Iliad's* twenty-four books, with one side now gaining the ascendency and then the other. The gods connive to assist their progeny or favorites, frequently tipping the balance to the invaders and then to the defenders. Athena and Hera nurse an implacable rage against the Trojans, because Aphrodite, the winner of the beauty contest, continues to flaunt her charms and protect Paris who awarded her the golden apple. Apollo, the archer god who presides over healing, music, and the Muses, also staunchly favors the Trojans, as does Ares, the god of war. Achilles rejects entreaties by Odysseus, Diomedes, and his old mentor Phoinix to come to the aid of the flagging Greeks, even when Hector leads the Trojans to the ships and sets some on fire. But he consents to send Patroclus, his childhood friend, companion, and charioteer, to fight in his stead and gives him his armor.

Patroclus proves unstoppable on the battlefield, and once again the tide of battle turns. But he is tricked by Athena in believing he is invincible and recklessly carries the fight to the walls of the city. Rallying to Troy's defense, Hector slays Patroclus and mutilates his body. Enraged at the desecration, Achilles vows to return to battle. Fearful for her son's life, Thetis goes to Hephaestus, the god of metallurgy, to receive divine armor to replace the weapons the Trojans have taken from Patroclus's body. The smithy god fashions a magnificent shield and Thetis brings it back to her son. In the climatic combat episode in the *Iliad*, Achilles slays Hector, ties his body to his chariot, and drags it around the city. The horrified Trojans implore the Achaeans to return the corpse for proper burial. But Achilles vows to feed Hector's remains to the dogs. Finally, King Priam, Hector's father, is guided to the Greek encampment by Hermes, the messenger of the gods, and pleads with the implacable victor and kisses his hands. Touched by the old man's imploring request, Achilles returns the body. The *Iliad* ends with a brief truce allowing both sides to bury their dead and prepare for the inevitable final onslaught.

The actual fall of Troy, including the famous episode of the Wooden Horse, is told in the *Odyssey* by Demodocus, the blind bard in the Phaeacian court, and by Helen. The Greeks build a giant wooden horse and leave it outside the city gates. A note explains that the statue is a gift to Athena and the Achaean fleet has departed because the war had reached a stalemate and the men are all homesick. The unsuspecting Trojans wheel the wooden horse into their city, and the warriors hidden in the statue emerge under cover of darkness. Led by Odysseus, they open the city gates to their compatriots who have not sailed away for good after all. They slay most of the males, rape or abduct the females, and sack and burn the city.

In anger at the Argive war crimes, including the rape of Cassandra and the murder of Priam, who had both sought sanctuary at sacred altars, the gods now turn against the victors. Most of the returning expeditionary forces are shipwrecked or routed by serpents of the deep. Odysseus loses all his men in a sequence of magical misadventures. For ten years, Poseidon, the god of the sea, obstructs the Ithacan's voyage home to his wife Penelope and son Telemachus. The *Odyssey* tells the story of Odysseus's heroic homecoming. With the help of Athena, he survives encounters with ogres, monsters, seductive goddesses, and an angry sea god, visits the Underworld, and manages to reach his home island in the guise of a beggar. The epic ends with father and son massacring the suitors who are eating the family out of house and home, the reunion with Penelope and Laertes, his elderly father, and brief spiritual pilgrimage.

Eye-Shrouding Darkness

As a war epic, the *Iliad* is full of violence and mayhem. Nearly two hundred and fifty individual deaths are described in gory detail, including thirty-one by Hector, twenty-eight by Patroclus, twenty-four by Achilles, twenty-two by Diomedes, eighteen by Odysseus, sixteen by Ajax son of Telamon, thirteen by Agamemnon, seven by Menelaus, seven by Aeneas, and three by Paris. However, it is a mistake to liken Homer's graphic depiction of blood and guts to modern war novels, Hollywood movies, or video games. Unlike contemporary battle epics that feature hordes of cloned warriors and nameless antagonists, all the deaths in the *Iliad* are humanized. However briefly, each death is described meticulously, the victim is named, and the tragic consequences noted. Here are a few examples of how Homer personalizes each slaying:

> Now against you the goddess, grey-eyed Athena, has set
> this man: fool that he is, Tydeus's son's mind does not grasp
> the fact that there's no long life for a man who fights the gods—
> that Papa won't come back for his children to greet or cling
>   round
> His knees: no return from the wars and the bitter grind of battle.
> (5.405-09)

> Instead his arrow struck blameless Gorgythion,
> Priam's first son, in the chest: the mother who bore him
> had come as a bride from Aisyme, the beautiful Kastianeita,
> a woman most like to the goddesses in stature.
> His head dropped to one side: as a garden poppy sinks
> under the load of its seed and the springtime showers,
> so bowed his head sideways, weighted down by its helmet.
> (8.301-08)

> Then seizing [the spear] in one hand wide-ruling Agamemnon
> dragged it toward him mad as a lion, and wrenched it
> out of Iphidamas's grasp, slashed his neck with his sword,
> unstrung his limbs. So he fell, and slept the sleep of bronze,
> wretched youth, helping his countrymen, far from his wife,
> the bride that he had no joy of [yet] . . .
> (11.238-43)

> Wretched [Sokos], your father and lady mother will never

The Sleep of Bronze

close your eyes in death now: the flesh-eating birds of prey
will tear them out raw, wings beating madly around you—
                    (11.452.55)

When [Patroclus] had spoken thus, death's end enshrouded him,
and the soul fled from his limbs, fluttered down to Hades
bewailing its fate, youth and manhood all abandoned.
                    (16.855-57)

[Idomeneus] died himself at the hands of Hector, killer of men,
who hit him below the ear, in under the jawline. The spear
dashed his teeth out by their roots, cut his tongue at the midpoint.
                    (17.615-18)

Then Alastor's son Tros—who'd come up to clasp his knees
in the hope that he'd take him prisoner, let him live,
out of pity for one of his age group rather than kill him: the fool,
unaware that there wasn't a chance of ever persuading him,
since this was a man without kindness of mind or heart,
but raging to kill—flung his arms now around Achilles' knees,
tried to beseech him. A swordstroke found his liver,
the liver protruded, and black blood poured down from it,
filling his tunic's fold. Darkness shrouded his eyes
as he lost hold of life.
                    (20.462-71)

Can't you see what I'm like, how handsome and tall I am?
A fine father sired me, the mother who bore me was a goddess— . . .
so he spoke, and Lykaon's knees and heart were unstrung:
he let go the spear, and sat there, both hands outstretched
in supplication. But Achilles drew his sharp sword, and plunged it
in by the neck at the collarbone: the two-edged blade
sank in its full length, and Lykaon fell prone, law stretched out
there on the ground. His dark blood gushed, soaked the earth.
Achilles now seized one foot, flung him into the river
as flotsam, and vaunting, spoke winged words over him:
lie there now with the fishes, that'll lick the blood
from your wound, quite indifferent to you: nor will your
mother lay you out on a bier and wail over you: rather will Skamandros
roll you away in its eddies to the wide gulf of the sea,

and fish darting through the waves will surface amid
their black ripples to nibble Lykaon's white lustrous fat?
So die all, till we reach sacred Ilion's citadel,
With you in full flight, and I in murderous pursuit?
(21.108-20)

The Seven Levels of Consciousness

Menis, the opening word in the *Iliad*, means wrath: "Wrath, Muse, sing of Achilles Peleus's son's calamitous wrath, which hit the Achaeans with countless ills."

But *menis* means more than intense anger or rage. It is cosmic wrath, the righteous response to breaking the unbreakable laws of the universe. *Menis* primarily refers to the wrath of the gods. Throughout the Homeric saga, it is applied to Zeus's wrath against other immortals or mortals, as well as to the wrath of Athena, Apollo, and the other gods. When linked to demi-gods or mortals such as Achilles, it implies that they have exceeded not only human moral standards but also the cosmic order. In Greek, the heavenly mandate is known as *themis*, personified as a goddess of justice, right, and universal law. (Themis makes two cameo appearances in the *Iliad*.) Achilles overreaches and treads on divine prerogatives, as well as ignores human ones. This seals his fate.

The immediate cause of Achilles's wrath is Agamemnon's arrogance. As Achilles later admits, his boundless rage over the seizure of his bedmate Briseis is the cause of the enmity between himself and the Argive commander:

"Son of Atreus, was it really the best thing for both of us,
for you, for me, that we two, grief-filled as we were,
should rage on in heart-eating strife because of a girl?
I wish she'd been killed by an arrow from Artemis
That day at the ships when I chose her, after sacking Lyrnessos!"
(19.56-60)

Renouncing his wrath, Achilles vows to put on the divine armor that Hephaestus has forged for him and return to combat.

In contrast to Achilles who accepts personal responsibility for his misguided actions, Agamemnon is unrepentant:

"It's not I who am the one at fault,
but rather Zeus, and Fate, and some night-walking Fury,
who in the assembly cast wild delusion on my mind

that day when, acting along, I took his prize from Achilles.
But what could I do? It's a god that fulfills all matters:
Zeus's elder daughter, Delusion, who blinds all mortals—"

(19.86-91)

For good measure, Agamemnon goes on to boast how the Fury even deluded Zeus himself. He then denounces Hera, who "though only a woman, deceived by her crafty wiles" the king of the gods.

Passages like this suggest that the Homeric works are broadly allegorical. As in most scriptural and literary matters, there is a wide spectrum of interpretation. These range from literal readings that view the Olympian gods as completely autonomous actors to those who view them figuratively as psychological projections of human thoughts, wishes, and fears. In between, as Agamemnon's evasive passage suggests, most of the combatants in the war view life as governed by a combination of inscrutable deities, the elements of nature, and abstract forces or drives that lack personality and go by metaphorical names such as Delusion, Panic, and Rout.

Over the years, I have used the Seven Levels of Consciousness to analyze literature, history, and art, as well as the lives of individuals, cultures, and societies. According to this model, introduced by educators George Ohsawa and Michio Kushi, human beings pass through seven natural stages of consciousness, from autonomic or unconscious awareness to sensorial, emotional, intellectual, social, and philosophical or spiritual judgment. The crowning seventh level may be described as supreme judgment or universal consciousness.

Each level develops at a different period in life. During the embryonic or first stage, our growth and development proceed through autonomic, mechanical functions that we may call the primary and basic judgment of life. Upon birth and for the duration of our life, this primary judgment continues to function through all parts of our body such as unconscious nerve reactions, digestive and respiratory functions, circulatory and endocrine activities, execratory functions, and in other ways. However, in embryo and soon after our birth, we begin to develop sensory consciousness or the second level of judgment to deal with various kinds of stimuli from the other stages of existence: a sense of touch for the solid environment, a sense of taste for the liquid environment, a sense of smell for the gaseous environment, a sense of hearing for the vibrational environment, and a sense of sight for the world of light. The sensory experience further involves discriminating various physical states such as hunger and thirst, pain and pleasure, and heat and cold.

In the third stage, we develop emotional judgment, which deals with the feeling and distinction of beauty and ugliness, love and hate, joy and sadness, like and dislike, emotional attachment and detachment, emotional agreement and disagreement. The prototype for this stage also begins in the womb when the developing baby feels the emotional tone of the mother, father, and family's moods, even though it cannot understand the meaning of the words. Over time, after birth and through childhood, this metamorphoses into the world of popular culture, including literature and film, music and dance, and other artistic outlooks. In daily life, emotional awareness governs relationships with partners, paramours, children, parents, and friends. When it comes to art and taste, we may call this stage of development, in the more refined apprehension, aesthetic consciousness.

Through the repeated experience of sensory and aesthetic rise and fall, we grow and develop our judgment and consciousness to the fourth level: assumption and speculation, conceptualization and organization, analysis and synthesis, evaluation and definition, and other more objective mental activities. This stage typically begins with language as the child learns to correlate sounds objectively with things in his or her environment. In this level, which we may term the intellectual, logical concepts are formed, reasoning images are structured, organized systems are conceived, and comparative values are defined. This is intellectual judgment—the world of modern science and technology as well as social administration.

Our consciousness further expands toward understanding the relations among people and among groups of people, including societies, the environment, and the world as a whole. From individual human relations we further develop to understand and balance family relations; from family relations to community relations; from community relations to relations among humanity and other species. This fifth level of consciousness may appear in children and teens, but usually doesn't fully develop until adulthood. It may be called social judgment. The problems of ethics and morals, harmony and peace, world law and world order, energy and environmental policy, are among many other concerns at this level. From this stage we view personal life from the perspective of society and national life from the perspective of benefiting the world as a whole.

From many experiences and challenges, successes and failures in the first five levels, our consciousness further develops to the level of philosophical thought. We think deeply about such basic questions as: What is life? Where have we come from? Where are we going? What is the purpose of life? Who am I? We start to reflect upon the meaning of our own life, search for the secret of the universe, and strive to become one with eternal truth. The sixth level of consciousness is a door to the last level of consciousness. All traditional religions, spiritual doctrines, and teachings of the way of life begin at this level. While glimpsed at an early age, spiritual or philosophical consciousness traditionally occupies late maturity or old age after one's career has peaked and the children have grown up.

Through the constant search for universal truth, the meaning of life, and the origin and destiny of creation, we finally reach universal consciousness, which may be called Supreme Judgment. At this seventh level we understand the order of the universe and the achievement of universal love and absolute freedom. Living at the universal level has been described by different traditions as attaining Satori, reaching Nirvana, living in Grace, or entering into the Kingdom of Heaven. This consciousness does not conflict with any circumstances or point of view, embracing all contradictions in the relative world as complementary, understanding the paradoxical constitution of the entire universe, and beginning to exercise our real freedom. At that time, our consciousness starts to merge with the Absolute or God. We move or play freely among the previous six levels of judgment. We live with the spirit of endless gratitude and love and pray for all beings to realize eternally their endless dream. These, in brief, are the seven levels of consciousness through which a natural human being passes while living upon this earth.

There is a logarithmic temporal and spatial relationship among the different levels of awareness. In terms of time, mechanical responses change instantaneously, usually in a matter of seconds. Sensory changes take longer, usually a matter of minutes. Emotional feelings persist over a period of days, weeks, or months, while intellectual theories can keep their influence for years. Social ideas can last over a century, while philosophical products such as religions and doctrines can last a millennium. In terms of space, the lower types of judgment influence a fewer number of people over a narrower space, while the higher judgments influence a larger number of people over a wider space. Yet all results and influences produced by the first six levels of consciousness are relative, ephemeral, and all eventually disappear, producing the opposite effects. Supreme judgment or consciousness alone acts beyond the limits of time and space, and its influence is universal and everlasting.

Let's apply this basic model to the *Iliad*. The first or bedrock level of consciousness, the autonomic, concerns survival. Preservation of life under mortal threat and realizing an objective, such as storming the walls of Troy or turning back the invaders, are the goals of this level. Most violence and war are conducted at this level. In the march of history, combat has become increasingly mechanized and impersonal. In the heroic Bronze Age, single combat between evenly matched opponents is the ideal. Thus the match up between Achilles and Hector is the battle of the millennium. Throughout the epic, slaying an enemy with the bow is considered dishonorable because the arrows are shot at a distance, or dipped in poison. Fighting at close quarters with spear and shield, in contrast, is deemed honorable. Sheer might or brawn largely informs this level, but it is guided by sensory, emotional, and higher levels of judgment, especially reason. Odysseus's resourcefulness and wiliness refer primarily to his mental prowess, though he is a seasoned warrior and physically imposing. What would Homer and the ancient Greeks make of modern war when combatants no longer engage in face-to-face fighting, and bombs, long-range artillery, drones, and other faceless harbingers of death and destruction prevail?

If we look at the *Iliad's* roster of immortals and mortals from this perspective, we find that the majority of gods and people act from the first, second, and third levels of awareness. Most of our daily life has to do with: Level 1) securing the basics (food, shelter, clothing, etc.) or developing our physical skills, (flexibility, mobility, and balance). Level 2) living comfortably and satisfying our sensory drives and desires (sex, warmth, pleasure, etc.). Level 3) satisfying our emotional needs (love, friendship, hobbies, beauty, and other preferences). We also use our mental facilities (Level 4) to understand the world around us and how it functions. But when it comes to relationships, eating, and other daily choices, for the most part we let our hearts (Level 3) rule our heads (Level 4). Only a small percentage of people pick their partners on the basis of their minds (Level 4), commitment to social justice (Level 5), or spirituality (Level 6). Paris certainly didn't. Similarly, most people are aware that saturated fat and cholesterol are not healthy, but this seldom deters them from eating heavy artery-clogging meals and sugary desserts. Taste or sensory judgment (Level 2), as modern food manufacturers well know, trumps nutritional labeling (Level 4). The following list summarizes the levels of consciousness among the gods, spirits, and heroes, citing typical examples from the text:

Immortals

Zeus Universal order, Levels 1-7, with a focus on lust (2), Olympian rage (3), creating order among mortals and immortals (5), observance of the sacrifice (6), and inscrutable being (7); "Go quickly [Thetis], then, to the camp, and give your son [Achilles] this message: Say that he's angered the gods, that I, above all other immortals, am filled with rage, because in his maddened heart he's kept Hector by the curved ships, won't give him up" [24.112-15]

Hera Practicality and domestic arts, Levels 1-5, with a focus on jealously and revenge (2), love (3), and 5 (social order); "I who declare I'm the highest of all goddesses as the eldest born, and because I'm recognized as your consort—and you're the king of all the immortals! How, in my rage, could I not cobble trouble for these Trojans?"

Athena Wisdom, weaving, military prowess, and other skillful action, Levels 1-6, with a focus on resourcefulness, strategy, deception, disguise, (4) and justice (5)

Apollo Arts and sciences, especially music and dance, and medicine and healing, Levels 3-5, with a focus on aesthetics, reason, health, and community

Hermes Communications, commerce, and learning with a focus on efficiency (1), trade (5), and esoteric wisdom (6)

Aphrodite Pleasure and love, Levels 2-3, with a focus on attraction, intimacy, and protection of her son Aeneas; in one truce with Hera who sought charms to deceive Zeus the goddess of love "undid from her bosom the embroidered breast band intricately worked, with all kinds of allurement set in it—therein were love, and desire, and dalliance: beguilement that steals away the sharp wits (4) of even sensible people"

Ares Violence and war. Levels 1 and 2; Athena calls him a "ravening madman, a sick piece of work, a two-faced liar" and Zeus virtually disowns him because of his brutality; Homer also describes him as "the mindless one, who knows no things that are *themis*"

Hephaestus Arts and crafts, metallurgy, skillful means with a focus on efficiency (1), beauty (3), community (5), spirituality (6), and universality (7)

Themis The goddess of law, justice, and right, Levels 4-7; appears briefly twice in the epic, but as the mother by Zeus of Good Order, Justice, Peace, the Seasons, and the three Fates plays a key behind-the-scenes role in the *Iliad* and *Odyssey*

Personified Abstractions

Delusion and Prayers of Repentance Daughters of Zeus, as Phoinix, Achilles's old tutor, explains to him: "There are, too, Prayers of Repentance, great Zeus's daughter, lame and wrinkled, these—eyes furtive, sidelong glances—their task to keep close on the heels of Blind Delusion: but Blind Delusion is strong and swift-footed, so she by far outstrips them all, goes ahead of them over the whole earth, harming mortals; the healing Prayers follow on behind her"

Dream Zeus sends Agamemnon a destructive dream to mobilize his forces against Troy; Dream appears to him in disguise while sleeping and lulls him into unwise action

Panic Rout "[Ares'] dear son Panic Rout, the mighty and fearless who sends even the sturdiest warrior fleeing in terror"

Rivers Skamandros and Simoeis, the two rivers of the Trojan plain, are personified and pursue Achilles when he tries to storm the city

Sleep The brother of Death whom Hera takes by the hand to beguile Zeus and to whom she pledges in troth one of the Graces and a golden throne made by Hephaestus

Terror, Panic, and Strife The sisters and comrade of "man-slaying" Ares, who yoke his horses; Zeus dispatches Strife "that baneful spirit—cradling a portent of war in her hands and uttered a loud and terrible cry, shrilly, infusing great strength into every Achaean's heart, to engage in unceasing warfare and battle; so that to them, at once, war now became much sweeter than going back in their hollow ships to their own dear country"

Mortals

Achilles Acts primarily on the emotional level (3) with occasional rational insight (4) "Shrewdness serves woodcutters better than mere brute force"; challenges Agamemnon over keeping Chryseis and returns Breseis for the good of the expedition (5); and nods to the gods (6)

Agamemnon Sensory (2) and emotional (3); governed by fear, paranoia, and revenge; e.g. he rebukes Menelaus, for whose sake the war is being fought: "Menelaus, dear brother, what makes you care so much for these people? Did you get the best treatment in your home from Trojans? Not one of them should escape sheer doom at our hands, no, not even the child whose mother still carries him in her belly: let the people of Ilion all perish together, unmourned, eradicated!" (6.55-60); he finally self-reflects when Nestor convinces him to make peace with Achilles: "Since I was blinded, a slave to my wretched passions, I'm willing to make amends, to pay boundless compensation." In a glance at this sevenfold model, Homer has him offer Achilles seven tripods, seven women, skilled in fine handiwork, and seven well-endowed townships.

Hector Emotional (3) and a strong sense of safeguarding Troy (5)

Helen Emotional (3), intellectual (4), and occasionally social (5)

Menelaus Emotional (3), intellectual (4), and social (5); the king sympathizes with the Trojans, even though they have abducted his wife

Nestor The elderly patriarch of the Achaeans acts primarily out of social judgment or concern for the success of the expedition (5): "My friends, be men now, let shame into your hearts before other men; and remember each of you, your children and wives, your possessions and your parents, whether for you they are living or dead! On behalf of them, far distant now, who am here beseech you to make a strong stand, not to turn back in craven flight!"

Odysseus Wily, resourceful, and the Greeks' prime strategist, he is motivated primarily by intellect and cunning (*metis*) (4); he also displays emotion on behalf of his family (3), social concern for victory over Troy and the welfare of his men on the voyage home (5), and visits Hades and carries out the will of the gods (6)

Patroclus Emotional (3); when his ghost appears to Achilles and reviews his past life, he brushes aside "that wretched manslaughter business, the day that I lost my temper and killed Amphidamas's son, through childish folly, not meaning to, over a game of dice"

Paris Sensory and emotional (2-3) and social (5), but when rebuked as "so handsome, made for woman, seducer" by Hector, he takes it to a higher level (6): "Do not bring up against me the sweet gifts of golden Aphrodite. Not to be cast aside are the gods' illustrious gifts, of whatever sort—even if no man would choose them" (3.63-66)

Priam Emotional (3), social (5), and spiritual (6), grieving for his sons, but he is primarily motivated to preserve Troy and honor the gods

Spinning the Thread of Life

Applying the paradigm of Seven Levels of Awareness to wrath, the *Iliad's* main theme, we can classify it into seven types of ever wider, greater intensity:

1) Blind rage, an unthinking, visceral human emotion such as Achilles demonstrates after hearing of Patroclus's death

2) Rage accompanied by bodily pain and discomfort, also experienced by Achilles

3) Rage accompanied by feelings of sadness and loss, as further manifested in Achilles' response and vow to avenge Patroclus's death

4) Rage accompanied by a well-thought out plan of revenge or defense such as Thetis's strategic plan to seek divine weapons from Hephaestus for her son

5) Rage and revenge directed against an entire city or people such as Achilles's resolve to destroy Troy and all it inhabitants and hold them responsible for Helen's abduction

6) Rage sanctioned by prayer and sacrifice to the gods to uphold the mores of society and the proper boundaries between mortals and immortals, as Achilles does when he prays to Zeus over Patroclus's desecrated body and is aided by Athena, Poseidon, and other immortals; on the other hand he incurs Zeus's *menis* when he mutilates Hector's corpse

7) Cosmic rage meant to repair a breech in universal order that threatens to introduce chaos into the world of gods and mortals; it is akin to Aristotle's definition of tragedy as the imitation of an action rooted in the order of the universe that brings catharsis and elicits feelings of pity and fear.

At this supreme level, it may also be a transcendent experience such as the *Iliad* itself when it is sung, danced, observed, or read, creating a state of mind that unites subject and object so that Homer, Zeus, Hera, Achilles, Hector, and the other cast of gods and heroes, as well as ourselves the audience and performers, become indissolubly united.

The role of Zeus in the epic raises many questions. He is the ruler of heaven, but he is not all-powerful like Yahweh in the Hebrew Bible, God the Father in the New Testament, and other supreme beings. Zeus shares dominion over the world with his two brothers. Zeus rules the heavens, Poseidon rules the oceans, and Hades presides over the Underworld. Together the three siblings share the earth. Zeus is also constantly looking over his shoulder and to the horizon. On the one hand, he fears his father Cronus and other Titans incarcerated in Tartarus, a sunless realm deep in the earth, will break free. On the other, he fears one of his progeny will grow up and overthrow him as he dethroned his father.

While Zeus's overall goal is to maintain celestial order, he can't control his libido and engages in endless affairs, rapes, and seductions of nubile goddesses, women, girls, and even animals. His sister and wife Hera nurses the archetypal rage of a scorned spouse and gives him no peace. After Patroclus's death, she demands that Troy be burnt to the ground. Zeus is reluctant to see the entire city destroyed to satisfy Hera or Achilles' wrath, and he admires Hector's valor and Priam's devout sacrifices and prayers for his protection. Finally, the relentless queen of heaven proposes a swap. She will give Zeus a chit to destroy three cities dear to her heart if he will surrender Troy's fate to her. Worn down by her henpecking, the exasperated cloud-shaker finally agrees. In the end, Troy's fate comes down to a lovers' spat in the heavenly bedchamber. Like playing hearts or swapping baseball cards, the two immortals reshuffle their closely held hands of cards. The end result upends the chessboard below them. Their offhand agreement shapes and influences the lives of millions, determines the course of Western history, and leads to the founding of Rome and Britain. As Achilles confesses to Priam when he comes to collect his son's body: "Let's allow our distress to lie at rest in our hearts, for all our grieving, for there's no profit accrues from numbing lamentation: that's how the gods spun life's thread for unhappy mortals—to live amid sorrow, while they themselves are uncaring"

As the above compendium shows, allegory permeates the *Iliad*. Besides direct appearances by Dream, Sleep, Prayer, Panic, Rout, and others, the gods themselves mirror human qualities. As the embodiment of rational thought, Athena appears to mortals now as wisdom, now as delusion. For example, Hector meets his match in single combat with the son of Peleus and dies of a spear thrust to the throat and collarbone. But as Homer observes, he was "slain through Achilles' hands, by grey-eyed Pallas Athena." Hector's courage, however noble, is based on his "towering strength." He is brought low by craft, reason, and higher levels of awareness. When Achilles himself is later killed, Paris shoots the arrow, but as Homer observes, it was Apollo who wields the bow. Allegorically, Achilles—the soul of rage and mercilessness—is slain by reason, art, and healing—the domains Apollo reigns over. Paris, in turn, is later killed in combat by the Greek warrior Philoctetes. He is hit by arrows in the bow hand, the eye, and the heel, three locations that can be viewed as karmic justice for slaying Achilles and being dazzled by Aphrodite's eye-popping beauty and promise of the most beautiful woman in the world. As often noted, Athena only appears to Odysseus in the *Odyssey* when he's thinking clearly, not when he's angry.

Zeus himself often represents a projection of cosmic order or chaos, depending on the subject's level of consciousness. To Priam, he manifests as compassion when he orchestrates the return of Hector's body. When he remains inconsolable over Patrocles's death, Achilles laments over Zeus's mercilessness. In the opening of the *Odyssey*, Zeus addresses the Olympian gods: "My word, how mortals take the gods to task! All their afflictions come from us, we hear. And what of their own failings? Greed and folly double the suffering in the lot of man."

When Zeus encourages the immortals to take sides in the war, Poseidon pairs off against Apollo. The seas, which Poseidon rules, are a traditional symbol of the unconscious, or the first level of awareness. Apollo, the sun god, represents the light of reason and logical thinking, as well as the arts and healing. It is natural that consciousness and unconsciousness should square off. Athena is attacked by Enyalios, an ancient god of war. As a battle goddess herself, theirs is a manifestation of repulsion (like repelling like), as well as a natural polarity between yin and yang—the crafty, subtle, feminine arts of war and the direct, hard, masculine show of strength. Hera, the queen of domesticity, goes after Artemis, the goddess of the hunt. As goddess of marriage, Hera incarnates fertility, while the single, unattached Artemis remains chaste. Leto, the mother of Artemis and Apollo, fights Hermes, the Olympian herald. As a Titan, goddess of motherhood, and consort of Zeus, Leto is abhorred by Hera, and in this encounter Hermes does Hera's bidding. Finally, Hephaestus, the god of fire, combats the River Xanthos. The personification of water almost succeeds in drowning Achilles until the divine smithy arrives and encircles the raging current with flame, allowing the Argive hero to escape.

As these match ups suggest, the *Iliad* has a strong allegorical layer and is crafted on a foundation of complementary opposite energies in the natural world. In Greek myth and philosophy they are described as love (*philotes*) and strife (*neikos*). In the Far East, they are known as yin and yang. Homer does not deny the existence of the gods or the spiritual world, as did many skeptical Greek philosophers, dramatists, and authors who came after him. But the way he fashions the mental landscape, sculpts his characters, and weaves their destinies shows that consciousness is seamless, comprehensible, and multi-textured.

Beyond the whims of the gods, the passions of mortals, and the seven-step ladder to Olympus is there any order in the Homeric universe? There are brief displays of compassion, such as the meeting between Achilles and Priam, but does the arc of the moral universe, as Rev. Theodore Parker, the nineteenth century abolitionist so eloquently contended (later paraphrased by Martin Luther King, Jr.), bend toward justice? To Achilles' Shield, the divine weapon that enabled the Achaeans to defeat Hector and turn the tide of war, we now turn.

2
ACHILLES' SHIELD

The relentless battlefield violence and brutality in the *Iliad* is broken by intermittent truces to bury the dead, parleys among the Olympians, and a few scenes of domesticity. We are treated to occasional portraits of Helen or Andromache, the wife of Hector, weaving or conversing with other Trojan women. In his tent, far from battle, Achilles plays the lyre and ponders sailing home and living a long, but inglorious life in Pythia. But these tranquil episodes are rare. The most extended meditation on peace and harmony is Homer's vivid description of the divine shield wrought by Hephaestus.

Following Patroclus's death, Achilles' mother, the immortal nymph Thetis, is terrified that her wrathful son will seek revenge on Hector and perish in the attempt. She knows that if he continues to pursue a warrior's path he is destined for a short, but glorious end, and she is fated to an eternity of grieving. To safeguard him, at least from the mightiest of the Trojan spearmen, she seeks out Hephaestus, the god of metallurgy, to fashion heavenly weapons. Hephaestus welcomes her warmly because his mother Hera cast him out of Olympus on account of his lameness, and Thetis and Eurynome, the daughter of Ocean, rescued him from the sea. As a child, he was brought up in their cave where he learned to fashion necklaces, brooches, and other beautiful objects. As he tells Charis, his bright-veiled wife, "I have a great need to repay fair-tressed Thetis fully for having saved my life."

Bewailing her fate, long-robed Thetis clasps Hephaestus's knees and begs him to "make my short-lived son a shield and a helmet, and a corselet and fine greaves equipped with ankle-pieces" to replace those Patroclus lost when he was slain by Hector.

The god of fire reassures her that he would hide her son if he could "away from grievous death." But since that is impossible, "he'll get fine new armor, such gear that in time to come all humankind will be thunderstruck at the sight of it."

In his workshop, he begins to fashion the mighty Shield, the centerpiece of the weaponry. As he limps around the studio, he casts bronze, tin, silver, and gold into the fire and works it on his anvil with a weighty hammer and forging tongs. With consummate skill, he forges the Shield, enormous and sturdy, with five layers of protection and a bright rim with three strands of metal topped with silver baldric.

First, on the huge hield, Hephaestus "fashion[s] the earth, the sea, and the heavens, the unwearying sun, the moon on its increase to full, and every constellation with which the heavens are crowned." In the center, he sets the Pleiades, the Hyades, Orion, and the Bear or Wain "that revolves in one place, keeping a watchful eye on Orion, and alone never sinks into the baths of Ocean."

Second, the god of the forge fashions two cities of peace and war. The first depicts marriage and banquets, including a torchlight parade and dancing in the streets. Amid the celebrations a dispute arises between two men over the blood-price of a man who has been killed. One of the men claims to have paid it all, but the other swears he received nothing. As the dispute is referred to an assembly to arbitrate, some citizens of the city back one side, and some the other. The elders, or judges, sit on polished seats of stone in a sacred circle. Each holds a herald's staff and one by one rises to give his opinion. Two talents of gold are set between the competing parties for the victor.

Around the second city two contingents of troops encamp. The choice before them is whether to destroy the city by fighting or share the city's wealth and make peace. The besieged resolve to fight and instruct the women, children, and old men to man the ramparts while the able-bodied men prepare for battle led by Athena and Ares.

The attackers then set up an ambush in a riverbed by a watering place for flocks and herds. Two herdsmen playing their pipes come along with their sheep and cattle and are slaughtered. The besieged hear the animals in distress and join battle on their "high-stepping horses" and with bronze-tipped spears. Strife, Tumult, and the baneful Death-Spirit mix amid the two sides and sow mayhem. One man is "dragged through the turmoil, dead, by the feet."

Third, Hephaestus fashions a second circle of human activity depicting a "broad field of rich plowland" worked by many farmers and their draft animals. At the edge of the field they are each handed a cup of honey-sweet wine. As they toil, Homer writes, "the field grew black, as though it had really been plowed, though made of gold: here indeed was marvelous artistry." Other country folk reap a harvest on a royal estate, cutting "swathes some were falling in rows, along the line of the furrow, while others the sheaf-binders were tying with twists of straw." The king stands by, "staff in hand and happy at heart" while a feast is prepared for the harvesters by the women with a great sacrificial ox lavishly sprinkled with white barley.

Fourth, Hephaestus creates another circle with a grape orchard with a profusion of vines entwined on silver poles holding clusters of grapes. Around the vineyard he inscribes a ditch done in cobalt enamel and a fence made of tin. An array of boys and girls "all innocently light-hearted" carry the honey-sweet fruit in wicker baskets while a boy in the center sings the Linos song and makes sweet music on a clear-toned lyre, while they stamp to the beat and shout and dance in unison. Linos was the first human to be given the gift of divine song, but slain by Apollo out of jealousy.

On this circle, the divine craftsman also sets a herd of straight-horned cattle made of gold and tin. Four herdsmen accompany them with nine shepherd dogs, but among the lead cattle two fearsome lions get hold of a bellowing bull. The men and dogs follow in pursuit but are afraid to attack as the bull is devoured. In the distance, the god makes a pasture with grazing sheep and their sheepfolds.

Fifth, Hephaestus creates an inlaid dancing floor like the one "in spacious Knossos that long ago Daedalus fashioned for fair-tressed Ariadne." Here many young men and women, robed in fine tunics and linens, dance. The girls wear garlands and the boys gold and silver adornments. They proceed to dance in a circle, "feet well-skilled, very lightly," in the manner a potter sits at a wheel and tests the clay. A crowd of spectators cheers as they approach each other in a dancing line, while a "sacred bard sang to his lyre" and two acrobats whirl among them "taking the lead in all their sport and pleasure."

Sixth, finally the smithy god sets the mighty stream of Ocean to run round the outer rim of the magnificent shield.

The Ages of Humanity

Given the loving detail Homer devotes to describing Achilles' Shield, this elaborate art work may hold the key to understanding the *Iliad* as a whole. However, many scholars view the scene as a digression from the main battlefield action, or as an antiquated heraldic device similar to mythical shields described by Hesiod, Virgil, and other classical writers. One common interpretation holds the Shield's tableaux focusing primarily on rural peace and prosperity symbolizes everything that Achilles stands to lose by returning to battle. Unlike Agamemnon's shield which brandishs fearsome images of the Gorgon "with her stare of terror," Achilles's is predominantly peaceful. At birth it was prophesized that he could either enjoy a long peaceful but unheroic life, or die young bravely in war. In *The War That Killed Achilles*, in which she contends that Homer is essentially a pacifist, Carolyn Alexander observes that the Shield "eschews the motifs most predictably associated with warfare and furnishes the *Iliad* with the most memorable images of peace.... The shield Hephaestus forges for Achilles carried all of life. It underscores all he is to lose—which is all of life."

Homer's description of the Shield is one of the lengthiest scenes in the epic. As Oliver Taplin contends in "The Shield of Achilles Within the *Iliad*," the Shield places warfare into perspective with the rest of life: "On the shield the *Iliad* takes up, so to speak, one half of one of the five circles. It is as though Homer has allowed us temporarily to stand back from the poem and see it in its place—like a 'detail' from the reproduction of a painting within a larger landscape, a landscape which is usually blotted from sight by the all-consuming narrative in the foreground." Throughout the poem, Taplin goes on, "Again and again, pain and destruction and violent death are compared to fertile agriculture, creative craftsmanship, useful objects and tasks, scenes of peace and innocent delight....The similes thus let us—indeed make us—look through the war to the peace that lies behind it, to the peace that the warriors have abandoned and which many of them will never know again. The similes make us see war as wasteful and destructive, the blight of peace and pleasure....[The Shield] makes us think about war and see it in relation to peace....The *Iliad* owes its tragic greatness to Homer's ability to appreciate and sympathize with both aspects of heroic war. He shows how for every victory there is a defeat, how for every triumphant killing there is another human killed. Glorious deeds are done, mighty prowess displayed: at the same time fine cities are burned, fathers lose their sons, women lose their families and freedom."

In still other insights about the Shield, Gregory Nagy, a leading Homeric scholar, sees the scene about arbitrating the dispute in the Circle of the Cities of War and Peace as the genesis of the *polis*, or democratic political unit, in early Greek jurisprudence. Leonard Muellner, another critic, sees the Shield upholding the absolute value of life that Achilles upholds when he rejects the Achaean embassy to return to battle compared with the ethos of the warrior: "For me, to be alive, has nothing to match it, not all the fabled wealth of Ilion . . . to bring a man's life back neither raiding nor victories suffice once it has fled beyond the barrier of his teeth." "The possibility that there is no way to compensate for the loss

Achilles' Shield 51

of life keeps alive the issue of the relative value of *kleos* [a warrior's epic glory] and *psukhe* 'life's breath' in the world of Achilles' Shield," observes Muellner. W. H. Auden's poem *Achilles' Shield* draws on scenes in Hephaestus's handiwork as a metaphor for modern totalitarian society and the inhumanity of war.

Looking back, I don't remember the Shield from my childhood book on Greek mythology or later reading of Homer. Nor did it make an impression on me in college when I studied the classics. But when I turned to the *Iliad* while writing *One Peaceful World* with Michio Kushi, I immediately recognized its significance. The Shield depicts the cycle of the axial precession of the equinoxes and the four major epochs of human history over the last 25,800 years. Instead of dividing his circular diagram into quadrants as Michio did in his lectures, Homer fashioned four concentric circles within a larger circle. In the macrobiotic model, the stars and constellations are featured around the outside of the circle. In the Greek model, they dwell in the center. The two diagrams represent the same thing. They simply offer complementary opposite perspectives.

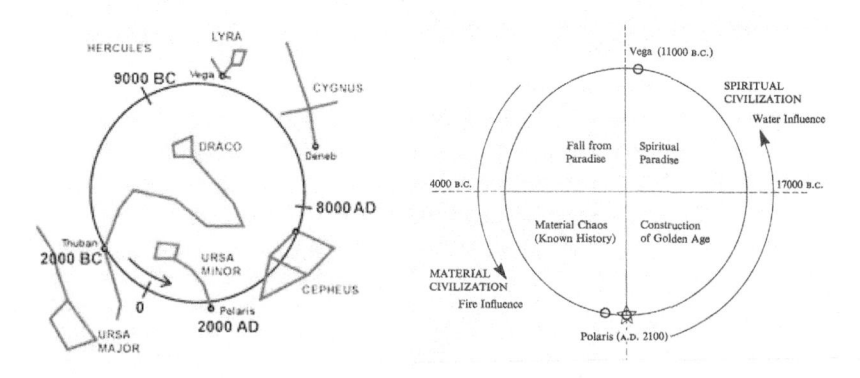

There are slight differences. Homer's first circle depicts the present day: the cities of war and peace. Then it returns to the agricultural origins of humanity (the Circle of Agricultural Peace and Plenty and the Circle of Vintage and Pasturage) and concludes with the approaching Circle of the Dance. The Vega Cycle starts with paradise and proceeds sequentially through the historical cycle, ending with building the new golden age.

	Vega Cycle	**Achilles' Shield**
Pole Star	Northern constellations with Vega and Polaris as the primary Pole	Northern constellations with the Bear pointing to the North Star

	Stars	
Quadrants or Circles	1. Paradise	1. Circle of the City of Peace and the City of War
	2. Wilderness or Paradise Lost	2. Circle of Agricultural Peace and Plenty
	3. Material Chaos	3. Circle of Vintage and Pasturage
	4. Construction of the Golden Age	4. Circle of the Dance

The traditional Ages of Humanity also correspond with these two models of history. In the West, Hesiod, a near contemporary of Homer, presents the classical description of the ages in *Works and Days*. The first era saw the creation of a golden race of mortals by the Olympian gods. It was presided over by Cronus (the Roman god Saturn), Zeus's father, and is known as the Golden Age. Humans lived like gods, "carefree in their hearts, shielded from pain and misery." People lived long, happy lives, without aging. The "barley-giving earth" brought forth a plentiful harvest without toil. People lived in "peace and abundance as lords of their lands rich in flocks and dear to the blessed gods."

Eventually, in the course of time, "the earth covered this race" and the mortals of the Golden Age became holy spirits watching over the eras to come. Following their reign, the gods fashioned a second race, "a much worse one," this time of silver. They were nurtured as playful children for a hundred years. When they grew up, they could not refrain from conflict and violence. During this era, seeds of grain were placed in the ground for the first time since humans now had to produce their own food. (Genesis tells a similar story.) In time, Zeus, who now ruled the skies, was angered and buried the Silver Race because they failed to honor the gods.

The Bronze Age followed the Silver Age. Created from hard ash trees, people in this era were "dreadful and mighty and bent on the harsh deeds of war and violence." They ate no grain and their "hearts were tough as steel." Their weapons, homes, and other tools and implements were all made of bronze. But their minds were bent on destruction, and "black death claimed them for all their fierceness." Following their extinction, Zeus made a divine race of heroes "better and more just." As sons and daughters of immortals and mortals, these demigods nevertheless engaged in "evil war and dreadful battle wiped them all out." They included all the men who "sailed to Troy for the sake of lovely-haired Helen." In that distant land, "death threw his dark mantle over them." A few heroic Achaeans and Trojans survived, thanks to Zeus's favor, and lived long, happy lives. Upon death, their spirits went to the islands of the blessed where they enjoyed "three times a year the barley-giving land [that brought] forth full grain sweet as honey."

The Iron Age followed the Bronze and Heroic Ages. People of this era, which includes our own, "waste away with toil and pain." Children do not resemble their fathers and "there is no affection between guest and host and no love between friends or brothers." Children disobey and treat their parents cruelly. They will even "sack one another's city." "Right and shame will vanish," and the rare person who keeps his oath and is just and good will be dishonored. Envy prevails and people "take joy in the ruin of others."

Ages of Humanity	**Achilles' Shield**	**Vega Cycle**
1. Golden	Circle of Agricultural Peace and Plenty	Paradise
2. Silver	Circle of Vintage and Pasturage	Wilderness
3. Bronze/Heroic and Iron	Circle of the City of Peace and City of War	Material Chaos
4. New Golden	Circle of the Dance	Construction of the new Golden Age

Hesiod's Five Ages are often condensed into four epochs with the Bronze and Heroic combined followed by the Iron Age. This schema corresponds with the circles on Achilles' Shield and the seasons or quadrants of the Vega Cycle. Hesiod does not describe the future era, represented by the Circle of the Dance or the Construction of the Golden Age. The Greek view of history as cyclical is paralleled in other traditions. In Vedic India, the Four Yugas begin with the *Satya*, in which virtue rules supreme. It is followed by the *Treta*, in which morality declines by 25 percent; the *Dvapara*, in which good and evil are on an equal footing; and the *Kali*, the current era in which vice governs. In Sanskrit literature, the four ages are also described as the Golden, Silver, Bronze, and Iron as in the Greek schema. In Mesoamerica, there are five ages known as Suns. In the ancient Maya, Inca, and Aztec cosmology, however, the ages progressively increase in virtue, while in the Eurasian paradigm, the eras decrease in morality and spiritual insight.

Microcosm and Macrocosm

Achilles' Shield not only depicts the cosmos, the precession of the equinoxes, and cycle of human history, but it also illustrates highlights of the *Iliad* itself. Let's look at some of these parallels.

"The Shield begins," as Leonard Muellner perceptively notes, "like the *Theogony*'s cosmogony, with the making of earth and sky, Gaia and Ouranos." Furthermore, the depiction of the sun, moon, and constellations in the center of the Shield portrays the precessional march of the North Star. This is the star pointed to by the "Bear or Wain that revolves in one place, keeping a watchful eye, and alone never sinks into the baths of Ocean." Interestingly, this passage probably refers to the Little Bear or Little Wain, not the Big Bear or Big Wain. In Mycenaean times, the star Kolchab in the Little Bear (better known as the Little Dipper) served as the North Star. It was succeeded by Polaris, which continues to serve today as the Pole Star. In either case, the Bear reference points directly to the bright star at the center of the firmament that remains unmoved and never sets on the horizon in the life of any individual or society.

The two cities of humankind refer broadly to the checkerboard pattern of war and peace that has characterized human history. With the rise of urbanization, periods of peace and plenty have been followed by times of war and famine, as depicted on the Shield. The two cities also represent the Achaeans and the Trojans. The "besieged" with their "high-stepping horses" are clearly the Trojans, known for their mighty steeds and excellent horsemanship. The "bronze-tipped spears" situate the action in the Bronze and Heroic Ages. Strife, Tumult, and the baneful Death-Spirit depicted on the Shield frequently make their appearance in the epic narrative. The description of the women, children, and old men manning the rampants on the Shield is later echoed by Hector: "Let the boys who are in their first youth and the grey-browed elders take stations on the god-founded bastions that circle the city; and as for the women have our wives each one in her own house, kindle a great fire; let there be a watch kept steadily lest a sudden attack get into the town when the fighters have left it."

The dispute over the blood-price glances at the death of Patroclus and the compensation on the battlefield Achilles will extract from Hector and the Trojans. The assembly of elders, or judges, nods at the immortals on Olympus. Homer uses the same epithet to describe them sitting in council on "well-shaped or polished stones" as he does the masonry in Zeus's palace. The desecration of Patroclus's corpse violates *themis*, or the principle of cosmic order, and warrants retribution. The question is how much? Thetis, Athena, and some of the gods supporting the Achaeans want Zeus to let Achilles, not only avenge his companion's death, but also live and avert his fated death. Aphrodite, Ares, and those aligned with the Trojans call for a more measured response. The mention of Athena and Ares, the champions of the Argives and Trojans respectively, reinforces this interpretation. The scene on the Shield may also point to Ajax, who in an earlier episode entreats Achilles to return to the fray, contrasting his savage fury and stubbornness to a man who "accepts recompense even from his brother's or his own son's murder . . . and the kinsman's emotional passion is duly tempered by the blood-price he has received." The image also foreshadows the assembly at the end of the epic in which a settlement is reached between Odysseus and the relatives of the suitors.

The ambush and murder of the two herdsmen on the Shield glances at Odysseus and Diomedes who slaughter Dolon, a Trojan spy, and Rheus, a Thracan king, on the way back to the main Achaean camp after visiting Achilles in his hut. As emissaries of Hector, the "people's shepherd," they are herdsmen.

The second circle of the Shield depicts an idyllic era of peace and plenty. The rich fields of barley are lovingly tended by the community as a whole and yield an abundant harvest. In addition to the golden grain, the reapers enjoy cups of golden honey-sweet wine. The king, "staff in hand and happy at heart," presiding over the estate is Cronus (Saturn), Zeus's father, and god who ruled over the Golden Age. Cronos's symbol, the scythe, is alluded to not only in the staff which the king wields, but also in bringing in the sheaves.

The third circle on the Shield depicts a vineyard with vines of ripe grapes propped up on silver poles. A group of boys and girls "all innocently light-hearted" assist the pickers. These images point at the Silver Age, when children will be nurtured for one hundred years, and foolishness will lead. In the midst of the children a boy sings sweetly and plays on a clear-toned lyre. The tune he performs, the Linos song, owes its name to a legendary musician who was slain by Apollo. As the deity who presided over the Muses and was the god of music, he resented Linos, who received the divine gift of song. Linos mirrors Achilles, who plays the lyre in his hut on the beach while sulking over Agamemnon's arrogance and refusing to fight. Like Linos, Achilles was fated to be slain by Apollo.

The next scene around the third circle on the Shield depicts a group of long horn cows and sheep being led to pasture. But two fearsome lions attack the lead bull and tear out its entrails. The herdsmen and their dogs hold back in fear. The scene glances at Patroclus who leads the Argives to the Trojan gates and is set upon by Hector and Aeneas. It also looks ahead to the *Odyssey* in which Odysseus's crew rebels and devours the cattle of the Sun and disturbs his flock of sheep. The ringleaders, Eurylokhos and the helmsmen, mirror the two lions, while Odysseus himself holds back in fear of divine retribution. The violent incident dooms the men and reflects the decline of virtue and morality in the Bronze Age as humanity descends into violence and bloodshed.

The fourth circle on the Shield depicts an "inlaid dancing floor" like the one that Daedalus fashioned for Adriane. Daedalus, the master craftsman and artist, built the Labyrinth in Knossos, the capital of ancient Crete and the Minoan civilization. Originally it was a large dance studio, but it later became the lair of the Minotaur that demanded a periodic sacrifice of seven youths and seven maidens. The Athenian hero Theseus embarked on a quest to kill the ferocious beast. But brave men had entered the maze before and failed to emerge. Adriane, the daughter of King Minos of Crete, fell in love with the young knight and gave him a ball of thread to find his way out. In this passage, mention of the myth reinforces the precessional symbolism of humanity's turn from an epoch of savage violence to one of peace and happiness. Homer compares the long Bronze and Iron Age of violence and war to the bloodstained Labyrinth that is destined to return to its original virtuous state as a theater or haven for music, dance, art, and the other fruits of peace and prosperity.

The other scenes in the fourth and final circle on the Shield reinforce this joyful imagery with scenes of young men and women dancing, laughing and singing together in a circle. They are likened to "a potter [that] sits at a wheel that matches his hands' grasp, and tries it, to see how it will run." This glances not only at Hephaestus, the archetypal divine craftsman, but also at Homer, the poet weaving his epic verse. Further, the image depicts a craftsman preparing to fashion something new—the return of the Golden Age. The young male dancers carry "daggers of gold, suspended from silver baldrics." These reinforce the Golden Age imagery and the cyclical order of return to paradise from the silver era to the golden one. The "sacred bard" who is singing on his lyre in the center of the dancing circle glances at Homer the epic poet who channels the Muses. Like fractals or stacking Russian dolls, the bards sing the *Iliad* and *Odyssey* within the *Iliad* and *Odyssey*.

In this way, Achilles' Shield portrays the four Ages of Humanity, ending on a positive, joyful depiction of the coming era of peace and an end to all conflict, violence, and warfare. Marlowe, a close student of Ovid's tales and Arthur Goldberg's translation of Homer, may have had this image in mind when he wrote about "the merry songs of peace." The phrase refers to the dawn of a new golden age with the birth of Elizabeth, England's future queen.

Shield and Sword

Shields play a prominent role in the *Iliad* and other early Greek literature. They came in a variety of sizes and were typically round, oval, or rectangular. Some had small scalops cut out of the sides for better mobility with a spear, and huge ones could be used to protect the entire body and were described by Homer as being as big as a wall. Primarily defensive, shields were occasionally used to ward off blows or arrows, or assist others as when Ajax covers and protects his brother. They were also wielded offensively, as when the Achaeans advance behind Achilles with their shields resting on shoulders in the tortoiseshell formation. Most shields were made with layers of oxhide, though some like Achilles' contained thin layers of metal. The most common epithets used to describe Iliadic shields are "well balanced," "gleaming," "embossed," or "man-enclosing." The code of the Bronze Age warrior rewarded chivalric behavior. At one point in the action, the mighty Achaean warrior Diomedes and the able Trojan Glaucus propose to "exchange armor and be guest-friends." In a later bromance, Ajax and Hector reach a stalemate in their man-to-man combat, call a truce, exchange weapons, and "depart in friendship."

The other divine armor that Hephaestus fashions is not described in the *Iliad*. Other than the fabled ash spear of his father, spears and swords play no special role in the epic, as they do in the Arthurian romances, Samurai tales, and many other cultural traditions. Ash is especially hard and is to wood what bronze and iron are to metals. In Hesiod's catalog of the Ages, humans were (re)created from hard ash trees in the Bronze Age.

Unlike mortals, the gods sow confusion among their enemies with the elements, including storms, mist, floods, fires, and other natural phenomena. They also use the bow, as in the case of Artemis and Apollo. Poseidon wields a trident. Zeus's thunderbolt, a particularly potent weapon, can smite mortals and paralyze immortals. The cloud-shaker also wields the Aegis, a divine shield or supernatural animal skin that wards off all danger. Athena, the only other god who wields the aegis, brandishes the head of the Gorgon, a monster whose look turned the beholder to stone, on her aegis. In the *Iliad*, on one occasion she places her aegis around Achilles's shoulders and fashions a golden cloud and shining flame around his head.

With this divine protection, he issues a war cry "as clear as the trumpet" that sows panic among the Trojans and their horses. On another occasion, Zeus lends the aegis to Apollo, who enveloped in a cloud, leads Hector in a successful counterattack. The aegises were originally made by Hephaestus. The epic also notes that he made a corselet for Diomedes, a private chamber for Hera, and the stone porticos of Zeus's Olympian abode. He also fashioned the armor for Peleus, Achilles' father that he inherits and later lends to Patroclus. It is stripped from his body by Hector and, of divine origin, plays a major role in the *menis*, or cosmic wrath, of the gods against Troy.

After Thetis gives the mighty Shield to her son, it is instrumental in turning the tide of war. "Arm yourself for battle. Be clad in valor," she tells Achilles, filling him with dauntless strength and dripping ambrosia and nectar to preserve Patroclus's body. As soon as he receives the divine gear, Achilles accompanies Odysseus and Diomedes to a council of the Argives and renounces his wrath against Agamemnon.

He then puts on "the god's gifts that Hephaestus made for him." The Shield, "huge and sturdy," "so fine, so intricate," gleamed afar "a brightness like the moon's" and sent a shaft of life skyward. It fits perfectly, and as Homer attests, "buoyed him like wings." Then the Achaean warrior takes up his Pelian ash spear, weighty and massive, that Cheiron, gave his father. Cheiron was the youthful centaur that, like Apollo, carried a bow and had the gift of healing and prophecy. Fully suited, Achilles appears "agleam in his battle gear like Hyperion the bright Sun."

Yoking his two immortal horses, Xanthos and Balios, Achilles prepares for battle. Xanthos addresses him and prophesizes his death due "to a great god and all-mastering Fate": "But you yourself are destined to be laid low by a god's might, and a man's," alluding to his death at the hands of Apollo and Paris. The Furies cut off Xanthos's power of speech, and Achilles mounts his steed.

In the fighting on the beach, Aeneas throws a rock at Achilles and hits "the shield that kept him from grim death." In a lull in the action, Achilles sets aside his new Shield and seizes twelve Trojan youths from the water to sacrifice for the killing of Patroclus and sets his mind on slaughter. It is unclear whether the boys are assisting their elders or are innocents caught in the fighting. But they are unarmed. In a murderous fury, Achilles then mercilessly slays Lykoan, a young Trojan warrior whom he once knew. Having thrown down his weapons, Lykoan clasps his knees in supplication and is ruthlessly dispatched by Achilles' "long spear." Note that in both these heinous acts, Achilles sets aside the Shield in keeping with its function as a defensive weapon and an emblem of peace and reconciliation.

Achilles' Shield

As the fighting picks up, Asteropaios lets fly two spears at Achilles's Shield "but failed to break through: the gold layer, a god's gift, held it off." Then in the most extended battle scene with the son of Peleus other than the climatic fight with Hector, River goes after Achilles, "its crest crashing into his shield [and] forced him back." In a breathtaking chase, Achilles leaps back with the swoop of a black eagle, the hunting falcon, while the River strives mightily to drown him. When Achilles prays to Zeus, Poseidon and Athena speed to the rescue. The River, known as Scamandros, is the principal tributary of Troy. With the other major waterway, Simoeis, it rises up to defend its homeland. "For I tell you neither [Achilles'] violence nor his good looks will save him," River promises his fellow river, "nor his fine armor, which in some flooded pool of mine will lie, all coated with mud." Vowing to "entomb him in silt," River rushes turbulently at the valiant warrior, "surging high, seething with foam and blood and slaughtered corpses." But as the enraged current towers over Achilles for the deathblow, Hera darts to protect him. The queen of heaven calls upon Hephaestus, her lame son and creator of the Shield, to create a ring of fire, while she raises gale-force winds, to enclose the watery abyss. In obedience, Hephaestus raises "a marvelous conflagration," and soon the entire Trojan plain is ablaze, as well as the riverbanks and the rivers' teeming fish and eels. The divine intervention works magic. As the "sweet streams blazed and their water bubbled," River stops "with no will to flow further." In deference to Hera, River pledges not to protect the Trojans in the future, even if the city is set ablaze. River is vanquished.

The final trial begins with Apollo stirring up Agenor, a warrior of unmatched power, who hit Achilles's shin under the knee, but "the god's gift held it back." In the encounter with Hector, the leader of the Trojan army lets fly his far-shadowing spear and "struck Pelus's son's shield in the middle, didn't miss it, yet the spear bounced back off the shield." As his missile falls harmlessly aside from the mighty Shield, Hector realizes that he has been deceived by Athena, and Achilles has been given divine protection.

Achilles then rushes at him, "heart full of wildly raging strength, with his Shield—fine intricately wrought"—out in front to protect his body, "while the bright helmet, four-plated, nodded above, and waving all round it, the lovely gold plums that Hephaestus had set thick about its crown, like that star that goes among other stars at nightfall, the star of evening, the loveliest star in the heavens, was the gleam that shone from the sharp spear that Achilles brandished in his right hand, planning trouble for noble Hector."

The dazzling Shield not only saves Achilles from death on the battlefield, it also demoralizes Hector. Taking advantage of his opponent's confusion, Achilles spears the huge Trojan warrior in the gullet and he dies. Although he has triumphed thanks to the divine Shield, Achilles's wrath remains unappeased. Adding insult to injury, he then takes "the famous battle gear with him" and attaches Hector's body to his chariot. The mutilation of Hector's corpse, which he proceeds to drag around the walls of Troy, alienates the gods and seals his fate.

Vega Cycle Resonances

As in *Hamlet*, the Shield represents a play-within-the-play that reveals past, present, and future action. It is an *Iliad* within the *Iliad*. But the epic itself, or the poetic saga of the Trojan War, can also be viewed as part of a larger canvas: the 25,800-year cycle, known to later Greeks as the Platonic Year, and to us as the Vega or Vega/Polaris Cycle.

In this telling, the theme is humanity's sojourn through cycles of peace and feasting, war and famine, and then back to a state of primal abundance. As we have seen, the four large circles on Achilles's Shield correspond with the Four (or Five) Ages of Humanity described in early Western literature and found around the world.

According to this reading, Achilles and Odysseus stand for Everyman, or humanity in its perennial quest for a healthy, happy, meaningful existence. The two cities on the Shield are Troy and the Greek encampment. Throughout the narrative, the Achaean fortifications are described in urban terms. The beachfront where the hollow ships are moored is dotted with walls, gateways, ditches, and towers. The breastworks and "great wall" of the Argives sport buttresses and jutting timbers and constitute a rudimentary settlement for tens of thousands of warriors. It is furnished from the spoils of plundering the countryside and sacking cities allied with Troy. From a solitary hut, Achilles' abode metamorphoses into a "high-born cabin" with rough-cut fir-wood beans, and a roof." By the time Priam arrives and seeks an audience with Achilles, it is a teeming military nerve center with "a large courtyard" and a "close-set palisade." Though primitive compared to the elegant, towering citadel of Troy, the elderly king would have experienced it more as an urban than a rustic environment when he came to ransom his son. The two cities on the beach at Troy are also emblematic of the Spiral of History.

As a Bronze Age epic, considerable mention is made in the *Iliad* of this compound of copper and tin. In the Aegean, tin from Mediterranean trade networks was imported to Crete, renowned for its copper mining, from about 3200 BCE. The Minoan civilization used it for jewelry, tools, and cookware, and the Mycenaean added weaponry. The Late Bronze Age ended about 1200 BCE or several centuries before the Homeric epics reached final written form.

Apollo, Lord of the Silver Bow, bears an epithet harkening back to the Silver Age, when virtue has declined about 50 percent. Though a mighty god, he was born into the generation after Zeus and lacks the authority and power of his father. Hera became insanely jealous when Zeus seduced his mother Leto. Upon the birth of Apollo and his twin sister Artemis, the goddess caused all countries to shun her, and her babies were born on the island of Delos.

Iron was known since antiquity, but the process for working it was not perfected until after Homer's time. The poet mentions it in passing. But he would have been familiar from mythology of the prophesized Iron Age, and the durable metal figures in several pivotal scenes. When Achilles makes a funeral pyre for Patroclus, he covers the body from head to toe with animal fat, and then tosses four horses, two dogs, and most shockingly the twelve noble Trojan sons in the flames. Homer describes him as setting "fire iron's might" to consume the corpse and sacrificial animal and human victims. Just before dying, Hector's last words to Achilles are: "Truly the heart in your breast is of iron." In the course of the war, the son of Pelus has transformed from the honorable Bronze Age hero to the merciless warrior of the Iron Age. As we have seen, the poet describes him as setting his great Shield aside when he captures the unlucky Trojan youths. Now, once again bereft of divine sanction, he burns them alive. The era of Iron and tempered steel has arrived. The *Iliad* tells the story of how humanity has sunk into the basest evils through lust (thanks to Paris's choice of Helen), through anger (thanks to Achilles's relentless rage and desire for revenge), and through ignorance (thanks to Agamemnon's arrogance). In India, these evils are known as the Three Poisons and are associated with the coming of the Kali Yuga or Iron Age when vice prevails. As an artist, Homer intuited the arrival of the era that extends to our own day and will reach its zenith when Polaris peaks as the North Star.

Allegorically, the Trojan War is the war within the human breast for peace, justice, and right. The Achaeans and the Trojans represent our active and passive qualities, our strengths and weaknesses. In this inner yin-yang conflict, balance, harmony, and proportion are the keys to victory. Queen Helen in the epic embodies the Golden Age. She is the beautiful utopian first era of humanity—fresh, fair, bountiful. She is Paradise incarnate, and when she is abducted, she symbolizes Paradise Lost. The Greeks are catapulted into the Wilderness Age and forced to live without her. But they are heedless to fate, try to get her back by force, and disperse across the Aegean Sea.

The Trojans, representing a more refined, feminine-oriented culture and civilization, break the laws of hospitality, transgress patriarchal marriage rites, and are the target of the wrath of the gods. Many opportunities arise to make peace, including returning Helen to Sparta and avoiding defeat, but in their hubris the Trojans too court disaster. The end result is that the twin cities, originally at peace, go to war and needlessly destroy one another. In prophesizing his victor's death as he himself is slain, Hector warns: "It may be I who provoke the gods' wrath against you, that day when Paris and Phoebus Apollo kill you." The gods' *menis* against Achilles, Agamemnon, and the other Argives does not hinge on Hector's deeds, but rather on the Achaeans' own violation of cosmic order. Achilles, whose consciousness rarely rises above sensory and emotional judgment, is slain figuratively by love (Paris) and by art (Apollo). As the *Iliad* ends, the participants on both sides bury their dead, unaware that almost total destruction by fire and water awaits. Only a few, like Odysseus, Aeneas, and Helen, will escape unscathed and sow seeds of a brighter, more peaceful and humane culture and civilization.

Orpheus and Eurydice Revisited

The role of Helen, who sinks as well as launches a thousand ships, finds resonance in the myth of Orpheus and Eurydice. The greatest musician and healer of antiquity, Orpheus played the lyre and was celebrated for being able to charm the animals with his music and even cause stones to dance. But when his beautiful young wife Eurydice suddenly dies on their wedding day, he is devastated and resolves to go to the Underworld to get her back. After crossing the river Styx and entering the joyless realm, he meets Hades, the god of death; his wife Persephone, the maiden who was abducted from her mother Demeter and held in the world of darkness half the year; and the ghosts that dwell there.

Striking the strings of his lyre, he sings a heartfelt plea for the return of Eurydice. He asks the gods to allow her to live out her fair lifespan, or if the Fates refuse, to take his life as well. In Ovid's version of the myth in the *Metamorphoses*: "The bloodless spirits wept as he spoke, accompanying his words with the music. Tantalus did not reach for the ever-retreating water: Ixion's wheel was stilled: the vultures did not pluck at Tityus's liver: the Belides, the daughters of Danaüs, left their water jars: and you, Sisyphus, perched there, on your rock. Then they say, for the first time, the faces of the Furies were wet with tears, won over by his song: the king of the deep [Hades], and his royal bride [Persephone], could not bear to refuse his prayer, and called for Eurydice."

Orpheus joyfully accepts her return and the condition that on the way back, he must walk in front of her and not look back. But just as they arrive at the opening to the world of light, Orpheus turns around. In horror, Eurydice falls back into the abyss and is lost forever.

The Orpheus myth, one of the most famous tales of antiquity, has many levels of meaning, including the trials and tribulations of love, the virtues of perseverance, and the healing power of music and art. At a cosmic level, it tells the story of the first part of the Vega Cycle. Orpheus is Everyman, or humanity during the long precession of the equinoxes. Eurydice personifies the Golden Age. For a time, humanity enjoyed untold natural abundance, heightened spiritual powers, and heavenly peace on earth. But then the ancient scientific and spiritual civilization suddenly collapsed, as the Milky Way lost its ascendency in the Northern skies and declined low to the horizon. The shift coincided with tumultuous earth changes, including the scorching of northern latitudes by a gigantic comet in the Younger Dryas about 12,900 years ago, culminating in earthquakes, tsunamis, and a great flood. Humanity has to cope with an entirely new world as the Golden Age vanishes. But the memory of that idyllic time persists as the Wilderness years dawn, and humanity yearns for Lost Paradise.

The moral of the story is that Orpheus, or humanity, cannot look back, or live in the past, to enjoy the blessings of the Golden Age. Instead, it must always face forward as it goes through the processional cycle. Eventually, after passing through the Silver, Bronze, and Iron Ages, the bright, shining energy of the Milky Way will return, and a new Golden Age will be born. Eurydice—or Paradise—can accompany Orpheus—or humanity—on this journey in the form of memory, artistic or cultural artifacts, or faith in the order of the universe. But Lost Paradise cannot be possessed by living in the past. Humanity must go forward around the historical spiral and realize its destiny.

The biblical tale of Lot's wife looking back and turning into a pillar of salt glances at a similar truth. In the Homeric epics, Helen plays the part of Paradise, or the lost Golden Age. The Spartans, and by extension, Greece as a whole, have enjoyed her grace. All the men of the islands are naturally in love with her, and when Paradise is lost, they all vow to get her back, even in the face of death on a far distant battlefield.

Destruction by Water and Fire

Unlike the Greeks who dwell in the Bronze Age but deceive themselves into believing they the rightful heirs of the Golden Age, the Trojans inhabit a Silver Age. They are further back on the precessional cycle and have not regressed as much as the Achaeans. In the past, their city has been leveled by Heracles with the divine assistance of Poseidon and Apollo. This earlier war is alluded to throughout the *Iliad*. Troy is both a city of peace and a city of war. Paris—a symbol for humanity during this quadrant or circle—is enchanted by Aphrodite's promise of Paradise and awards the apple to the goddess of love. In return, she makes him irresistible to Queen Helen. But their love transgresses *themis*, cosmic order and right, that manifests in the laws of hospitality and other social norms.

In fighting over Helen—or Paradise—the Achaeans and Trojans elevate her into a goddess of beauty, a sex symbol, and a fetish. Neither side will give in, though almost all the combatants eventually recognize that the war is senseless. In the end, Troy is sacked and the gods turn against the Achaeans. Helen survives and is reunited with her husband Menelaus. Helen is depicted in Troy weaving an intricate robe with poignant scenes from the war. Like Hephaestus, she is portrayed as an artist who is sensitive to the deeper currents of life and the suffering around her. Helen's name comes from the Indo-European root for "sun," "torch," or "radiant." It is also a cognate of Selene, the Greek moon goddess, so "Helen" means shining heavenly daughter. Euripedes' play *Helen*, composed several centuries after Homer, presents the earliest account of Helen as the daughter of Zeus and Leda. The king of the gods took the form of a swan and seduced Leda, the wife of a Spartan king, and produced Helen from her egg. In some versions of the myth, Helen's sister was Clytemnestra, who later married Agamemnon, and her brothers were Castor and Pollux, the twins who became the constellation Gemini.

In sharp contrast to his brother Agamemnon and most of the other Greeks, Menelaus expresses compassion for his enemies. Morally, Helen and Menelaus reflect intellectual and social consciousness that enables them to weather a brutal, senseless conflict in which few of their countrymen or women survive. But they are the exception. After her husband returns from the Trojan War, Clytemnestra and her lover murder Agamemnon because he has sacrificed their daughter Iphigeneia in return for fair winds to sail to Troy. Orestes, their son, then kills the adulterous couple and avenges his father. Centuries of war between Sparta and Athens lie ahead, as well as a legacy of plunder, pitilessness to captives, and total war that was perfected in Troy. During their tete-a-tete, Hera agrees to let Zeus smite Sparta, Mycenae, and Argos at his future pleasure in return for destroying Troy. Like the modern world as a whole, the Aegean cultures and civilizations enjoy the fruits and blessings of rudimentary democracy, including innovations and advances in technology, communications, and transportation. But virtue and right sharply decline, leading to millennia of mindless Iron-Age suffering, violence, and war.

In the Vega Cycle, and many other myths and legends, the precessional round can be divided into eras that end with water or fire. In Plato's *Timaeus*, Critias says, "There have been, and will be again, many destructions of humankind arising out of many causes, the greatest have been brought about by the agencies of fire and water." In the New Testament, in the Second Epistle of Peter, it is said, "By the word of God the heavens existed long ago, and the earth was formed out of water and by water, through which the world at that time was destroyed, being flooded with water. But by His word the present heavens and earth are being reserved for fire, kept for the day of judgment and destruction of ungoldly men."

As this passage aludes to, about 13,000 years ago, following the rise of Vega as the North Star, a series of earth changes led to a great flood or series of floods, commemorated in the Babylonian account of Gilgamesh, the biblical story of Noah, and legends about the sunken continents of Atlantis and Mu. In this great inundation, almost all physical signs of past culture and civilization vanished. Humanity entered a long period of difficulty remembered as the Wilderness or Wasteland. Following the retreat of glacial ice and a warming trend, civilization blossomed in ancient China, Sumeria, India, Mexico, and Peru. Over time, the new Bronze Age gave way to the Iron Age. Over the last three thousand years, iron and steel have led to the rise and fall of mighty empires and made possible undreamed of inventions and material living standards. The Iron Age is the Age of Ideology. Instead of natural law religion, race, tribe, class, nation, sex, gender, genes, and other personal or social identifications govern. But modern Iron Age society is unsustainable, and now the planet faces a catastrophe by fire. The nuclear threat, industrial pollution, artificial electromagnet radiation, medical scanning, artificially grown and processed food, new viral epidemics, and global warming are all fire-like phenomena that threaten the future of our species. When Achilles' burns alive the twelve Trojan youths—emblematic of the twelve constellations of the Zodiac—he glances at the fiery half of the precessional cycle that is now coming to a peak. Today, global destruction by water is less threatening than by fire, but it still poses challenges. Beside a critical shortage of clean water for drinking, farming, manufacture, and other uses, water energy includes the circulation of money, ideas, and culture. These easily stagnate or become blocked, threatening international peace and prosperity. Rising sea levels, spreading toxicity, and other water-related climate change are also the cool yin counterpart to global warming's intense yang, hot, fire energy.

In the *Iliad*, the twin forms of destruction are depicted in the climax.

Hector and the Trojans take the offensive and set the Argive ships on fire. They are quickly put out. Indeed, Achilles has vowed to return to battle if the ships are set ablaze. This episode glances at the larger, more universal fire destruction that lies ahead unless the Achaeans—humanity—awakens in time and turns the tide of battle.

Conversely, Achilles' rout by River, an extended meditation on the destructiveness of the watery element, nods at the great flood during the time of Vega. To save her favorite, Hera intervenes and commands her son Hephaestus, the god of the forge, to create an enormous fire to scorch the riverbanks and halt the inundation. Homer's description of the gigantic torrents of water River raises against Achilles calls to mind the Great Wave in Hokusai's woodblock print. The episode pits the two elementary forces against each other, highlighting the twin challenges humanity faces on its precessional journey—subduing water and mastering fire.

Later, of course, Troy is sacked and burned, destroyed by fire. This points to the Iron Age destiny facing modern civilization. If it doesn't learn from the past and create a new vision of Paradise on earth, it is destined to collapse. The Achaean victors, for the most part, are destroyed sailing home from Troy by storms, pirates, monsters of the deep, and other watery elements. Odysseus is one of the few to return alive. His homecoming is ordained by Zeus, the wielder of the thunderbolt and cloud-gatherer who combines fire and water in his own supreme being. Aside from scenes of war and peace, the twin elements are depicted on Achilles's Shield as the sun, moon, and other celestial lamps in the center and Ocean encircling the world on the periphery. Thus the dance of Fire and Water whirls through the inlaid images and heroic verse of the Homeric epics, as well as our individual lives. Whether they are Furies or Graces is up to each person or generation to decide.

As Oliver Taplin asks in a perceptive essay on the *Iliad*, "Why is the shield of Achilles, instrument of war in a poem of war, covered with scenes of delightful peace, of agriculture, festival, song, and dance?" Clearly, the divine Shield Achilles receives is not an ordinary or even supernatural weapon. It is a tool of peace, an artistic rendition of harmony, an emblem of enlightenment that turns the tide of inner battle against anger, greed, and ignorance. The Shield is a mandala portraying humanity's past, present, and future. As Hephaestus reassures Thetis when she asks him to make the Shield for her son Achilles, "He'll get his fine new armor, such gear that in time to come all mankind will be thunderstruck at the sight of it." It offers the thread for the way out of the labyrinth of fear, violence, and war that has prevailed for the last thirteen thousand years.

3
The Grain-Giving Earth

The Original Mediterranean Diet

The *Iliad* begins and ends with a sacrificial feast, and food plays an important role in the epic, including the scenes of harvesting and banqueting on Achilles' Shield. The principal food of the Aegean, including the Greek isles and Troy, was barley. Barley had traditionally been eaten in the Mediterranean world for millennia. Wild barley was gathered and processed into cereal and baked goods for tens of thousands of years. The domesticated variety dates to about 8500 BCE, and by 4500 BCE it had spread north to Scandinavia. Barley was the principal grain of ancient Egypt. Large-scale bakeries and breweries made bread and beer, the staples for generations of pyramid builders in the Nile River Valley. Barley was also the principal grain in the ancient Near East, including Sumeria, Babylon, Assyria, and Canaan. In the Bible, barley and other grains are called the Staff of Life.

According to the Linear B tablets in Knossos, the capital of Minoan civilization, workers received rations of barley for their daily fare. The ritual use of the grain dates back to the Eleusinian Mysteries. *Kykeon*, a fermented drink given initiates, was prepared from roasted barley and herbs. The *Homeric Hymn to Demeter*, the goddess of the harvest whose name means "Barley Mother," refers to the concoction. Sacred precincts set aside for growing grain, planting orchards, or cultivating vineyards were known as *temeros*.

Barley appears throughout the *Iliad* and *Odyssey*. Homer refers frequently to "the grain-giving earth," "the nourishing earth," and "the grain-rich plowland," signifying this principal food. In the epic, as throughout the region, barley was eaten as whole grain porridge, soup or stew, and baked into bread or cakes of barley meal. White, or polished, barley was sprinkled on oxen or other animals during the sacrifice. Indeed, barley was so central to cultural identity that eating grain was a hallmark of being human. Compared to the gods who do not eat ordinary food, Homer describes the Greeks and Trojans as "mortals who eat Demeter's grain." On one occasion, Diomedes, one of the Argive's strongest warriors, taunts his opponent Glaucus: "I will not fight with the blessed gods but if you are of them that eat the fruit of the ground, draw near me and meet your doom." Great Ajax, son of Telamon, vows he "will yield to no man who is in mortal mold and eats the grain of Demeter, if bronze and great stones can overthrow him."

In one poignant episode, Lykaon, the young Trojan prince who has been taken captive, clasps Achilles's knees and pleads: "Zeus's nursling, I'm your supplicant, I deserve your respect, since you were the first with whom I tasted Demeter's grain on the day you captured me in our well-planned orchard, and shipped me far away from father and friends." Clasping the knees is a traditional gesture of seeking mercy or peace. Thetis clasps Zeus's knees in making a request early in the epic and once again when she comes to Hephaestus for divine armor. On that previous occasion, Lykaon was ransomed for 300 oxen. But this time, Achilles scorns his appeal and ruthlessly slays him. In a later, more chivalric age, the era of the Crusades, Christian and Islamic adversaries who broke bread with each other were forbidden to take up arms.

In addition to barley, wheat was grown and consumed throughout the region. However, because it was harder than barley, wheat was customarily milled and baked into bread. This added a costly step, and as a result wheat was eaten primarily by the nobility, or by the common people only on special occasions. As a well-to-do city, Troy consumed more wheat than usual. Homer mentions the "wheat-rich plains" several times and describes Menelaus, king of prosperous Sparta, "whose heart grew warm and melted like morning dew that coats the ears of grain where the plowland bristles with its ripe crop of tall wheat." The poet also mentions spelt, rye, and oats.

The traditional Mediterranean diet of that era also included beans and pulses, and chickpeas are mentioned in the *Iliad*. Vegetables complemented main foods, and onions, clover, parsley, and other wild herbs—a traditional delicacy in Greece known as *horta*—are noted. Chief greens included purslane, chard, mustard greens, chicory, pea shoots and the sprouts of amaranth. Stuffed vegetables (*gemista*) and vegetables stews (*ladera*) were also popular. Fruits too were enjoyed, the most notable, of course, being grapes, which were sacred to Dionysis and appear prominently on Achilles's Shield. Olives, sacred to Athena, also appear in the saga, not only as food and oil, but also as the wooden handle of a bronze battleaxe and an ointment Hera uses to seduce Zeus. Apple and fig trees too appear in passing. Though no nuts are described, the *Iliad* mentions beech, oak, pine, tamarisk, ash, and plane trees, some of which included edible nuts or seeds used in making flour. Seaweed was also eaten in antiquity, and Homer mentions it once, but not in a food context.

The most elaborate meal in the *Iliad* is worth quoting in full:

> When those others arrived at the hut of Neleus's son,
> they themselves dismounted onto the bounteous earth,
> while old Nestor's henchman Eurymedon unyoked his horses
> from this chariot. They dried off the sweat on their tunics
> standing to face the breeze from the seashore, then they went
> into the hut, and sat down on chairs, and for them
> lovely-tressed Hecamede mixed a posset—old Nestor
> had taken her from Tenedos when Achilles sacked it . . . .
> First she brought out a table and set it before them,
> a fine one, well polished, its feet enameled in cobalt,
> and set on it a bronze basket, with an onion as relish
> for their drink, and pale honey, and sacred barley-meal,
> with an exquisite cup, that old Nestor had brought from home,
> studded with golden rivets. Its handles were ears,
> four in number; round each a pair of golden
> doves were feeding: it rested upon a double base.
> Others needed to strain to hoist this cup from the table
> when full, yet Nestor, the old man, raised it without effort.
> In it, for them, this woman resembling the immortals
> now mixed a posset, grating goat's cheese on Pramnian wine
> with a bronze grater, and sprinkled white barley meal over it,
> and when she'd prepared this brew, desired them to try it.
> (11.618-41)

As the reference to grated cheese makes clear, the Greeks as a rule did not ordinarily consume cow's milk, cheese, or other dairy products. The region's hilly, rugged terrain was better suited to raising goats and sheep. The main sweetener in the epics was honey, as the above passage notes. Homer mentions "honey-sweet wine" on many occasions and uses the golden imagery of honey in several elaborate similes. Sugar was unknown in Europe until the Middle Ages.

As a maritime region, fish and seafood were enjoyed throughout the Aegean. However, compared to later times, fish consumption was small because it was labor-intensive to catch, transport overland was expensive, and it did not preserve as well as other foods. The combatants in the war are not described eating fish in the *Iliad*, though fish and eel are mentioned, like other foods, in striking similes illustrative of nature's bounty and life's lessons. For example, "Patroclus went up to him and drove a spear into his right jaw; he thus hooked him by the teeth and the spear pulled him over the rim of his car, as one who sits at the end of some jutting rock and draws a strong fish out of the sea with a hook and a line—even so with his spear did he pull Thestor all gaping from his chariot; he then threw him down on his face and he died while falling."

The traditional Greek diet—barley and other grains, beans, vegetables, fruits, honey, and a small amount of animal food, primarily fish or seafood—is healthy and nurturing. It contributed to "long life" or *macro bios*, a term first coined by Hippocrates in the 5th century BCE It is the origin of the term "macrobiotics" that represented an ideal of health and longevity up until the present time. As Antiphanes, an ancient Athenian food commentator, observed, "Our dinner is a barley cake bristling with chaff, cheaply prepared, and perhaps one iris-bulb or a dainty dish of sowthistle or mushroom or any other poor thing that the place affords us poor creatures." Poliochus, another ancient Greek food authority, remarked, "Both of us broke a bit of black barley bread, with chaff mixed in the kneading, twice a day, and had a few figs. Sometimes, too, there would be a braised mushroom, and if there were a little dew we'd catch a snail, or we'd have some native vegetables or a crushed olive, and some wine to drink."

In our own era, the Hippocratic dietary teachings of *macrobios* have been unified with parallel traditions in Japan and the Far East by George Ohsawa and Michio Kushi under the name of modern macrobiotics. The roots of the modern Mediterranean Diet—a healthy way of eating and living widely recognized today—go back to this timeless dietary pattern.

Diet and the Ages of Humanity

The ancient Greeks believed that a decline in diet during the historical cycle accompanied a decline in virtue and piety. During the Golden Age, grain flourished. According to Hesiod, "Helpless old age did not exist, and with limbs of unsagging vigor they enjoyed the delights of feasts, out of evil's reach. A sleeplike death subdued them, and every good thing was theirs; the barley-giving earth asked for no toil to bring forth a rich and plentiful harvest." The blessed gods also bestowed upon them rich flocks, and people in that era "lived in peace and abundance."

During the Silver Age, when people were "plagued by the pains of foolishness" and "could not refrain from reckless violence," they turned against each other and neglected to worship the gods or offer sacrifices. Food is not directly mentioned in connection with this era, but during the subsequent Bronze Age, people were "dreadful and mighty and bent on the harsh deeds of war and violence." They "ate no breads and their hearts were tough as steel." The lack of grain as staple food is directly linked with loss of morality and right, as well as the rise of violence and war. Since virtue in the Silver Age decreased by about one half, we can infer that people in that era ate about half as much barley and other healthful foods as they did in the Golden Age and proportionately less in the ages that followed.

The Age of Heroes, the fourth of Hesiod's five ages, a "better and more just" race emerged. Most of those who fought in Troy, however, were still governed by Bronze Age values and were wiped out by "evil war and dreadful battle." Many of the Achaeans survived the sack of the city, but perished at sea as "death threw his dark mantle over them." A few Zeus saved and settled in the Blessed Isles and "gave them shelter and food." These "blissful heroes" enjoyed thrice annually "the barley-giving land" that brought forth "full grain sweet as honey." The mini-Golden Age of heroes at the end of the catastrophic Bronze Age, in other words, saw a return to eating whole grains as principal food.

In the present Iron Age, almost all affection will be lost between parents and children, guests and hosts, brothers and sisters, and among friends. "Evil-doers and scoundrels will be honored," toiling humanity will be "blighted by envy," and people "will take delight in the ruin of others." The person "who keeps his oath, or is just and good" will lose favor, but he will be rewarded by Zeus "who sees afar" and does "not decree for them the pains of war." Their city will prosper and "youth-nurturing peace comes over the land." Whole grains vanish altogether.

For such righteous individuals, "the earth brings forth a rich harvest," including oaks teeming with acorns, busy bees, and fleecy sheep weighed down with wool. "Women [will] bear children who resemble their fathers. There is an abundance of blessings, and the grain land grants such harvests that no one has to sail on the sea." Once again, barley and other whole grains are the keys to peace and prosperity in our current age. The message is that children who grow up to resemble their parents will thrive not only because of faithfulness within the family, but also because they eat similar food. Sharing food within the family or community is a cardinal principle of modern macrobiotic healthcare. People who eat together develop a common mind and spirit that is passed on from generation to generation. Lack of grain and other fruits of the earth, as the passage relates, forces people to go to sea to fish and observe a maritime way of eating. Even such a moderate animal-based diet can have a strong impact on personal and social health. In the *Odyssey*, as we shall see, the oar is the key symbol of a nautical way of life that encompasses heavy animal-food consumption, piracy, and fleets of warships.

The Vega Cycle mirrors a similar dietary decline. In the Golden Age, wild grains constituted principal food and grew in abundance, leading to universal peace and plenty. Following the rise of Vega as the North Star, major earth changes, including a Great Flood and return of glacial ice, occurred. The traditional grain-based way of eating declined, and meat and other animal food began to be consumed to supply raw power to survive the elements, clear forests, and rebuild civilization. Conflict, violence, and tribal war arose during this period of hardship and difficulty known as the Wilderness. The rise of the constellation Heracles, associated with great trials and tribulations, governed this era. Following a warming trend, domestication of grains and livestock appeared in the Fertile Crescent, Vedic India, Shang Dynasty China, and Mesoamerica. The amount of grain consumed increased. However, it was not as vitalizing and energetic as wild grain, and the agricultural revolution introduced private property. Ownership led to territoriality, disputes over land, and eventually war, as surplus grain and the domestication of livestock led to the rise of kingship, nobility, and a standing army. This era saw Thuban, a star in Draco, rise overhead as the North Star. On the one hand, this era, the beginning of historical times, saw the introduction of the alphabet and written language, advances in metallurgy and transportation, and other progressive developments. On the other hand, violence and war became increasingly mechanized.

In the millennia since then, this trend has accelerated up to the present time. The modern diet, in which an animal-based way of eating replaced a plant-based one, arose and spread worldwide. The industrialization of food, including scientific breeding of cattle, gave birth to the Industrial Revolution, leading to rising living standards and technical expertise, but also increased violence and warfare. This era is now climaxing as Polaris reaches its zenith as the North Star. It will be succeeded by a new, more harmonious and peaceful era, in which a plant-based diet, centered once again on whole cereal grains, governs. Eventually, in about six to seven thousand years, this will lead to a new paradise on earth. The cycle of dietary changes is summarized in the following chart:

The Grain-Giving Earth

Ages of Humanity	**Achilles' Shield**	**Vega Cycle**
Golden: wild grain	*Circle of Agricultural Peace and Plenty*: Wild grain	*Paradise*: wild grain
Silver: less grain, more fish	*Circle of Vintage and Pastoral*: animal food	*Wilderness*: more animal food
Bronze/Heroic/Iron: Meat and alcohol-based	*Circle of the City of Peace and City of War*: Animal food and wine	*Material Chaos*: Animal food and sugar based
New Golden: grain and plant-based	*Circle of the Dance*: grain-and-plant-based	*Construction of the Golden Age*: grain-and-plant-based

The changes in diet during the Ages of Humanity and in the Vega Cycle parallel the passage from a peaceful to a violent era and back again. The *Iliad* and *Odyssey* chronicle a similar journey.

In discussing the primacy of grains in *The Cuisine of Sacrifice Among the Greeks*, Marcel Detienne observes:

> The very term *bios* [life], which Hesiod employs to indicate the ear of grain men use as their particular food, underscores a relationship between grains and the vitality peculiar to men, a relationship so intimate that we must speak of consubstantiality. The fabric of human life is cut from the same material that forms the food that sustains it. It is 'because they do no eat bread' that the gods are not mortals. . . . To go back to the terms of the Odyssey, barley and wheat constitute the *muelos andron*, men's marrow, the very substance of their life force.

Meat and Heroes

Homer often compares fallen warriors to harvested grain: "And now as a band of reapers mow swathes of wheat or barley upon a rich man's land, and the sheaves fall thick before them, even so did the Trojans and Achaeans fall upon one another." On another occasion, he likens Achilles' horses trampling the shields and bodies of his enemies to oxen trampling the barley on the threshing room floor.

The traditional macrobiotic/Mediterranean diet, however, is very different from the Bronze Age way of eating observed by the two armies in the epic. The principal food consumed by Achilles, Agamemnon, Hector, Aeneas, and the other warriors is the meat of ox, heifer, ewe, lamb, goat, or hog. The feasting begins in Book 1 of the *Iliad* when Chyrseis is returned to her father to placate Apollo and end the plague he has visited upon the Achaeans. Agamemnon, the arrogant Greek commander in chief, has refused to return the captive maiden to her father, a priest of Apollo, who offers a handsome ransom. After the archer god rains arrows of epidemic on his army, Agamemnon reluctantly yields. Odysseus leads the Achaeans in setting up a sacrificial altar. After washing their hands, they sprinkle barley, and Chryseis's father prays to Apollo to lift the scourge. The sacrifice, the first of nearly twenty in the epic, is worth quoting in full to glimpse the process:

> When they had prayed, and scattered the barley groats, first
> pulling back the victims' head, they slaughtered and flayed them,
> cut out the thighs, wrapped them up in a double layer
> of fat, and placed above them cuts of raw meat. The old man
> burned these over split billets, with fire-bright wine
> drizzled them, while beside him young men held five-pronged forks.
> When the thighs were well-broiled and they'd tasted the innards, next
> they chopped up the rest, threaded the bits on skewers,
> grilled them with care, then drew them all off. But when
> they were through with their work, and the meal had been got ready,
> they feasted, and no one's heart lacked a fair share in the feasting,
> but when they had satisfied their desire for food and drink,
> the young men topped up the mixing bowls with liquor
> and served it to all, the first drops in their cups for a libation.
> The whole day through with song these young Achaeans sought
> to appease the god, chanting their lovely paean,
> that hymned the deadly archer, whose heart rejoiced as he listened.
> (1.458-74)

The Trojans also engage in frequent sacrifices and gorge themselves on meat, wine, and other rich foods. In Book 6, the tide has turned against the defenders, and Queen Hecuba goes to the temple of Athena to pray for divine protection:

> "Lady Athena our city's protector, queen among goddesses,

> now break Diomedes' spear, now grant that he himself
> fall prone in front of the Skaian Gates, and at once
> we'll sacrifice in your shrine a dozen yearling heifers
> that have never felt the goad, in the hope that you may pity
> our town, and the Trojans' wives and infant children."
> So she prayed, but Pallas Athena shook her head in denial.
>
> (6.304-11)

Following a truce, both sides enjoy a rich feast accompanied by plenty of wine. Next to meat, wine or other alcohol was the mainstay of the warriors on both sides:

> Jason's son sent some special wine, a thousand measures,
> from this convoy the long-haired Achaeans bought their wine,
> some in exchange for bronze, others for gleaming iron,
> others again for hides, or the cattle themselves, and some
> in exchange for war captives. They set up a lavish feast,
> and then, all night through, the long-haired Achaeans
> feasted, as did the Trojans and their allies in the city:
> and all night through Zeus the counselor planned them harm,
> thundering fearfully, so that pale terror seized them.
> They spilt on the ground the wine from their cups: no one dared
> to drink more till they'd poured a libation to the almighty son of
> Cronos.
>
> (7.471-82)

When the fighting resumes and Hector and the Trojans force them back to their ships, Agamemnon chastises his men for their dietary indulgence:

> Shame on you, Argives, base cowards, good only to look at!
> What's become of our boats, when we swore we were the best—
> those empty public boasts you would utter on Lemnos,
> as you wolfed down plentiful meat of straight-horned cattle,
> and swilled the bowls that were brimming over with wine,
> that each man would take on in battle a hundred—no, two hundred!
> Trojans; but now we're not even a fit match for one."
>
> (8.228-34)

Later, after Achilles rejoins the fray to avenge the death of Patroclus and slays Hector, he returns to his tent and prepares a "heart-warming funeral feast" for the Myrmidons:

> Many sleek oxen now struggled around the iron knife
> while being slaughtered, many sheep and bleating goats;
> and many a white-tusked hog, bulked up with lard,
> was stretched out there to be singed in Hephaestus's flame,
> and around the corpse blood ran thick, by the cupful.
> (23.30-34)

At the funeral for Patroclus, Achilles covers his dear friend's body with a thick coat of animal fat. Then he slays a host of "shambling oxen" and "fattened sheep" to throw on the pyre, as well as a bevy of dogs and horses and the twelve noble Trojan sons. After this holocaust, the victorious Achaeans enjoy "a heart-warming funeral feast."

Throughout the *Iliad*, the principal warriors on both sides are compared to carnivorous animals in quest of meat. As the single combat between Paris and Menelaus commences, Homer relates:

> Now when war-minded Menelaus first caught sight of him
> emerging out of the crowd with his lengthy strides,
> then, as a lion rejoices at finding, when ravenous,
> some hefty carcass—an antlered stag or a wild goat—
> and eat it he must, despite being set upon by swift
> hunting dogs and tough youngsters, so Menelaus
> delighted at seeing Alexandros, divinely handsome,
> with his own eyes, and, hot for revenge on the wrongdoer,
> promptly sprang fully armed, from his chariot to the ground.
> (3.21-29)

On other occasions, Menelaus is compared to a lion "desperate for meat" and determined to "seize the fattest steer," while his brother Agamemnon is also likened to the king of the jungle. Odysseus wears a helmet inscribed with a boar's white gleaming tusks. On his shoulders, Hector wears the skin of a grey wolf. His divine protector, Apollo, is described as "the wolf-born" and in mythology one of his epithets was Lykeios. The name derives from *Lycia* (from the root word for wolf in Greek) where his cult may have originated.

Though he hosts sumptuous feasts for his men, Achilles himself rarely eats. Following Patroclus's death, he refuses to eat altogether. "Please, don't tell me to glut my heart with food or drink, now this terrible grief has come upon me." As he lapses into despondency, his mother Thetis grows alarmed. As the other men enjoy a big shaggy ram for breakfast, she darts down from Olympus and implores her son: "My child how long will you go eating your heart out with weeping and lamentation, thinking neither of food nor of bed?"

In contrast to Achilles, Odysseus is very pragmatic about food and eating. When Achilles offers a sumptuous repast to the embassy seeking to convince him to return to the fray, Odysseus replies: "There's rich plenty, all that our hearts could want to dine on. Still, tasty food is not our business now . . . It's a toss up whether we'll save or lose our well-benched ships—unless you array yourself in your might!" On a later occasion, influenced by Achilles's abstemiousness, Odysseus orders his men to eat before returning to the battlefield: "For in [food] is strength and courage....the man who's taken his fill of wine and food can fight with enemy warriors all day long."

Although he ignores his mother's entreaties, Achilles nurses a ravenous hunger for vengeance. As Hector falls in the climactic battle scene, he begs Achilles: "Do not let the dogs make a meal of me beside the Achaeans' ships!" and promises that his father King Priam will give him a generous ransom for the return of his corpse. Achilles insolently replies:

> Don't entreat me, you dog, by my knees or by my parents!
> I just wish there was a way for my raging heart to let me
> carve your flesh raw and eat it, in return for what you've done
> . . . no, dogs and birds will eat every last scrap of you."
> (22.345-354)

"Truly the heart in your breast is of iron," Hector sighs with his last breath, invoking the connection between the coming Iron Age and the final decline of virtue and compassion. As we saw, this coincides in Hesiod with the change from a grain-based diet to an animal-centered one.

The Trojans are only marginally more civilized. Fearful for her husband's fate, Andromache, Hector's wife, thinks foremost how his death will affect their son's access to rich foods. She fears he will be ostracized and treated as a beggar:

> One holds out his cup—long enough to wet his lips,
> yet not his palate. Then one
> with both parents alive will kick him out of the feast,
> punching him up, and reviling him in harsh terms: . . .
> Astyanax, who before, on his father's knee
> would eat nothing but marrow and rich fat of sheep,
> and when sleep came on him . . .

[Hector], coiling worms will devour you when the dogs have had
their fill"

(22.494-509)

When she hears Hector is slain, his mother Hecuba becomes inconsolable and like Achilles compares herself to a ravenous beast. She wails:

> You [Achilles] must have a heart of iron
> for once you are in his power, once he sets eyes on you,
> that treacherous raw flesh eater will show you no pity,
> or any respect. Let us rather lament far from him,
> sitting here in our own home. All-mastering Destiny
> surely spun a thread at his birth, when I myself bore him,
> that far from his parents he'd glut quick scavenging dogs
> after meeting a stronger man—whose whole liver I wish
> I could get in my jaws and devour? A fair requital, that,
> for my son.
>
> (24.205-214)

Priam is also heartbroken, but accepts Troy's fate as the will of the gods. He bravely makes his way by nightfall to the Achaean camp to retrieve his son's body. Embracing the warrior's knees and kissing his hands—"those terrible murderous hands that had killed so many of his sons"—Priam beseeches Achilles to release the corpse. The arrival of the aged king brings Achilles to his senses and in the old man he sees the likeness of his father. They embrace and together share a sacrificial meal:

> [Achilles] sprang up, and cut the throat
> of a white sheep: his comrades skinned it, butchered it neatly,
> cut up the meat with skill, threaded the bits on skewers,
> grilled them with care, then drew them all off. That done,
> Automedon brought bread and put in on the table
> in handsome baskets, while Achilles shared out the meat.
> So they reached out their hands to the good things ready for them;
> but when they'd satisfied their desire for food and drink,
> then Priam, scion of Dardanos, gazed in wonder at Achilles,
> his stature and beauty, how like the gods he appeared
>
> (24.621-30)

Note the meal includes bread, as well as meat, a symbol of culture, civilization, and human moderation and decency. In virtually all the other sacrificial meals, bread or grain is not mentioned, showing that the poet was aware of its energetic effects and symbol of peace and reconciliation. Over the meal, Achilles and Priam agree to observe nine days of mourning for their fallen comrades, a tenth day of burial, and public feasting on the eleventh day. On the twelfth, the fighting will be resumed.

The *Iliad* ends with Priam returning to Troy. On Hector's funeral pyre, the flame is quenched with "fire-bright wine." Afterwards, the white bones are gathered and laid in a golden casket and buried in a great mound. "When they'd raised the mound, they all went back, then sat down together and shared a glorious feast."

The Food of the Gods

Gods too feast, banquet, and enjoy eating. But they don't consume earthly food, they eat ambrosia and drink nectar. The celestial feasts are presided over by Themis, the goddess of cosmic order who was Zeus's second wife and sits next to him on the Olympian throne. In Book 1, the Nereid Thetis (not to be confused with Themis) explains to Achilles that Zeus "yesterday went to Ocean, to visit the blameless Ethiopians, for a feast." She says all the other Olympian gods accompanied him and will be gone for twelve days. But when they come back, she vows to clasp Zeus's knees and persuade him to listen to her son's petition. According to Herodotus, the Ethiopians were *Macrobioi*, or semi-divine, long-lived people who eat an ambrosial like food furnished by the gods. Along with Hippocrates' Oath and essays on diet, the Greek historian's chronicle was a major source of macrobiotic teaching on diet and health in the ancient world. The concept of *makro bios* may go back to the Abioi, the "most just of men," mentioned in the *Iliad* who abstained from war and enjoyed a life of sanctity.

After the twelve days are up, Thetis approaches Zeus and begs his favor. He honors her request but incurs the wrath of Hera. To end the quarrel from erupting into open warfare among the gods, Hephaestus gives a goblet to his mother and pours out sweet nectar. He clowns around the assembly hall with his lame foot, dispensing the heavenly beverage and causing merriment among the gods. As Homer relates, the crisis is soon averted:

> Then the whole day long until the sun went down
> they feasted and no one's heart lacked a fair share of the feasting,
> nor of the exquisite lyre that Apollo handled, nor of
> the Muses who sang sweet-voiced, responding one to another.
>   (1.601-04)

Ambrosia, the food of the gods, confers strength, longevity, and immortality. It is brought to Olympus by doves and represents the divine energy or vibration of the earth. Nectar is usually portrayed as a divine beverage, the celestial equivalent to wine. Not only the gods, but also immortal horses feed on ambrosia. In the *Iliad*, Iris, the rainbow messenger of the gods, unyokes her chariot and feeds her steeds ambrosia as fodder. On another occasion, the immortal river Simoeis makes ambrosia spring up from its streambed to nourish Hera's chariot horses. Ambrosia can also be used as an unguent. On one occasion, Hera uses ambrosia to clean her body, massages it with olive oil "specially perfumed for her ambrosial robe," and plaits "the shining tresses, fine and ambrosial" of her hair to seduce Zeus and get him to do her bidding. Ambrosia can also be used to forestall putrefaction of human corpses. Thetis drips ambrosia and red nectar through [Patroclus'] nostrils to keep his flesh "forever unspoiled." Aphrodite and Apollo minister to Hector in like fashion when Achilles drags his body around the walls of Troy and mutilates it.

Unlike mortals, the gods are bloodless. On one occasion, Hebe, the daughter of Zeus and Hera and cupbearer of the gods, serves nectar to her parents and the divine assembly while they debate the course of the war. After Zeus gives the gods permission to enter the fighting as combatants, Aphrodite is seriously wounded by Diomedes as she tries to protect the Trojans. In describing her injury, Homer contrasts the physiology of the gods with that of humans:

> The spear drove straight into her flesh—
> clean through the fragrant robe toiled on by the Graces themselves—
> at the base of her palm: out flowed the goddess's blood, immortal
> *Ichor*, such as flows in the veins of the blessed gods,
> for they neither eat bread nor drink fire-bright wine, and so
> are bloodless, and come thus to be called immortals.
>
> (5.337-42)

Ichor is an ethereal golden fluid that flows in the veins of the gods. It is the distilled essence of ambrosia and nectar. Although the gods are immortal, their deathless energy can be diminished or drained away, leaving them weak and incapacitated.

The Sacrifice

In the ancient Aegean world, diet and food customs were inseparable from sacrifice. In *Theogony*, the poem describing the origin and genealogy of the gods, Hesiod relates that the sacrifice began when Prometheus stole fire from heaven and gave it to mortals to cook meat. Instead of setting aside the choicest parts of the ox and bull for the immortals, he tricked Zeus into taking the bones and other inedible parts and kept the succulent flesh for humans. In anger, Zeus punishs Prometheus by chaining him to a rock, and every day an eagle eats his liver. As a deathless Titan, Prometheus's liver grows back each night, only to be devoured again the next day.

Over the millennia, a complex system of ritual sacrifice developed in the Mediterranean, as it did in Mesopotamia, Egypt, Vedic India, and other regions. In Greece, the primary animals sacrificed were oxen, cattle, and sheep. Goats and hogs were also ceremonially killed, but they enjoyed lesser status. In mythology, goats grazed on grapevines sacred to Dionysus, and swine ravaged harvests sacred to Demeter. Only domesticated animals were offered to the gods. Since wild animals eat each other indiscriminately and observe no laws or restraints, they were considered impure. Similarly, the Greeks wouldn't sacrifice animals that were sick, aged, or injured or killed by wild beasts.

By Homer and Hesiod's time, sacrificial rituals permeated Bronze Age society. They were held for all important undertakings, from military battles to peace treaties, from the convening of assemblies and installation of new officials to marriages, funerals, and other ceremonies marking the stages of life. All these events began with a sacrifice and ended with a meal. To found a colony, Greek tradition called for setting up a hearth, including a cooking spit and pots, with a portable flame from the home city.

Despite Prometheus's deception, the Olympians did not actually consume meat, or earthly food, as we have seen. They imbibed only the smoke of the charred bones and flesh and the aromatic fragrance of herbs and spices, while the edible parts were reserved for humans. In Hesiod, the Blessed Immortals dine on ambrosia and the wafting smoke of sacrificial offerings. However, the gods did not automatically accept whatever was offered. For example, once when Hector implores divine assistance, Homer relates:

> [The Trojans] brought from the city both oxen and fattened sheep
> quickly, provided themselves with honey-sweet wine
> and bread from their homes, and gathered plentiful wood,
> and offered full rich sacrifices to the immortals, so that
> the wind bore the smell of them skyward, up from the plain,
> savory, sweet: but the blessed gods did not share it,
> nor did they wish to: hateful to them were sacred Ilion,

and Priam, he of the good ash spear, and Priam's people.
(8.545-52)

After Hector's death, Apollo addresses the assembled gods and eloquently pleads for them to restrain Achilles's wrath and spare further desecration of the Trojan's body:

> A hard-hearted lot you gods, and destructive! Did Hector never
> burn for you thighs of oxen, then, or of unblemished goats?
> Yet you couldn't be bothered to save him, dead though he is. . .
> Achilles has lost all pity, and has no respect in him—
> a great source to a man of both harm and benefit....
> Great though he is, he should watch out for our anger:
> through this fury of his he's outraging the silent earth.
> (24.33-54)

Over Hera's objections that Achilles is the offspring of a goddess, while Hector nursed at a woman's breast, Zeus rules in favor of Apollo:

> Hector/was more dear to the gods than all other mortals in Ilion!
> To me at least, for he never failed me with gifts I enjoyed—
> not once did my altar lack its fair share of the feasting,
> the libations, the burnt fat our accepted privileges!
> (24.66-70)

Informed Animal Consent

Sacrifice establishes and reinforces communion between humans and animals. In the ancient world, it was recognized that animals played an indispensable role in the fabric of life, giving their flesh, fur, bones and teeth, and other features for food, clothing, shelter, tools, and other uses. To maintain the moral and spiritual equilibrium between the human and animal worlds, traditional cultures and societies entered into a covenant. They agreed to honor and respect the animals in return for giving their lives so humans might live. Of course, the gods were also part of this cosmic order, and the sacrificial rites recognized the unity and reciprocal duties and responsibilities of all three domains.

Since the cosmos was based on order and harmony, not chaos and violence, it was imperative to get the animal's consent to be sacrificed. To this end, the Greeks poured pure water and sprinkled barley groats on its head. Taken by surprise, the animal shuddered with the splash of cold water, and the grain caused it to shake its head from left to right, signaling consent.

Then the priest or sacrificer suddenly slit the animal's throat. The knife was hidden in a basket of barley and salt, so that the entire procedure took place before the animal realized what had happened. As we have seen, the Homeric epics describe this in detail. Indeed, as scholars have pointed out, Patroclus is slain in exactly the same way as an animal sacrifice with an oblique, stunning blow. Achilles's companion serves as a ritual victim, but one who willingly gives his life for his friend. In some cultures, kings, queens, and other nobles were sacrificed for the welfare of the community. In the epic cycle, Agamemnon sacrifices his daughter Iphigeneia in return for favorable winds when his expedition sets sail for Troy. In Christian theology, Jesus is the paschal lamb that sacrifices its life for the sins of humanity.

Grains play an important role in purification. After a funeral in which the corpse is burned and animals sacrificed, the fire is extinguished and meat eating is suspended. Relatives or friends are expected to bring an equal amount of grain to exchange for meat, and a new pure flame must be kindled from a neighbor's hearth. As Marcel Detienne explains, "Cereals precede and prefigure meat and fire because they are naturally cooked by the brightness of the sun. They can serve as a substitute for animal flesh as well as announce the cooking action of the hearth."

The Homeric epics are not vegetarian, but they uphold and reflect the natural grain-based order of eating described in Hesiod and portrayed on Achilles's Shield. In the Golden Age, whole grains and other plant foods grew in abundance. A similar state reigns in Genesis. Only after the Flood (and the rise of Vega as the North Star) do human beings start to eat meat and set up sacrificial altars to the gods.

Humanity itself is a product of cooking. According to one myth, humans were born out of the ashes of the war between Zeus and the Titans. The Olympian ruler's thunderbolts ultimately destroyed this ancient rebellious race, and from the lightning, thunder, and charred earth emerged the first humans. When Prometheus, a Titan who had been pardoned by Zeus, subsequently stole fire to cook meat, humanity crossed the red or uncrossable line between humans and animals and between mortals and immortals. Incurring his *menis*, or wrath, for upsetting the cosmic order, the ruler of the gods punishes Prometheus by having his liver devoured every day by an eagle (a bird sacred to Zeus). Liver congestion and blockages, leading to resentment, anger, wrath, and violence, is a well-known consequence of heavy animal food eating, especially consuming meat that is poor quality or unsanctified. In the conventional interpretation of the myth, such as I was taught as a child, Zeus unjustly punishes Prometheus for stealing fire and giving it to humanity. Mastery of fire distinguishes us from the animals and allows us to cook, keep warm, and forge metals. These are plainly true. However, a close reading suggests that Zeus's *menis*, or wrath, was incurred not through the unauthorized gift of fire per se, but its improper use to cook unsanctified meat and other animal foods, as well as neglect of grains, leading to the end of the Golden Age and the fall of humanity. Prometheus's liver troubles were simply the inevitable consequence of disobeying natural law and losing his health and sound judgment. In the *Odyssey*, as we shall see, slaying and eating the forbidden cattle of the Sun dooms Odysseus's crew, and indiscriminate feasting seals the fate of the suitors.

Another association with the liver in the Homeric epics is the frequent reference to clasping the knees. In the *Iliad*, as we have seen, Dolon, a defeated Trojan, clasps Achilles's knees and begs for his life. In the *Odyssey*, upon reaching Phaeacia, Odysseus clasps the knees of Queen Arete and implores her help in getting home. There are many other examples. In Far Eastern medicine, the knees correspond with the liver, whose meridians pass through the knees. Knee problems signify liver problems and treating the corresponding organ or feature will usually enhance the other. Clasping the knees, a sign of submission and appeal to put aside anger for mercy, evidently arose out of this understanding.

Wine, the yin to meat's yang, also plays a corrosive role in the epic, as it has throughout history. In moderation, wine, honey, and other extremely expansive foods are part of a healthful Mediterranean diet. But in excess they can lead to weakness, loss of focus, dullness, and other deficiencies. In combination with meat and other heavy animal food, such fare can lead to angry, explosive outbursts and violent behavior. The ancient Greeks recognized the dangers of consuming too much extreme food of this kind as well. In one myth, Zeus makes Cronos drowsy with honey and disarms and castrates him. The better known version of this tale has Gaia, the goddess of the earth, cut off Cronos's testicles with an iron sickle. The sickle glances at the Iron Age. Cronos (or Saturn) presided over the Golden Age, and after he was overthrown, Zeus ruled over the Silver, Bronze, and Iron Ages with their successive decline in virtue and morality.

The sacrificial covenant between humans and animals steadily declined over the millennia. Today's factory farming that inhumanely breeds, raises, and slaughters millions of cows, chickens, and other animals without any regard to their suffering or spiritual well being is the antithesis of traditional sacrificial rites. At the height of the Iron Age, as Hesiod and Homer predicted, whole grains would be forgotten, and humans would no longer eat wholesome bread or other cereal products. Sympathy, pity, and respect for natural order would virtually disappear.

4
The Long Way Home

"The power of heaven showed him the long way home."

The *Odyssey*, an epic about *nostos*, or homecoming, is lighter, brighter, and more peaceful than the *Iliad*. Despite the loss of all his men and massacre of the suitors, Odysseus's story is essentially a romance or comedy and has a happy ending. In contrast, Achilles's tale is consistently tragic. The Trojan War saga has elements of love, compassion and wisdom, and Achilles' Shield envisions a joyful future. But the horrific gore and bloodshed saturate the *Iliad* in hues of black and crimson. In contrast, peaceful scenes of hospitality, feasting, and family reunion in the seafaring chronicle overshadow its surreal trials, tribulations, and episodic violence. The *Odyssey's* accent on life, peace, and domestic tranquility is the fruitful yin counterpart to the *Iliad's* stress on death, war, and hard yang finality.

Before analyzing the second of the two great epics, it is helpful to review the narrative action. The *Odyssey* begins in the tenth year after the sack of Troy. Odysseus still hasn't returned home, and everyone in Ithaca,

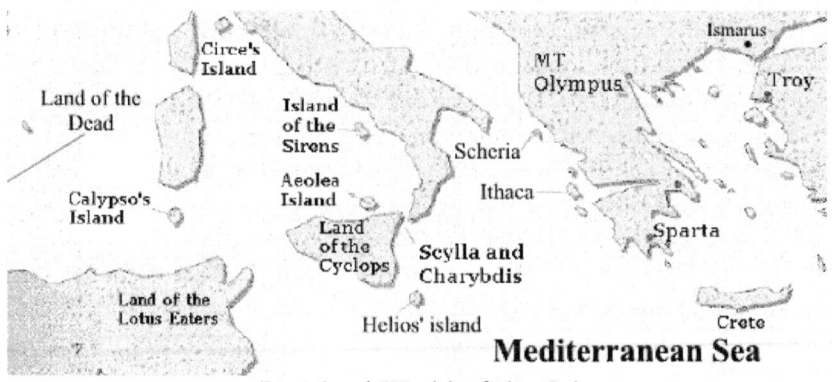

Imagined World of the Odyssey

his homeland, including his own family, thinks he is dead. Penelope, his lonely, long-suffering wife, is being pressured to remarry by a legion of princes and well-to-do young men. Before he left, Odysseus told her that if he had not returned by the time their infant son was grown, she should remarry. Now Telemachus is twenty and himself growing weary of the suitors who have overrun the palace, feasting every night, and eating them out of house and home. For three years, Penelope has cleverly postponed selecting a new husband. By day, she weaves a burial shroud for Laertes, her elderly father-in-law, who has retired to a farm. By night, she unweaves the tunic, but one of her unfaithful maids alerts the courting suitors to her deception, and she is forced to complete her handiwork.

On Olympus, the goddess Athena discusses Odysseus's fate with Zeus. Poseidon, the lord of the deep, has destroyed his ships and drowned all his men after they blinded his son Polyphemus, the Cyclops. In disguise, Athena visits Telemachus and urges him to seek news of his father. The next day, he sets sail to visit survivors of the Trojan War. In Pylos, on the Greek mainland, he meets with Nestor, the elderly king and councilor to Agamemnon, and then in Sparta receives a warm welcome by Menelaus and Helen, who are now reconciled. Menelaus regales him with stories of his own seven-year-long return via Egypt and other exotic lands, and reports that Odysseus was captive of the nymph Calypso. Telemachus hears firsthand the fate of Agamemnon, Menelaus's brother, who was murdered on his return home by his wife Clytemnestra and her lover Aegisthus.

As the Telemachy, or story of Telemachus's search, unfolds, Zeus sends Hermes, the messenger of the gods, to Calypso's island to seek Odysseus's release. The beautiful nymph adores her human lover and has kept him captive for seven years, promising him immortality if he will marry her, but he pines for home and return to Penelope. Heeding Hermes's directive, Calypso frees Odysseus and gives him clothing, food, and drink to take as he sets out on a rough-hewn raft that he builds. Still wrathful, Poseidon gets wind of the seafarer's release and promptly destroys the raft. But with the help of a veil given to him by the sea nymph Ino, Odysseus swims ashore on Scheria, home of the Phaeacians. Awakening the next morning on the beach, he encounters Nausicaa, a young princess who is washing her clothes with her attendants. She is the daughter of King Alcinous and Queen Arete, the rulers of the island, and offers the famished stranger hospitality. Later that day, Odysseus is welcomed at the palace and refreshes himself with food and drink. Over the next couple days, he participates in a pentathlon and listens to the blind bard Demodocus sing about the Trojan War, including the story of the

Wooden Horse in which he played a pivotal role. The strange visitor tries to conceal his tears in his cloak, but the king picks up on his distress. At last revealing his identity, Odysseus begins to narrate his return from Troy and the harrowing loss of all his ships and men.

After leaving Troy, Odysseus and his crew engage in a pirate raid on Ismarus in the land of the Cicones. But they are soon repulsed, and the storm winds blow them to the land of the Lotus-Eaters. Several of the men eat the wondrous lotus fruit whose narcotic effect makes them forget their homecoming. Hastily departing this island that threatens to sap their will, Odysseus and his men make landfall on a hilly shore dotted with caves. After his men help themselves to the cheese and wine they find in one grotto, the occupant, Polyphemus, returns and slays a couple of the crew. The giant cannibal bars the exit from the cave with a boulder and devours several more men before falling asleep. Devising a clever stratagem, Odysseus whittles a stake and drives it through the Cyclop's eye, boasting that his name is Nobody. When his fellow Cyclopses come to the rescue and ask who is punishing him, Polyphemos replies, "Nobody," and they leave. The next morning, when the giant moves the boulder away to allow his flock to go to pasture, Odysseus and his men conceal themselves by holding on to the underside of the sheep. Polyphemos pats down the animals, but fails to catch them and they escape. But once out of the monster's clutches, Odysseus recklessly boasts that it was he Odysseus who outwitted the Cyclops and taunts him with his real name. The brute prays to his father Poseidon, who curses the Greek seafarer with ten more years of wandering.

Next the Achaeans are befriended by Aeolus, the lord of the winds, who gives them a bag of winds, including the gentle West wind, to take them home. But while their captain sleeps, the greedy crew open the bag thinking it contains gold and unleash a tempest that blows them further off course. Encountering the cannibalistic Laestrygonians, Odysseus loses eleven of his twelve ships and fleeing for his life makes landfall on the island of Circe, the sorceress. Feeding the remaining crew cheese and wine, she turns them into swine. Thanks to Hermes, who gives him *moly*, a magic herb, Odysseus resists her spell. He forces her to restore his men in exchange for becoming her lover. After a year, the homesick wanderer begs her for divine assistance, and she tells him that he must sail to the mouth of the Underworld and see the shade of Tiresias, the wisest man of antiquity. In Hades, Odysseus meets the seer, who prophesies his safe return to Ithaca after further sorrows, and tells him of a final pilgrimage that he must take with an oar over his shoulder. The Greek captain also converses with the spirits of his mother Antikleia, Achilles and

Agamemnon, and with a legion of illustrious nobles.

Returning to Circe's abode, the sorceress advises him on the next stages of his journey. Steering clear of the Sirens, seductive maidens that lure sailors to their deaths with their beautiful singing, Odysseus plugs up the ears of his crew with beeswax and orders that he be tied to the ship's mast to resist temptation to join them. Scylla, a six-headed monster, and Charybdis, a deadly whirlpool, present the next challenge. Though losing six men to Scylla, Odysseus and his men skillfully steer between the twin dangers. On the island of the Sun, they disembark to replenish their stores. Both Circe and Tiresias have warned them on pain of death not to eat the cattle of the Sun. Ignoring this advice, the men slay, roast, and consume the kine. The Sun god complains to Zeus, and the father of heaven raises another tempest that capsizes their remaining ship and drowns all the men save for their captain. Clinging to a fig tree, Odysseus washes ashore on the island of Ogygia, where he remains as a love slave to Calypso for seven years until Zeus orders his release.

Enthralled by Odysseus's tale, the Phaeacians agree to help ferry him home. Deposited on an isolated stretch of Ithaca, Odysseus is met by Athena who helps him disguise himself as a wandering beggar and guides him to the hut of Eumaios, his old swineherd. Pretending to be a Cretan veteran of the Trojan War, Odysseus assesses the lay of the land and the loyalty of his old servants. With Athena's assistance, Telemachus returns safely home from Sparta despite plans by the suitors to ambush his ship and kill him. In Eumaios's hut, father and son are reunited and Odysseus reveals his identity. Still disguised as a beggar, Odysseus arrives at the palace, and most of the suitors and servants ridicule and treat him rudely. Antinous, an especially arrogant suitor, flings a stool and other objects at him, and Odysseus strives to keep his temper.

In their first meeting, Odysseus tests Penelope's loyalty. The only ones to recognize him are Argos, his old dog, who promptly dies, and Eurykleia, his childhood nurse and caretaker, who glimpses an old scar on his thigh from a youthful hunting accident. The next day, at Athena's unseen prompting, Penelope consents to marry the suitor who can string Odysseus's mighty bow and shoot an arrow through a dozen axe heads lined up in a row. None of the suitors can handle the bow and hoot in derision when the old beggar asks to take part in the competition. Odysseus easily strings the great bow and sends an arrow through the aligned axe heads. Then he turns the shafts on the suitors and with the help of Athena, Telemachus, and the loyal swineherd and cowherd slays the suitors. A bevy of the disloyal female servants who have been consorting with the suitors are hung, and the goatherd, who has mocked and humiliated him, is gruesomely slain.

Finally Odysseus reveals himself to Penelope, but still hesitant to accept him she orders that his bed he put in the hallway until his identity can be confirmed. Odysseus sees through her verbal trap and reminds her that their marriage bed was carved from an olive tree in the ground around which they built their house. Only then does she accept him as her true husband. Athena commands the Night to hold back the dawn to prolong their lovemaking. In the morning, Odysseus tells Penelope there is one final act he must perform. To ensure a long, happy life together, as Tiresias instructed him in Hades, he must make a pilgrimage to the mainland with an oar on his shoulder and pray to Poseidon. Only then will his homecoming be over.

Later that day, Odysseus visits Laertes, and son and father are reunited. The townsfolk, including families of sons who never returned from Troy and relatives of the slain suitors, call an assembly and demand justice. A few angry relatives resort to arms and pursue Odysseus and Telemachus to his father's orchard. After consulting Zeus, Athena intervenes and convinces both sides to give up their rancor and live in peace.

Resourceful Odysseus

Like Achilles, Odysseus is courageous, a leader of men, and an accomplished warrior. However, he is not as physically imposing or as strong as the hero of the *Iliad*, nor as reckless in his actions, or heedless of the advice of others. Over and over, Odysseus's character is described as resourceful, crafty, devious, and many-faceted. The Wooden Horse, which he proposed, is the classic example of his ingenuity. But the way he outwits the Cyclops, the Lotus-Eaters, the Sirens, and other subhuman and superhuman protagonists also demonstrate his innate cleverness.

In Greek, the quality of wise cunning is known as *metis*. The name originates from the goddess Metis, who was Zeus's first wife. According to the *Theogony*, she gave the young god a potion to trick his abusive father, Cronus, into vomiting out his siblings. Afraid that in turn she would sire a son who would overthrow him, Zeus swallowed Metis. But she was already with child, and their offspring, Athena, was born, fully grown and armed, from his mighty head. Shrewdness became Athena's trademark. But as a female, she was no threat to Zeus's rule, and father and daughter become close confidants. Athena, of course, is Odysseus's protector, and as she teases him they are "two of a kind, we are connivers both."

Odysseus also has a temper and strives to curb his anger. But it doesn't rise to the level of *menis*—or cosmic outrage—as in the case of

Achilles, and he almost always subdues his emotions. For example, when he returns home disguised as a beggar and retires for the night at the palace and sees some of Penelope's maids sneak out to sleep with the suitors, Odysseus becomes enraged. Muttering to himself, he says punningly: "Down; be steady. You've seen worse, that time the Cyclops like a rockslide ate your men while you looked on. Nobody, only guile, got you out of that cave alive." Then Homer adds: "His rage held hard in leash, submitted to his mind."

As the supreme deity, Zeus perfectly combines in himself *metis* and *menis*—the ultimate yin and yang qualities of character and judgment. The Homeric epics explore these twin themes, with the accent on divine wrath in the *Iliad* and on wise cunning in the *Odyssey*. In the former, the goal of the warrior is *kleos*, or imperishable glory enshrined in epic poetry, myth, and legend. In the latter, the purpose of the wanderer is reuniting his *oike*, or his household or family. *Oike* is the Greek root word for "ecology," or as Gary Snyder rendered it his book of poems *Earth Household*.

Compared to the realistic action in the *Iliad*, Odysseus's voyage transpires across a mythic landscape. During his travels, he encounters a variety of fabulous beings that are allegorical or symbolic. Before he reaches Scheria and the hospitality of the Phaeacians, the first half of the epic is largely a dream or fantasy. Throughout the ages, readers and commentators have drawn inspiration from Odysseus's wiles in dealing with the giants, ogres, sorceresses, and other mythical beings he encounters. For example, Scylla and Charybdis are viewed as the dilemma of being "caught between a rock and a hard place," "choosing between two evils," or finding oneself "twixt the devil and the wine dark sea."

From a literary view, the hero's homecoming is a spiritual journey. In the course of his adventures, Odysseus navigates the seven levels of consciousness. But his path is the complementary opposite of Achilles. The son of Peleus advances from ignorance to enlightenment, but his final *satori* is a tragic one. It ends in momentary oneness with Priam, who comes to claim Hector's body, followed offstage by implacable death in the final assault on Troy and eternal glory. Odysseus's journey to wisdom ends in supreme happiness and union in life. He achieves his *nostos* and *oike*, or homecoming and reunion with Penelope, Telemachus, and Laertes. Unlike Achilles, who goes to Hades and bewails his fate, Odysseus is destined for a long, happy life and a peaceful death.

Marauding Seafarers

The brief first leg of Odysseus's journey is overlooked in most accounts of his adventures, as it includes no supernatural beings or monstrous villains. From Troy, Odysseus and his twelve ships sail west to Ismarus, a stronghold of the Cicones on the Thrace mainland. There the Achaeans plunder the town, kill the men who resist, and enslave the women. While cavorting on the beach, butchering the sheep, getting drunk on plundered wine, and violating the wives and daughters, the crew is attacked by the main force of Cicones and narrowly escapes after losing six men in each ship.

The Ithacans' horrific act of piracy merits moral censure, and an enraged Zeus responds with two and a half days of storms that nearly capsize the fleet. But raiding is part and parcel of daily life in the late Bronze and early Iron Ages, so the Stormgather's gusty rebuke amounts to a slap on the wrist. For nine years prior to the final assault on Ilium, the Greeks have been raiding the Aegean islands and coastline with impunity. Briseis, Chryseis, and other captives who figure prominently in the *Iliad* are just several of the young women abducted in the campaign against Troy and its allies.

As the foundation of consciousness, the first level properly includes all autonomous activities such as breathing, digestion, heart rate, blood pressure, nervous functioning, and other unconscious or instinctive responses. Without basic physical strength and vitality, life is not possible. Survival and efficiency are the goals at this level. The plateau of awareness that gives rise to Odysseus's attack on Ismarus is mechanical or unthinking jugment. It represents blind pursuit of hunger, thirst, sex, and other bodily drives. It differs little from that of the lower animals or what the *Theogony* views as the realm of the beasts. Today, psychologists equate this kind of reflexive thinking and robotic behavior with the hind, rear, or what is popularly called the reptilian brain. This region governs the flight or fight response, characteristic of snakes, alligators, and other reptiles that see life as "eat or be eaten." After ten years of war, the Achaeans still have an aggressive mentality. The world to them is divided between the strong and the weak, and as the victors they feel they are entitled to the spoils.

Escape from Lotus Land

After nine days of drifting, Odysseus and his men round the Malea coast and come to the land of the Lotus Eaters. While stocking up on fresh water, several crew members are sent into the interior to learn about the natives. They report that the inhabitants are harmless and live on the sweet flower of the lotus. They are offered the honeyed plant to eat and immediately come under its narcotic spell. The search party never cares to come back to their ship nor return home. They long to stay forever and enjoy the fragrant native bloom of the flower. Odysseus drags the howling men back to the ships and ties them to the rowing benches. Then he gives strict orders to the rest of the crew not to taste the lotus or lose their hope of homecoming.

Homer does not describe the specific physiological effects of the lotus. But it is similar to mescaline, LSD, and other psychedelic drugs that alter cognition and perception. The lotus yields heightened colors, richer textures, sharper contours, more vibrant sounds, more fragrant smells, more satisfying tastes, and other enhanced sensory effects. The realm of sensory awareness naturally develops from infancy and childhood through maturity and old age. On psychotropic drugs, short-term memory is generally impaired, though emotional and intellectual insights may also be heightened. The lesson at this level is to avoid sensory indulgences that can override common sense and lead to apathy, sloth, inertia, and other extreme yin states of mind. Odysseus wisely recognizes the symptoms of excess and spirits his men away before they forget their purpose and dream in life. The man of many turnings will encounter higher octaves of this state later in his quest when he comes under the sway of Circe and Calypso.

The Lawless Cyclops

From lotus land, the voyagers arrive at the country of the Cyclopses—giants, louts, and cannibals who live "without a law to bless them." Each one dwells in his own mountain cave, "dealing out rough justice to wife and child, indifferent to what the others do." Their land remains untilled and the herds of wild goats untouched. The Cyclopses, however, tend to herds of domesticated sheep and goats. Venturing inland, in a cave, Odysseus and his men stumble upon a drying rack with cheeses and vessels full of whey. The men want to confiscate the rich foodstuffs and return to the ships, but Odysseus is curious about the caveman. Polyphemus, the Cyclops, returns eventually with his flock and milks the ewes. In the dim light of the campfire, he spies the intruders and asks them whether they engage in a "fair traffic" or "cast your lives like dice, and ravage other folk by sea?"

Odysseus introduces himself and his crew as Achaeans, returning from Troy, blown off course. He asks the Cyclops to extend hospitality and warns that Zeus protects unoffending strangers and will avenge them if they are harmed. Polyphemus replies to this veiled threat by saying he cares "not a whistle for your thundering Zeus." Suddenly, the Cyclops catches two men in his enormous hands, beats their brains out, and eats them raw. Shocked and terrified, the Greeks pray to Zeus and keep their distance in the darkened cave. At one point, Odysseus considers stabbing the ogre in the liver, but realizes that if he dies, they will never be able to move the gigantic boulder blocking the way out of the cave.

In the morning, the Cyclops seizes several more men to make his breakfast. After praying to Athena, Odysseus comes up with a plan. From a large olive branch lying on the floor of the cave he fashions a stake with a pointed edge. In the evening, after losing two more men, the resourceful seafarer offers his tormentor some strong liquor. As the greedy oaf drains three bowls of wine, Odysseus tells him that his name is "Nobody." Drunk, the Cyclops promptly falls asleep, only to have his one bulging eye put out by the sharpened pike. Howling in pain, Polyphemus attracts the attention of other Cyclopses living in nearby caves. They gather around his entranceway inquiring what ails him. "Nobody tricked me. Nobody has ruined me." he replies. The neighboring Cyclopses shrug and return to their own dwellings.

Odysseus laughs mightily to see "how like a charm the name deceived them." But he still has to come up with a stratagem to slip out of the cave alive. "I drew on all my wits, and ran through tactics, reasoning as a man will for dear life, until a trick came," he later explains to the Phaeacians. Using cords of willow from the ogre's bed, he ties each man under a sheep and lines them up with another sheep on each side. In the morning, when the blind Cyclops lets them out to pasture he feels the tops and sides of the flock but misses the men riding underneath and Odysseus who clings to his favorite ram.

In this way, they make their way back to the ships and safety. But then Odysseus "let my anger flare" and as they row out to sea yells: "Cyclops, if ever mortal man inquire how you were put to shame and blinded, tell him Odysseus, raider of cities, took your eye." Polyphemus pronounces a curse on the Ithacan and prays to his father, Poseidon, never to let him see his home, or failing that, at least lose all companions and suffer bitter days.

The Cyclops episode illustrates the interplay between the heart and the head, the emotional and intellectual levels of awareness. Odysseus wisely keeps still in the cave, humoring the giant and keeping his own emotions in check. Relying on his intellect, he comes up with a bold plan and executes it perfectly. At one point, he goads the giant with emotional taunts, but this serves only to increase Polyphemus' thirst for wine, a necessary ingredient in rendering him senseless and ripe for blinding. The Cyclops, of course, operates on Levels 1 and 2, mechanical and sensory judgment. However, his initial question to the Achaeans—"Are you honest men or pirates?"—contains a deep kernel of truth and rises to the level of Cyclopean *satori*, or level 5 social judgment.

After overcoming an obstacle, Odysseus makes the cardinal mistake of looking back and turning emotional. He becomes enchanted with his own mental prowess, forgetting that it is Athena, or higher powers of reason and intuition, that have saved the day. In boasting of his victory and revealing his true name, he incurs a curse that will cost him another ten years of wandering and the lives of all his men. Poseidon's *menis*, or cosmic wrath, is now raised, and he does everything possible to thwart the Ithacans' return. Even Zeus is disgusted at Odysseus's arrogance and disdains the offering that is set out before the men set sail.

Gone with the Wind

Since most people's lives revolve around mechanical, sensory, emotional, and intellectual awareness, the challenges often repeat themselves in new guise. Life moves in a spiral, unfolding in a slow circular direction, now forward, now back, not in a direct linear ascent. In the next series of adventures, Odysseus and his crew encounter obstacles and opportunities akin to those in the first leg of their voyage but more challenging.

From the land of the Cyclops, they make landfall on Aeolia, domain of Aeolus, the wind god. The island is another earthly paradise, given to royal feasting every day in a sumptuous palace with beds of filigree. The returning warriors spend a month enjoying this luxury in return for telling tales of Troy and their plans to sail home. The hospitable monarch presents the departing captain with a mighty bag containing the storm winds. Only Zephyr, the West wind, is not enclosed, allowing it to blow Odysseus and his men gently home.

For nine days, the travelers sail peacefully homewards until on the tenth they draw offshore of Ithaca and can see their fellow countrymen building fires on the shore. Elated at arriving at their destination, Odysseus falls asleep. But while he is in deep slumber, the men open the bag, suspecting that it contains gold and silver. Their folly releases all the winds, and a hurricane blows the ships all the way back to Aeolia. Surprised to see the Achaeans again, Aeolus turns down Odysseus's request to make good their loss. "Take yourself out of this island, creeping thing," the king commands. "No law, no wisdom, lays it on me now to help a man the blessed gods detest—out! Your voyage here was cursed by heaven!"

In Greek myth, the four winds are portrayed as horses kept in the stables of Aeolus, the storm god. As an airy element, wind is a traditional symbol for air, breath, thought, and spirit. Possession of the bag of winds suggests firm control of the mind, a steadfast will, and unswerving purpose and direction. To get home, all Odysseus has to do is awaken to the fifth, or social, level of judgment, that governs his relation with nature and tireless devotion to the welfare of his crew. But at the critical moment, with his goal in sight, he falls asleep at the helm and misses his chance.

On the one hand, his failing flows from a combination of exhaustion (Level 1, or decline of vitality and efficiency) and indulgence on Aeolia (Level 2, or sensory awareness). Certainly, the greed of the crew in opening the precious bag in hope of finding gold, silver, and other hidden riches represents these lower levels of consciousness. When Aeolus calls Odysseus "a creeping thing" "without law and judgment," he strikes a nerve.

Mastery of the winds confers absolute freedom of movement and a successful voyage. Yet both captain and crew take their eyes off the prize for lesser rewards—a dreamless sleep in Odysseus's case and a dream like fantasy of infinite riches in the case of the crew. Wind is also a traditional symbol of karma. High, gusty, or stormy winds that interrupt, forestall, or wreck cherished plans stand for bad karma. Light, fair winds that speed you on your way are the opposite. Aeolus recognizes that the gods have cursed Odysseus when the very winds that he held in his hand blow him back to where he started. The Achaeans sow what they have reaped.

Driven out of Aeolus, the voyagers row for six days and nights before making landfall on the far stronghold of Lamos. In hindsight, Odysseus recognizes that they have brought this dire turn of events on themselves: "no breeze, no help in sight, by our own folly." In Lamos, where the sun never sets, they moor their ships inside a narrow cavern of the bay and set out to investigate the locals. On a wagon road, they meet a young girl, a daughter of Antiphates the Laistrygon, on her way to fetch water at a fountain. She directs them to her father's dwelling where, in the gloom, they spy a loathsome woman, the queen, who beckons to her husband. Without a greeting, he seizes one man, tears him apart on the spot, and makes a meal of him. As the Achaeans rush back to the black ships fearing for their lives, Antiphate summons the entire howling tribe of Laistrygonians, who rain giant boulders down on the ships. Odysseus escapes with his flagship and crew as it alone is harbored on the sea side. The other eleven ships are smashed to bits and the men slaughtered. It is the biggest disaster yet.

In the land of the perpetual sun, the barbarous Laistrygons represent extremism that never rests. As Odysseus observes, they have no cultivated land. Like the Cyclopses, the earlier cannibals they encounter, the denizens of Lamos live only on raw meat and have no culture. They are paranoid and distrust strangers, unlike mainstream Aegeans who believe in extending hospitality to visitors because they may be gods traveling in disguise. One day too they inevitably will be travelers and expect the same treatment. Hospitality to strangers is the social glue that holds Aegean culture together. Hence karma again is a major consideration. Understanding and acting upon karma, or the law of cause and effect, begins in Level 4 intellectual judgment and extends through Level 5 social judgment to Level 6 philosophical or spiritual awareness. The Trojan War itself is precipitated when the laws of hospitality are flouted. Paris abducts Helen, and the Trojan elders refuse to return her or the treasure they took with them, and these reprehensible acts incur the cosmic wrath of the gods. In the *Odyssey*, the laws of hospitality are also constantly being tested, broken, and renewed. Ironically, most of the men from Ithaca who have given ten years of their lives to uphold the laws of hospitality find themselves slain by a race of inhospitable brutes that know no law or judgment.

The Isle of Enchantment

The fates take Odysseus and his remaining ship to Aiaia, the island of Circe. The goddess is the daughter of Helios, the sun, and Perse, a sea nymph. Her brother is Aietes, keeper of the Golden Fleece. After several days of wandering in the wild, the main search party comes upon her smooth stone hall, guarded by tame wolves and mountain lions. Inside, Circe is singing a beguiling song and weaving on her loom. Welcoming the men, she seats them on thrones and prepares a meal of cheese, barley, and honey mixed with wine. But unknown to the revelers, she spikes their food with "a vile pinch," and they soon lose all desire or thought of their homeland. As they feast, Circe flies after them with her long wand and turns them into swine.

Fearing a snare, Eurylokhus, the squadron leader, alone declines to enter Circe's abode, and runs back to the ship to report to Odysseus the dire turn of events. On his way to Circe's mansion, Hermes appears and warns him of her enchantment. The messenger of the gods gives Odysseus an antidote, a magic plant known as *moly* that has a black root and a milky flower. The plant will "keep your mind and senses clear," Hermes promises. He urges him to overpower Circe with his own sword when she attempts to whip him into submission. When the goddess's golden cup of wine fails to incapacitate Odysseus, and she comes at him with her long stick, he draws his sword, holds it to her throat, and gets her to swear a firm oath of cooperation. Circe duly submits on condition he becomes her lover. Turned back into men, Odysseus's crew is restored to their natural form "younger, more handsome, taller than before." "Loveliest of all immortals," the goddess then convinces the wanderers to remain for a while from the "inhuman sea" and share her bounty. Even Odysseus succumbs to her charms, sharing her "flawless bed" each night for a year. Finally, one of the crew awakens him from his reverie: "Captain, shake off this trance, and think of home—if home indeed awaits us."

Keeping her word, Circe agrees to release the Ithacans and provision their ship. But to fulfill their destiny, she warns them that they must first visit the Underworld and heed the prophecy of Tiresias. The journey will take them by a death-dealing rock, but Circe discloses how to minimize its peril. Just before they disembark, Elpenor, the youngest Greek crewman, falls off her roof and dies. He has been slumbering there after a night of drinking and loses his footing on the ladder. Grieved at this loss and the prospect of sailing to the "cold homes of Death," Odysseus and his remaining crew, "cheeks all wet with tears," take to their oars and set sail.

Like many fairy tales, this episode involves breaking a spell or enchantment. Though blindsided by Circe, Odysseus's crew continues to be portrayed as pleasure seeking and gluttonous. Their swinish behavior is mirrored in their transformation into hogs. Enchantment also signifies loss of memory and identity of one's true nature and dream in life. Like the lotus-eaters, the men forget their homeland and yield to sensory indulgence. As the most beautiful of all goddesses, Circe proves irresistible to mortals. Her charms exceed even those of Helen, whose beauty sparked the Trojan War, and she almost bedazzles Odysseus into abandoning his homeward quest.

To overcome her snares, divine assistance comes to the Achaean captain in the form of *moly*. The plant's black root and white flower represent complementary opposites, yin and yang, or what George Ohsawa and Michio Kushi call the Unifying Principle. This begins at Level 4, or intellectual consciousness, and is the realm of reason, analysis, comparison, evaluation, logic, and conceptualization. Odysseus counters her seductive female beauty, distilled in the spiked honeyed wine, with his own male prowess, symbolized with the drawn sword. In myth and folklore, the sword stands for intellect and wisdom that cuts through to the heart or core of a problem. A classic instance is young Arthur, who pulls the sword out of the stone and becomes king of England. In turning the tables on Circe, matching her poison (yin) and violent threats (yang) with his own, Odysseus subdues the goddess, and she yields to the strength of his mind and virility. For a year, they enjoy each other's company, even producing a son, according to a later Greek myth. But remaining at the romantic or intellectual level of awareness eventually leads to stagnation. Soon it is time to move on. Elpenor's fall from the roof signifies the fall from the ladder of consciousness that Odysseus himself is gradually scaling. Unless he keeps his wits about him, he too will tumble from grace and lose his homecoming. Elpenor parallels a character in the Gilgamesh epic who died accidentally, received no burial, and stalks the Underworld.

Visit to Hades

Following Circe's directions, Odysseus and his crew sail north to the realm of perpetual night. At the mouth of the Underworld, they are met by the souls of the dead who throng around the votive pit. The spirits represent a cross-section of humanity: brides and young men, old men in pain, and tender girls unused to grief, as well as many warriors "battle-slain, bearing still their bloody gear." The first shade to approach, Elpenor, the crewman who fell to his death from Circe's roof, begs Odysseus to return to the island and bury his body. It has been neglected in their haste to depart. The resourceful wayfarer agrees to Elpenor's request and promises to plant an oar on his burial mound—an instance of social judgment. Next, the seer Tiresias appears and warns Odysseus that he has run afoul of Poseidon, lord of the sea, for blinding his son the Cyclops. Tiresias strongly cautions him not to allow any of his men to eat the cattle of the Sun when they next make landfall on Thrinakia. "Avoid those kine, hold fast to your intent, and hard seafaring bring you all to Ithaca," he foretells. "But if you raid the beeves, I see destruction for ship and crew." Finally, after meting out justice to the suitors, he advises Odysseus to journey overland while carrying an oar on his shoulder and make sacrifice to Poseidon. "My life runs on then as the gods have spun it," the long-suffering adventurer vows in compliance.

The remainder of the visit to the Underworld consists of brief appearances by other shades near and dear to the hero. First, his mother Antikleia brings Odysseus news of his wife, son, and father and confides how she died in loneliness, pining for his return. Three times son tries to embrace mother but grasps only air. Antikleia tells him such is the common fate of mortals and encourages him to make the most of his life in the world of light. A contingent of lovely female shades, including former queens and princesses, parades by and announce their names and lineages. The ghosts of illustrious comrades from Troy follow, beginning with Agamemnon, who reveals his grisly fate at the hands of his wife and lover. Then the spirit of Achilles appears and, as we saw earlier, bitterly laments his death in battle. Rather than dying early and winning eternal renown, he tells Odysseus, he would prefer serving as the lowliest farm laborer tilling the fields. The last among his former men-in-arms to appear is Ajax, son of Telemon. The colossal warrior is still furious that Odysseus beat him in a contest for Achilles's arms after he was slain by Paris. "The Lady Thetis, mother of Achilles, laid out for us the dead man's battle gear, and Trojan children, with Athena, named the Danaan fittest to own them," Odysseus recalls. The two great warriors tie for the laurels after several athletic competitions, and at the prodding of Athena, the judges—Trojan waifs and orphans—award him the trophies. Angry and despondent, the towering warrior then falls on his own sword. In Hades, Ajax gives no reply to Odysseus's apology and turns back to the world of darkness.

A throng of nefarious shades then pass by, including the giant Tityos, who like Prometheus, is condemned to have vultures peck out his liver (for raping one of Zeus's mistresses); Tantalus put to the torture of eternal thirst and hunger confined just out of reach of clear running water and luscious overhanging fruit; and Sisyphus, fated to roll a tremendous boulder to a great height, only to have it fall back down again. On a brighter note, Odysseus encounters not the ghost, but a projection, of Heracles, the hero who became immortal after a long series of tribulations similar to his own. The fabled warrior and his comely wife Hebe, the cupbearer of the gods, are feasting on Olympus. But he sends Odysseus a vision (or what today we would call a digital avatar) of himself in which he stresses how perseverance and reliance on Athena and Hermes saw him through. As phantoms by the thousands now assail him, Odysseus fears Persephone, queen of Hades, like Circe, designs to detain him. Beating a hasty retreat, he returns to his ship. The hawsers are cast off, oars are lifted, and the wind takes them back to the world of the living.

Odysseus's visit to Hades serves as a literary model for Virgil, Dante, and other pilgrims seeking insight and understanding into the nature of death and the world of spirit. This subject is properly the concern of Level 6, philosophical and spiritual consciousness. Curiously, Homer's Underworld is like a civic amphitheater or holding pen for departed souls. It resembles Circe's pigsty, described in the previous episode, where disturbed souls are crowded together, each ruing a lost opportunity, sleight, or victimization in life. Regrets dominate the conversations, and Odysseus's encounters with Agamemnon, Achilles, and Ajax reinforce the wisdom of the path he has chosen—to follow the way of *metis* rather than *menis*, the triumph of intellect over emotion.

In Hades, we find all seven levels of consciousness. For the most part, the souls throng together mechanically, bewail their misery, and rue their sensory and emotional choices or limits. Intellectual, social, and spiritual awareness are embodied in Tiresias, whose prophecy steels Odysseus's will and provides a larger roadmap for the realization of his dream. Heracles alone transcends the darkness and sorrow of Hades. As a mortal, he persevered in his own mighty labors and was transformed into an immortal. His attainment of universal consciousness and happy union with Hebe offers a shining example for Odysseus and Penelope.

Achilles's Shield also figures in this episode, linking the *Iliad*'s most sublime scene with the *Odyssey*. First, the shades that greet Odysseus—

brides and young men, old men, tender girls, as well as legions of warriors—appear like characters depicted on Hephaestus's Shield, especially in the circle of the cities of war and peace. Second, as we learn when Odysseus meets the spirit of Ajax, the goddess Thetis, who commissioned the Shield, organized a competition after Achilles's death for her son's armor. After a panel of children, almost certainly swayed by Athena, awards the palm to Odysseus, the colossal warrior commits suicide. Odysseus assures Ajax that the "accursed calamitous arms" mean nothing to him. "When you died by your own hand, we lost a tower, formidable in war. All we Achaeans mourn you forever, as we do Achilles; and no one bears the blame but Zeus. He fixed that doom for you because he frowned on the whole expedition of our spearmen." Ironically, the sword Ajax kills himself with is the one presented to him by Hector during a friendly truce in the fighting.

Odysseus's peace offering to Ajax's soul is another example of his *metis*, or inspired deceit. It is almost certainly a lie. Odysseus is much too competitive not to have given his utmost and won the armor on his own merits, including prayers to Athena, his guardian deity. Compared to the wily Ithacan, the humongous Ajax is not very bright. Indeed, in Hades, Odysseus rebukes him for his indignation and stubborn pride. The key point is that the Shield passes from Achilles, the hero of the *Iliad*, to Odysseus, the hero of the *Odyssey*. Achilles uses the Shield to defeat the invincible Hector and turn the tide of battle. But he does not really understand or appreciate its spiritual significance. Now that the Shield—with its magnificent artwork depicting heaven and earth and the Ages of Humanity—comes into Odysseus's possession, it remains to be seen whether he will grasp and apply its universal message.

The oar, another major prop in the *Odyssey*, also carries sublime significance. We will look at its deeper meaning in Chapter 6. But as Tiresias's final prophecy—echoing Elpenor's request that an oar be planted on his burial mound—the nautical implement is fraught with import. Heracles's admonition to rely on Athena and Hermes—practical wisdom and mystic knowledge—as he did will win Odysseus his homecoming and return to paradise.

The Sirens' Song

Returning to Aiaia, Odysseus and his men bury Elpenor's body and feast again with Circe. The goddess warns them of the Sirens, deadly harpies, who lie squarely in their ship's path. To avoid their bewitching songs, she advises Odysseus to plug the ears of his oarsmen with beeswax and have them tie him to the mast. Beyond their abode, littered with the bones of sailors who succumbed to their charms, lie the Prowling Rocks or Drifters. Nearby, Scylla, a six-headed monster, dwells in a cave. No ship can pass without losing some of its crew to her triple serried rows of fangs. On the opposite point, Charybdis, a gigantic whirlpool, sucks everything in her wake down into the sea three times a day. "Better to mourn six men than lose them all, and the ship, too," Circe instructs, encouraging him to pay Scylla her due and steer clear of Charybdis.

Odysseus follows her guidance, sacrifices six men to the monster, and arrives at Thrinakia, the island where the sacred cattle of the Sun graze. Helios the Sun god is Circe's father, and her dire warning to avoid killing the animals, seconded by Tiresias in the Underworld, proves true. When his crew runs out of food "and lean days wore their bellies," they round up the wild heifers, sacrifice to the gods, and enjoy their fill. Strange signs appear when they flay the carcasses. The cowhides start to crawl and the beef, both raw and roasted, lows like cattle upon the spits. For six days they feast on this forbidden food, and on the seventh, at Helios' angry behest, Zeus launches a thunderbolt and sinks the ship, with loss of all the crew except Odysseus.

 Clinging to the debris, the hapless captain lashes the mast and keel together and floats back toward Charybdis. After drifting all night, he manages to grasp the bough of a great fig tree that grows on the island. As the whirlpool sucks everything down to the ocean floor, Odysseus clings grimly to the branch. At twilight, he drops into the foam beside the timbers of his ship, rows hard with his hands, and passes safely through the strait. Nine days later the ocean currents take Odysseus to Ogygia, the island of the nymph Calypso. Here, as we have seen, he is marooned for seven years, enjoying her enchanting songs, handwoven tunics, and bed and board. Resisting her promise to make him immortal, Odysseus longs for home and reunion with Penelope. The stalemate between him and the nymph is finally broken when Zeus sets him free.

The last leg of Odysseus's magical journey witnesses further lessons in emotional and intellectual judgment. The Sirens combine the sensory delights and sumptuousness of lotus land and Circe's palace. In tacking toward Scylla and avoiding Charybdis, Odysseus shows that he has learned to control his emotions and suffer necessary losses. But when the crew continues to defy destiny and dine on the cattle of the Sun, the *menis* or wrath of the gods destroys them. Their transgression is similar to the children of Israel who create a Golden Calf in the Wilderness. (According to Rabbinical Judaism, Moses lived until 1271 BCE, the same decade archaeologists date the Trojan War.) Like Odysseus's men, the Israelites set up an altar and make burnt offerings to heaven while their absent commander Moses receives the Ten Commandments. But Yahweh—a storm god like Zeus—is not placated with their sacrifice. He punishes them with forty years of wandering and denies homecoming to Moses, their faithful shepherd.

Dancing in Scheria

After building a raft with Calypso's help and floating for many days, Odysseus catches sight of Scheria, the island of the Phaeacians. But just before the castaway makes landfall, Poseidon spies him on his return from Ethiopia. Realizing that Odysseus has been released from bondage by Zeus, the lord of earthquakes and thunderheads brews one final torrential storm to sink the mortal who has blinded his son. Stirring up the winds and waters with his trident, Poseidon destroys the raft and sends Odysseus into the swirling deep. But the nereid Ino spies him and gives him her veil as a buoy to prevent him from drowning. For two more days, he bobs helplessly in the swells, but on the third day with Athena's help makes shore. Naked and deathly spent, Odysseus looses the veil, letting it drift back to Ino, and kisses the soil of the earth. In an olive grove, he fashions a leaf bed and collapses exhausted while Athena showers "quiet sleep" and "seals his cherished eyes."

On Scheria, Odysseus is graciously received by Nausicaa, the young princess, and her parents, King Alcinous and Queen Arete. Their warmth and hospitality are the first selfless kindness he receives since leaving Troy ten years earlier. Circe and Calypso befriend him, but both desire him as their lover and harbor ulterior motives for their aid. Even Tiresias in the Underworld has to be placated with a blood offering in return for his prophecy.

Scheria marks a return to human culture and civilization. Indeed, the land of mariners is inhabited by a golden race and embodies the Circle of the Dance on Hephaestus's Shield. In describing how Odysseus came upon the island, Homer rhapsodizes:

> Now the great seaman, leaning on his oar,
> steered all the night unsleeping, and his eyes
> picked out the Pleiades, the laggard Ploughman
> and the Great Bear, that some have called the Wain,
> pivoting in the sky before Orion;
> of all the night's pure figures, she alone
> would never bathe or dip in the Ocean stream.
> These stars the beautiful Calypso bade him
> hold on his left hand as he crossed the main.

> Seventeen nights and days in the open water
> He sailed, before a dark shoreline appeared;
> Scheria then came slowly into view
> like a rough shield of bull's hide on the sea.
>
> (5.279-91)

Note that this passage begins with a description of the stars and constellations exactly as they are portrayed on Achilles's Shield. The North Star that "never bathes or dips" is singled out. The land itself resembles a shield, and as Odysseus discovers on making landfall in Scheria is populated mainly by young people dancing, singing, and enjoying the fruits of peace. Even the oar—a mighty symbol of the entire spiral of consciousness—appears in the opening line and the Phaeacians are later described as "oar-loving."

In a brief history, Homer tells us that the Phaeacians originated in Hyperieia, "a country of wide dancing grounds." To avoid the pillage of invading Cyclopses, they migrated across the sea "to settle a New World" on Scheria. Their founder walled the promontory, built their homes and shrines, and "parceled out the black land for the plow." Alcinous, the son, succeeded his father and now presides over their paradisal new homeland. The Phaeacians' love of the arts, especially music, dance, and storytelling, figures prominently in this episode. In seeking permission to go the beach, Nausicaa tells her father that she would like to wash her brother's clothes so they will have fresh linens when they go dancing. On the beach she picnics with her friends, sings and dances, and plays catch with a large ball. When the ball goes amiss and lands in a whirling stream, the girls's shouts awaken Odysseus. He quickly sizes up the situation, but unsure whether Nausicaa is a mortal or a goddess, compliments her graciously:

> If you are one of earth's inhabitants,
> how blest our father, and your gentle mother
> blest all your kin. I know what happiness
> must send the warm tears to their eyes, each time
> they see their wondrous child go to the dancing!
>
> (6.165-69)

After giving him some linens to cloak his nakedness, Nausicaa invites him to visit her parents. Arriving at the spacious palace, he is impressed by the fine workmanship of the rooms "airy and luminous." In another glance at the Shield, Homer tells us, the artwork reminds him of "the skill and ardor of Hephaestus." As skilled as the men are at navigation, the women are gifted in grinding yellow barleycorn and weaving upon their looms. Outside, he passes an orchard with pear trees, pomegranates, apples, figs, and olives, ripe for the picking:

> Fruit never failed upon these trees: winter
> and summer time they bore, for through the year
> the breathing Westwind ripened all in turn—
> so one pear came to prime, and then another,
> and so with apples, figs, and the vine's fruit
> empurpled in the royal vineyard there. . . .
> After the vines came rows of vegetables
> of all kinds that flourish in every season,
> and through the garden plots and orchard ran
> channels from one clear fountain, while another
> gushed through a pipe under the courtyard entrance
> to serve the house and all who came for water
> these were the gifts of heaven to Alcinous.
>
> (7.124-41)

Mention of fruit that grows year round, summer and winter, glances at the Golden Age when crops grew in abundance regardless of season. Gold and silver dogs created by Hephaestus also guard Alcinous's palace. Described as "deathless and ageless," they too nod at the Golden and Silver Age heritage of the Phaeacians.

For a moment, trouble threatens to erupt in paradise when Seareach, a hot-tempered young Phaeacian, insults Odysseus at court and says he is unfit to participate in their sports competition. The weary traveler upbraids him for his arrogance, explaining that the gods bestow their gifts appropriately on people, regardless of birth, brains, speech, or age. Picking up a discus, he promptly heaves it beyond all others. King Alcinous apologizes for the affront at "our peaceful games." Continuing Odysseus's train of thought, he agrees that the gods reward each person or culture proportionally to their bents:

> Our prowess . . . our skills, given by Zeus,
> and practiced from our father's time to this—
> not in the boxing ring nor the palestra
> conspicuous, but in racing, land or sea;
> and all our days we set great store by feasting,
> harpers, and the grace of dancing choirs,
> changes of dress, warm baths, and downy beds,

O master dancers of the Phaeacians!
Perform now: let our guest on his return
tell his companions we excel the world
in dance and song, as in our ships and running.
Someone go find the gittern harp in hall
And bring it quickly to Demodokus!   (8.256-69)

Not only does Alcinous describe his realm in terms of artistic and musical achievements, but he also offers his daughter Nausicaa in marriage to Odysseus. Marriage festivities, of course, are also a major theme depicted on Achilles' Shield. The blind bard whom the king summons, as most commentators agree, probably constitutes a self-portrait of Homer, who according to tradition was sightless and glances at the bard and his lyre depicted on Hephaestus's fresco. And the song that Demodokus then sings tells the tale of how Hephaestus outwitted his wife Aphrodite and her lover Ares. Once again, the divine craftsman and forger of the Shield, makes his appearance in a chapter that more than any in the two epics points to the dawn of the new Golden Age. As a coda to this artistic display, Alcinous calls upon two of his sons to demonstrate a special dance involving a soaring, round, shield-like ball, while a circle of boys dance in a circle around them keeping time to a steady, stamping beat. "O majesty, model of all your folk," Odysseus marvels, "your promise was to show me peerless dancers; here is the promise kept. I am all wonder." Twelve princes of the realm then present Odysseus with sumptuous gifts and the evening ends in a feast. Searach, the impetuous young man who offended Odysseus, presents him a valuable sword. The great tactician replies, "My hand, friend; may the gods award you fortune. I hope no pressing need comes on you ever for this fine blade you give me in amends." The scene contrasts sharply with the *Iliad* in which Odysseus slays Lyocan, the prince who has beseeched his forgiveness on the battlefield, and Achilles slays twelve captive Trojan princes to avenge Patrocles's death. The twelve princes in each epic point to the twelve constellations of the precessional cycle. The soaring ball in the Odyssey, representing the spiraling earth, makes the image even more visual.

Homeward Bound

When Dawn's rosy fingertips usher in the morning, Odysseus sets sail with the Phaeacians, and after a smooth voyage they drop him off the next day by an isolated cove on Ithaca. After hiding his treasure in the roots of an olive tree, Odysseus encounters Athena in the guise of a shepherd. At first he doesn't recognize her and spins a tall tale about being a Cretan castaway. But finally she confides: "I am Pallas Athena, daughter of Zeus, I that am always with you in times of travail, a shield to you in battle, I who made the Phaeacians befriend you, to a man." Urging patience, the goddess promises to help him mete out justice to the suitors.

Disguised as an old beggar, Odysseus arrives at the hut of Eumaios, his old swineherd, and tests his loyalty. South into Lakedaimon "into the land where greens are wide for dancing," Athena speeds to bring Telemachus back to Ithaca. Soon reunited, father and son plot, with the goddess's help, the suitors' doom.

Arriving at the palace, Odysseus endures taunts and blows from the impudent suitors and sees for himself how they are plundering his estate. In his first meeting with Penelope, he continues to present himself as a shipwrecked Cretan, but one who befriended Odysseus on his way to Troy. Penelope responds sympathetically to his tale and relates a dream she had in which an eagle kills twenty fat geese that have come to feed beside her house. In the dream, Odysseus drops out of the sky and comforts her: "Be glad renowned Icarios's daughter: here is no dream but something real as day, something about to happen. All those geese were suitors, and the bird was I. See now, I am no eagle but your lord come back to bring inglorious death upon them all." The canny visitor assures her that it is a true dream, but Penelope interprets it as an illusion—a dream of glittering ivory rather than honest horn. The next day, she announces, she will decree a contest for her hand. She will marry whoever can string Odysseus's great bow.

The following morning, Odysseus grows despondent. Though he is a powerful warrior, battling 108 suitors appears beyond even his strength and *metis*. Athena rebukes his faint-heartedness, and other omens steel his resolve. Public heralds announce the competition, and the suitors gather in the great hall to try their hand at the bow as Penelope and Telemachus watch. When all fail even to string the mighty bow, Odysseus tries his hand. To the jeers of the glum suitors, as Homer relates:

> The man skilled in all ways of contending
> satisfied by the great bow's look and heft,
> like a musician, like a harper, when
> with quiet hand upon his instrument
> he draws between his thumb and forefinger
> a sweet new string upon a peg: so effortlessly
> Odysseus in one motion strung the bow.
> Then slid his right hand down the cord and plucked it
> so the taut gut vibrating hummed and sang

a swallow's note.

(21.460-70)

As amazement spreads across the faces of the suitors, Zeus sends a thunderclap overhead as a sign of impending doom. Carefully notching an arrow, Odysseus sends it "clean as a whistle through every socket ring, and grazed not one, to thud with heavy brazen head beyond." What the suitors fear the most has come to pass. Odysseus, king of Ithaca, has returned. Vowing that it is now time to settle affairs, the master of the manor says the time for "song and harping that adorn a feast" is over. With the help of Telemachus and the loyal swineherd and cowherd, the suitors are massacred. As promised, the goddess of wisdom enters the fray. "At this moment that unmanning thunder cloud, the aegis, Athena's shield, took form aloft in the great hall. And the suitors made with fear at her great sign."

The sole survivors are the minstrel, who clasps Odysseus's knees and pleads: "My gift is song for men and for the gods undying," and a herald who cared for Telemachus in boyhood. A dozen of the serving women who lay with the suitors are hung in the roundhouse. Though respecting their humanity, as he does all the dead and dying in Troy, Homer couches their end in rhythmic terms:

> [Telemachus] tied one end of a hawser to a pillar
> and passed the other about the roundhouse top,
> taking the slack up, so that no one's toes
> could touch the ground. They would be hung like doves
> or larks in springes triggered in a thicket,
> where the birds think to crest—a cruel nesting.
> So now in turn each woman thrust her head
> into a noose and swung, yanked high in air,
> to perish there most piteously.
> Their feet danced for a little, but not long.
>
> (21.517-26)

In the second half of the *Odyssey*, encompassing his arrival in Scheria and return to Ithaca, Odysseus learns to develop and extend his social consciousness. Washing up naked on the shield-like island symbolizes his rebirth and transformation after losing all his ships, men, treasure, and hope of homecoming. Odysseus is stripped of everything he holds dear, including his identity. He finds himself a true Nobody—the name he proclaimed for himself in the Cyclops' cave. In this utopian enclave, he is reborn into a true human community. Peace and prosperity prevail; music, dance, and the other arts are valued more highly than physical prowess; and violence and war remain a distant memory. In sharp contrast to Troy and Ithaca, life on Scheria embodies a budding golden age and the last circle on Achilles' Shield.

On Ithaca, Odysseus must summon all of his wits and cunning to clean house, mete out justice to the suitors, and reunite with his family. Restoring order to his household and homeland requires mastery of social skills. As on the battlefield in Troy, he has to sacrifice his own individual needs to the community he serves. Biting his tongue while the arrogant courtiers plunder his estate, lust after his wife, and mock his son and himself is a supreme lesson in controlling the emotions and developing intellectual, social, and spiritual awareness.

Equally fascinating is Penelope's evolving consciousness. As a grieving wife, she functions primarily at an emotional level. After twenty years, she still has not come to terms with altered circumstances and is stuck in the past. But in loyal service to Odysseus's memory and dream of future reunion, she devises an ingenious strategy to deceive the suitors. Weaving and unweaving the shroud displays her *metis*, or practical wisdom, as her intellect triumphs over her emotion. "She may rely too long on Athena's gifts—talent in handicraft and a clever mind; so cunning—history cannot show the like." Homer dwells on her "thoughtful beauty" and describes the conflict in her breast as "Penelope, most worn in love and thought." The suitors call her "deep-minded queen." Does she recognize the old beggar as her husband before the archery contest? Some readers and commentators think so. Her final test, ordering their unmovable bed to be moved into the hallway, cleverly forces Odysseus's hand. Until that moment, both man and wife have been spinning tall tales to one another. The long delayed moment of truth now arrives.

Odysseus's return to the world of ordinary reality in Scheria and Ithaca contrasts with the magical first half of the epic. But the symbolism of the Shield shines through. Indeed, we learn that he not only inherits Achilles's great armor with its mandala of past, present, and future, but he also begins to don the cloak of divine *metis* fashioned by his protector. Athena's cunning wisdom is his Shield, as she reminds him, and will see him through. In the thick of the battle, the goddess wields her own great shield, the divine aegis, to strike down the suitors. Their end is bloody, but not undeserved. The innocent are spared, and as we shall see in Chapter 6 "Odysseus's Oar," the epic ends in a climactic vision of the return of love and peace and the dawn of the new golden age.

5
Plowlands Kind with Grain

> The sun rose on the flawless brimming sea
> into a sky all brazen—all one brightening
> for gods immortal and for mortal men
> on plowlands kind with grain.
> —*Odyssey* 3.1-4

Like the *Iliad*, the *Odyssey* begins and ends with lessons in eating, proper food preparation, and mealtime etiquette. The opening lines introduce the dietary theme:

> Sing in me, Muse, and through me tell the story
> of that man skilled in all ways of contending,
> the wanderer, harried for years on end,
> after he plundered the stronghold
> on the proud height of Troy.
>   He saw the townlands
> and learned the minds of many distant men,
> and weathered many bitter nights and days
> in his deep heart at sea, while he fought only
> to save his life, to bring his shipmates home.
> But not by will nor valor could he save them,
> for their own recklessness destroyed them all—
> children and fools, they killed and feasted on
> the cattle of Lord Helios, the Sun,
> and he who moves all day through heaven
> took from their eyes the dawn of their return.
>   (1.1.16)

The epic ends, of course, with the massacre of the suitors, "that wolf pack . . . who prey upon [Odysseus's] flocks and dusky cattle," "drain bowls of water and wine," and "butcher whole carcasses for roasting."

In between, there are encounters with cannibals, monsters, and other fantastic beings that do not eat grain or other human food. As a Bronze Age staple, animal food plays a major role in the story. But it figures substantially less in the second of the two Homeric poems, while fruits, vegetables, sweets, and wine—lighter, more feminine foods—move to the forefront. On his voyage back to civilization, Odysseus encounters a series of goddesses, women, and girls who nurture and assist him in his ascent on the ladder of food and consciousness.

The Staying Power of Oarsmen

Barley, the main grain in the Aegean world, appears throughout the *Odyssey*. Disguised as Mentor, a boyhood friend, Athena advises Telemachus to set sail to learn news about his long lost father. "Go on home, as if to join the suitors, but get provisions ready in a container—wine in two-handled jugs and barley meal, the staying power of oarsmen, in skin bags, watertight." Odysseus's son duly follows her advice and packs twenty bushes of finely ground barley meal and twelve *amphorai*, or flasks, of wine.

In Sparta, where he meets Menelaus, Telemachus is impressed by the suitability of the landscape for cultivation: "My lord, you rule wide country, rolling and rich with clover, galingale, and all the grains: red wheat and hoary barley. At home we have no level runs or meadows, but highland, goat land—prettier than plains, though. Grasses, and pasture land, are hard to come by upon the islands tilted in the sea, and Ithaca is the island of them all."

Meanwhile, as his son presses Menelaus and Helen for the latest intelligence, Odysseus washes up on Scheria, the shield-like island of the Phaeacians. In welcoming him, the princess Nausicaa offers him bread and wine from her picnic basket. Yearning for human companionship after years of captivity by a goddess, Odysseus expresses his gratitude. In recounting his adventures to King Alcinous and Queen Arete, he emphasizes the primacy of grains and moderate eating.

In the land of the Lotus-Eaters, the wanderer reports, he strictly avoids eating any of their seductive fruits that caused his crew to forget their homeland. On their next stop, searching for provisions in a cave, they come across the Cyclops, whom he describes as "knowing none but savage ways, a brute so huge, he seemed no man at all of those who eat good wheaten bread." While his men greedily devour the giant's cheese, whey, and milk, Odysseus abstains. In tricking the cannibal into getting drunk, he offers him some fiery brandy that he received as a gift from Maron, the son of the priest of Apollo in Ismarus, for kindness he showed in sparing him and his wife and child. As Odysseus tells his listeners, he had an intuition that the wine would come in handy: "In my bones I knew that some towering brute would be upon us soon—all outward power, a wild man, ignorant of civility." The enraged ogre, whom he tricks with wordplay, vows to avenge the loss of his eye by eating him raw as he did several of his crewmen: "Nobody's my meat." But Odysseus and his men cleverly pass through the entryway concealed beneath the sheep and escape the cannibal's reach.

After encountering another man-eating race, the Laestrygonians, whom Odysseus observes have no cultivated land for growing grain, the voyagers come to Circe's abode. Once again, the gluttonous crew stuffs itself with cheese, sweets, and wine and is turned by the sorceress into swine. Only Odysseus, who abstains from this rich fare and drunkenness, escapes this fate. Thanks to Hermes's magic plant, *moly*, he is able to counter Circe's seductive tincture. Only after they reach an understanding does the goddess serve her visitors barley loaves and other plant-quality food.

After leaving Circe's paradise, Odysseus and his men thread the needle between Scylla and Charybdis. The man-eating monster with six heads catches her prey "like hooking a fish and ripping it from the surface." The deadly whirlpool, which gratefully they are able to avoid, devours whole ships in one gulp—a metaphor of consumption run wild.

In the Underworld, Elpenor's spirit beseeches Odyssey to bury him properly and invokes the sanctity of grain: "Now hear the grace I pray for, in the name of those back in the world, not here—your wife and father, he who gave you bread in childhood, your only son, Telemachus." Also in Hades, Achilles famously tells Odysseus that he would rather till the grain-giving earth and eat simply than preside over the glorious dead. Like the gods, the souls in the Bronze Age Underworld do not eat material food. They thrive on human blood and the fragrance of animal sacrifices, and only after they sip at the votive pit will they converse with their visitor.

On the island of the Sun, as the resourceful captain relates, his men live on barley and wild plants—vegan style—supplemented by wine, for as long as they can:

> As long as bread and good red wine remained
> to keep the men up, and appease their craving
> they would not touch the cattle. But in the end,
> when all the barley in the ship was gone,

hunger drove them to scour the wild shore
with angling hooks, for fishes and sea fowl,
whatever fell into their hands; and lean days
wore their bellies thin.

(12.417-24)

But fish and poultry don't suffice, and temptation gets the better of Odysseus's crew, and they slay the forbidden cattle. The unsanctified beef proves lethal. Indeed, its strange effects appear on the spits, as the immortal animals crawl, moan, and express their horror at being killed and eaten. In a vain effort to appease the Sun god, the crew carries out a sacrifice, but they lack "barley meal to strew on the victims" and ensure a voluntary death. Their arrogance soon rebounds on them as Zeus smotes their ship. All except Odysseus, who alone does not eat the unsanctified beef, drown.

Washing up on Scheria, half dead and ravenously hungry, Odysseus is greeted by Nausicaa, the comely princess, who gives him loaves and wine—human food—after days and weeks of subsistence living and near starvation. Arriving at the palace of her parents, he is delighted to see fifty maids-in-waiting seated by the round mill, grinding yellow barleycorn, and the orchard with its abundance of fruit. Inside, Alcinous's mistress of provisions greets him "with bread and other victuals, generous with her store." The banquet, during which he relates his odyssey, is richer and includes animal food, but grains are always served, symbolic of the high culture and civilization of this Aegean utopia.

Upon being dropped off by the Phaeacians at a remote cove on Ithaca, Odysseus doesn't at first recognize his home country. Athena in disguise as a shepherd boy tells him that the island is unsuitable for training horses—a reference to Troy, the land of spirited steeds. "But there is nothing meager about the soil, the yield of grain is wondrous," she emphasizes.

At the cottage of Eumaios, his old swineherd, Odysseus is greeted with bread and modest fare. Pretending to be a castaway from Crete, the lord of the manor uses a grain-based metaphor for his downtrodden appearance: "My strength's all gone, but from the husk you may divine the ear that stood tall in the old days."

The forester in turn tells the visitor of his own lineage and saga of woe. He relates that he is a native of Syrie "rich in grain" and other products of the earth. "No dearth is ever known there, no disease wars on folks, of ills that plague mankind." When people reach old age, "Apollo with his longbow of silver comes, and Artemis showering arrows of mild death." Though a veritable golden race inhabits the country, it is vulnerable to unscrupulous visitors. As a child Eumaios is abducted by a seafaring merchant who sells him into slavery. Fortunately, he ends up in the service of Laertes, Odysseus's father, who has always treated him kindly.

The day he sets out for the palace, Homer depicts Odysseus as a cook preparing breakfast with the forester: "There were two men in the mountain hut—Odysseus and the swineherd. At first light blowing their fire out, they cooked their breakfast, including "heaped up willow baskets full of bread" and "an ivy bowl of honey-hearted wine." Among his many talents, Odysseus is a cook and a baker. Who knew?

Cooking Their Lordships' Mutton

The *Odyssey* reaches its climax with the massacre of the suitors in the banquet hall and the reunion of Odysseus and Penelope. Food, cooking, and dining metaphors permeate the climactic scenes of the epic. From the opening of the story, the suitors are described as reckless young men with unrestrained appetites, who are devouring the food stores of the palace, plundering the livestock, and behaving in a rowdy, gluttonous manner. Every day, they force the swineherd and cowherd to bring fresh animals to the manor to supply their nightly feasting. "Three hundred and sixty [fine porkers] now lay there at night, guarded by dogs like wolves."

In a typical description of their priorities, Homer sings:

> Swaggering before Odysseus' hall,
> the suitors were competing at the discus throw
> and javelin, on the level measured field.
> But when the dinner hour drew on, and beasts
> were being driven from the fields to slaughter—
> as beasts were, every day Medon spoke out:
> Medon, the crier whom the suitors liked;
> he took his meat beside them.
>
>   "Men," he said,
> "each one has had his work-out and his pleasure,
> come in to Hall now; time to make our feast.
> Are discus throws more admirable than a roast
> when the proper hour comes?"
>
>   At this reminder
> they all broke up their games, and trailed away
> into the gracious, timbered hall. There, first,
> they dropped their cloaks on chairs; then came their ritual:
> putting great rams and fat goats to the knife—
> pigs and a cow, too.

> So they made their feast.
> (17.210-29)

On seeing the chaos in the banquet hall for himself, Odysseus decries "the wine drunk up in rivers, sheer waste of pointless feasting, never at an end!" To this, Telemachus replies:

> And so you see why enemies fill our house
> in these days; all the princes of the island...
> eating our house up as they court my mother.
> She cannot put an end to it, she dare not
> bar the marriage that she hates; and they
> devour all my substance and my cattle,
> and who knows when they'll slaughter me as well?
> (16.142-50)

Ironically, it is Odysseus's own feigned hunger and appetite for food that the suitors most ridicule. Because of his age, dress, and poverty, they dismiss him as a nobody unfit to share their company at table.

The wily tactician plays along with Antinous, the leader of the suitors and his chief tormentor, and pretends to be malnourished: "There's no part of a man more like a dog than brazen Belly, crying to be remembered . . . My hunger drives me to take this food, and think no more of my afflictions." Rebuking Antinous for his lack of civility, Telemachus says scornfully: "Give him [Odysseus] a loaf. Am I a niggard? No, I call on you to give. And spare your qualms as to my mother's loss, or anyone's—not that in truth you have such care at heart: your heart is all in feeding, not in giving."

Eurymakhos, the next most obnoxious suitor, hurls a wine pitcher at Odysseus. In response, the seething, but ever patient, master of the manor laments his age and infirmity and challenges him to a contest of scything a deep hayfield or plowing a field and cutting a straight furrow. Odysseus's choice of competitions glances at tilling the grain-giving earth before he left for Troy and swerved to avoid his infant son who was placed in his way by the army recruiters.

Ktesippos, an especially rich and arrogant suitor, fishes a cow's foot from a basket at the table and throws it at Odysseus who adroitly ducks. Taunted by another suitor, the old beggar insists on a boxing match and to everyone's astonishment wins the contest. Antinous now regards him with new eyes and gives Odysseus some of his blood pudding, made from goat stomachs stuffed with blood and fat, and some wine.

The only suitor linked to barley or wheat is Amphinomos, and he is the sole young noble who respects Odysseus and tries to make peace. As Homer notes, he "comes from grainlands on Dulikhion, and he had lightness in his talk that pleased Penelope, for he meant no ill." "Here's luck, grandfather, a new day; may the worst be over now," Amphinomos tells Odysseus, offering him some bread and refreshment.

"No man should flout the law but keep in peace what gifts the gods may give," the man of many turns replies appreciatively to Amphinomos. But he delivers a stern warning to leave before the day of reckoning arrives: "I see you young blades living dangerously, a household eaten up, a wife dishonored—and yet the master will return, I tell you, to his own place, and soon; for he is near. So may some power take you out of this, homeward, and softly, not to face that man the hour he sets foot on his native ground. Between him and the suitors I foretell no quittance, no way out, unless by blood, once he shall stand beneath his own roofbeam."

That evening, Penelope agrees to meet the mysterious stranger who brings news of her husband. In the first words to his wife in twenty years, Odysseus invokes the blessings of grain and the fertility of the earth:

> My lady, never a man in the wide world
> should have a fault to find with you. Your name
> has gone out under heaven like the sweet
> honor of some god-fearing king, who rules
> in equity over the strong: his black lands bear
> both wheat and barley, fruit trees laden bright;
> new lambs at lambing time—and the deep sea
> gives great hauls of fish by his good strategy,
> so that his folk fare well.
>
> (19.128-136)

Pretending to be a Cretan merchant who befriended Odysseus on his way to Troy, the stranger continues his fable. He reports he gave barley and wine to her husband, as well as sacrificed to the gods, when he visited.

Penelope relates a puzzling dream she just had in which twenty fat geese came to feed on the grain beside her house. A mountain eagle with great wings and crooked beak storms in to break their necks and strew their bodies. In the dream Odysseus comes to her and explains that the geese are suitors and will face his retribution. In the dream, grain clearly symbolizes wealth, prosperity, and peace—all of which are being devoured by the suitors.

At the end of their brief conversation, Penelope says his words are comforting but she must take her rest. Her response also glances at the cultivated earth and its nourishing grains. "But mortals cannot go forever sleepless. This the undying gods decree for all who live and die on earth, kind furrowed earth."

That night, Odysseus sleeps fitfully as his emotions vie with his intellect. Mindful of the blood pudding that Antinous gave him, Homer compares the returned wanderer to a giant sausage:

> His rage held hard in leash, submitted to his mind,
> while he himself rocked, rolling form side to side,
> as a cook turns a sausage, big with blood
> and fat, at a scorching blaze, without a pause,
> to broil it quick: so he rolled left and right,
> casting about to see how he, alone,
> against the false outrageous crowd of suitors
> could press the fight.
>
> (20.22-30)

The simile is a perfect Homeric example of "you are what you eat."

On the morning of the climactic contest of the bow, Odysseus prays for an augury, and Zeus responds with a rousing peal of thunder. Another omen immediately follows. An elderly servant woman "grinding out whole grain and barley meal, the pith of men" hears the thunderclap and prays, "Let this day be the last the suitors feed so dainty in Odysseus's hall! . . . May they feast no more."

The next day at the manor, as preparations are made for the contest for Penelope's hand in marriage, the servants set out fresh joints of meat and red wine for the suitors to steel their resolve. Though bulked up on heavy animal food, none of the contestants can string the great bow, much less send an arrow through the dozen axe heads.

Over the jeers of the suitors, Odyssey takes a turn. He easily handles the mighty bow and hits the target. Then signaling Telemachus and the two loyal servants to take up arms, he proclaims the suitors' doom invoking a culinary metaphor: "The hour has come to cook their lordships' mutton—supper by daylight. Other amusements later, with song and harping that adorn a feast."

Odysseus's first arrow hits Antinous under the chin and punches up to the feathers through his throat. As Homer relates, "Backward and down he went, letting the winecup fall from his shocked hand. Like pipes his nostrils jetted crimson runnels, a river of mortal red, and one last kick upset his table knocking the bread and meat to soak in dusty blood." In an example of poetic justice, the chief suitor is struck in the gullet, and upsets the dinner table where he has feasted for the last three years!

The other suitors quickly offer to restore all the meat and wine they have consumed along with twenty oxen and gifts of bronze and gold. But Odysseus scorns their remorse as too little too late. Eurymakhos, the next most insolent suitor, then admonishes them to hold up their tables to deflect Odysseus's arrows. The irony of the desperate young nobles futilely wielding the feasting tables as shields is not lost on the poet. Homer describes how Odysseus proceeds to send an arrow into Eurymakhos's liver, the organ most affected by heavy consumption of meat and alcohol. Then the hapless suitor "lurched and fell aside, pitching across his table. His cup, his bread and meat, were spilt and scattered far and wide." One by one, the suitors are dispatched to Hades, including Amphinomos, the respectful suitor, whom Telemachus slays with a spear. Unfortunately, he does not heed Odysseus's advice to go home before the hour of reckoning.

When the servant women are finally summoned to scrub and purify the hall, Eurykleia, the old nursemaid, finds Odysseus "spattered and caked with blood like a mountain lion when he has gorged upon an ox, his kill—with hot blood glistening over his whole chest, smeared on his jaws, baleful and terrifying—even so encrimsoned was Odysseus up to his thighs and armpits." He is still clearly under the influence of the blood sausage.

As she rejoices at the slaughter, Odysseus rebukes her: "To glory over slain men is no piety. Destiny and the gods' will vanquished these and their own hardness. They respected no one, good or bad, who came their way. For this, and folly, a bad end befell them."

Later that day, Odysseus and Penelope finally reunite. She recognizes him when he correctly describes their marriage bed carved from a live olive tree. The tree symbolizes being rooted in the earth and the strong, unbreakable love and respect that unites them.

The final meal in the *Odyssey* portrays father, son, and grandson dining on a modest homemade dinner as the outraged relatives of the dead suitors rise up in arms. Alarmed that an unnecessary new spiral of violence will arise, Athena—goddess of the olive branch and the original Mediterranean diet—goes to Olympus to consult with Zeus. She advises him to make peace. Descending from heaven in one spring, she arrives in Ithaca "just as the company of Odysseus finished wheat crust and honeyed wine."

Ritual Sacrifice

Animal sacrifice plays a central role in the Odyssey as it does the *Iliad*. The epic opens with Zeus traveling to the lands of the rising sun to visit his loyal subjects "regaled by smoke of thighbones burning, haunches of rams and bulls, a hundred fold." We are told he "lingered delighted at the banquet side."

In the opening chapters, Telemachus also makes libation to the gods with sacrificial wine before setting off in quest of news of his father. Off the coast of Pylos, he observes black bulls being offered to Poseidon "the blue-maned god who makes the islands tremble." Indeed, it is the largest sacrifice in either epic: nine congregations consisting of 500 citizens each lead nine bulls apiece to the altar. The size of the offerings qualify it as a hecatomb. Technically a hecatomb is the ritual slaying of one hundred cattle. However, in practice, it could consist of twelve or more. At the end of the Olympic games in classical Greece, a hecatomb was offered to Zeus. Homer mentions hecatombs several times in his poems.

Telemachus's host, old Nestor, offers his skewered red beef and wine that have been dedicated to Athena. Conveniently, Athena appears at the banquet in the guise of Mentor. She advises Nestor, "Why not slice the bulls' tongues now, and mix libations for Poseidon and the gods?" She is the only one present aware that the god of the sea and earthquake has cursed Odysseus and thwarted his homecoming.

After making libations of sweet red wine, mellowed eleven years, to Athena, Nestor orders one of his son to get a young heifer to prepare a ritual feast for the lord of the deep and other immortals:

> The smith now gloved each horn in a pure foil
> beaten out of the gold that Nestor gave him—
> a glory and delight for the goddess' eyes—
> while Ekhephron and Stratios held the horns,
> Aretos brought clear lustral water
> in a bowl quivering with fresh-cut flowers,
> a basket of barley in his other hand.
> Thrasymedes who could stand his ground in war
> stood ready, with a sharp two-bladed axe,
> for the stroke of sacrifice, and Perseus
> held a bowl for the blood. And now Nestor
> strewing the barley grains, and water drops,
> pronounced his invocation to Athena
> and burned a pinch of bristles from the victims.
> When prayers were said and all the grain was scattered

great-hearted Thrasymedes in a flash
swung the axe, at one blow cutting through
the neck tendons. The heifer's spirit failed.
then all the women gave a wail of joy.......

(3.471-89)

This passage glances at capital punishment through the centuries based on this sacrificial model. For example, in Tudor England, on the scaffold, the executioner would ask the condemned to forgive him. The long sword was customarily hid from view and the victim's attention diverted, so that when it was wielded, death struck suddenly and painlessly.

On the next leg of his journey, Telemachus meets Menelaus and Helen. The king of Sparta explains that his brother Agamemnon, the commander of the Achaeans, was slain like a sacrificial animal: "He [Aegisthus] led him [Agamemnon] in to banquet, all serene, and killed him, like an ox felled at the trough; and not a man of either company survived that ambush in Aegisthus' house." Sacrifice also accompanies Odysseus on his voyage home. In the Cyclops' cave, he and his men make a burnt offering and pray for deliverance. After escaping confinement, he slays the prize ram that he seized from the ogre's flock and burns his long thighbones, but Zeus disdains the offering. On Aeolia, they spend time with Aeolus and his family, who enjoy a royal feast each day accompanied by fumes of sacrifice. On Circe's island, the sorceress serves primarily plant-quality food after turning the crew back from swine into men. On their departure, she leaves Odysseus and his companions a black ewe and ram.

Hades is the site of the most dramatic sacrifice in the epic. After digging a votive pit at the entranceway, Odysseus sets out sweet milk and honey, sweet wine, and clear water. Then he scatters barley and, addressing the surging dead, vows to slaughter his best heifer for them when he reaches home in Ithaca. For Tiresias, the blind seer, he swears to sacrifice a black lamb. Then slashing the two animals that Circe has given him, he lets their black blood stream into the well pit. Commanding his officers to flay the sheep, he makes burnt offerings to the gods below, as well as to Hades, lord of death, and his pale bride, Persephone. As the aroma of burning meat wafts into the opening, Odysseus crouches with drawn sword to keep the swirling phantoms from the bloody pit till Tiresias appears.

On the island of the Sun, the men cannot resist temptation and slay the cattle sacred to Helios. They attempt a ritual sacrifice to the gods to allay the prohibition, but it is not accepted. The divine cattle begin to squirm and exhibit grotesque movements. Their similarity to condemned criminals in our own era who are subjects of botched executions is striking.

The loss of all his men finds Odysseus castaway, alone and half drowned in the wine-dark sea. On Scheria, he is delighted to discover human foods—grains, vegetables, fruits, and other mostly plant-quality fare. At the banquets, his hosts propitiate the gods with nightly sacrifices. On one occasion, King Alcinous puts twelve sheep to the knife, eight boars, and a pair of oxen. Before the minstrel Demodokus sings, he also offers an ox to Zeus. The soul of hospitality, the Phaeacians selflessly transport their visitor home to Ithaca. But on the return journey, Poseidon destroys the ship because they have thwarted his plan and conveyed Odysseus home. To assuage the god's *menis*, Alcinous sacrifices twelve choice bulls and prays that the watery lord will not wreck further retribution on their city.

When Odysseus makes his way to the swineherd's hut, Eumaios slaughters two young porkers and serves them along with barley meal and wine to his visitor: "This is your dinner, friend, the pork of slaves. Our fat shoats are all eaten by the suitors, cold-hearted men, who never spare a thought for how they stand in the sight of Zeus..... Not a night comes under Zeus, but they make butchery of our beeves and swine. Not one or two beasts at a time, either. As for swilling down wine, they drink us dry." At another meal, the forester sacrifices a boar and sets aside one portion for the wood nymphs and Hermes.

At the palace, the suitors' meals are conspicuous not only for the enormous amounts of meat they stuff themselves on, but also because they rarely if ever make sacrifice. When he returns safely home from Sparta, Telemachus tells his mother to pray and burn offerings so that Zeus will aid them in their revenge.

As a Bronze Age epic, meat, wine, and other rich food figure prominently in the narrative. However, Homer makes a clear distinction between those who cook their food and eat grains as their principal fare and those who do not. He also distinguishes those who pray to the gods when they slay and sacrifice animals and those who don't. Both grain-eating and respectful, voluntary slaughter of animals for feasting are hallmarks of culture and civilization, moral vision, and spiritual awareness.

In many ways, Odysseus's crew and Penelope's suitors are the mirror image of each other. They are both governed by their appetites. They prefer meat, dairy, and other rich fare to grains and othe plant foods. They ignore or incorrectly carry out the sacrificial rites that respect the spirits of the victims, eliciting their willing participation and minimizing their suffering. These customs are central to upholding *themis*, or cosmic order. The Bronze and early Iron Ages worshipped the sacred bull. Zeus,

Poseidon, and Hades are all lords of bulls. In the form of a white bull, Zeus abducts Europa, a beautiful Phoenician woman. As the earth-shaker, Poseidon is identified with bulls, the domestic animal that most embodies power, ferocity, and virility. Recently in southwest Anatolia, not far from Troy, a cave was excavated where inhabitants sacrificed bulls to Hades. Archaeologists described it as an entrance to the Underworld.

7 Levels of Food

Food in all of its dimensions—from agriculture and vintage to pasturage and ritual slaughter, from cooking and eating to feasting and drinking—fills the epic canvas of the *Odyssey*. To summarize the seven levels of dietary awareness:

The first, or mechanical, level governs basic hunger and thirst. Its goal is survival and proficiency. Throughout the story, the food of human beings is contrasted with that of monsters, beasts, and subhuman races that live to eat rather than live to eat. For the most part they live on raw as opposed to cooked food and are cannibals. In his own palace, Odysseus cultivates the persona of a hungry beggar whose primary motivation is filling his own belly.

The first level is also the domain of the unconscious. As psychologist Carl Jung observed, "The sea is the favorite symbol for the unconscious, the mother of all that lives." In this case, Father Poseidon (and his nereids and nymphs) fulfills the role of awareness that is below the surface and the repository of sunken treasures, hidden reefs, and other mysterious depths of the psyche. At a dietary level, Poseidon's wrath against Odysseus and his crew mirror their arrogance and ignorance of uniquely human food and hospitality customs, including prayer and sacrifice, after ten years of hard-fought war and loss of their humanity.

The second level involves eating for sensory enjoyment. At this stage, taste, texture, aroma, and other visual, audio, tactile, or olfactory concerns are foremost. The intoxicating flower of the Lotus-Eaters is the classic example. However, Circe's tincture, Helen's potion, and the sacrificial smoke that rises to the Olympian gods also fall in this category.

Level three, aesthetically prepared food, is represented by Aeolus's banqueting, Calypso's dainties, and the Phaeacians' lush orchards and sumptuous table.

Level four, healthful food, begins with grain and, as we have seen, is served whenever hospitality, culture, and civilization are found in Homer's tale. This kind of food leads to clear thinking, sound judgment, and optimal physical health and vitality.

Level five, crops that yield peace and prosperity, represents social judgment and a society that values order over chaos and tranquility over conflict. The many references to the "grain-giving earth" glance at this level. Odysseus consistently invokes the blessings of grain throughout his wanderings and judges each land he visits on whether it cultivates barley and wheat. Penelope's attraction to Amphinomos, the most cultivated and peaceful of the suitors, and the one from the "grainlands of Dulikhion, is another example.

Level six, food ways that contribute to philosophical or spiritual insight and understanding, primarily involves the sacrifice. Meat and wine are offered to the gods before feasting in recognition of their divine origin and destiny. Those who eat unsanctified food, including Odysseus's crew and Penelope's suitors, come to a violent end. For the most part, they are eaten or slaughtered like the animals they have abused or neglected.

Level seven, universal consciousness, glances at ambrosia and nectar. The food of the gods plays less of a role in the *Odyssey* than in the *Iliad*. The chief instance is when Hermes comes to Calypso (who plays vegan chef to Circe's paleo) and relays Zeus's command that he be set free. She sets a table of ambrosia and stirs a cup of ruby-colored nectar for him.

Another instance is when Athena bathes Penelope's cheeks, throat, and brow with ambrosia to make her more presentable to her disguised husband.

A third reference comes in the scene after the massacre in which the souls of the slain suitors enter Hades. They are greeted by Odysseus's dead comrades in the Trojan War. In a conversation between the two Greek commanders, Agamemnon tells Achilles how respectfully his body was treated after his death. He says the daughters of Poseidon wailed and wrapped ambrosial shrouding around him. In this way, even the fiercest former enemies make up in the calm, peaceful aura of celestial nourishment.

The Golden Age

The Golden Age is glanced at in Odysseus's visit to Scheria, as we saw in the last chapter. The Ages of Humanity are also hinted at in the narrative. Mortals with golden accessories include Nestor, with his famous wine cup, Arete who gives Nausicaa a golden flask with olive oil to take to the beach, and Penelope who gave Odysseus a golden brooch on his departure to Troy. The couple's great olive bed has gold and silver fittings.

On the wayfarer's return journey, Aeolus ties the bag of winds to Odysseus's ship with a silver thread. This is emblematic of the Silver Age in which virtue has declined by about one half. Aeolus is generous until the reckless crew opens the bag and releases the winds, and the ship is blown back to his island. Then he turns coldly on his visitors rather than give them another chance.

Menelaus gives Telemachus a silver wine bowl on his visit to Sparta. Queen Helen presents Odysseus's son with a golden shuttle and a royal robe adorned and brilliant with embroidery for his future bride. As one of the few survivors of the Achaean expedition, Menelaus represents a flawed but virtuous monarch. Helen, a symbol of the Golden Age, looks forward to the return of peace and felicity in Ithaca when Telemachus marries and one day becomes king.

The gods and goddesses are invariably identified with gold—a symbol of permanence or immortality. Dawn rises on her golden throne. Both Athena and Hermes wear golden sandals and carry golden wands. Circe serves Odysseus from a golden bowl, and Calypso weaves his tunics with a golden shuttle. The nymph also dons a golden belt when she bestows on him the double-bladed axe. Foretelling the sojourner's destiny, the shade of Tiresias carries a golden sceptor in the Underworld.

Echoes of the Bronze and Iron Ages continue to ripple through the *Odyssey* as in the *Iliad*. The two baser metals figure in the sporadic violence and slayings in the story. As Athena admonishes Odysseus when his resolve flags upon his return to Ithaca: "Where is your valor, where is the iron hand that fought at Troy for Helen?"

Iron appears most prominently in the contest of the bow. The blades of the weapon are made with iron, and the axe heads are forged from a combination of bronze and iron. The composition of the arrows is not described except for being "spiked with coughing death." The massacre anticipates the Iron Age in which all virtue is lost; extermination, ethnic cleansing, and genocide prevail, and no witnesses are left alive.

Destruction by fire and water—the twin means of apocalypse in the precessional cycle—also play a cardinal role in the epic. Hermes relates to Calypso how Athena initially caused a black wind to blow and the seas to rise when the Achaeans wronged the goddess by desecrating her temple in Troy. As a result, many victorious warriors never made it home. The Trojans' fate is to have their city sacked and burned. The Greeks' is to suffer a watery death.

For the Achaeans's sacrilege, Helios, the Sun god, threatens to withhold his life-giving rays when his sacred cattle are slain and eaten by Odysseus's crew. Only the promise of Father Zeus, wielder of the thunderbolt, to strike Odyssey's ship with chain-lightening and drown the disobedient crew prevents the "sun-warmed earth" from turning deathly cold. Poseidon also swamps the wanderer's raft and nearly drowns him in the briny deep.

The other great manifestation of fire and water comes following the massacre of the suitors. Odysseus orders the servant women to scrub away the blood and guts with water and when that is done calls for fire: "Bring me brimstone and a brazier-medicinal fumes to purify my hall . . . Let me have the fire." The apocalyptic fate of the suitors constitutes a mini-Vega or precessional cycle of destruction and purification by complementary opposite elements.

The *Odyssey* ends with Athena and Zeus conferring on Mt. Olympus how to end the violence and bloodshed. As Odysseus, Telemachus, and Laertes prepare to battle the advancing townsfolk and relatives of the slain suitors, Athena disguised as Mentor calls a halt to the fighting on both sides: "Break off this bitter skirmish; end your bloodshed, Ithacans, and make peace." Terrified at the authoritative voice of the goddess, the combatants drop their weapons. Zeus reinforces her edict by hurling a smoking thunderbolt of dazzling fire at her feet.

Athena then turns to Odysseus:

> "Son of Laertes and the gods of old,
> Odysseus, master of land ways and sea ways,
> command yourself. Call off this battle now,
> or Zeus who views the wide world may be angry."
>
> He yielded to her, and his heart was glad.
> Both parties later swore to terms of peace
> set by their arbiter, Athena, daughter
> of Zeus who bears the stormcloud as a shield—
>
> (24.601-13)

The *Odyssey* ends with the image of a celestial shield of wisdom and understanding conferring peace and prosperity on Ithaca. The goddess's aegis of *metis*, or practical wisdom, is the perfect complement to Hephaestus's divine Shield in the *Iliad*. Indeed, we learn that Achilles's wondrous armor depicting the Ages of Humanity came into Odysseus's possession. Although it is lost when his ship capsizes, he now possesses the kernel of its universal teachings as he scales the ladder of consciousness leading to laying the foundation for the construction of the new Golden Age. But for this to come to pass, Odysseus must make one final journey.

6
Odysseus's Oar

Odysseus's Oar is to the *Odyssey* what Achilles's Shield is to the *Iliad*. The oar is both a tangible physical object in the narrative and a symbol of wisdom and spiritual enlightenment. Like Achilles, who is assisted by his mother, the goddess Thetis, Odysseus is aided by Circe, the goddess who guides him to Hades. In Achilles's case, the gods bestow the divine armor on him to turn the tide of battle in the Trojan War. In Odysseus's case, the spirit of Tiresias discloses to him his fate and instructs him to shoulder his oar to complete his homecoming, harmonize with the immortals, and lay the foundation for a healthy, peaceful world.

Compared to Achilles's magnificent Shield with its mural of the cosmos and human history, the humble, unvarnished oar is an improbable symbol of supreme insight and understanding. Indeed, there is no single memorable oar in the *Odyssey*, nor one that Odysseus regards with special significance. In contrast, the mighty bow with which he slays the suitors is also a major symbol of deliverance and described in loving detail. But archery does not figure in Tiresias's augury, even though the feat rises to the level of universal consciousness.

Despite the lack of a great oar in the story, the many small oars create a potent symbol. In this chapter we shall explore its moral and spiritual calculus as Odysseus carries out his last task.

Bronze Age Ships

To understand the role the oar plays in the story, we must look at Bronze Age ships and Aegean seafaring. When the *Odyssey* begins, Odysseus commands a fleet of twelve ships. Each ship has fifty oars, so he sets sail for home from Troy with about 600 men. Along the way, he loses individual men to the Cicones, the Cyclops, the Laestrygonians, and Scylla. After the crew slays the cattle of the Sun, Zeus smites his last ship. By the time he reaches Calypso's island, he has lost even this vessel and all of his remaining men.

The long hollow ships described in the epic were called *pentekonter*, a name that stems from their crew of five times ten, or fifty rowers. Their length was 30 meters or about 100 feet, and their width about 4 meters. They were low, narrow, and sleek to minimize wind resistance. Some vessels sported a deck and others lacked a deck and were open. The oars fit into oarlocks built into the benches that the rowers sat on. The men, who all doubled as warriors, faced backward as they rowed, reaching as far back as they could and inserting the blade of their oar in the water. The oars swept the water backwards, providing forward thrust. The crew was led by a helmsman on the steering platform in the stern. He controlled a steering oar and tiller that jutted out on the diagonal that kept the ship moving in the right direction. This pilot also used his hands and voice to set the rhythm of the rowers. There was a lookout platform and windscreen in the bow, and a stem post often bore the head of an animal, bird, or hero. The original mounting of the famous Hellenistic statue of *Winged Victory of Samothrace* had Nike standing on a ship's prow. A piper kept time for the rowers. In the *Iliad* the ships are routinely depicted as black, from the tarring of their keels. A large square sail in the middle of the ship propelled the vessel when the wind was up and blowing in the right direction. Homer also portrays the ships as shallow drought vessels that could be beached in sandy bays. Hence, much of the fighting in the *Iliad* takes place by the Achaean encampment on the Trojan shore where they have drawn up the ships and formed a defensive wall around them. According to the Catalog of Ships in the *Iliad*, over one thousand ships took part in the siege of Troy, and the number of invaders exceeded one hundred thousand.

In the pentekonters, the rowers were divided into two rows of twenty-five each. Leather screens protected their heads and extended over the open bulwark. Their long oars were usually made of polished pine and had a flat blade at the end. Rowing was an exacting chore, requiring physical strength and endurance, mental alertness, and superior concentration. In the *Iliad*, rowers are described as experiencing numbness in their legs and arms and praying for favorable winds so they could hoist the sail. Gear and provisions were stowed under the benches. Grain was kept in leather bags and water and wine in clay jars or bottles fashioned from animal skins. Weapons and naval pikes, used to battle other ships, were also kept on board.

A prototype for Odysseus's ships was the *Argo*, the boat Jason and his crew sailed on in quest of the Golden Fleece. In that epic, the shipbuilder was Argus—hence the ship's name—and like the hero of the *Odyssey* he was aided by Athena. In the *Argonautica*, a later epic poem, his father

Laertes is portrayed as a member of Jason's expedition to obtain the Golden Fleece. The *Argo* was built from the pine trees of Mount Pelion and from talking oak trees of Dodone and enjoyed the gift of speech, much like Achilles's horses. It took an architect and twelve carpenters about six months to make a single galley. The Greek ships were almost entirely military. The Argives left trade to the Canaanites and Phoenecians, whose ships and knowledgeable pilots plied the Mediterranean and Aegean.

Oars in the *Iliad*

As an epic about a war fought on land, the *Iliad* only mentions oars in passing. In the opening chapter, for example, after the plague has struck their camp, Agamemnon reluctantly agrees to ransom Chryses's daughter. Homer tells us that Odysseus captains a smaller vessel with a crew of only twenty oarsmen to take her home.

When Odysseus leads the embassy to convince Achilles to return to battle, the son of Peleus rejects their pleas and threatens to row home:

> But now, since I have no wish to fight against noble Hector,
> tomorrow I'll offer sacrifice to Zeus and all other gods,
> then haul my ships down to the sea and load them up,
> and you'll see—if you want to, if it concerns you at all—
> at first light, sailing over the teeming Hellespont,
> my flotilla, its rowers all eagerly plying their oars.
> (9.356-61)

When Hector and Paris, hungry for battle, charge out of the city gates, Homer invokes a nautical simile: "Just as a god will provide eager sailors with a more than welcome tailwind, when they're weary of thrusting back seawater with polished pinewood oars, the labors loosened their limbs, so these two now appeared before the eager Trojans."

When Aeneas and Achilles exchange insults in their encounter, the Trojan prince tells him that even a 100-oared galley would not hold all the taunts they fling at each other. When the Trojans attack the Achaean ships on the beach, Ajax steps back on the seven-foot benches of the oarsmen and with his long spear valiantly prevents the Trojans from setting the ship on fire.

None of these passages is particularly noteworthy. However, there is a memorable description of Menelaus when he prepares to engage in single combat with Paris that resonates with the primary reference to the oar in Tiresias's prophecy:

Priam's son hit Menelaus in the chest with his arrow,
on the plate of his corselet, and off it the bitter arrow glanced.
Just as off a broad shovel on a big threshing-floor
the dark-hued beans or chickpeas fly through the air
before the shrill storm blast and the sweep of the winnower,
in such wise from the corselet of glorious Menelaus
the bitter arrow glanced off, and flew wide of the mark.
(13.586-92)

As we shall see, the winning shovel is a major symbol in the *Odyssey*. The image is echoed in Tiresias's instructions about the oar in Hades and in Odysseus's final conversation with Penelope.

Oars in the *Odyssey*

As a maritime epic, oars appear throughout the *Odyssey*. In the opening chapters, Athena assists Telemachus in setting sail to inquire about his absent father. "Telemachus, your crew of fighting men is ready at the oars, and waiting for you," she advises him. "Come on, no point in holding up the sailing." Almost simultaneously, the goddess of wisdom appeals to Zeus to release Odysseus from Calypso's bondage: "He lives and grieves upon that island in thralldom to the nymph; he cannot stir, cannot fare homeward, for no ship is left him, fitted with oars—no crewmen or companions to pull him on the broad back of the sea."

Zeus consents to her request, and orders the beautiful nymph to release her captive. Calypso gives Odysseus an axe, auger, and other tools to build a boat. He fells twenty tall alder, poplar, and pine trees. After fashioning the hull, the decking, and the mast, Homer relates, "Odysseus shaped a steering oar to hold her steady." With the help of a warm landbreeze the goddess conjured, the great seaman sets sail, leaning on his oar, steering all night via the constellations and North Star.

The celestial compass brings him to Scheria, the shield-like island. But Poseidon is still aggrieved and churns up hurricane winds and raging seas. Toppled by a great wave, Odysseus plunges into the sea, "the oar-haft wrenched from his grip." Fortunately, the nereid Ino throws him her veil to cling to, and Athena checks all the winds except one that blows him to the shore. Begging mercy from the local river god, Odysseus loosens the veil, letting it drift back to the nereid, and kisses the earth. He has landed among the hospitable Phaeacians. The trajectory of his lifeline is interesting: oar, veil, and earth. They are the same elements that figure in Tiresias's charge to him, except Ino's serendipitous arrival is replaced by the stranger he meets on his journey inland. Instead of a veil, he will be asked a veiled question that will mark the place where he plants the oar, marking the end of his wandering.

On Scheria, Odysseus learns that the Phaeacians excel in ship design. But unlike Aegean seafarers, they have no warships. In keeping with their Golden Age heritage, they have only ships that ply the seas for peaceful trade and missions of mercy. After Demodokus the bard finishes his songs, King Alcinous explains to Odysseus the realm's unique ships:

> Tell me your native land, your coast and city—
> sailing directions for the ships, you know—
> for those Phaeacian ships of ours
> that have no steersman, and no steering oar,
> divining the crew's wishes, as they do,
> and knowing, as they do, the ports of call
> about the world. Hidden in mist or cloud
> they scud the open sea, with never a thought
> of being in distress of going down.
>
> (8.594-602)

The monarch's description of his country's surreal fleet echoes the fruit in the royal orchards that grows and ripens year round. Like the *Argo* in the Golden Fleece myth, the ships have a mind of their own and need no human pilots or maps. They represent a half-way station between the magical seascape of the adventures and Odysseus's return to Ithaca. They obey the will of their crew or passengers and intuitively know the way home.

In relating his tale to his hosts, Odysseus focuses on the hardships he and his men endured after leaving Troy. The oar symbolizes their struggles and their means of survival. For example, after sneaking out of the cave and taunting Polyphemus, the Cyclops heaves a titanic boulder at the departing men, but it falls just short of the black-prowed ship's steering oar. After stealing the ogre's flock of sheep, they feast on mutton and sweet wine, sleep on the beach, and set out the next morning:

> When the young Dawn with finger tips of rose
> touched the world, I roused the men, gave orders
> to man the ships, cast off the mooring lines;
> and filing in to sit beside the rowlocks
> oarsmen in line dipped oars in the grey sea.
> So we move out, sad in the vast offing,
> having our precious lives, but not our friends.
>
> (9.612-18)

After reaching Aeola, they receive the bag of winds, a treasure more precious than gold, because it blows them home. Although the crew need not row, Odysseus himself mans the steering oar for nine straight days to make sure the ships stay on course. But through carelessness, he falls asleep, and they are blown back to the island of the wind god. A surprised Aeolus recognizes they have been cursed and withdraws his breezes, forcing them to man the oars harder than ever. "He drove me from the place, groan as I would," Odysseus recalls, "and comfortless we went again to sea, days of it, till the men flagged at the oars—no breeze, no help in sight, by our own folly." Backbreaking oaring—a scourge of sailors, tradesmen, and galley slaves for millennia—is now their lot.

Their exhausting labors finally take them to the land of the Laestrygonians. But instead of welcome and a respite, they encounter cannibals. Losing more men, Odysseus orders a hasty retreat:

> "Men," I shouted,
> "man the oars and pull till your hearts break
> if you would put this butchery behind!"
> The oarsmen rent the sea in mortal fear
> and my ship spurted out of range, far out
> from that deep canyon where the rest were lost.
> So we fared onward and death fell behind,
> and we took breath to grieve for our companions.
>   (10.141-148)

The next round of strenuous rowing takes them to Circe's island. After winning her cooperation and spending a year feasting, Odysseus and his crew sail to Hades. Thanks to the sorceress's magic, they are borne directly to the Underworld. As the captain relates, "We made fast the braces, took our thwarts, and let the wind and steersman work the ship with full sail spread all day above our coursing."

In Hades, the oar figures prominently in the encounters with Elpenor and Tiresias. The shade of the crewman who fell off Circe's roof and died without proper rites pleads:

> O my lord, remember me, I pray
> do not abandon me unwept, unburied,
> to tempt the gods' wrath, while you sail for home;
> but fire my corpse, and all the gear I had,
> and build a cairn for me above the breakers—
> an unknown sailor's mark for men to come.

Heap up the mound there, and implant upon it
the oar I pulled in life with my companions.

(11.80-87)

Elpenor's plea is reminiscent of the ghost of Patroclus, who beseeches Achilles to cremate and pray over his remains in the *Iliad*. Odysseus vows: "Unhappy spirit, I promise you the barrow and the burial."

Tiresias then appears and foretells his destiny. The blind seer warns him to avoid raiding the cattle of the Sun on Thrinakia or lose all his crew and risk many years wandering before he comes home. He prophesizes Odysseus will return home to his wife and son and make the insolent suitors atone in blood. But that is not the end of his journey.

But after you have dealt out death—in open
combat or by stealth—to all the suitors,
go overland on foot, and take an oar,
until one day you come where men have lived
with meat unsalted, never known the sea,
nor see seagoing ships, with crimson bows
and oars that fledge light hulls for dipping flight.
The spot will soon be plain to you, and I
can tell you how: some passerby will say,
"What winnowing shovel is that upon your shoulder?"
Halt, and implant your smooth oar in the turf
and make fair sacrifice to Lord Poseidon:
A ram, a bull, a great buck boar; turn back,
and carry out pure hecatombs at home
to all wide heaven's lords, the undying gods,
to each in order. Then a seaborne death
soft as this hand of mist will come upon you
when you are wearied out with rich old age,
your country folk in blessed peace around you.
and all this shall be just as I foretell.

(11.132-52)

Returning to Circe's isle with a favorable wind and sea swell, Odysseus makes good on his promise to Elpenor: "Then we heaped a barrow lifting a gravestone on the mound, and fixed his light but unwarped oar against the sky." The upright positioning of the oar echoes the task Tiresias assigns to Odysseus, except in the latter case he erects it for himself—and all humanity.

The next leg of their journey takes them by the seductive Sirens. Heeding Circe's advice, Odysseus plugs the ears of all his oarsmen with beeswax. Then the crew furls the sail and poises "the smooth oar blades and sent the white foam scudding." Tied to the mast, the resourceful captain hopes to avoid the beautiful sea-maidens' deadly song. But as Circe predicts, the melodies are too alluring, and he orders the crew: "Untie me!" But the men bend steady to the oars until the singing dwindles away.

Once safely past the Sirens, the crew puts down their oars. But scarcely have they removed the wax from their ears when the sound of waves in tumult terrifies them. As Odysseus recalls, "Oars flew from their hands; the blades went knocking wild alongside till the ship lost way, with no oarblades to drive her through the water." Through the sheer force of his personality, Odysseus calms the men down and promises to "use my wits to find a way out for us." He orders them to "get the oarshafts in your hands; hit these breaking seas." But he doesn't tell them they are heading toward Scylla and Charybdis lest they "[drop] their oars again, in panic, to roll for cover under the decking."

When Scylla makes her strike, she whisks six men and their oars from the ship. "I happened to glance aft at ship and oarsmen and caught sight of their arms and legs, dangling high overhead." By skirting the underwater maelstrom completely, they avoid Charybdis and total destruction and row on. Only then does Odysseus tell them of Tiresias's prophecy and give a strong warning about raiding the cattle of the Sun. "Nothing but fatal trouble shall we find here. Pull away, then, and put the land astern."

But Odysseus's relentless pace strains the men to the breaking point. Eurylokhus, his deputy and brother-in-law, complains angrily:

Are you flesh and blood, Odysseus, to endure
more than a man can? Do you never tire?
God, look at you, iron is what you're made of.
Here we all are, half dead with weariness,
falling asleep over the oars, and you
say "No landing."
(12.358-63)

Forcing the crew to swear a great oath to respect Helio's herd, Odysseus pilots the ship into a bay. But after exhausting their stores and local fish and wild game, the gluttonous men disobey and slay the cattle of the Sun.

Unlike the biblical story of creation, Zeus rests for six days while the men feast. But on the seventh, when they set out to sea again with a favorable breeze, he piles a thunderhead above the ship, stirs up gale force winds, and capsizes the vessel. The mast topples, bashing in the skull of the chief oarsman in evident karmic punishment for steering the expedition in the wrong direction. Then Zeus unleashes a thunderbolt that flings the survivors into the sea where all but the captain drowns.

Odysseus manages to lash together part of the mast and keel, which he straddles to ride out the storm. Passing Scylla and Charybdis again, he manages to catch hold of the bough of the great fig tree that grows on their shoals. After an eternity of waiting, the submerged mast and keel bob back up to the surface.

> Now I let go with hands and feet, plunging
> straight into the foam beside the timbers,
> pulled astride, and rowed hard with my hands
> to pass by Scylla. Never could I have passed her
> had not the Father of gods and men, this time
> kept me from her eyes.
>
> (12.565-70)

Odysseus drifts in the open sea, using only his hands as oars, for nine days. Buoyed up by the gods, he finally washes ashore on Scheria.

Such is the account the wayfarer gives to the Phaeacians. After several days of welcome and festivities, King Alcinous places a ship at Odysseus's disposal to take him home. The gracious hosts bestow valuable gifts on their visitor, including a chest of garments, gold in various shapes and adornments, and a bevy of tripods and deep-bellied cauldrons. The provisions consist of loaves and red wine. In keeping with their Golden Age pedigree, no weapons, even ceremonial ones, are taken on the voyage, nor meat or other animal food stocked for refreshment.

> "When you came
> here to my strong home, Odysseus, under
> my tall roof, headwinds were left behind you.
> Clear sailing shall you have now, homeward now,
> however painful all the past."
>
> (13.4-8)

After wishing the monarchs a life of felicity, Odysseus boards the Phaeacian vessel and lies down on a rug and linen placed for him on deck that he might sleep in peace.

> Now he himself embarked, lay down, lay still,
> while oarsmen took their places at the rowlocks
> all in order. They untied their hawser,
> passing it through a drilled stone ring; then bent
> forward at the oars and caught the sea
> as one man, stroking.
>
> (13.91-96)

After leaving the harbor, the ship makes for the open sea and soon goes on auto, or magic, pilot:

> How a four-horse team
> whipped into a run on a straightaway
> consumes the road, surging and surging over it!
> So ran the craft and showed her heels to the swell,
> her bow wave riding after, and her wake
> on the purple night-sea foaming.
>   Hour by hour
> she held her pace; not even a falcon wheeling
> downwind, swiftest bird, could stay abreast of her
> in that most arrowy flight through open water,
> with her great passenger—godlike in counsel,
> he that in twenty years had borne such blows
> in his deep heart, breaking through ranks in war
> and waves on the bitter sea.
>
> (13.100-113)

Reaching Ithaca, the Phaeacians draw into a cove and run the ship's keel half its length to shore, glancing at the Achaean warships beaching themselves on Troy. Unloading the ship, they carefully hide their passenger's precious treasure around the roots of a tall olive tree. Then they move Odysseus, still fast asleep, on his bed cover and blanket to the grove and depart without waking him.

The journey ends in tragedy. On their way home, an irate Poseidon turns their ship to stone and threatens to send an earthquake and raise a mountain around their port city. King Alcinous recalls his father's prophecy that one day just such a tragedy would strike. Knowing their magic is unequal to the angry sea god's, the ruler promptly orders a hecatomb and prays for mercy. He also vows in the future never to give safe conveyance to stranded passengers. Like Aeolus, the wind god, he knows bad karma when he sees it.

Once Odysseus reaches Ithaca, the oar recedes into the background. Disguised as a castaway, he spins a yarn about his maritime background to Eumaios, telling the old forester that "I reveled in long ships with oars." Telemachus makes several passing references to oars upon his return. In the palace, the saucy servant girl, upbraids Odysseus, disguised as a vagrant: "Instead of going out to find a smithy to sleep warm in—or a tavern bench—you stay putting your oar in, amid all our men." Losing his temper at this taunt, Odysseus threatens: "One minute: let me tell Telemachus how you talk in hall, you slut; he'll cut your arms and legs off!" It is unclear whether he takes offense at the slur on himself, sailors in general, the possible double-entendre, or all of the above.

Curiously, the images of the oar and bed—rowing and sleeping, remembering and forgetting—soon surface again in his talk with Penelope:

> Honorable lady, wife of Odysseus Laertiades,
> a weight of rugs and cover? Not for me,
> I've had none since the day I saw the mountains
> of Crete, white with snow, low on the sea line
> fading behind me as the long oars drove me north.
> Let me lie down tonight as I've lain often,
> many a night unsleeping, many a time
> afield on hard ground waiting for pure Dawn.
>
> (19.394-402)

Penelope has just asked her maids to make a warm, comfortable bed for the stranger with colored rugs and coverlets. But until he is in his own marriage-bed, rooted to the earth (and able to wield his own oar, so to speak), Odysseus scorns the substitute.

Finally, after the massacre and their tearful reunion, Odysseus confides to Penelope his one remaining task:

> "My dear, we have not won through to the end.
> One trial—I do not know how long—is left for me
> to see fulfilled. Tiresias's ghost forewarned me
> the night I stood upon the shore of Death, asking
> about my friends' homecoming and my own.
> --
> But now the hour grows late, it is bedtime,
> Rest will be sweet for us; let us lie down."

(23.279-85)

To this Penelope replies, continuing the metaphor:

> "That bed,
> that rest is yours whenever desire move you,
> now the kind powers have brought you home at last.
> But as your thought has dwelt upon it, tell me:
> What is the trial you face? I must know soon;
> what does it matter if I learn tonight?"

(23.287-92)

In reply, Odysseus paraphrases the seer's words:

> "My strange one,
> must you again, and even now,
> urge me to talk? Here is a plodding tale;
> no charm in it. No relish in the telling.
> Tiresias told me I must take an oar
> and trudge the mainland, going from town to town,
> until I discover men who have never known
> the salt blue sea, nor flavor of salt meat—
> strangers to painted prows, to watercraft
> and oars like wings, dipping across the water.
> The moment of revelation he foretold
> was this, for you may share the prophecy:
> some traveller falling in with me will say:
> 'A winnowing shovel, that on your shoulder, sir?'
> There I must plant my oar, on the very spot,
> with burnt offerings to Poseidon of the Waters:
> a ram, a bull, a great buck boar. Thereafter
> when I come home again, I am to slay
> full hecatombs to the gods who own broad heaven,
> one by one.
>   Then death will drift upon me
> from seaward, mild as air, mild as your hand,
> in my well-tended weariness of age,
> contented folk around me on our island.
> He said all this must come."
>   Penelope said:
> "If by the gods' grace age at least is kind,

we have that hope—trials will end in peace."
(23.294-321)

Only after revealing this mysterious errand with the oar does Odysseus "mingle in love" with Penelope. All night they exchange stories about their trials and enjoy sweet sleep while Athena holds back the Dawn.

Either Oar

The meaning of Tiresias's final charge and the symbolic meaning of Odysseus's oar has puzzled generations of readers and listeners. The main theories incorporate one or more of the following elements: 1) the gods want the hero to retire or abandon a seafaring life, 2) Odysseus finally appeases Poseidon's wrath with a sincere act of pilgrimage and sacrifice, 3) Odysseus undergoes a psychological transformation and learns that not everyone sees things as he does, 4) Odysseus sheds the last vestige of his identity and undergoes a spiritual rebirth, 5) Odysseus brings the blessings of a maritime society, including worship of Poseidon, to a backward, inland culture, 6) Odysseus treads the path of an ordinary sailor and learns to empathize with the hardships of his rowers, and 7) the traveler discovers a true Scheria, or utopian society, and resettles his family there far from the maddening crowd in Ithaca.

Elpenor's fate foreshadows Odysseus's. Indeed, the two oars are introduced in the same scene in which the hero visits Tiresias in Hades. Clearly, the seaman's oar is emblematic of his profession—a lowly sailor and rower boy. Though the youngest crewman, he fully shares the difficulties and rewards of the sea voyage, including rowing away heroically from the Lotus-Eaters, the land of the Cyclops, the wind god's stronghold, and the realm of the man-eating Laestrygonians. The oar is an appropriate talisman of his vocation and hard physical labor. Like helmets placed on crosses in modern times, erecting an oar on his burial mound is a fitting tribute.

Odysseus, however, is no ordinary seaman. True, as captain, he is in overall charge of his fleet. After losing most of his ships and small clusters of men, he mans the steering oar and tiller and takes a hand with an oar on the benches. Following the capsizing of his last ship, he is marooned on Calypso's island. Released at Zeus's command, he builds his own boat and fashions his own oar. Then when Poseidon smites his life raft, he rows with his hands. If the oar is a symbol of his identity, he loses it well before returning to Ithaca when he washes up on Scheria naked, famished, and half-drowned.

In fact, seafaring is only a small part of Odysseus's *kleos* or glory. In

Troy he wins the epithet "sacker of cities," and his prowess in battle informs his view of himself far more than sailing. He is also a seasoned diplomat and the "equal of Zeus" in counsel. As a wrestler, boxer, and discus thrower, he is also unsurpassed. And as he tells King Alcinous, his favorite weapon is the bow. He also identifies closely with his family and sees himself as a husband, father, and son. Clearly, the inward journey Tiresias foretells glances at a loss of the familiar seascape and landscape. But the man of many turns would easily take it in stride. He is the master of cunning and deceit, passing himself off as someone he is not to all three of his dearest relatives, as well as the suitors and his old servants. Only his old dog, Argos, is not fooled. He immediately recognizes his master and dies. Among all his strengths and accomplishments, the oar appears to be one of the lesser implements, objects, or symbols associated with Odysseus. He could just as well carry a spear, bow, or even a lyre on his shoulder.

Let's look more closely at Tiresias's prophecy. First, he instructs Odysseus to walk on foot overland until he comes to a region where men have "never known the sea, nor seen seagoing ships, with crimson bows and oars that fledge light hulls for dipping flight." As part of the Mediterranean and Aegean worlds, ancient Greece was primarily a maritime society. Nearly all inhabited regions were on or near the sea. Until modern times, seafaring ships, small boats, or riverine craft conducted most trade and travel because of a lack of roads and reliable year round ground transport. Pilgrimaging to an area where people didn't know the sea would not have been easy. As the seer implies, the journey would be a matter of days or weeks.

Odysseus would have set off from Ithaca, his homeland. By contrast, Ithaca is a small island in the Ionian Sea off the northeast coast of Kefalonia, a larger island, and due west of the Greek mainland. During the late Bronze Age, Thaki (as residents referred to their island) served as the capital of a powerful Ionian kingdom-state, including surrounding isles. Known as formidable navigators and explorers, the Ithacans launched bold expeditions beyond the Mediterranean Sea. In size, the island covers 45 square miles, and at its maximum extends 29 miles long by 4 miles wide. It is slightly larger than Nantucket. But unlike the isle off the Massachusetts coast, Ithaca consists of two peninsulas about equal in size joined by the Isthmus of Aetos (the Eagle). Molos, a sweeping bay, divides the two long and narrow halves of the island. The highest peak on the island, Mount Neritos, rises about a thousand feet. The *Odyssey* describes the island as "shining Ithaca":

My home is on the peaked sea-mark of Ithaca
under Mount Neion's wind-blown robe of leaves,
in sight of other islands—Doulichion,
Same, wooded Zacynthos—Ithaca
being mostly lofty in that coastal sea,
and northwest, while the rest lie east and south.
A rocky isle, but good for a boy's training;
I shall not see on earth a place more dear.
(9.24-31)

From this shining isle, Odysseus's journey would have taken him inland. In telling Penelope about this quest, he embroiders Tiresias's words and says he is to walk "from town to town." This could imply that he goes south to Peloponnesus, the southernmost region of Greece that is shaped like a large hand and juts into the Cretan Sea. However, the Peloponnesus is actually an island, separated from the mainland by a thin isthmus and well peopled, so it is unlikely he would have been able to carry out his mission there. More likely, Odysseus would have set forth on the mainland coast and traveled northeast into Aeolia, or modern day Thessaly. Its vast plain was the site of Mt. Olympus and the battle between the Titans and the Olympians. Here he would probably have found farming villages that had little or no knowledge of the sea. By the second century BCE, the region exported surplus grain to the Roman Empire.

In an essay "Odysseus and the Oar," William Hansen offers one of the most influential contemporary interpretations of the tale. Drawing on comparative folklore, he shows that the sailor and the oar is a common motif in oral narratives. From among thirty versions of the story that he has collected, he presents sixteen that are similar to Homer's. For example:

> St. Elias was once a seaman. On account of his endless rowing, the man got tired (rowing while eating, that's the way they had it in those days). He put his oar on his shoulder and left to go to find a place where they didn't even know the name of it. He walks to the village, he asks, "What is this called?" "An oar," they say. He walks to another village, he asks, "What is this called?" "An oar." What the devil! He became desperate. Keeping on with his inquiry he finally asks at one village situated at the very top of the mountain, "What is this called?" "A piece of wood." Thank God! He sets the oar straight up, builds a hut, and resolves to remain there for the rest of his life. For this reason, they always put St. Elias on mountaintops.

All of the examples Hansen presents are from the nineteenth and twentieth centuries. (The latest is from an American comic strip drawn in 1977.) Since there are no extant examples of oral folklore before that time, he says he is unable to document how far back the story goes. However, there are many fairy tales from Europe, India, China, and other cultures that have parallel themes (e.g., Cinderella and the lost slipper), but none features a mariner shouldering an oar. Hence, all the examples he discusses probably derive from the *Odyssey* itself and millennia of Aegean folklore. In any event, Hansen takes a literalist approach and concludes that Homer's tale, like the modern versions, is an old sailor's lament. It reflects seamen's age-old weariness with what Homer calls "the bitter sea" and yearning for retirement or a pleasant life on land. "Planting the oar simply marks the end of the quest," he concludes, "and is not a fetish of the god Poseidon or have some other cultic significance."

Classicists tend to interpret Odysseus's trek in more figurative terms. They see the pilgrimage and sacrifice as the final step in making peace with the god of the sea. Ever since Odysseus put out his son Polyphemus's eye, Poseidon is determined to thwart his return. He manages to capsize his final ship and drown all of his crew. But it draws the Earth-Shaker into conflict with Zeus and Athena and threatens to upset the cosmic order. Only a magnanimous sacrifice on Odysseus's part will finally lay the issue to rest. The oar is a symbol of the sea, Poseidon's domain, and the perfect object for this purpose.

A variation carries this interpretation a step further. It contends that Odysseus is colonizing a new region for Poseidon's worship and spreading his domain from the sea to land. For example, Seth L. Schein in *Reading the Odyssey* states, "Odysseus must make his ultimate peace by bringing the knowledge of ships and the worship of the sea god Poseidon to inland agriculturalists among whom they are yet unknown." Archaeologists have found evidence of several mainland temples dedicated to Poseidon. Advocates of this theory contend that Odysseus is an agent of cultural, or even religious, diffusion.

At the end of his quest, Odysseus clearly appeases Poseidon and, if Tiresias is right, puts an end to their quarrel. But this doesn't explain the other elements of the tale. In a perceptive essay "Unmarked Space: Odysseus and the Inland Journey," Alex Purves offer a sophisticated psychological and semantic reading. He suggests that the inland journey is an inward journey. He says the blind seer's charge has nothing to do with spreading the worship of Poseidon, but rather is designed to strip Odysseus of his persona, or outward identity, and end the epic on a note of ambiguity or suspension of belief.

"What makes this final landscape of the *Odyssey* so different from the other spaces in the poem is its complete and systematic erasure of the border between land and sea," Purves writes. "For Odysseus to become truly lost, he must leave the orienting order of the sea behind, entering a region where he will relinquish not only his own sense of direction and reference but also his identity in the context of Homeric poetics."

He reminds us that the Greeks rarely ventured inland and tended to settle and travel in close proximity with the coast. "When he takes up an oar on his shoulder and walks inland until he meets a people who have never tasted salt—then, and only then, will Odysseus truly lose his way in both world and poem." Most of the adventures in the epic, he continues, take place in an "imaginary zone of untold and unplaced time" but for the most part located on the horizon, or periphery, of the familiar, mapped world. Now, at the very end of the epic, Odysseus travels to the center: "The narration of Odysseus's story had previously traveled as far as the edges of the world. Now as his projected story crosses the boundary of the poem's end, it also shifts from the space of sea and edge to a new site, that of land and interior. It is at this point, when Odysseus loses control over the physical trajectory of his path through space, that he will also lose control over the coordinates of his narrative."

When the stranger mistakes the oar for a winnowing shovel, Purves asserts, a single object takes on two opposite meanings. "Odysseus, in other words, is instructed to get as lost in language as in space." This ambiguity dismantles or deconstructs Homeric metaphor, and the epic loses its own anchor. He likens this to Odysseus's bed that is fixed by being rooted in the earth, but instantly loses its meaning when in Penelope's cunning test she suggests to Odysseus that it has been moved. "The bed and the oar of Book 23, both complement and undo one another: the bed creates narrative resolution and closure because, as a *sema* [divine omen], it remains fixed in place, while the oar throws not only the ending of the poem but also its whole system of meaning into question because it moves ever further away from its original position on (the shores of) the ocean."

Far from colonizing the region and extending Poseidon's realm, Purves contends, Odysseus's planting of the oar and sacrifice remain anonymous. Unlike Elpenor's oar that marks his life, death, and role in the Trojan War, Odysseus's oar heralds the final loss of his own name and glory. Until his final errand in the wilderness, the Greek hero manages to exert linguistic control over the people and strange beings he encounters. His lies and deceits, most notably the Wooden Horse and the inscription that accompanies it, always win him the day. On the return journey, he tricks Polyphemus with clever wordplay. With *moly*, he bends Circe to his spoken will. In Hades, he promises sacrifices to Tiresias and the other spirits in return for foreknowledge of future events. On Scheria, his bard-like eloquence moves the Phaeacians to build him a ship and convey him home. But on his inland quest, he becomes a true "Nobody," the name he gave himself when he taunted the Cyclops.

By portraying Odysseus losing linguistic control over speech and the meaning of words, Purves concludes, Homer subverts the goal of epic verse whose purpose is to sing the eternal glory of gods and heroes. Odysseus

> fails to take into account the logical consequence of Tiresias's prophecy: there exists somewhere upon the earth a group of people who, although they are human and 'eaters of bread,' have never heard of the Trojan War, much less a man named Odysseus. The Inlands must be eaters of bread if they mistake the oar for an agricultural tool, and, since it is impossible to narrate the story of the Trojan War without the mention of ships, they must also be a people ignorant of Homeric verse. The oar that Odysseus eventually plants thereby marks a 'lost' or invisible space in terms of epic narrative's ability to cover the entire earth with its *kleos* [glory].

Purves's reading is provocative and takes the ending of the *Odyssey* to a deeper, more inward level. But its aesthetic conclusion is unnecessarily complicated and abstract. It also ignores the possibility that a transformation, rather than confusion, takes place when the oar is recognized as a winnowing shovel.

Let's summarize the multiple meanings of the oar and their correspondence with the stages in the journey of the soul to wisdom:

The Oar and the 7 Levels of Consciousness

Level	Symbol or Goal	Examples from the Epic
1. Mechanical	Transport and survival	Odysseus and his crew row for their lives
2. Sensory	Hard work	Backbreaking labor or relaxation during times of high winds and sailing
3. Emotional Aesthetic	Identity	Loss of name and ignorance of the sea; identification with

		beauty or horror
4. Intellectual	Direction	Steering and piloting the ship
5. Social	Community	Carrying out a common task
6. Spiritual	Sacrifice	Use in burials, prayers, and sacrifices
7. Universal	Unity	Becoming one with sea, sky, and earth

The Winnowing Shovel

Before exploring the meaning of the oar further, a linguistic mix up needs to be clarified. Most modern English translations of the *Odyssey* depict the stranger as identifying the object Odysseus carries as a winnowing fan. A winnowing fan is a shallow wicker basket in which harvested grain is thrown up to separate the kernel from the chaff. A winnowing shovel has a long handled flat blade with three to five short teeth and is fashioned from wood. Both objects are used to winnow grain, but the winnowing shovel is clearly the tool confused with an oar in the *Odyssey*. In the Bible, both winnowing fans and shovels appear, and the same confusion prevails. For example, in the *King James Bible*, Matthew prophesizes that Jesus will appear in the end time with a "winnowing fan" in his hand to separate the good from the wicked. In the *New Revised Standard Version*, it is called a "winnowing fork." In the *Wycliffe Bible*, it is called a "winnowing cloth" and in the *Weymouth Bible* a "winnowing shovel."

In "Odysseus's 'Winnowing-Shovel' and the Island of the Cattle of the Sun," S. Douglas Olson focuses on the symbolism of the winnowing shovel. He shows that it is a metaphor for Odysseus's entire journey:

> On the island of the cattle of the Sun, Odysseus and his men are put to the test by the appearance of high winds, and when he goes apart from them, they are quickly marked out for destruction. That Odysseus' oar is mistaken for a winnowing-shovel is thus a sign not only of how far from the sea he has come but also of the scrutiny he has undergone. He alone of all the crew has in the end been saved.

The episode separates the wheat from the chaff. Odysseus is the wheat, the crew is the chaff. He is obedient to the will of the gods, they are not.

Olson says this interpretation is confirmed by Tiresias's use of the word *atherelogos* for the winnowing shovel. *Athere* is the Greek word for "meal" or gruel, and *logos* is the word for "reason" or the controlling principle of the cosmos. It is a synonym for the word used in the *Iliad* to describe the threshing of the beans and chickpeas in the granary. He also shows that *thrinax,* another common word for a winnowing shovel, appears to be the root for the name of Thrinakia, the island of the Sun. As he concludes:

> The spot where the winds separate Odysseus from his worthless crew, in other words, is precisely "Winnowing-Shovel Island," and it accordingly comes as no surprise that the sign which will mark the moment when the hero can at last make his peace with Poseidon will be an oar mistaken for a "destroyer of chaff."

Thrinakia, by the way, is usually translated as Trident Island, so the resemblance to a winnowing shovel clearly fits. The trident (a pitchfork with three teeth), of course, is the symbol of Poseidon. He wields it to govern the seas; bring clear, cloudy, or tempestuous weather; and stir up earthquakes, tidal waves, and hurricanes. We might also keep in mind that the episode with the cattle occurs precisely in the middle of the *Odyssey*. It is also highlighted in the opening passage of the epic when through Homer the Muses relate:

> He [Odysseus] saw the townlands
> and learned the minds of many distant men,
> and weathered many bitter nights and days
> in his deep heart at sea, while he fought only
> to save his life, to bring his shipmates home.
> But not by will nor valor could he save them,
> for their own recklessness destroyed them all—
> children and fools, they killed and feasted on
> the cattle of Lord Helios, the Sun,
> and he who moves all day through heaven
> took from their eyes the dawn of their return.
>   (1.6-16)

Note how the Muses's prologue emphasizes the central importance of Tiresias's warning to avoid killing and eating the cattle of the Sun. It also glances at the night of Odysseus and Penelope's reunion when he relates how "Tiresias told me I must take an oar and trudge the mainland, going from town to town, until I discover men who have never known the salt blue sea, nor flavor of salt meat." This echoes the lines: "he saw the townlands and learned the minds of many distant men." Like the three-pronged trident, the cattle of the Sun appear symbolically at the beginning, middle, and end of the epic. Also, note the cattle form seven herds, nodding at the seven levels of consciousness.

The mention of salt, or the lack of it, in the diets of the inlanders is another key element in unraveling the meaning of his final quest. Other translations describe this as inhabitants who "do not mix salt with their food." The word "meat" derives from *meal*, meaning principal or daily food, and is not necessarily animal flesh. There are several interpretations of this phrase: 1) the people in the region eat no salt whatsoever, 2) they do not eat meat, fish, or dairy food that is salted, 3) they do not use sea salt but do eat rock salt, 4) they do not salt food at the table but use it in cooking.

It is unlikely that the inland dwellers do not use any salt since no known human culture or civilization has lived without salt. More likely, they eat little meat (and no fish or seafood). Salted meat, including fish and seafood, is a staple of maritime societies, including ships that ply the Mediterranean or Aegean and carry provisions for days and weeks at a time. It is much tougher, harder, and more contractive than non-salted meat and, especially in combination with wine or honey, salted meat or other salty food can give rise to aggression and violence. Indeed, the nickname for a sailor is "old salt," and the world over navies have a reputation for being more brutal and violent than armies. Also, some commentators have observed that food offered to the gods by the ancient Greeks was unsalted, hence the inlanders are a supernatural race. This goes too far.

The sense of Tiresias's charge is that Odysseus should walk to a place where people eat little if any animal food, especially salted meat or fish. In this remote inland region, the people farm for a living and will be unfamiliar with the sea, including oars, ships, sea salt, and the saltier, meatier diet of islanders and coastal people. Their main food, of course, symbolized by the winnowing shovel, is barley, wheat, and other whole grains, beans, and other predominantly plant quality foods.

The Oracle of the Oar

The key to understanding Odysseus's Oar is recognizing that the oar is a symbol of war as well as emblematic of the sea. For twenty years, the hero has been engaged in marauding, piracy, battles, and other violent and bloody adventures. The oar is a symbol of the fearsome black, hollow Achaean ships that rain violence, bloodshed, and captivity on coastal and island peoples. All warriors double as oarsmen, and as Odysseus's fateful voyage home shows, skill in rowing is instrumental to carrying out and surviving raids on towns and cities, as well as close encounters with ogres and angry gods. The spear and shield wield death and destruction, but without the oar and the synchronized rowing of many men and ships to the scene of battle, the bronze implements would be useless. Although not a weapon itself, the oar is an indispensable part of the ancient Greek armory. As Athena advises Telemachus as he sets out to obtain news of his lost father: "Telemachus, your crew of fighting men is ready at the oars, and waiting for you." In *The Rape of Troy*, Jonathan Gottshall observes:

> Fast ships with shallow drafts are rowed onto beaches and seaside communities are sacked before neighbor can lend defensive support. The men are usually killed, livestock and other portable wealth are plundered, and women are carried off to live among the visitors and perform sexual and menial labors. Homeric men live with the possibility of sudden, violent death, and the women live in fear for their men and children, and of sails on the horizon that may harbinger new lives of rape and slavery.

Odysseus's return from the Trojan War is all about his return to humanity. For ten years, he lives a fierce, dog-eat-dog life in the campaign to retrieve Helen. He slays countless opponents, including some like Dolon who are unarmed and defenseless. He employs guile to deceive the Trojans, put the city to the torch, and abduct women and children. By ancient standards, he is a war hero. By modern standards, he is a war criminal. As mythologist Joseph Campbell perceptively notes, Odysseus is unfit for ordinary life, especially the domestic life of marriage and fatherhood and the civic life of ruling a small kingdom. Odysseus needs ten years of encountering the feminine principle—in the form of various sorceresses, monsters, goddesses, and humans—to decompress and return to normal.

Odysseus is too macho to fit into society, even a patriarchal one. In Far Eastern terminology, he is too yang—or hard, tight, and contracted—to function peacefully. Like many modern veterans, the Greek survivors are susceptible to PTSD (post-traumatic stress disorder). The entire episode with the Sirens and their seductive songs glances backwards, invokes an image of rowing, and appeals to Odysseus's nostalgia for battle:

> Sea rovers here take joy
> Voyaging onward,
> As from our song of Troy
> Greybeard and rower-boy
> Goeth more learned.
> All feats on that great field
> In the long warfare,
> Dark days the bright gods willed,
> Wounds you bore there,

Argos' old soldiery
On Troy beach teeming,
Charmed out of time we see.
No life on earth can be
Hid from our dreaming.

(12.232-45)

Flashbacks of past hardships and glories overwhelm Odysseus, and he orders the crew to untie him from the mast. But, for once, the men obey his earlier command and bind him all the tighter. Only when they are out of sight and hearing of the deadly maidens does "my faithful company [rest] on their oars now, peeling off the wax that I had laid thick on their ears; then set me free." In this episode, oars are the tools of deliverance from the harpies and their temptation to drown one's sorrows by living in the past.

Odysseus's final quest, or post-*Odyssey* odyssey, recapitulates the entire voyage. In Ithaca, the starting point, he starts his journey with an oar, a symbol of war, on his shoulder. After trudging inland for several days, he comes to a farming region where violence and war, as well as oars and ships, are unknown. The implement on his shoulder is mistaken for a winnowing shovel, a farm tool used to separate the barley or wheat from the chaff. Grain, as we have seen throughout the Homeric epics, is a symbol of peace and plenty.

In the course of his inward journey, a weapon of war transforms into a tool for peace. It parallels Isaiah's famous prophecy:

> And He shall judge among the nations, and shall rebuke many people: and they shall beat their swords into plowshares, and their spears into pruning hooks: nation shall not lift up sword against nation, neither shall they learn war any more.

(2:3–4)

A plowshare is the metal blade of the plow used to till the soil to sow barley and wheat, while a pruning hook is a tool with a long curved blade for clipping grapevines. Isaiah's words are directed at a Bronze Age civilization in the Near East that is every bit as bloody as in the Aegean. Like the Biblical text, the Homeric epics end with a vision of an end to war and the metamorphosis of a weapon of war into an implement of peace. Coincidentally, Isaiah was a contemporary of Homer. He flourished in the kingdom of Judah in the mid-8th century BCE. Like Newton and Liebniz (the calculus), Darwin and Wallace (evolution), and Edison and Tesla (electricity), Homer and Isaiah simultaneously give voice to the same universal vision. The idea of converting a military weapon or technology for peaceful civilian use is the same in the Greek poem as in the Hebrew scripture.

The close relationship between food and peace is illustrated in the Far Eastern word for peace. In China and Japan, the ideogram for peace and harmony is *wa*. It is composed of two characters: 1) grain (millet or rice) and 2) mouth. Eating a whole grain-based diet leads to the development of a strong, healthy body; calm, clear mind; and sound judgment.

The English word "grain" derives from the Latin *granum*. The Greek word *karyon*, meaning seed or kernel, is the root of "corn." Corn originally referred to barley (barleycorn) and other whole grains, and eventually came to be exclusively identified with maize. "Cereal," another name for edible grain comes from Ceres, the Roman name for Demeter, the Greek goddess of grain. Demeter's name comes from the Minoan word *dea*, or barley, and the proto-Indo-European *meter*, or mother. She is the Mother of Barley.

As the goddess of the harvest, Demeter appears six times in the Homeric epics. In the *Iliad*, Protesilaos is the first man to be killed in the Trojan War. He was from Pyarson, a precinct of Demeter. His death suggests that proper nourishment is the first casualty of the war. In Book 5, we read that the Achaeans do not break their ranks or separate like the grains of Demeter on the threshing floor. As the fighting progresses, Homer notes that mortals such as Ajax eat "the bread of Demeter" as opposed to the ambrosia of the immortals. When Hera seduces Zeus, he tells her that he loves her more than any of his previous lovers, including "Demeter of the lovely tresses." She begs a favor of Aphrodite, her beautiful rival, to give her a seductive garment that "steals away the sharp wits of even sensible [gods]." In this way, Zeus, like Paris, is bewitched by female beauty to an act that brings disastrous, unforeseen consequences. When Lykaon begs Achilles for his life, he reminds him that they once enjoyed together "the yield of Demeter," or bread. In the *Odyssey*, Calypso reminds Hermes that Demeter was allowed to take Iasion as a lover until Zeus struck him down with a thunderbolt. Calypso would keep her captive indefinitely, but accedes to the divine decree.

Despite these minor appearances, Demeter's spirit permeates the epics in upholding the primacy of grain, especially barley. As the principal food for human beings and the foundation of a peaceful, prosperous society, grain figures prominently on Achilles' Shield and in the journey with the oar. By the time the stranger appears and asks why he is carrying a winnowing shovel on his shoulder, Odysseus will have traversed into the heart of a farming community. As we have seen, he probably ends up in

Thessaly, the inland region of northern Greece that is the breadbasket of the Aegean. In all likelihood, he plants the oar on the side of the road in a field of ripening barley. In this way, the long-separated family—the human family—returns to its agricultural roots and, in the words of Homer, attains "blessed peace."

As a symbol of the unconscious, the sea is the treasure house of personal and collective desires, impulses, myths, and dreams. Its teeming profusion harbors swells and currents, waves and tides, dark and sunny weather, high winds and stillness, and other complementary opposites. Now raging, now calm, now frigid, now balmy, the sea glances at humanity's origins and destiny. On the Shield, Ocean encircles the rest of the cosmos, and in the *Iliad* and *Odyssey*, rivers, nymphs, and other watery elements are personified as immortal.

As god of the sea, Poseidon represents the bedrock of consciousness—the unconscious out of which more refined levels of awareness emerge. On the spiritual journey, the wild, teeming inner chaos is progressively tamed by rational thought and faith in higher powers. Drives and instincts give way to emotions and thoughts. Social justice replaces personal revenge. Terrestrial law mirrors cosmic order. Transcendental wisdom embraces all.

In relation to the sea, the oar controls and traverses the waters. In the realm of the psyche, it symbolizes the self, ego, or I that navigates through the autonomic contents of the mind that are not accessible to introspection, including repressed feelings, subliminal perceptions, thoughts, habits, desires, forgotten memories, and dreams. The oar churns through these states of cognition, sets a direction, and reaches a goal. On the journey of life, the oar represents mastery over the levels of consciousness and the voyage from ignorance to knowledge, from suffering to bliss.

The oar is also a symbol of memory or wakefulness. Falling asleep on the benches or at the helm can be fatal to the expedition, as Odysseus found to his regret when in sight of Ithaca for the first time he dropped his oar, dozed off, and lost his homecoming.

Axis Shift

The metamorphosis of the oar from a symbol of the sea and the unconscious to a tool for growing grains, sowing peace, and mounting the ladder of consciousness is also reflected in its shift from a horizontal to a vertical orientation. In most traditional cultures, horizontal energy symbolizes the earth and vertical energy heaven. Horizontal encompasses the realm of daily activity, including transporation by land or sea, trade, communication, and other practical affairs. Vertical represents higher, more refined artistic, intellectual, and spiritual pursuits. Horizontal energy moves in a heavy, downward and inward, centripetal spiral. Vertical energy moves in an light, upward and outward, centrifugal spiral. Except for human beings, who walk upright, all other mammals proceed horizontally on all fours or stoop like primates.

The union of horizontal and vertical is emblematic of balance. Examples include the cross in Christianity, the totem pole in Native American culture, and yin and yang in Chinese philosophy. In the post-*Odyssey* odyssey, the horizon of the pilgrim changes from horizontal to vertical, as the oar that lies flat on the traveler's shoulder is planted upright in the ground. In the water, oars are also wielded horizontally to row across great expanses of sea. After setting up the oar in the soil, Odysseus is instructed to sacrifice a ram, a bull, and a boar to Poseidon. The three animals all have a horizontal, onward rushing orientation. Like the barley kernels—which grow upright and are customarily sprinkled on the sacrificial victim's head to win its consent—the upright oar-cum-winnowing shovel rises over, or transcends, the horizontal plane.

In the waters, though pulled horizontally, the oar is dipped diagonally, a tilt toward the vertical and balance between sky and earth, sea and land, light and dark, and other manifestations of yin and yang. When planted upright, it also points directly overhead at the North Star, the center of the cosmos that governs the cycles of history, the ages of humanity, and the destiny of individuals, families, and nations.

In the epics, Homer subtly weaves horizontal and vertical imagery to depict the hero's journey through the seven levels of consciousness. In the *Iliad*, the fighting takes place for the most part on the Trojan plain, a level beachhead, and the action is primarily horizontal. The opening plague scene, involving the coming and going of Chryses's ship, the later embassy to Achilles' camp, and the concluding ebb and flow of the combat, culminating in Achilles dragging Hector's body around the walls of Troy, take place in this dimension. The major vertical symbol, of course, is Achilles's Shield, which is painted upright by Hephaestus and held perpendicular to the flat thrusting spears of Aeneas, Hector, and other Trojans. Later, as we learn in the *Odyssey*, after Achilles dies, Ajax and Odysseus vie in a competition for his divine Shield. Believing that he has lost to the Ithacan unfairly, Ajax fixes his sword in a small mound—like the ones Odysseus later erects for Elpenor and Poseidon—and falls on it, committing suicide. In death, his corpse lies flat and is buried or burned, while his spirit rises and is conveyed to Hades by Hermes.

In ancient Greece, as in many cultures, the universe was seen as structured vertically, with the heavens above, the earth in the middle, and the afterworld below. The gods dwelt on Mt. Olympus, the highest mountain in Greece, which was emblematic, like most mountains in myth, poetry, and literature, of the spiritual ascent. Atlas, the primordial Titan, holds up the *axis mundi*, or great column that supports the celestial sphere. Calypso is his daughter, and in the *Odyssey* her island Ogygia is the *omphalos*—the navel or center of the world. When he washes up on her shore, Odysseus completes about half of his journey. Though she offers him eternal youth and immortality, he rejects the goddess's proposal to return home and reunite with his own mortal wife, Penelope. Homer subtly contrasts the wooing of Odysseus, by Circe, Calypso, and Nausicaa, with the suitors' pursuit of Penelope.

In the *Odyssey*, the delineation between the two axes is more sharply drawn than in the *Iliad*. Throughout the tale, Odysseus falls asleep at inopportune times and suffers for his carelessness. On the journey home from Aiola, he can't keep awake, and the crew seizes the opportunity to open the bag of winds. In sight of Ithaca, the ship is blown off course and their homecoming is lost. On Circe's island, Odysseus dozes off and the sorceress turns the crew into swine. On Thrinakia, he slumbers when his men slay the cattle of the Sun. On the way back to Ithaca, the wanderer falls into a deep sleep, and after dropping him off the Phaeacian ship is turned to stone. The first night at the palace in Ithaca, Odysseus sleeps fitfully and awakes more wrathful than ever. While the massacre of the suitors is a foregone conclusion, a less troubled sleep may have led him to pardon Amphinomos, the kindly suitor, and possibly some of the disloyal servant women.

In contrast to horizontal slumber, vertical postures accompany major moments of deliverance. When Odysseus's ship capsizes, he saves himself by grabbing hold of the solitary fig tree that grows on Scylla's island. On Circe's island, he grants Elpenor's last wish and erects an oar on his burial mound. In resisting the temptation of the Sirens, Odysseus has himself lashed to the mast. Freed from Calypso's thralldom, he fashions a raft from a tall pine tree. When Poseidon sends swelling seas to destroy it, the hero survives by clinging to the mast. When winning the archery contest, the hero displays his masterful command of the great bow that is wielded vertically. All of these upright episodes prefigure the final planting of the oar on his last journey.

Directionology also figures in Penelope's motions. She is portrayed frequently as ascending or descending a staircase in the palace. In her first appearance in the Odyssey, we read: "She came, then, down the long stairs of her house, this beautiful lady, with two maids in train attending her as she approached the suitors; and near a pillar of the roof she paused." The staircase and pillar symbolize the ladder, or spiral, of consciousness. Weaving plots against the suitors, she shuttles among the middle levels of consciousness, now descending to her courters' low, sensorial awareness, pining emotionally for Odysseus, devising stratagems to delay a marriage or win gifts, and ascending to social judgment in securing her son's succession. The loom on which she weaves is also vertical in orientation—slightly taller than the weaver—and compared to the high beams of a ship. The first time they meet, Odysseus in disguise greets his wife: "Your name has gone up to heaven like the sweet honor of some god-fearing king, who rules in equity over the strong: his black lands bear both wheat and barley." In matters of food, grains grow vertically, livestock is raised horizontally.

When she awakens, Penelope is portrayed as hesitant and fearful. Her disturbing dream of the eagle slaughtering the geese arises from horizontal slumber. But the story ends on an upward, joyful note. Odysseus and Penelope's marriage bed is carved from an olive tree that "grew like a pillar," whose roots extend to the earth and whose upright trunk serves as the bedpost. Recognition of the pear tree and other upward growing plants in Laertes' orchard serve to reunite father and son.

In raising a cairn to Poseidon and planting the oar as he did for Elpenor, Odysseus creates a burial mound for his former self. He inters his life of violence and war. He raises a tomb for his old unconscious or semi-conscious self and frees himself from the past. Penelope alludes to the connection when after listening to her husband describe Tiresias's prophecy, she replies: "If by the gods' grace age at least is kind, we have that hope—trials will end in peace." The Greek word for hope *elpis* comes from the same root as Elpenor, whose name and memorial oar mean Hopeful.

The final ritual of the oar, accompanied by prayers to Poseidon, the god of the unconscious, marks an end of humanity's attachment to lust (the ram), power (the bull), and ignorance (the boar). The entire odyssey can be viewed as a spiritual journey in which Odysseus passes through the evolutionary stages of life:

1. In the sea Odysseus and his crew are likened to fish, especially when they are speared by the Laestrygonians and devoured by Scylla. After Odysseus's raft capsizes, he is likened to an octopus

2. Washing up on land, Odysseus goes through the amphibious, reptilian, and bird stages when he crawls ashore on Scheria, hides under a pile of olive leaves, and is adorned with bright hair and other features by Athena

3. In the palace at Ithaca, Odysseus is likened to a mammal, specifically

a mountain lion, when he slays the suitors

4. On his final journey, Odysseus assumes a fully upright position, hiking into the interior, completes his return to humanity, and develops as a fully mature, upright, and peaceful human being

Tiresias's prophecy foretells that when Odysseus unshoulders his heavy battle oar and weighty warlike past and adopts a simple, peaceful life, his journey will be over. He will enjoy a happy old age and gentle death. This is precisely the quiet life devoid of glory that Achilles laments in Hades for not choosing. Right after Odysseus meets the blind seer, the spirit of Achilles appears and reinforces Tiresias's edict: "Odysseus, light of councils. Better, I'd rather be a laborer for some poor country farmer and live on bread than rule over the breathless dead."

On his visit to the Underworld, the hero of the *Odyssey* receives three closely related *sema* or signs of his destiny: 1) Elpenor's request to be properly buried and for an oar to be placed on his grave. (Recall the young rower died after indulging in wine and other rich foods and losing his balance.) 2) Tiresias's charge to journey inland with an oar and plant it in the earth when it is mistaken for a winnowing shovel. 3) Achilles's regrets that he did not follow a similar path and retire to a quiet life of farming. Odysseus's youngest crewman and rower boy, the wisest man in antiquity, and the bravest, most powerful Achaean warrior combine to give him sound advice and clear guidance to abandon war, adopt the way of life of a simple, farming culture, and cultivate the life-giving grain and other crops that yield "blessed peace."

7
Calypso's Butterfly Axe

After leaving Ogygia, Calypso's island, on a raft and capsizing in the sea, Odysseus eventually washes ashore on Scheria, the island of the Phaeacians. In contrast to the lotus-eaters, Cyclops, Circe, Sirens, and other fabulous beings he has encountered, Phaeacia marks Odysseus's return to human culture and civilization. Indeed, the land of mariners is inhabited by a golden race whose main activities are dancing, fashion, shipbuilding, and navigation.

At a banquet, King Alcinous explains to his bedraggled guest that the Phaeacians excel in the arts of peace, not war. After an evening of dance and song, the Phaeacian princes present Odysseus with splendid gifts, and the evening ends in a sumptuous feast. Seareach, an impetuous young man who earlier offended Odysseus in a sporting competition, presents him a valuable sword. The great tactician replies, "My hand, friend; may the gods award you fortune. I hope no pressing need comes on you ever for this fine blade you give me in amends."

Odysseus also learns that the Phaeacians excel in the nautical arts. But unlike Aegean and Mediterranean seafarers, they have no warships. In keeping with their harmonious heritage, they have only vessels that ply the seas for peaceful trade and missions of mercy. As King Alcinous reveals, the island's unique ships have neither steersman nor oars, but navigate by "divining the crew's wishes, as they do, and knowing, as they do, the ports of call about the world."

As his visit comes to an end, Odysseus tactfully turns down an offer from the monarch and his noble queen Arete to marry Nausicaa, their industrious daughter and young woman who cared for him when he washed ashore. The Phaeacians graciously bestow valuable gifts on their illustrious visitor and transport Odysseus home. In keeping with their Golden Age pedigree, no weapons, even ceremonial ones, are taken aboard ship on the voyage.

Unfortunately, for the Phaeacians, no good deed goes unpunished. On their way home, an irate Poseidon, god of the sea, turns their ship to stone and threatens to send an earthquake and raise a mountain around their home port. King Alcinous recalls his father's prophecy that one day just such a tragedy would strike.

Pax Minoica

Phaeacia nods at the Golden Age described by Hesiod, and its ships also play a role in the story of Jason and the Argonauts. But it is not a fantasy island like most of the surreal places visited by Odysseus homeward bound. Life on Scheria closely parallels the culture of the ancient Minoans.

Minoan civilization flourished in Crete, a Mediterranean island, located equidistant between Greece, Egypt, Anatolia (Turkey), and Canaan, from about 3600 to 1500 BCE. A mountainous island with peaks up to 8000 feet and fertile valleys, Crete was settled by Neolithic farmers about 7000 BCE. Its towns and villages developed into a complex agrarian and mercantile society with multi-storied houses, lush courtyards, paved streets, and indoor plumbing with piped water and flush toilets. As a powerful, maritime power, Minoan civilization extended from Spain in the west to Syria, Mesopotamia, the Black Sea, Afghanistan, and possibly the Indus River Valley in the east. Its superbly built ships controlled the Bronze Age trade in copper, tin, and other valuable metals, as well as grain, olive oil, wine, fabric, jewelry, pottery, and luxury goods. In one of his tall tales to Penelope, a disguised Odysseus describes his visit to the island: "There is a land called Crete, in the midst of the wine-dark sea, a fair, rich land, begirt with water, and therein are many men, past counting, and ninety cities." He also mentions the great city Knossos, where King Minos reigned and conversed with his father Zeus. Odysseus also passes himself off as a Cretan merchant to Athena and Eumaios, the swineherd.

The monumental structure at Knossos contained more than a thousand rooms. But there is no record of a Minoan king by the name of Minos or that of any other ruler. The name "Minoan" was bestowed on this ancient sea power in honor of the mythical king by Sir Arthur Evans, who excavated the site in the early twentieth century. The ancient Egyptians referred to Crete as *Keftiu*. The palatial building and other Minoan architecture contain beautiful frescoes, ceramics, and seals depicting leaping dolphins, soaring swallows, twined octopi, undulating snakes, and other animals; and colorful lilies, crocuses, and other delicate flowers. The complex at Knossos also harbored workshops for making pottery, storerooms for grain, olive oil, and other staples, and halls for celebrating.

The pastel frescoes vividly portray the natural world and daily life with an emphasis on fashion, sports, dancing, harvesting, and other joyful pursuits. Females play a key role in Minoan society, and the women are depicted as attractive and stylish. They are attired in embroidered dresses, adorned with flowers in their hair, and often have open blouses displaying their breasts. Some figurines are suggestive of goddesses or priestesses, and the Minoans appear to have venerated the Great Goddess in her many guises, including earth mother, sun goddess, and moon deity.

Minoan society shows a high degree of organization and wealth, but there is no evidence of monarchy, royalty, a central authority, or a military elite. There is no archaeological, artistic, or literary evidence of an army, offensive weapons, or defensive fortifications. Nor is there evidence of war, battles, or social violence over the span of a millennium and a half. This contrasts sharply with ancient Sumer, Egypt, Babylon, Assyria, and other contemporary city-states and kingdoms—and with later Mycenaean and Classical Greek culture—that glorified war and conquest. There are beautifully wrought daggers, swords, and spears in Knossos and other Minoan sites, but these appear to have been used solely on ceremonial occasions, as Homer suggests in describing Seareach's gift of a sword to Odysseus at the farewell banquet.

The Double-Axe and Labyrinth

The Minoan double-axe, known as the *labryns*, has been likened to the cross in Christianity and the crescent in Islam. It appears prominently in Cretan paintings, pottery, and seals. However, the Minoan double-axe is not linked to actual military use or animal sacrifice. It was the same shape as the blade of the hoe used to grow grains and other crops on the island. In later Greek mythology, the double-axe was associated with Zeus and other male storm gods. But in Crete, it was a symbol of goddesses or priestesses and symbolizes a butterfly (the symbol of change and transformation). The *labrys* may also represent the goddess and her male consort, representing sexual and gender equality. The shapes also glances at the female sexual organs (a symbol of fertility, birth, and rebirth).

In the *Odyssey*, Calypso gives Odysseus a tool to fell trees to build the raft that will take him home (by way of Phaeacia). "She gave him a great axe of bronze, easy to wield, with keen double blade; its haft was of olive, handsome and fitting close." Her gift of the double-axe—the ancient Minoan symbol of rebirth and of respect and harmony between the sexes—symbolizes the spiritual quest.

The *labrys* is linked etymologically to the Labyrinth, which means the House of the Double Axe. According to Greek legend, King Minos regularly sacrificed seven Athenian youths and maidens to the Minotaur, a terrifying creature half human and half bull. To slay the beast, who inhabited the center of an impenetrable maze, the Athenian youth Theseus won the heart of a Cretan maiden Adriane, who gave him a double-axe and a ball of thread to unwind as he entered the labyrinth and then find his way back. From a spiritual view, the labyrinth symbolizes the twists and turns, dead ends, and ever-changing spirallic movement of life. It is the journey into the deepest recesses of the soul and triumph over fear and desire. From a historical perspective, the defeat of the Minotaur by a Greek hero represents the ascendency of the Mycenaeans over the Minoans. The Mycenaeans, the first advanced culture in mainland Greece, colonized Crete after the catastrophic collapse of Minoan civilization.

In about 1628 BCE, an enormous volcano on Thera, a small island north of Crete, erupted in one of the largest explosions in recorded history. The eruption buried Akrotiri, a city on Thera, sent a plume of ash twenty miles into the stratosphere, and sparked a tsunami that was a hundred feet or more in height. The explosion was preceded by tremors and rising steam, so the Therans were able to evacuate before the eruption. Loss of life on Crete, which received the brunt of the tidal wave and earthquake, was also minimal. However, the large communal center at Knossos, as well as most standing structures, were destroyed along with most of the fleet. There was a brief recovery and partial reconstruction, but within fifty years, Crete was overrun by the Mycenaeans, a martial culture from the Greek mainland. The glorious Minoan Golden Age vanished, to be remembered only in myth and legend.

The catastrophic event on Thera is alluded to in the *Odyssey* when the Phaeacian vessel that transports Odysseus home is turned to stone and Poseidon threatens to bury the island under a mountain. The Greek warrior had incurred the wrath of Poseidon, the god of the sea, by maiming his son, the one-eyed Cyclops, and the sea god vowed vengeance. Volcanoes with their circular craters may have been personified as "one-eyed" monsters, or Cyclopses. *Phaeacia* derives from "phaios," the Greek word for gray and may signify volcanic ash.

At the Phaeacian court, Odysseus learns that the inhabitants migrated to their island paradise after the cannibalistic Cyclopses plundered their original homeland. The Homeric epic also notes that after defeating the Minotaur, Theseus took Adriane, a native Minoan, to Naxos, a Cretan colony on the tip of the Greek mainland. Naxos was a safe haven, whereas resettling Adriane in Mycenaean Greece, the warlike region to the north, would have been dangerous. Homer, living in the 8th century BCE, about eight hundred years after the end of the Minoan era, incorporated myths and legends about Crete in his epic. In the *Odyssey*, Phaeacia appears to be a colony established by Minoans after fleeing the huge volcanic eruption and its aftermath.

The Minotaur too may hearken back to this cataclysmic disaster, as a bellowing bull was also an ancient symbol for an erupting volcano. Cretan bulls played a central role in sporting events, but unlike later European bullfighting were never killed. Minoan acrobats, primarily female, competed to leap on their backs. With their inferior gymnastic skills, Athenian athletes, who participated in this proto-Aegean Olympiad may have been injured, or even killed, in the dangerous competition. In Athens, their sacrifice could have given rise to the Minos story. The horns of the bull and cow (as all ancient cattle had horns) were associated with the moon. The Minoan bull leaping feats also glance at the constellations of Perseus and Andromeda. While Orion confronts Taurus in the night sky, Perseus somersaults over the bull's back to rescue Andromeda.

On an even larger canvas, the sudden implosion of Minoan civilization appears to have caused an axis shift in the relation between the sexes. Until this time, Cretan society honored women and very likely observed a matrilineal social structure in which inheritance and male leadership went through the female line. According to this view, Minos was not the name of a tyrant or king, but an office and the consort of the leading female priestess or votive goddess. The goddess's companion, a strong, virile young man may have served as the Lord of the Animals and presided over the world of the dead like Osiris and other early Mediterranean and Middle Eastern male divinities.

The Minoans' written language, known as Linear A, remains undeciphered after 5000 years, so much about the society remains speculative. Historians and scientists theorize that the monumental structure excavated at Knossos was a 1) royal palace (presided over by either a queen, king, or both), 2) a temple and center of religious worship and cultic practices, 3) a community center devoted to the wonders of nature and the arts, sciences, and trade, or 4) some combination of the above. In the *Odyssey*, Homer notes, "Daedalus in Knossos once contrived a dancing-floor for fair-haired Ariadne." This suggests that the architect of the labyrinth originally designed it for musical and artistic pursuits, perhaps bull-leaping. In a surviving fragment, the later philosopher Empedocles describes the Minoan as largely a pacifist and vegan culture: "Not then with unmixed blood / Of many bulls was ever an altar stained; But among men 'twas sacrilege most vile / To reave of life and eat the goodly limbs."

Whether or not the Minoans worshipped the earth mother Rhea and an older generation of Aegean goddesses, after the collapse of Cretan civilization, patriarchy came to dominate the region. Following the collapse of Minoan society, the three brothers Zeus, Poseidon, and Hades—the chief Greek male gods—rose to power. They symbolized the three volcanic elements—thunder and lightning, tempestuous seas and earthquakes, and merciless death—that roiled the Aegean and destroyed Thera and Crete. As Craig S. Barnes surmises in *In Search of the Lost Feminine*, a penetrating study of early Greek mythology, the earth mother, the moon goddess, and other female deities that ruled the region until now were regarded as powerless to save the Minoans from the apocalypse. The new father gods, along with their questing sons, took control of religious and civil life and instituted cultic virginity, patriarchal marriage rites, and inheritance of property through the male line. Conquest, male valor and glory, and the sanctity of marriage replaced fertility, female nurture and community, and rebirth and renewal as guiding principles. During the 400 years of Mycenaean ascendency, Barnes explains, cyclical time, lasting peace, and a blessed afterlife gradually gave way to linear time, perpetual war, and a dark Underworld of wandering spirits. Peaceful agrarian rhythms that looked to recurrent cycles of the moon, sun, and stars yielded to piracy, land raids, and wars of conquest in which power, violence, and opportunism observed no temporal limits.

A close reading of the Greek classics shows a constant friction between the old spiritual order and the new. There are several stories concerning the origin of the name of the Aegean Sea. The first is that it comes from Aega, the manifestation of the Great Goddess in the form of a goat. Second, the name may derive from Aegea, the queen of the Amazons, a legendary race of strong women whose culture didn't include males. Third, Aegean stems from Aigaion, a mythical giant known as the "sea goat" who fought the Titans and later the Olympians. A fourth legend holds that Aegean is named after Aegeus, the father of Theseus, who drowned himself when he thought his son had been killed by the Minotaur. The myths follow a historical progression from Minoan to Mycenaean to Homeric times.

Diet and the Minoans

The traditional Cretan diet also offers a clue to the peace and prosperity at the heart of Minoan civilization. As in other parts of the Aegean and Mediterranean worlds, barley was the main grain and wheat, spelt, and rye secondary cereals. Grains were enjoyed in whole form and porridge at meals as well as bread, pasta, and baked goods. Lentils, chickpeas, black-eyed peas, and other beans were also consumed regularly, along with *horta* or wild vegetables, including artichoke, asparagus, chicory, endive, radish, leeks, mustard, purslane, vetch, and okra. Grapes, olives, figs, dates, quince, almonds, sesame, poppy seeds, and other fruits, seeds, and nuts also formed an important part of the daily way of eating.

Special Cretan dishes included *rusk*, a crunchy biscuit made with barley, wheat, or rye flour and double-baked. Sprinkled with oregano, olive paste, eggplant chickpea dip, or other topping, it is enjoyed saturated with olive oil and enjoyed as an appetizer, salad, or entire meal. Other favorites included *xinochrontros*, a sour thick frumenty or boiled, cracked wheat; *eftazymo* or chickpea leavened bread; *kolokithokeftedes*, or fried patties of mashed zucchini; *marathopita* or fennel pie; and *yemistra* or stuffed vegetables.

The Minoans cooked on small charcoal braziers that were placed on a table inside or outside. As a rule, Cretan cooking was mild and not spicy. The principal herbs were thyme, basil, and oregano. In an island with many goats and sheep, cultured diary products such as yogurt were enjoyed. But creamy sauces and butter in cooking were largely avoided in favor of olive oil. Honey, the main sweetener, figured in snacks and desserts such as *xerotigana*, or fried dough strips with honey and nuts. From time to time, especially on festive occasions, seafood such as sea bass, barnacles, sea snails, and fish roe, were prepared. Modest amounts of meat and poultry were also consumed, as well as beer and wine. The roots of the healthy, modern Mediterranean Diet go back to this era. Today, Crete has the lowest heart disease and cancer rates of any country in the world.

In contrast to the plant-based Cretan diet, the Bronze Age way of eating that succeeded the Minoan, emphasized heavy animal food. The change can be seen in the Homeric epics, composed nearly a millennium later. The Greeks are constantly feasting on bulls, cows, rams, sheep, goats, and swine. Many of these domesticated animals are slaughtered ritually and offered first to the gods as an offering for auspicious winds, courage in battle, and final victory. The roots of animal sacrifice extend to the Paleolithic, and sacrifice was practiced on a modest scale in Crete. But as Empedocles notes, bulls were never sacrificed, and overall consumption of animal food was limited.

As Indo-European patriarchy replaced the matrilineal Minoan and wider Aegean society, animal sacrifice developed into a major cottage and cultic industry. Kings, military commanders, and individual warriors competed to win the favors of the gods. *Hecatombs*, or large public sacrifices, were common. At the start of the *Odyssey*, Odysseus's son, Telemachus, sets off in quest of news of his father and off the coast of Pylos observes black bulls being offered to Poseidon "the blue-maned god who makes the islands tremble." It is the largest sacrifice in either epic: nine congregations consisting of 500 citizens each lead nine bulls apiece to the altar. At the end of the Olympic games in classical Greece, a *hecatomb* was offered to Zeus.

Energetically, meat gives a burst of immediate power and energy, qualities prized by warriors and plunderers. Meat also stimulates the liver and gallbladder, the traditional seat of courage, righteous anger, and vision. Achilles's wrath, the governing emotion in the *Iliad*, is kindled by his frequent sacrifices, and Patroclus and he cook choice cuts of meat for their comrades in arms. Though the immortal Olympian gods dine on nectar and ambrosia, they enjoy the scent of burnt offerings consecrated by mortals. In an effort to balance their heavy meat intake, the Greek warriors downed enormous amounts of wine and other alcohol.

In contrast, the Trojans, situated in Asia Minor (in present day Turkey), retained elements of a matrilineal civilization. Worship of the Great Goddess was still strong among many of their allies, including Lemnos, Lesbos, Pedaissos, and Lynessos, and they did not regard marriage vows as sacrosanct like the Greeks. Hence, when Helen eloped with Paris, according to the Trojan version of the tale, the ancient Minoan ideal of free love came into play. The patriarchal Greeks, led by Agamemnon, the king of Mycenae, vowed to get her back. He had won the competition for Helen's hand on behalf of his brother, Menelaus, so Helen's marriage was one of territorial alliance, not love, to begin with. All peace entreaties and offers to pay ransom by the Trojans were rejected. As Barnes concludes in *In Search of the Lost Feminine*, the marriage bond—including the sanctity of virginity, the legitimacy of sons, and property rights it upheld—was inviolate in the new masculine order.

Zeus, the ruler of the gods, grew up on Crete and as a baby was fed milk from a wild goat's horn by Agea or Amaltheia, a nymph on Mount Ida, and honey by Melissa, the bee goddess. Rhea, Zeus's mother, hid him there to protect him from his father Cronus, who had swallowed all his previous children at birth lest a prophecy that he would be overthrown by one of his own offspring come true. Rhea gave Cronus a stone to swallow instead. When he came of age, Zeus confronted his father, made him regurgitate his siblings (Hestia, Demeter, Hera, Hades, and Poseidon) and in a titanic battle defeated his father and fellow Titans. A triumphant Zeus then released their prisoners from the Underworld. These included the Cyclopses, who gratefully gave Zeus thunder, the thunderbolt, and lightning. The three victorious brother gods drew lots to divide the world among them. Zeus got the air and sky, Poseidon the waters, and Hades the realm of the dead. They divided earth, the provenance of their grandmother Gaia, between them. Hence Poseidon became known as the Earth-Shaker as well as the god of the sea. The older female gods went into exile or were demonized as the Furies, Medusas, and Sirens.

Zeus's early Cretan diet shaped and influenced his later rule. Goat's milk, yogurt, cheese, and other products are very energizing. Like a goat, the young ruler of the heavens was very strong, feisty, and resilient. Goats are also very horny, or feeling sexually aroused, and Zeus was notorious for his love affairs, seductions, and rapes. In the form of a white bull, he abducted Europa, a Phoenician princess, after whom the continent of Europe was named and who gave birth to Minos, the future king of Crete.

Honey conveys a dreamy bee-like quality and creates an attraction to strong females. Hera, Zeus's wife, filled the role of Queen Bee on Mount Olympus, jealously protecting her turf from other consorts and paramours. Originally an earth or moon goddess, Hera was shackled to Zeus in an unhappy marriage when the patriarchy came into power. In the *Odyssey*, once when she disobeyed her husband, Zeus hung her from the sky with gold chains and two anvils suspended from her feet until she relented.

Among Zeus's many offspring, Athena stands out. Her mother, Metis (Thought or Cunning), was swallowed by Zeus, as Cronus swallowed his children before him. Like father, like son. A new prophecy foretold that one of Zeus's offspring would displace him. But since Zeus lacked a womb, the baby was born by Caesarean section when Hephaestus, the smith of the gods and another of Zeus's children, removed him from his head. Tellingly, the surgical tool he used was the *labyrns*, or double-axe, glancing at Minoan culture. Athena, the goddess of weaving, war, and wisdom, represents a synthesis of Minoan artistry and Mycenaean martial skill. By remaining single, unmarried, and celibate, she largely transcended the volatile dynamic related to gender and the balance of power between the sexes. However, even she was often forced to take sides. On returning home from Troy, Agamemnon was slain by his wife Clytemnestra and her lover. She was irate that he had sacrificed their daughter Iphigeneia in return for favorable sailing winds to Troy and for murdering her first husband and abducting her. Clytemnestra clearly observed the flexible ancient Minoan customs relating to partnership, and according to one version dispatched Agamemnon with the double axe. (In the Homeric epics, animals are sometimes sacrificed with this instrument as well.) When Orestes, their son, subsequently slew his mother and was tried for murder, Athena cast the deciding vote to acquit him. In contrast, after the Trojan War, Helen, Clytemnestra's sister, reconciled with her husband, Menelaus. As the queen of Sparta, she came from a region influenced by flexible Minoan values and customs (e.g., long hair), which helps to explain why she eloped with Paris.

Calypso's Concealment

Ogygia, Calypso's abode, is described as the naval or center of the earth. The island contains many varieties of birds, trees, and flowers, as well as meadows of soft violent and parsley. Vines of grapes adorn the grottoes, and four springs of white water flow in the cardinal directions. Calypso's name derives from *kalypto*, which means "to cover" or "to conceal." Calypso is portrayed as an enchantress who uses her charms to turn Odysseus into her consort and prevent him from realizing his quest. Like many mothers or lovers, she seeks to keep her beloved safe from physical harm and the vicissitudes of life. Another example in Western myth and legend from the Holy Grail cycle is Herzeloyde (Heart's Sorrow), who hides her son Parzival, from all knowledge of combat and war after her husband is slain in battle. In effect, Calypso's island and hollow cave is a womb—a safe, nourishing space—in which Odysseus will remain stillborn. Naturally, he rejects her offer to keep him her immortal boy toy and strives to be released, or reborn, and realize his own destiny.

In addition to her beauty and sexuality, Calypso consciously uses food to sap his strength. With her attendant nymphs, she prepares relaxing food for him, especially dainties, or sweets, that she makes sure to pack on his departure in one final attempt to weaken his resolve. Calypso's yin, or smothering/mothering approach, is diametrically opposite to Circe, the other enchantress, who attempts to bend Odysseus's will through violence or strong yang methods. In contrast to Circe's vegan cooking, Calypso offers primarily Paleo cuisine. Her spicy dishes and heavy viands turn his men into swine. In both cases, the sorceresses' spells are broken by Hermes, the messenger of the gods, who represents higher wisdom. In Circe's case, he gives Odysseus *moly*, the black and white herb representing the unifying principle. The magic flower gives him the power to match her violence with his own. In Calypso's case, Odysseus eventually tires of her physical and emotional attractions and falls into weeping and depression. Like a sailor steering by the pole star, he keeps his mind focused on returning home to Penelope and his family. Interestingly, the seven years Odysseus spends with Calypso and one year with Circe correspond with the traditional spiral proportion of 7 parts yin to 1 part yang or a 7:1 ratio.

When Hermes arrives with orders from Mount Olympus to release her stranded lover, Calypso laments:

"O you vile gods, in jealousy supernal!

> You hate it when we choose to lie with men—
> immortal flesh by some dear mortal side.
> So radiant Dawn once took to bed Orion
> until you easeful gods grew peevish at it,
> and holy Artemis, Artemis throned in gold,
> hunted him down in Delos with her arrows.
> Then Demeter of the tasseled tresses yielded
> to Iasion, mingling and making love
> in a furrow three times plowed; but Zeus found out
> and killed him with a white-hot thunderbolt.
> So now you grudge me, too, my mortal friend.
> But it was I who saved him—saw him straddle
> his own keel board, the one man left afloat
> when Zeus rent wide his ship with chain lightning
> and overturned him in the wine-dark sea.
> Then all his troops were lost, his good companions,
> but wind and current washed him here to me.
> I fed him, loved him, sang that he should not die
> nor grow old, ever, in all the days to come.
> But now there's no eluding Zeus's will.
> If this thing be ordained by him, I say
> so be it, let the man strike out alone on the vast water. Surely I
>   cannot 'send' him.
> I have no long-oared ships, no company
> to pull him on the broad back of the sea.
> My counsel he shall have, and nothing hidden,
> to help him homeward without harm.
>
> [5.124–151]

Odysseus's tears, as much as Zeus's threats, move the goddess to cooperate, and she unselfishly gives him the double axe to construct his raft, as well as provisions, clothing and "a fair wind behind you to let you reach your own land unharmed."

If the Achaean warrior has softened during his sojourn on Ogygia and gotten in touch with his feminine side, Calypso has also changed. Though Odysseus rejects her immortal gifts, she comes to respect his temporal love for Penelope and her human flaws. No doubt Odysseus often told her that life on her island, however idyllic, did not make him happy. As he tells the Phaeacians:

> There is no boon in life more sweet, I say,

> than when a summer joy holds all the realm,
> and banqueters sit listening to a harper
> in a great hall, by rows of tables heaped
> with bread and roast meat, while a steward goes
> to dip up wine and brim your cups again.
> Here is the flower of life, it seems to me!
>
> [9.5–11]

Calypso comes to recognize that man's dream (changing society and embarking on a quest) is different from woman's dream (eternal love) and gives him the double axe, the ancient Minoan symbol of equality and harmony, to realize his goal. In the process, as her heartfelt lament to Hermes shows, she voices the unfairness and frustration that goddesses and nymphs, as well as women and girls, feel in a male-dominated cosmos. Whether immortal or mortal, they reject the double standard that allows males to choose their own partners and even abuse, abduct, and rape them with impunity.

Ironically, Odysseus himself is a master of concealment, a feminine quality not usually prized in warriors. The Wooden Horse, whose concealed warriors sprang out and turned the tide of the war, is his idea. On the journey home, he constantly uses trickery and subterfuge to survive. He conceals himself and his men as sheep to outwit the Cyclops. He fails to tell his men about Scylla and sacrifices several of his crew for the greater good. He has his men tie him to the mast of his ship to avoid the enticements of the Sirens. He disguises himself as an old beggar to gain admittance to his own palace and gain an audience with Penelope. Even then he continues to feign false identities and spin yarns to all he meets. The only mortal who sees through his subterfuges is Argos, his old dog.

Daughter of Atlas

There is also an astronomical dimension to the episode on Ogygia. Calypso is the daughter of Atlas, a Titan who was condemned to hold the earth on his shoulders for eternity after the Titans lost the war with the Olympians. The conflict can be viewed as a struggle between the older pantheon presided over by Gaia, Mother Earth, and the newer Indo-European sky gods.

In Homer's words, Atlas "holds the high pillars that keep the earth and the sky apart" and "knows the depths of the sea in its entirety." In this role, he represents the world tree or *axis mundi* that connects heaven and earth. Calypso's island serves as the naval, or center, of the world around which the constellations and other stars turn. Fathers can also be protective, especially of their daughters.

In a display of her astronomical knowledge, Calypso advises Odysseus to keep *Ursa Major* (the Big Dipper) on his right when he sails from her island. Her sky lore glances at the Minoans, who controlled Mediterranean and Aegean seafaring, and had an advanced system of celestial navigation. Like many megalithic sites, structures and stones on Crete were oriented to the equinoxes, solstices, and heliacal rising or setting of individual stars, especially Arcturus, a bright star in Bootes, the guardian of the Bear. In Knossos, the first rays of the rising sun on the vernal equinox silhouette an inscribed double axe on the concave stone in what archaeologists call the Corridor of the House Tablets.

Calypso's role as a midwife in Odysseus's rebirth is reinforced by references to her as a nymph as well as a goddess. Nymphs were minor female nature deities who dwelled in the ocean, rivers, lakes, springs, meadows, groves, caves, and mountains. Described as "daughters of Zeus" in the epics, they have altars and receive offerings and sacrifices. Overall, nymphs are beneficent and assist mortals in arriving and settling into new environments. In Greek, the word also refers to a mortal woman who exerts a nurturing influence, especially a young woman just before marriage. Penelope, as a future bride, also qualifies as a nymph.

Throughout the *Odyssey*, Odysseus is surrounded by these sylvan beings. The epic opens with Odysseus dwelling with the nymph Calypso. Though she welcomes and succors him, he feels like a prisoner. After she releases him and Poseidon destroys his raft, Odysseus is saved from drowning by the nymph Ino, who throws him her magic veil. On Scheria, Nausicaa, a marriageable young princess, rescues him and takes him to the palace. She is likened to Artemis, the huntress goddess, and her nymphs. In the Phaeacian court, before King Alcinous and Queen Arete, Odysseus relates his earlier adventures, including several encounters with nymphs. After outwitting the Cyclops, he was befriended by nymphs on Goat Island who assisted his crew in locating food. On the island of the Sun, nymphs served as shepherdesses of the sacred cattle and assisted the crew in berthing their ship in a hollow sea cave where they held beautiful dance performances. The Phaeacians drop Odysseus off on Ithaca at the Cave of the Nymphs. The secluded shelter houses stone amphoras and mixing bowls in which bees store their honey and looms on which the nymphs weave purple mantles. Athena reminds him that he used to sacrifice hecatombs to the nymphs on earlier homecomings. Odysseus prays with outstretched hands to the island's nymphs, a gesture soon repeated by Eumaios, the old herdsman with whom he seeks shelter.

In the epics, Homer portrays the sea as both nourishing and terrifying, feminine in its placidity, patriarchal in its implacability. At one point, Odysseus is compared to an octopus, the iconic sea creature whose wily nature and "many feet" mirror his own craftiness and "many turnings." Cast adrift, alone and naked, in the sea, the Greek warrior is tossed to and fro by gigantic waves and tempests provoked by Poseidon. In a glance at Calypso, Homer describes the angry sea god as "covering" the sea and land with clouds to further torment him. At Zeus's command, Poseidon has vowed not to kill Odysseus, but torments him as long as he can. In the briny deep, the beleaguered warrior regrets not dying on the battlefield in Troy, at the summit of his glory, when he retrieved the corpse of Achilles.

On the raft, before it capsizes, Homer compares Calypso's provisions and sail to thistles that "cover" precious seeds. Like a pollinated seed, Odysseus is blown by the winds and will have to release his protective shell and hull in order to germinate. As Ann Bergren notes perceptively in *Weaving Truth: Essays on Language and the Female in Greek Thought*. "Almost at once, Odysseus is moved off this dead center by the intervention of Ino. In the symbolism of rebirth, her role is that of a midwife, facilitating his separation from those elements, previously protective, that now inhibit his emergence from the sea. She urges him to take off the garments from Calypso that have 'covered' him like a placenta, but now hold him back, and to abandon his raft, likened before to a thistle's sheltering case. As an alternative lifeline, a figural umbilical cord, she offers an 'immortal veil' to fasten below his chest and then to cast off, once he reaches dry land."

Comparing Odysseus to a germinating grain, Homer continues with the simile:

> A gust of wind, hitting a pile of chaff,
> will scatter all the parched stuff far and wide;
> just so, when this gigantic billow struck
> the boat's big timbers few apart. Odysseus
> clung to a single beam, like a jockey riding,
> meanwhile stripping Calypso's cloak away;
> then he slung round his chest the veil of Ino
> and plunged headfirst into the sea. His hands
> went out to stroke, and he gave a swimmer's kick.
> [5.381–388]

As the outer shell or husk of the budding new life within, the raft shatters like the outside covering of a seed. Athena, the wayfarer's guide and symbol of the *anima* or feminine side of his soul, invisibly guides Odysseus to land. Curiously, as Bergren notes, "Instead of its usual identification with motherhood, the earth here is likened to a father. Failure to reach this land would mean the loss of what only the father confers in father-ruled society, home and legitimate adult identity. Despite its distance from Ithaca, Phaeacia is now psychologically the 'father-land' of Odysseus. To set foot on this island is to achieve separation from the mother and identification with the father, to emerge, that is, as a male child. Accordingly, it is to children that Odysseus is compared, children nearly orphaned, too young to assume their patrimony."

In this way, with the help of several nymphs, Odysseus emerges from a liquid into an air environment and evolves from a primitive creature of the sea to a human being.

The Dance of the Sexes

In the new age of bronze, women were regarded as subservient to men, little more than property of their fathers, husbands, and sons. This is especially true in the *Iliad* where the Achaeans consider the women and girls of Troy and their allies fair game for abduction, rape, and slavery. Warriors on both sides cow each other and their own recalcitrant troops by calling them females. For example, when the tide turns against them, Menelaus rallies his forces: "Ah me, you empty braggarts, you women, not men, of Achaia! This will be an embarrassing business, deep, deep disgrace, if no Danaan now steps forward to stand against Hector!" The Trojan hero engages in the same taunts. To Diomedes, he challenges: "Son of Tydeus, the swift-horsed Danaans used to honor you above all, with meat, full cups, a privileged seat; but now they'll despise you—it seems you're a woman at heart! On your way, craven dolly!" Agamemnon offers captive women to share the bed of Greeks who distinguish themselves in battle—not unlike the virgins of paradise promised in some later religions for those who give their lives in holy war. After slaying Hector, Achilles sponsors an athletic competition and as a prize offers a captive woman skilled in handiwork worth four oxen. The *Odyssey* portrays the same hierarchal structure. In the opening book, we learn from Telemachus that Eurykleia, the sage old servant who later identifies his father by his scar, was purchased by Laertes from her father for the equivalent of twenty oxen.

In the course of his adventures, Odysseus's relationship to women goes through a profound change. At the start of his journey, the hero still regards women primarily as booty, as the raid on Ismarus shows. Unlike the crew, he is not motivated primarily by pleasure or sexual fulfillment, as his indifference to Circe and Calypso and their sensory and emotional wiles indicates. His masculine prowess and *metis*, or crafty intellect, overcome their seductive beauty. The Sirens tempt him, not so much by their loveliness, as for their enchanting voices and recitation of his past glories. Appealing to his ego and desire for *kleos*, or eternal glory, is more seductive than physical satisfaction. In contrast, Scylla and Charybdis, the she-monsters of the deep, offer no special attraction, but serve as examples of extreme feminine contraction and expansion, or yang and yin, through whose midst Odysseus must find a middle way. In Hades, this intellectual challenge is compounded when the spirit of his mother Antikleia appears. He gently postpones their emotional reunion in order to speak first with Tiresias and not lose his chance to learn his destiny. In the land of the Phaeacians, he almost succumbs to lovely Nausicaa's gentle demeanor, kindness, and hospitality. But he remembers his dream and sends her ahead to the palace alone, blessing her:

> And may the gods accomplish your desire:
> a home, a husband, and harmonious
> converse with him—the best thing in the world
> being a strong house held in serenity
> where man and wife agree. Woe to their enemies,
> joy to their friends! But all this they know best.
> [6.194-99]

Arriving at the palace, Odysseus clasps the knees of Arete, Nausicaa's mother and queen, and begs her mercy on his castaway status and long suffering. He clearly perceived that she served as the true power in Phaeacia—another vestige of ancient Minoan rule. On Ithaca, Penelope too receives the stranger gracefully and proceeds to match wits with him, fulfilling his homily to Nausicaa on the marriage of true minds.

The only other woman with whom Odysseus has a companionable relationship is Helen. On his foray into Troy after Achilles's death, Helen recognizes him in disguise. But homesick, she then plots with him against her adopted city. She draws him a bath, gives him a massage, provides him with fresh clothes (evidently woven on her own loom) and then helps him and Diomedes steal the Palladium. This wooden statue of Athena was kept in Troy and prophesized to keep the city safe so long as it remained in its possession. Later Aeneas took it to Rome. Odysseus also gains the advantage when Helen circles the Wooden Horse imitating the voices of the wives and sweethearts of the men inside. To preserve silence, Odysseus clamps his hand over one of the concealed warriors, foreshadowing how he later strives to save his crew by putting beeswax in their ears and other stratagems. Though originally queen of Sparta, Helen may be influenced by the cult of the ancient Near Eastern mother goddess, with strong roots in Anatolia, and grows more assertive while living in Troy. Though she clearly admires Odysseus and honors his son, there is no hint that she seeks to possess him like most of the other women and goddesses in the *Odyssey*.

Rituals reenact myths, and in traditional societies boys and girls are initiated into the adult community through special ceremonies in which they learn or discover their place in the world. For males, this is primarily farming, hunting, healing, or serving as a seer or shaman. For females, the ritual focuses on nurture, giving birth, and raising children, taking into account woman's unique gifts and talents.

As Joseph Campbell explains, after they have been inducted into the adult community, young initiates typically join other members of the tribe, culture, or society in ritual circle dances. The men customarily form a ring around the outside and the women twirl inside. The Homeric epics were originally performed to the accompaniment of rhythmic dancing as the poet or bard recited the text and played the lyre. Such performances hearkened back to the lost Minoan golden age. The architecture, frescoes, and other artwork on Crete display circle dances and a male bard playing the lyre. To visualize ancient round dances, A. P. David, author of *Dance of the Muses: Choral Theory and Ancient Greek Poetics*, created a video demonstration of the way in which a modern Greek syrtós, a dactylic circle dance, evolved from ancient performance and reflects Homeric hexameter. The dancers circle in clockwise spiral motions that accord with the planets, or heavenly gods, as seen from the earth. The video clip (http://danceofthemuses.org/ Home.html) includes recitations from the Catalogue of Ships in the *Iliad* and dancing in the court of Alcinous, where a pair of soloists plays with a ball, in the *Odyssey*.

The Corn God

The triumph of patriarchal society and the rise of violence in daily life may not be based solely on misogyny arising from an extreme animal-food based diet. Ancient female-oriented cultures honored a male vegetarian deity whose life, death, and rebirth mirrored the agrarian cycle of planting, harvest, and reseeding. In sacred ceremonies, the corn god's male representative was ritually dismembered, the parts scattered, and then reassembled as in the myths of Osiris, the Egyptian deity; Dumuzi, the Mesopotamian consort of Innana; and Tezcatlipoca, the Aztec god of night and sorcery. Sir Arthur Evans, who excavated Knossos, discovered a cache of children's bones in the palace that had knife marks suggestive of human sacrifice. Recent archaeological evidence from Chania in Crete suggests further cases dating to 1280 BCE. This would have been during the Mycenaean era centuries after the collapse of Minoan culture. While traditional Cretan civilization appears to be egalitarian, peaceful, and life-affirming, it is possible that in its long history, some priestesses and women engaged in extreme rituals. Under the influence of poppies, a major medicinal plant on the island, they could have enacted ecstatic trances and dances in which boys and men were the willing—or unwilling—victims. In the *Odyssey*, the lotus-eaters, Circe's drugs that turn men into swine, and Helen's potion that drowns all sorrow suggest that male apprehension and fear of feminine energy was not wholly unjustified.

In a provocative nutritional hypothesis, John Younger, a classicist at the University of Kansas, speculates that Minoan depictions of women with blue streaks in their eyes wearing saffon colored clothing, had high, or at least adequate, levels a vitamin A and B, while men's eyes, showing red streaks, may have been low in these nutrients. A major source of saffron and these nutrients is the crocus flower. In artwork, the crocus is associated solely with females. Younger believes that the Minoan civilization was a matriarchy and that practices like this could have "made the men angry and driven them to revolt." Just before or in anticipation of the Mycenaean takeover, he finds evidence that most farms and houses on the island were destroyed as the possible result of a revolution or revolt against female rule.

Later Greek mythology, when the sacrificial shoe was on the other foot, tells of the offering of many maidens to ward off plague, famine, war, or other disaster. The founding myth of Athens is based on the sacrifice of Chthonia, the youngest daughter of Erechteus, one of the founding rulers of the city, and the stone carvings of the Parthenon, the great temple dedicated to Athena, tell her story. Although not mentioned by Homer, the sacrifice of Iphigeneia, the daughter of Agamemnon and Clytemnestra, constitutes a central theme of the Trojan War. When high winds and choppy seas prevented the Acheans from launching their flotilla, Calchas the chief priest told Agamemnon that his daughter would have to be sacrificed. The Greek commander complied with the oracle, the elements abated, and the fleet sailed. However, the sacrifice appears to have driven both parents mad and helps to explain Agamemnon's hard, cruel behavior on the battlefield and Clytemnestra's thirst for revenge. Agamemnon lured his daughter to the camp on the pretext of marrying her to Achilles, and then slew her himself. Clytemnestra murdered her husband on his return from Troy many years later. Curiously, the deity who required the sacrifice was not a male, but a female—Artemis, the goddess of the hunt, who demanded the sacrifice after Agamemnon slew a deer from her sacred grove.

Despite its demonizing of women, Bronze Age society regarded the cosmos as primarily feminine. While the three divine brothers ruled the sky, waves, and afterlife, they each had spouses, and often multiple female partners, children, and offspring who wielded power behind the scenes. Besides the Olympian goddesses—Hera, Aphrodite, Athena, Demeter, Hestia, and Artemis—there were the many nature spirits, including the Nereides (sea nymphs), Naides (fresh water nymphs), Oceanides (ocean nymphs), Oreades (mountain nymphs), Horae (goddesses of the seasons), Aurai (nymphs of the breezes), the Hesperides (nymphs of the sunset, west, and evening), and nymphs of the Pleiades and other constellations. The Primordial goddesses, Titanesses, Muses, the Charities, and other groupings round out the female pantheon. Bronze and Iron Age males still lived in a largely feminine cosmos.

However, according to the natural laws of balance and harmony, ideological extremes fear, or seek to control, and even destroy, their opposites. Hence, extreme patriarchal society fears natural femininity and fosters a submissive ideal. Vice versa, in excess, matriarchy strives to control, subdue, or suppress true masculinity.

Most of the familiar Greek myths are misogynist. In Hesiod's *Theogony*, for example, Pandora is demonized as the source of evil in the world (like Eve in the Bible). From a Minoan or feminist perspective, the Greek myths are not hard to decode. The rape of Europa by Zeus symbolized the Mycenaean conquest of Crete and is often exact to the smallest details. The great storm god saw the beautiful maiden gathering flowers in a meadow with some nymphs and fell in love. Changing himself into a bull, Zeus breathed a crocus—the symbol of Minoan girls and young women—from his mouth and carried her to Crete. The product of their union was the Minotaur, the half-human, half-beast that has haunted Europe in many guises—Griffin, Centaur, Harpy, Siren, Vampire, Frankenstein's monster—ever since.

Coincidentally, Crete also figures in Helen's abduction or elopement. Coming to Sparta on a diplomatic mission for his father, Paris meets Menelaus and Helen. The young Trojan prince is smitten by Helen—the most beautiful woman in the world—and after Catreus, Menelaus's grandfather, suddenly dies and the Spartan king goes to Crete for his funeral, the two lovers flee to Troy. Catreus, a Cretan king, was a son of King Minos and Queen Pasiphae. Hence, Menelaus's extended family includes the Minotaur, the monstrous offspring of Minos. Though the Minotaur was by now dead, Helen may have decided not to accompany her husband to the Cretan funeral in order to avoid unpleasant memories associated with the dark bull of the family.

In the world of many turns and twists, truth is an elusive commodity. Three times after returning to Ithaca, Odysseus feigns to be a merchant from Crete. To Athena, Eumaios, and Penelope he weaves a fanciful identity as a traveler from "the land called Crete in the midst of the wine-dark sea." After being nourished for seven years by Calypso, he receives the blessings of her *labrys*, or double axe, the archetypal symbol of lost Cretan civilization and the equality between the sexes. At some level, if not the Olympian heights, Odysseus has transformed into a Minoan wayfarer with newborn respect for females and for the feminine principle within himself.

Minoan Culture and Achilles' Shield

As we have seen, Achilles' Shield mirrors both large cycles of history and small ones. On a macroscopic level, it corresponds with the Four/Five Ages; on the microscopic, with the events in the *Iliad* itself. In between, the Shield may also glance at the rise and fall of Minoan civilization.

For over a millennium, the wealthy, peaceful Aegean and Mediterranean sea power constituted a Golden Age, as depicted in the Circle of Agricultural Peace and Plenty on the Shield, when the fruits of the earth grew themselves (and even the ships had a mind of their own). The Silver and Bronze Ages are glanced at in the opposing Cities of Peace and War and in the Circle of Vintage and Pasturage with the children playing music and singing while two lions devour a bellowing bull. In the *Iliad*, Achilles, Menelaus, and Diomedes are described as lion like, and the Lion Gate, portraying two lions, was the entranceway to the Greek city of Mycenae. The bull was a principal symbol of strength and virility in Crete, and bull leaping a favorite pastime. The lions attacking the bull nod at the Mycenaean plunder of Minoan civilization. From the Greek perspective, slaying the Minotaur, or bull like monster that lived in the Labyrinth, and overthrowing the effeminate Cretan culture, may have justified their rule.

In the very next sentence in the *Iliad*, introducing the fourth and final Circle of the Dance, Homer segues into describing how Daedalus fashioned a dancing floor at Knossos. This entire quadrant, given to music, the arts, and joyous celebration, nods at the return of Minoan values and practices in a future epoch. The bard playing the lyre, the two acrobats, and other details in this circle mirror Minoan festivities and perfectly accord with the musical and gymnastic demonstrations the Phaeacians, a putative Minoan colony, arrange for Odysseus on his return.

The Authoress of the *Odyssey*

Homer's views of women have been debated since antiquity. Not surprisingly, in a work of universal literature, they range from extremely pro-female to violently anti-female. Samuel Butler, the English novelist and classicist, contended that the author of the *Odyssey* was a woman. "It was not till I got to Circe that it flashed upon me that I was reading the work, not of an old man, but of a young woman—and of one who knew not much more about what men can and cannot do that I had found her know about the milking of ewes in the cave of Polyphemus," Butter relates in *The Authoress of the Odyssey*.

Butler, author of *Erewhon* and other Victorian satires, was dead serious about his thesis that the real life Nausicaa composed the second of the great Greek epics. He cites the maiden's advice to Odysseus to bypass her father Alcinous and go straight to the seat of power, Queen Arete: "Never mind my father, but go up to my mother and embrace her knees; if she is well disposed towards you there is some chance of your getting home to see your friends again."

Butler describes many feminine touches in the story. In Hades, for example, "I do not think a male writer would have put the brides first, nor yet the young bachelors second." There follows encounters with a procession of illustrious wives and daughter of great princes. Only as an afterthought, at Alcinous's request, does he mention meeting the shades of Agamemnon, Achilles, and Ajax. In the story about Helen and the Wooden Horse, Butler notes, "A man might have made Helen walk round the horse, pat it, and even call out the names of the heroes, but he would never have thought of making her mimic their wives."

"I do not believe any man living could wash Odysseus's feet and upset the bath so delightfully as Eurykleia does," he avers. The same with how she folds Telemachus's clothes. As for fumigating the great hall after the final massacre, "The first thing a woman would have thought of after the suitors had been killed was the dining room carpet." Nor would a man have remarked about all the food and wine spoiled "by the upsetting of the tables at which the suitors had been sitting."

The same desire to extol women appears in "making the Sun leave his sheep and cattle in the sole charge of the two nymphs Lampetie and Phaethusa who, by the way, proved quite unable to protect them. But then the Sun was a man, and capable of any folly."

As for Calypso, in Butler's view, she is clearly "the master mind, not Odysseus; and, be it noted, that neither she nor Circe seem to have a manservant on their premises." He wonders if the Greek castaway were really so sagacious why didn't he discover Calypso's axe and auger and fashion a raft years earlier without her finding out about it. "As for the provisions, if Odysseus was not capable of accumulating a private hoard, his cunning has been much overrated. Though the authoress chooses to pretend that Odysseus was dying to get back to Penelope, she knew perfectly well that he was in no great hurry to do so."

As for Athena, "in the *Iliad* she is a great warrior but she is no woman: in the *Odyssey* she is a great woman but no warrior."

The writer of the *Odyssey,* Butler concludes, "is nothing if she is not young, self-willed, and unmarried… The poem is such a *tour de force* as none but a high-spirited, head-strong girl who had been accustomed to have her own way would have attempted, much less carried to such a brilliantly successful conclusion."

In an early twenty-first century study, Andrew Darby concludes in *Rediscovering Homer*, that a female poet most likely wrote both epics. "A woman singer, the most skillful of her generations, had already produced the *Iliad*, the quintessence of the old oral tradition. With added confidence and greater maturity, she was now able to create something newer and freer, a poem that would quietly and subversively build a woman's viewpoint into the traditional framework."

In a new translation of the *Odyssey* (U of California Press, 2018), Peter Green notes that the author may have been a she: "We do not know for certain who Homer was, or where he lived, or when he wrote. We cannot be absolutely certain that the same man (if it was a man) wrote both the *Iliad* and the *Odyssey*, or even that 'wrote' is a correct description of the method of composition involved."

In another new translation of the *Odyssey* (Norton, 2018), the first in English by a woman, Emily Wilson dismisses Butler's thesis: "It is more plausible to view the *Odyssey* as the product of archaic male imaginations, questioning and defending the inequalities of male dominance within the status quo." However, she does acknowledge that the portrait of Calypso, "a powerful but emotionally open female character, frustrated in her desire for the human she has rescued, is one of the most memorable sequences in the poem." With Campbell, she agrees that the epic raises questions about whether Odysseus will "bring the battlefield home with him." "In returning to Ithaca and to [the olive] bed, Odysseus has chosen a world in which his own work is part of something larger than himself, and where he is woven into relationships that are both rooted and changing." Wilson's translation takes a distinctly softer, more nuanced register than her male counterparts, and she portrays more humanely non-Western people and fabulous beings than previous translators. One of her most evocative insights is that "the cult of Athena in Greece may have originated from that of a Minoan owl goddess."

8
Return to Paradise

The Loom of History

In Greek mythology, the loom and shuttle symbolize domesticity, loving kindness, craft—and bondage. The Fates (Morai) spin the threads of fortune and misfortune on their distaffs and weave the destiny of life. In Cretan myth, Adriane gives Theseus the double axe to slay the Minotaur and the golden thread to lead him back safely. Weaving is a major motif in the Homeric poems, and Athena is the goddess of weaving. Beside Penelope—Helen, Andromache, Circe, Calypso, and Arete labor at their looms.

Weaving is exclusively woman's work. In the opening of the *Iliad*, Agamemnon replies insolently to Chryses, the priest of Apollo, who comes to ransom his daughter: "I will not free her. She shall grow old in my house at Argos far from her own home, busying herself with her loom and visiting my couch; so go, and do not provoke me or it shall be the worse for you." When Andromache begs him not to go forth in battle, Hector admonishes her, saying it is a man's duty to fight, even if he loses his life, and she and their son are taken into captivity: "It may be that you will have to ply the loom in Argos at the bidding of a mistress, or to fetch water from the springs Messeis or Hypereia, treated brutally by some cruel taskmaster; then will one say who sees you weeping, 'She was wife to Hector, the bravest warrior among the Trojans during the war before Ilium.'" On another occasion, he orders her: "Go, then, within the house, and busy yourself with your daily duties, your loom, your distaff, and the ordering of your servants; for war is man's matter, and mine above all others of them that have been born in Ilium." When Hector is finally slain, Andromache is the last to know: "Hector's wife had as yet heard nothing, for no one had come to tell her that her husband had remained without the gates. She was at her loom in an inner part of the house, weaving a double purple web, and embroidering it with many flowers."

In the opening of the *Odyssey*, Telemachus upbraids Penelope who objects to a minstrel singing a song of woe about the Achaeans lost on their return from the Trojan War: "Make up your mind to it and bear it; Odysseus is not the only man who never came back from Troy, but many another went down [to Hades] as well as he. Go, then, within the house and busy yourself with your daily duties, your loom, your distaff, and the ordering of your servants; for speech is man's matter, and mine above all others—for it is I who am master here." On the visit to Sparta, Telemachus distributes presents to Helen, including a golden distaff, a silver workbox full of fine spun yarn, and a distaff with violet colored wool laid upon its top.

The goddesses are also proficient in the textile arts. Arriving on Aeaea, Odyssey's men find the sorceress Circe singing beautifully "as she worked at her loom, making a web so fine, so soft, and of such dazzling colors as no one but a goddess could weave." Similarly, when Odysseus arrives at the nymph Calypso's, "She was busy at her loom, shooting her golden shuttle through the warp and singing beautifully."

In the city of the Phaeacians, Odysseus observes weaving at court: "There are fifty maid servants in the house, some of whom are always grinding rich yellow grain at the mill, while others work at the loom, or sit and spin, and their shuttles go, backwards and forwards like the fluttering of aspen leaves, while the linen is so closely woven that it will turn oil."

When he arrives in Ithaca and is dropped off by an isolated cave, Odyssey finds "great looms of stone on which the nymphs weave their robes of sea purple." Telemachus tells him that Penelope "does not often show herself even to the suitors, but sits at her loom weaving in an upper chamber, out of their way." In the palace, as the archery contest gets under way, Telemachus again rebukes his mother: "Go, then, within the house and busy yourself with your daily duties, your loom, your distaff, and the ordering of your servants. This bow is a man's matter, and mine above all others, for it is I who am master here."

Of course, the primary weaving symbol is Penelope's work on Laertes's burial shroud. As Antinous, the chief suitor, complains to Telemachus in the opening of the story:

> Here is an instance of her trickery:
> She had her great loom standing in the hall
> and the fine warp of some vast fabric on it;
> we were attending her, and she said to us:
> "Young men, my suitors, now my lord is dead,

> let me finish my weaving before I marry,
> or else my thread will have been spun in vain.
> It is a shroud I weave for Lord Laertes,
> when cold death comes to lay him on his bier.
> The country wives would hold me in dishonor
> if he, with all his fortune, lay unshrouded,"
> we have men's hearts; she touched them; we agreed.
> So every day she wove on the great loom—
> but every night by torchlight she unwove it;
> and so for three years she deceived the Achaeans.
> But when the seasons brought the fourth around,
> one of her maids, who knew the secret, told us;
> we found her unraveling the splendid shroud.
> She had to finish then, although she hated it.
> [2.100-118]

Intellectually, the husband and wife are well matched. Penelope is said to "weave a device," and Odysseus begs Athena to "weave a plan" to defeat the suitors. As Joseph Campbell observes, Odysseus and Penelope represent the sun and moon—the revolving, or weaving celestial bodies. The Greek warrior is in his nineteenth year when he comes home. Nineteen corresponds with the metonic cycle, a nineteen-year conjunction between the solar year and the lunar, or synodic, month. The cycle figures in Babylonian astrology, Chinese astrology, and the intercalary months of the Hebrew calendar. It is also found in the Antikythera mechanism, an ancient Greek analog computer, with multiple wheels and gears, that dates to about the third century BCE. The four years Penelope engages in this deception glance at the four phases of the moon and the end of a lunar cycle.

The much longer Vega/Polaris cycle also has four quadrants, and the *Odyssey* as a whole, like the *Iliad*, mirrors the four Ages of Humanity. The first stage, the Golden Age, is linked to Helen, the world's most beautiful woman, whom we earlier identified with Lost Paradise when she was abducted or eloped with Paris. Helen, like Penelope and the other women and goddesses, is an accomplished weaver. She is described in the epic as weaving a great purple tapestry displaying the horse-taming Trojans and the Achaeans fighting. Her artistic talents exceed even those of Penelope, whose "splendid" design for Laertes's shroud is not described, or Andromache's simple patterned flowers. Homer does not go into further detail about the elaborate scenes or pictures Helen creates. But in size and scope on her loom her artistry glances at Achilles' Shield, the outstanding mural in the epics.

The loom itself, in its size, grandeur, and intricacy, is a symbol of the cosmos, as frequent mention of the Fates spinning the threads of life and the destiny of people and nations attests. The weaving frame is also emblematic of the spiral of history, including the 25,800-year cycle of the precession of the equinoxes. In China, weaving figures prominently in the love story of the Weaving Maiden and the Cowherd. Zhinu, the weaver girl, and Niulang, the cowherd, fall in love, but the Goddess, the girl's mother, forbids their marriage, and they are banished to opposite sides of the Silver River. Once a year, on the seventh day of the seventh lunar month, a flock of magpies takes pity on the separated pair and forms a bridge to unite the lovers for one day. Celebrated today on July 7, the myth is the basis for major festivals throughout China, Japan, and the Far East.

The tale dates back 2600 years, about the same time as Homer. From the beginning the Weaving Girl was identified with Vega, a bright star in the constellation of Lyra and the then North Star; the Cowherd with Altair, the brightest star in the constellation of Aquila; and the Silver River with the Milky Way. The myth points to the gradual shift in the heavens. Once the Milky Way streamed directly overhead, showering its energy to earth, and ushered in an era of peace and plenty that was remembered ever after as the age of paradise. At this time, the two lovers were united. But about thirteen thousand years ago, Vega rose and assumed the throne of the celestial ruler or pole star. The lovers were separated as the Milky Way declined on the horizon and Altair moved to the other side. In the *Iliad*, Helen plays the role of the Weaving Maiden and Paris, a shepherd, the Cowherd. In the *Odyssey*, Penelope and Odysseus fulfill the roles. In his pre-Trojan war days, Odysseus raised animals, and his estate now teems with cattle, sheep, and goats. If he sets out with his oar right after the massacre and armistice with the townsfolk, it will be just one day that the two lovers reunite before separating again.

The Ages of Humanity

In the *Iliad*, Achilles's Shield depicts the universe, the Four Ages, and the history of humanity. The *Odyssey* also incorporates a cosmic dimension, culminating in the errand into the wilderness with the oar. The twelve ships en route to Ithaca, as Joseph Campbell further observes, represent the Zodiac. Like the sun, Odysseus is the solar force that shines brightly day in and day out. Like the moon, Penelope is the waning and waxing lunar orb who weaves and unweaves the shroud to conceal her true intentions. The oar itself resembles the Great Bear, the constellation in the Northern Sky that points to the Pole Star. Calypso bids Odysseus to hold these stars on his left as he pilots his raft. The Wain (a farm cart) and Plough were other traditional names for the constellation. Coincidentally, with its long handle and flat blade, this star cluster also resembles a gigantic oar rowing through the celestial waters.

Like Heracles's 12 Labors, Odysseus experiences a dozen adventures on his Return, emblematic of passing through the twelve constellations. Another heavenly symbol is the contest of the bow in which an arrow is shot through the socket rings of twelve axes. All of these astrological links point not only to the earth's annual journey through the Zodiac but also to the larger cycles of human history, culture, and civilization.

The three animals Odysseus is told to sacrifice after planting his oar are a ram, a bull, and a boar. These creatures glance at the Age of Aries the Ram, which coincides with the Bronze and early Iron Ages and the era in which the Homeric epics take place; the Age of Taurus the Bull, the previous era, coinciding with the Golden Calf in the Bible; and the Boar, the Eastern equivalent to Pisces the Fish, which followed the Homeric era and is ending today. They represent past, present, and future—the same order as depicted in the concentric circles on Achilles' Shield. These animals also appear prominently in the narrative. Odysseus escapes the clutches of the Cyclops by holding on to the underbelly of a ram. His crew defies the gods and feast on the bulls and cows of the Sun. Eurykleia, the old nursemaid, recognizes her master from the scar on his thigh that was inflicted in his youth by a wild boar. She also recognizes it while bathing his feet, which are ruled by Pisces in astrology. Odysseus's men are also turned into swine, a domesticated type of boar.

Today, we are approaching the dawn of the Aquarian Age. In Greek mythology, the concept goes back to Ganymede, the Trojan shepherd boy. Entranced with his beauty, Zeus swoops down in the form of an eagle and brings him back to Mt. Olympus where he serves as the cupbearer to the gods dispensing nectar and ambrosia. In this capacity, he is immortalized as the constellation Aquarius the Water Bearer. Odysseus is also linked to this sign because of his seaborne adventures, his devotion to Zeus, Athena, and the other gods, and his role in restoring order in Ithaca. On Scheria, he receives a flask of olive oil and a pitcher of wine from Nausicaa, symbolizing Aquarius's two jugs and the unifying principle of yin and yang, the complementary opposite energies that make up all things. The "blessed peace" promised him by Tiresias is nothing less than the dawn of the new Aquarian or Golden Age.

Each of the twelve astrological ages lasts 2150 years. Together they make up 25,800 years. The precessional cycle, as we have seen, is based on the slight wobble of the earth on its axis, as it courses through the heavens and the North Star gradually changes. This cycle is also known as the Ages of Humanity, the Platonic Year, and the Vega/Polaris Cycle.

Metals play a significant role in the *Odyssey* as they do in the *Iliad*. The main difference is that bronze figures prominently in the first epic, while iron is highlighted in the second. Let's look at some instances: Odysseus is consistently described as hard and strong-willed as iron. After hearing of his father's daring from Menelaus, Telemachus declares that he must have "iron in his breast." In putting out the Cyclops' eye, Odysseus tempers the spike "the way they make soft iron hale and hard." In bidding farewell to her captive, Calypso contrasts her love to his: "There are hearts made of cold iron—but my heart is kind." On his return to Ithaca, Odysseus's fashions a fake identity for himself as a merchant from Crete dealing in metals. Athena counsels Odysseus to show "iron patience." In her initial encounter with her husband, Penelope notes his lack of outward emotion: "His eyes might have been made of horn or iron for all that she could see." Later, Odysseus returns the observation, "Her heart is iron in her breast." Directing the swineherd to lock up the weapons in the hall, Odysseus moralizes, "Tempered iron can magnetize a man." The twelve axes set out in the contest of the bow are made of bronze and iron, glancing at the transition from the Bronze to the Iron Age and the coming era of lawlessness and vice. As the stranger tells Penelope, Odysseus will arrive in time for the contest "long before one of these lads can stretch or string that bow or shoot to thread the iron."

The precious metals play a minor role in Odysseus's return. Telemachus receives the gift of a wine bowl wrought with silver and lined with gold on his visit to Menelaus and Helen. Made by Hephaestus, the forger of the Shield, it suggests a quasi-ethical Silver Age court. More significantly, Odysseus and Penelope's great bed is inlaid with gold, silver, and ivory. The metals of the first and second age of higher spirituality and social justice are tempered by ivory. In describing her dream, Penelope declares there are two types: true dreams that enter through the gate of horn and false dreams of ivory. In this case, the inlaid ivory on their bed symbolizes *metis*, combining intellectual cunning and ethical ju-jitsu, the trait that allows both to survive, defeat the suitors, and reunite.

Like the two types of dreams, the Vega Cycle features one of two modes of destruction at each pole (every twelve to thirteen thousand years): the first by water or flood and the other by fire. In the Odyssey, these figure in Zeus's utter destruction of Odysseus's last ship: "Zeus let fly with his bright bolt and split my ship, rolling me over in the wine-dark sea." Washed up on Calypso's island, he is freed after seven years and departs on the raft he fashions only to capsize once again: "For blows aplenty awaited me from the god who shakes the earth. Cross gales he blew, making me lose my bearings, and heaved up seas beyond imagination—huge and foundering seas." Unlike Zeus, Poseidon does not wield a thunderbolt, but he shakes a trident. Returning from the "Sunburned land" in Asia, where the hot sun provokes his wrath, he churns up the deep "with both hands on his trident." Losing his oar—his direction in life—Odysseus is rescued by Ino, the Nereid, who "like a diving bird" breaks the surface of the waters and gives him her veil. The bird is a symbol of higher consciousness, or vision, and the divine veil guides him to Scheria, the Minoan-like island and symbol of the construction of the new Golden Age.

The number of suitors also has an astrological correlate. 108 is the product of the twelve houses (Ares, Taurus, etc.) and the then known nine planets. All around the world 108 is a sacred number. In Hinduism there are 108 beads on the *mala*, or Hindu rosary. In Chinese astrology, there are 108 sacred stars. In the *Odyssey*, meting out justice to the 108 suitors signifies conquest or mastery of the universe, similar to shooting the arrow through the socket rings of the twelve axes. At a spiritual level, 108 represent the number of sins, defilements, or delusions. In Buddhism, there are 108 earthly temptations a person must overcome to achieve nirvana. At the end of the year, temple bells in Japan are rung 108 times to finish the old year and ring in the new.

The cosmic dimension to Odyssey's final task is further alluded to when he tells Penelope of his meeting with Tiresias:

> Wife, we have not yet reached the boundary of all our trials,
> But still a labor that will be unmeasured,
> Manifold, and difficult, remains for me to complete.

"Unmeasured" means vast, all-embracing, universal. It is to the supreme, most sublime level of awareness that Odysseus is guided and the epic concludes.

Helen's Magic

Helen's name means "bright," and as the embodiment of the Golden Age, she symbolizes the radiance the Achaeans fight for after its loss. But looking back, as Orpheus does at Eurydice, another avatar of this paradisical era, is to contravene the cosmic law. It is to go backward, rather than forward, around the Shield of the Four Ages and the spiral of history. Since the Trojans also dwell in the past (a mythic world of taming horses and unlimited abundance), they are also doomed. In contrast, Helen is always present. Her kindly, compassionate nature shines throughout the epics, as she sympathizes with warriors and their families on both sides. In the end, the Greeks triumph, and she returns to Sparta and reunites with Menelaus, her first husband, and daughter Hermione. Their kingdom is no golden age, but it has elements of silver, or partial virtue, as symbolized by the several references to this metal during Telemachus's visit. Their marriage is sonless, so the future of their realm is problematic, and like most Greek city-states will decline ethically and spiritually in the Iron Age.

In contrast to both Circe and Calypso who seek to keep their visitor for themselves, Helen's chief role in the *Odyssey* is to affirm Telemachus's budding manhood and give him the confidence to return to Ithaca, stand up to the suitors, and help his father restore order in the palace. Until then, he only daydreams about governing in his own right. Despite declarations to his mother that "I am master here," Telemachus is at heart still an adolescent tied to Penelope's apron strings and loom. As in the *Iliad*, Helen continues to berate herself for her role in sparking a horrific war. But she is consistently kind and gracious. To Telemachus and the others traumatized by the conflict and its aftermath, she drops in the wine an anodyne—"mild magic of forgetfulness"—that frees her guests from all worries for a day. This elixir glances at the forgetfulness that the lotus flower and Circe's rich fare bring to Odysseus's crew. The potion replaces remembering—painful as it is and genuine self-reflection—with oblivion and a false paradise. Homer implies that if everything were perfect, there would be no growth and development, no insight or understanding, no trespasses and forgiveness, no enlightenment and meaning—no human life. It is the bargain Odysseus rejects when he turns down Calypso's offer of immortality and eternal youth for a harrowing return to Ithaca and a beloved wife who may or may not be faithful and whose outward beauty will fade. As the shade of Agamemnon warns him in Hades, Penelope may follow the example of Clytemnestra, his wife, who slew him with her lover Aegisthus upon his return from Troy.

In Hades, Odysseus is shocked when the shade of Achilles tells him that he would rather have been a simple farmer and lived to a ripe old age than a renowned warrior cut down in the prime of his life. Such an admission is heresy to the male Bronze Age code in which *kleos*, or eternal glory was attained by mortal combat. To reawaken his martial spirit, Odysseus regales Achilles with news of the glorious role his son, Neoptolemus, played in the final defeat of Troy. For a moment, Achilles is pacified.

This prevailing masculine ethic is also alluded to when Athena in disguise asks Telemachus if he is truly Odysseus's son. She means psychologically or spiritually in the sense of rising to the challenge and outwitting the suitors. The young man takes her question literally and replies: "I'll try, my friend, to you a frank answer. Mother has always told me I'm his son, it's true. But I'm not so certain." Iron-clad paternity and male succession were the lynchpin of evolving patriarchal Mycenaean and Classical Greek culture.

The Song of the Bow

Archery is another iconic theme in the Homeric epics. The *Iliad* begins with Apollo unleashing a plague on the Achaeans with his arrows, and the *Odyssey* ends with the contest of the bow and the slaying of the suitors. As we have seen, from the largest perspective, the contest of the bow represents the arrow of time spiraling through the twelve world ages, or the precession of the equinoxes and the destiny of humanity. The composite bronze and iron axes signify the passage from the Bronze to the Iron Age.

In addition to the final massacre, the bow plays a crucial role in the Trojan War saga. After the deaths of Hector and Achilles, we learn from Sophocles' play *Philoctetes* and the *Little Iliad*, a non-Homeric sequel, Odysseus ambushes Helenus, one of Priam's sons who is a seer, and under torture forces him to predict that victory will come to the Achaeans when Philoctetes, a Thessalian warrior, joins the fray with his bow and arrows. Philoctetes has a powerful bow once owned by Heracles, but on the way to Troy ten years earlier had been bitten by a snake and abandoned on an Aegean island. Odysseus rushes back to find Philoctetes, help him heal, and bring him back to Troy. With his mighty bow, Philoctetes slays Paris, who ironically is an archer himself. In the Bronze Age, archers were considered cowardly because they fought at a distance and did not engage in hand-to-hand combat. Hector and the other Trojans humiliate Paris for hiding behind a bow in the same way he hides behind Helen's skirt. Paris's death does not immediately end the war, but it marks a major propaganda victory. Odysseus goes on to select Philoctetes as one of the men he conceals in the Wooden Horse.

Odysseus's bow also has an illustrious history. As Homer relates, it was originally owned by Eurytos, king of Oechalia, and given to Odysseus by his son Iphitos after his father's death. In their youth, Eurytos and Odysseus meet in Messenia and exchange gifts. Odysseus receives the bow in return for a lance and sharp sword. Soon after, Iphitos is slain by Heracles, who covets his mares and colts. As a keepsake in memory of his friend, Odysseus decides not to take the weapon to Troy but leave it at home. He considers it a sign of peace and friendship, not war and enmity. Also the bow is inlaid with horn, probably from an ibex, which gives it its tensile strength. As Penelope explains to him in her dream, horn is a sign of honesty or deeds. Ivory, in contrast, is linked to teeth and represents lying and false promises. Because of disloyal, eavesdropping servants, Penelope converses with her husband obliquely, only hinting at the archery contest and the bow of horn when she describes the two types of dreams.

The test of the bow is foreshadowed in the *Iliad*. After Hector's death, Achilles sets out ten double axes of dark iron and ten single axes and some way off the mast of a ship set in the sand to which he tethers a fluttering pigeon. "Whoever hits the fluttering pigeon will get all the double axes to take back home as prizes, while the man who misses the bird, but hides the cord, will win the single axes, since his shot's the less accurate." Meriones, a Cretan warrior, wins the competition, and the bird, hit by his arrow mid-breast falls on the mast of the dark-browed vessel very much like Odysseus clinging to the mast of his capsized boat. Earlier, Meriones gave Odysseus a bow and quiver, a sword, and a helmet with the design of a wild boar's gleaming tusks. All of these gifts also prefigure Odysseus's return to Ithaca. Curiously, in the *Iliad*, the helmet is described as once owned by Autolykos, Odysseus's grandfather. Autolykos gave Odysseus his name, meaning "pain" or "trouble," and on one occasion visiting his grandfather he was gored by a wild boar. The scar, of course, figures in Eurykleia's recognition of the mysterious stranger when he comes to the palace in Ithaca. Penelope, by the way, asks the old servant woman to bathe the visitor, showing that she probably recognizes him at first sight and knows she will discover the scar and confirm the stranger's identity.

In the *Odyssey*, as we saw, Calypso gives Odysseus a bronze double-axe to fell a tree to build the raft that will take him home (by way of Phaeacia). The tool's shape and form (two complementary blades) suggest a yin/yang equality between the sexes. Learning to harmonize with feminine energy is the central theme of the *Odyssey*. As mythologist Joseph Campbell explains, after ten years in the killing fields of Troy, Odysseus is unfit for ordinary life, especially the domestic round of marriage and fatherhood and the civic life of ruling a small island. On the journey home, Odysseus needs ten years of encountering the feminine principle—in the form of various goddesses, monsters, sorceresses, and humans—to decompress and return to normal. Calypso's gift of the double-axe—the ancient Minoan symbol of harmony between the sexes—symbolizes the quest. In the course of the Trojan war and his journey home, Odysseus encounters a constellation of females: Circe, Scylla, Charybdis, the Sirens, Antikleia (his mother), Calypso, Ino, Nausicaa, Arete, Athena, Eurykleia, and

Penelope. Shooting an arrow through the dozen double-axe heads symbolizes successfully integrating the feminine energy of these twelve into him psyche. Twelve—the archetypal number of the Zodiac—represents wholeness and completion.

Odysseus's Encounter with Feminine Energy

Female	Symbol	Challenge	Resolution
1. Circe	Drugs, whips	Poison, spells	Threats, force
2. Charybdis	Whirlpool	Mass destruction	Middle way
3. Scylla	Monster	Selective destruction	Sacrifice
4. Sirens	Seductive songs	Hubris, glory	Self-control
5. Antikleia	Grief	Guilt	Acceptance
6. Calypso	Double axe	Immortality & eternal youth	Sorrow & tears
7. Ino	Veil	Attachment	Detachment
8. Nausicaa	Beach ball	Kindness	Gratitude
9. Arete	Elegant clothes	Nobility	Respect
10. Athena	Aegis, olive	Wisdom	Skillful means
11. Eurykleia	Bath	Obedience	Humility
12. Penelope	Loom	Loyalty	Trust

In Scheria, Odysseus relates his athletic prowess in several sports but tells Alcinous and his court that he is best with the bow. In Ithaca, when Odysseus disguised as a beggar, takes his turn with the bow, Homer describes it in musical terms:

> ... the man skilled in all ways of contending,
> satisfied by the great bow's look and heft,
> like a musician, like a harper, when
> with quiet hand upon his instrument
> he draws between his thumb and forefinger
> a sweet new string upon a peg: so effortlessly
> Odysseus in one motion strung the bow.
> Then slid his right hand down the cord and plucked it,
> so the taut gut vibrating hummed and sang
> a swallow's note.
> [21.460-469]

The bow is stored and shot upright, but strung sitting down. As Benjamin Haller observes in "The Gates of Horn and Ivory in Odyssey

19: Penelope's Call for Deeds, Not Words," the reason none of the suitors can string it is because it has to be strung in a kneeling posture and held horizontally. The vertical/horizontal polarity glances at the transition from lower sensory and emotional consciousness to higher intellectual and social awareness. As its comparison to a musical instrument indicates, the bow marks the return of art, culture, and justice to Odysseus's household and to Ithaca as a whole. It is a token of memory, peace, and friendship. Beyond restoring order to his household, Odysseus is probably thinking of Iphitos, the comrade of his young adulthood and first peace mission, when he strings the bow.

The idea for the archery test is Penelope's. She may devise this stratagem because she realizes that only Odysseus knows the secret of how to string the mighty implement. Like young Arthur who pulls the sword from the stone, he alone has the knowledge and saving grace to bend the bow to his will.

The massacre takes place on the feast day of Apollo, a fitting bookend to the opening of the *Iliad* with the archer god raining arrows of plague on the Achaeans. The Greeks have brought down his *menis*, or wrath, for refusing to ransom Chryseis, the captive daughter of a priest of Apollo. Odysseus leads the embassy that reverses Agamemnon's folly and returns her safely to her father. Though Apollo favors Troy and protects Paris through most of the fighting, he respects Odysseus's honorable action and befriends him when he returns to Ithaca, especially after he spares one of his priests following the sack of Ismaros. The gods do not hesitate to change sides when it serves their interests. Athena, for example, has been the staunchest supporter of the Achaeans in the siege of Troy. But when Lorcrian Ajax takes her statue and violates sanctuary by abducting Cassandra from Athena's temple in the sack of Troy, she wrecks vengeance on the entire expeditionary force, and few reach home.

As stringed instruments, the bow and the lyre share a similar form and construction. Both are also linked to healing. Apollo is not only the divine archer. He is the god of music and the god of medicine. (The Hippocratic Oath begins, "I swear by Apollo, divine physician . . ."). The plague he rains on the Greek camp in the opening of the *Iliad* is an example of an extreme remedy he inflicts to purge the body politic. In the *Odyssey*, the suitors—a plague infesting Ithaca and on a larger canvas representative of an epidemic of idleness and unsustainable consumption spreading virally until modern times—is cleansed with the purifying arrows of Odysseus, the master bowman and reciter of his own poetic epic. The fire and brimstone used to purify the great hall—the planet—glance at the destruction by fire and water at the end of the Vega cycle.

The contest with the bow wonderfully illustrates how the *metis*, or craft, of husband and wife complement each other and demonstrate conclusively that Odysseus has come home and deserves to reunite with Penelope and rule the island. It is equivalent to a thunderclap and lightning bolt from Zeus. But the subsequent massacre is little more than an expression of Odysseus's wrath, or *menis*, the same titanic rage that overcomes Achilles. Only with Hector's death and mutilation of his corpse can Achilles avenge Patroclus's death and appease the demons in his own breast. Against this background, it is imperative for Homer to add the post-Odyssey odyssey—foreshadowed by Tiresias's prophecy in Hades—and its Golden Age conclusion. It is integral to the entire journey and not an interpolation or tacked on ending. Otherwise the *Odyssey* is just another Bronze Age epic.

The Circle of the Dance

Music, song, and dance permeate the Homeric epics beginning with the opening lines. The word "sing," "voice," or "tell" is the first word in the *Odyssey* and, in some translations, the first word in the *Iliad* as well:

Odyssey
Sing in me, Muse, and through me tell the story—Robert Fitzgerald
Tell me, Muse, of the man of many ways, who was driven—Richard Lattimore
Sing to me of the man, Muse, the man of twists and turns—Robert Fagles

Iliad
Sing, goddess, the anger of Peleus' son Achilleus—Richard Lattimore
Anger be now your song, immortal one—Robert Fitzgerald
Rage — Goddess, sing the rage of Peleus' son Achilles—Robert Fagles

"Muse" in the opening invocation of the Odyssey refers to one of the nine goddesses of literature, sciences, and the arts who speaks or sings through the poet. The goddess addressed in the *Iliad* may be Calliope, the muse of epic poetry, or one of the other muses in Homer and Hesiod's canon. Several lines later, in the opening passage of the *Odyssey*, Homer repeats his request to the Muse, daughter of Zeus, to sing the story of Odysseus and his adventures. In the court of the Phaeacians, the blind singer Demodokos, beloved by the Muse, entertains Odysseus, who opines that all singers and poets are to be cherished because a Muse has taught them. Demodokos proceeds to sing how the Achaeans sailed away from Troy, leaving the Wooden Horse behind. In Hades, the spirit of

Agamemnon tells the shade of Achilles that all nine Muses mourned his death and one sang at his funeral, reducing all the Argives to tears. In the *Iliad*, the Olympian gods listen to Apollo and the Muses sing after banqueting. Several times, Homer invokes their aid, for example, in telling how Hector set fire to the Achaean ships. We also learn that the singer Thamyris boasted he could sing better than the Muses, and his memory was taken away for his arrogance.

Of course, not all music is divine, as the enchanting songs of Circe and the Sirens attest. The suitors too are portrayed as singing and dancing every night during their wanton feasts, and several times death and dying are likened by Homer to dancing, as when the treasonous servant women are hung. Exuberant singing or dancing is usually linked to alcohol. In later Greek myth, wine is associated with Dionysis, god of the grape harvest, fertility, and divine madness or ecstasy, but he is scarcely mentioned in the Homeric epics. While spinning tales to Eumaios, the old swineherd, Odysseus confesses: "Here's a wishful tale that I shall tell. The wine's behind it, vaporing wine, that makes a serious man break down and sing, kick up his heels and clown, or tell some story that were best untold."

Whether or not wine loosened Odysseus's tongue, Eumaios later confides to Penelope that the newly arrived stranger has bardic gifts:

> There was no end to what he made me hear
> of his hard roving and I listened, eyes
> upon him, as a man drinks in a tale
> a minstrel sings—a minstrel taught by heaven
> to touch the hearts of men. At such a song
> the listener becomes rapt and still. Just so
> I found myself enchanted by this man.
>
> [17.577-83]

Like Odysseus, Achilles is also linked to music. In his tent, he plays the lyre, which he confiscated on the raid that took captive Briseis, the young woman whose attachment sparks the feud with Agamemnon. Like Paris and Helen, the best of the Achaeans risks all for a woman whose beauty and grace have captivated him. After saving Paris from defeat by Menelaus in single combat, Aphrodite whisks him back to Helen's bed and tells her: "You wouldn't think he'd just come from fighting a man, but was off to a dance, or had just finished dancing." One night, Agamemnon grows apprehensive viewing the campfires of the Trojans and the sound of their flutes and pipes. On another occasion, Ajax raises the alarm: "Can't you hear the way that Hector's firing up all his troops in his consuming passion to set the ships ablaze? It's not to a dance he's inviting them but to battle!"

Memory and forgetfulness are one of the great themes of the epics. In the *Iliad*, Achilles's wrath causes him to forget his humanity. In the throes of combat, most of the other warriors on both sides also turn bestial and carry out the worst atrocities. Remembrance is the dominant motif of the *Odyssey* as Odysseus continually strives to remain awake physically and spiritually to fulfill his quest. The crew falls prey to the lotus flower, the Cyclops' provisions, Circe's table, and the succulent flesh of the cattle of the Sun. These foods weaken their resolve, lead them to forget their homeland, and ultimately bring their destruction and deaths.

Only on Ithaca, whose landscape he can't recall upon landing, does Odysseus's memory, like the bow he stretches, fully contract, and his resolve, like the arrow he later shoots, prove true. In a gesture of gratitude, he kisses the grain-bearing earth, and with Athena weaves a strategy to defeat the suitors. With the possible exception of Penelope, only Argos the aged dog recognizes him at first sight. Only when she sees and remembers the scar does Eurykleia realize her master has returned. Telemachus is too young to remember his father and only recognizes him when Athena enhances and brightens his countenance. Laertes too has forgotten his son, but Odysseus jogs his memory with details of his beloved orchard.

The preeminent symbol of memory in the epics is Achilles's Shield with its mandala of the cosmos and the circles of human culture and civilization. Music and dance, the blessings of the Muses, whose mother Mnemosyne is the goddess of memory, appear in each of the quadrants. In the first, depicting the circles of peace and war, the townsfolk celebrate marriages and banquets. Young men dance to the accompaniment of flutes and lutes. In the other half of this circle, as soldiers wait in ambush, a pair of herdsmen playing their pipes walks into the trap. Soon their merry tunes are replaced by the discordant sounds of Strife and Tumult, and their blood runs scarlet by the riverbed.

In the next circle, the Golden Age, the plowmen tend their rich fields of grain, as the king watches them bring in the sheaves. Heralds prepare a feast, while the women lavishly sprinkle white barley upon the fatted ox for the farmhands' dinner. Music and dance are not directly mentioned, but prayers and chants would have accompanied the sacrifice and libations, and pipes, harps, and perhaps drums accompanied the banquet.

In the third quadrant, the Circle of Vintage and Pasturage, the grape pickers are serenaded by a boy with a clear-toned lyre whose sweet music and voice "soft and exquisite." Hephaestus describes him as singing the

Linos song glancing at the legendary musician and first mortal given the gift of divine song and slain in jealously by Apollo. While harvesting the honey-sweet fruit, the reapers stamp their feet to the beat, shout, and dance along with him.

In the fourth quadrant, the Circle of the Dance, young men and women dance together, with hands on each other's wrists. Their space is likened to the dancing floor in Knossos that Daedalus, the great architect, fashioned for Ariadne. Indeed, all four quadrants glance at the joyful, peaceful Minoan civilization that was displaced by the Mycenaeans and later Hellenes. Using the Four Ages as a template, we may say the virtue of the golden and silvery Minoan culture declined by one-half following the volcanic eruption on Thera and the arrival of Bronze Age warriors and Indo-European values from the mainland. It decreased another quarter during the Age of Heroes and the war between the Achaeans and Trojans. It will vanish altogether with the approaching Iron Age and return in a new Golden Age of song and dance, peace and plenty, in the long course of the Spiral of History.

In an elaborate description of Hephaestus's handiwork in the circle of the dance, we are told:

> Now they would dance in a circle, feet well-skilled,
> very lightly, as when a potter sits at a wheel that matches
> his hands' grasp, and tries it, to see how it will run;
> and now they'd approach each other in dancing lines
> while a crowd of spectators stood round them, much enjoying
> such an element dance, and among them a sacred bard
> sang to his lyre, and two tumblers whirled among them,
> taking the lead in all their sport and pleasure.
> [18.599-606]

The last circle on the Shield glances at the construction of the new Golden Age. The unifying principle of yin and yang is symbolized by the two dynamic tumblers in the above passage. Today we are at the cusp of the end of the Iron Age and the start of a new precessional cycle. The supreme task we face today is finding a way out of the labyrinth of our own devising. As Joseph Campbell explained, the mythic quest is to die to our animal nature, open our heart chakra or central energy channel, and transform into compassionate human beings. The *Iliad* and *Odyssey* are Bronze Age epics set in an era of widespread marauding, violence, and war. The biological foundation for this disorder and forgetfulness, then as now, is excessive animal food consumption. In the ancient world, sacrifices and libations to the gods tempered this excess. But the heavy, contracted energy of cattle, sheep, and swine, complemented by the overly expansive energy of hot spices, wine, and lotus-like drugs creates a volatile mind and spirit. Wrath—the governing emotion of the Homeric epics and the succeeding Iron Age—is directly connected with liver problems and excessive meat consumption. In the Far East, the word for "anger" is "liver disease."

A major turning point on Odysseus's journey comes on Aiaia, Circe's island. Hermes gives him *moly* "a great herb with holy force to keep your mind and senses clear." The plant has a black root and milky white flower, symbolizing the union of opposites. Armed with knowledge of the unifying principle, the hero confronts the sorceress and remains immune to the mischievous drug and magic spell that turned his men into swine. Combining light and dark, horizontal and vertical, and yang and yin, *moly* contributes to intellectual development and mastery of the senses and emotions. As a gift of Hermes, the god of transitions and boundaries, *moly* embodies the power and wisdom of the higher plant kingdom. Its contrast with the lotus flower is striking. The lotus flower, eaten alone, consists of a single, extreme energy and leads to forgetfulness and separation. The *moly* flower is balanced with its root and contributes to remembrance and unification. On Odysseus's journey, this hermetic herbal represents the transition from a warrior's meat-centered diet and behavior to a citizen's plant-centered way of eating, thinking, and living. The final errand with the oar represents a higher octave of the same transformation.

Today, factory-farmed beef, pork, chicken, fish, and dairy have replaced traditional free-range livestock and animal products. Sacrifice is unknown in modern slaughterhouses, and the spiritual covenant with the animal world has long been severed. On the other end of the food spectrum, sugar, high-fructose corn syrup, and GMO sugar beets have replaced honey as principal sweeteners, and alcohol, opioids, and other drugs have also increased in potency many times. Combined with monocropping, chemical fertilizers, pesticides, and additives, as well as high energy processing methods and electrical cooking, microwave, and other artificial forms of fire, the modern food and agricultural system is in danger of no longer sustaining human life and the environment.

In contrast, Odysseus learns to respect the divine and animal kingdoms. He rejects the cannibalistic practices of the Cyclops, Laestrygonians, and Scylla. By controlling his appetites and remembering his return, he begins to transform human suffering into understanding and compassion.

Odysseus's own name means "pain" and "sorrow" and was bestowed on him by his grandfather Autolykos, a great thief and swindler. On a visit to his grandfather, young Odysseus went hunting on Mt. Parnassus and was gored by a wild boar. The wound healed but symbolically marked him for the rest of his life. It signifies his initiation into adulthood. In the *Iliad*, he gives free play to this wild, swinish nature and inflicts pain and brings sorrow to others. The following description of a wild boar could equally apply to Homer's hero: "Intelligent, equipped with keen senses, enduring, swift, wise to the ways of humans, wary, feisty, and aggressive when cornered, all of this makes the wild boar one of the most challenging and difficult game animals." In the *Odyssey*, Odysseus gradually dies to his boar-like nature and develops human qualities. In slaughtering the suitors and servant women he reverts to his lower nature. He behaves like a wild boar, slashing with his tusk-like bow and spear. He only comes to his senses when Phemios, the minstrel, clings to his knees:

> "Mercy, mercy on a suppliant, Odysseus!
> My gift is song for men and for the gods undying.
> My death will be remorse for you hereafter.
> No one taught me: deep in my mind a god
> shaped all the various ways of life in song.
> And I am fit to make verse in your company
> as in the god's."
>
> [22.386-93]

Odysseus spares Phemios and Medon, Telemachus's herald and boyhood caretaker. As this episode suggests, song, music, and dance offer a way out of the labyrinth. They help awaken and bring people into community with each other. They help drown out personal anger and sorrow. In the ancient Aegean world, from ancient Crete and Thera to utopian Phaeacia, piping and tunes accompanied all daily activities, from planting seeds to harvesting the grain and baking bread, from rowing galleys to competing in athletic competitions, from marriages and banquets to sacrifices and burials. Today the music of the terrestrial and celestial spheres has all but disappeared.

After the rest of the suitors are slain, Odysseus orders the harpist Phemios to choose a tune for dancing: "Some lighthearted air, and strum it. Anyone going by, or any neighbor, will think it is a wedding feast he hears." In one of his last displays of *metis*, or cunning, Odysseus deceives the town into thinking that the marriage rites for Penelope are being observed. This will give him and his family time to rally and decide their next move in defusing the anger of the relatives of the suitors, as well as the families whose fathers, brothers, and sons did not return with him from Troy. Thanks to Athena and Zeus's intervention, further conflict is avoided. As Homer relates:

> Athena cast a grey glance at her friend and said:
> "Son of Laertes and the gods of old,
> Odysseus, master of land ways and sea ways,
> Command yourself. Call off this battle now,
> or Zeus who views the wide world may be angry."
> He yielded to her, and his heart was glad.
> Both parties later swore to terms of peace set by their arbiter,
> Athena, daughter of Zeus who bears the storm-cloud as a shield.
> [24.606-13]

The ending of the Odyssey invokes the magnificent vision on the divine Shield. The assembly Hephaestus depicts to decide the legal case before it applies as much to Ithaca as it does to Troy. The assembly, a council or elders that decides matters peacefully, is also described as a circle, glancing at the ring dances and other joyful celebrations of daily life. As history unfolds after Homer's time, the assembly of elders metamorphoses into primitive all-male democratic and republican bodies in Athens and Rome, Magna Carta, Kouroukan Fouga (the great thirteenth century Mandan Charter of West Africa), the rights of the commons, the Declaration of Independence and U.S. Constitution, and the United Nations Declaration of Human Rights. If the earth is to survive, tribal, ethnic, religious, and national divisions and boundaries of all kinds will have to be erased as humanity unites to create a planetary commonwealth.

Return to a more natural way of life, based on natural and organic farming and a grain-centered, predominantly plant-based way of eating is the key to change at all levels. As the United Nations' report *Livestock's Long Shadow* (FAO, 2006) concluded, the global cattle and other livestock industries are the single biggest contributor to global warming, more than all the cars, trucks, buses, trains, and planes combined. This is truly devouring the cattle of the Sun and paying the supreme price!

The Bronze Age was a violent, brutal era, and meat eating was the norm among rulers, the aristocracy, and heroes. As Barry Strauss points out in *The Trojan War*, ordinary soldiers were the ones who "never got the best cuts of meat, if they got meat at all; the ones who never tasted fish; the ones who lived mainly on a diet of beans and barley . . . They washed down the food with young, unseasoned wine, rather than the fine Thracian vintages brought by ship to Agamemnon daily; they mixed their wine and water in wooden rather than silver bowls, and drank from plain pottery cups." During this era, vegetarianism was virtually unknown in Greece. In subsequent centuries, followers of Pythagoras and Orpheus rejected meat eating and the cult of sacrifice built up around it.

Yet despite being a product of his times, Homer consistently honors grain as true human food throughout his poems. All of the personal, social, and planetary benefits of a sane agriculture and food system are implied in the post-Odyssey odyssey. By journeying inward into his own psyche and planting the oar upright by the field of ripening barley or wheat, Odysseus completes his transformation into a fully conscious human being. He dies to his animal nature and is reborn as a peaceful, compassionate husband, father, son, ruler, and wanderer. His transformation is the culmination of a life-long spiral dance whose center is everywhere and whose circumference is nowhere. He honors the personal and collective unconscious, symbolized by Poseidon, the primordial sea from which the seven levels of awareness unfold. At its extreme, yin changes into yang, and yang into yin. Out of the horrific massacre of the suitors and servant girls emerges the path to enlightenment.

The Olive Garden

The olive, sacred to Athena and a traditional symbol of peace and harmony, plays a vital role in the *Odyssey*. Odysseus uses an olive stake to blind the Cyclops Polythemus, Circe massages his men with olive oil, and Calypso gives him the Minoan double axe with an olive wood handle to build the raft that enables him to leave her island. On Phaeacia, Odysseus washes ashore and conceals himself in leaves in a bed of wild and cultivated olive trees. Nausicaa anoints herself with olive oil on the beach, and her parents grow olives in their marvelous garden. When the Phaeacians reach Ithaca, they drop him off at a large olive tree at the head of an isolated harbor. Later Odysseus and Athena sit under the olive tree and plot the demise of the suitors. Finally, he visits his father, who like Penelope, is unsure of his true identity. He proves it by correctly describing the fruits trees in Laertes's orchard and olive grove.

In the climactic scene when Odysseus reveals himself to Penelope as her long lost husband, she hesitates to accept his identify, because other men have impersonated him and tricked her. She orders him to move his bed into the hallway for the night until his identity can be confirmed. Odysseus sees through her verbal cunning and reminds Penelope that their marriage bed was carved from an olive tree in the ground around which they built their house years ago. Only the two of them know this secret, and only then does she accept him as her returned spouse. In a divine demonstration of the relativity of time, Athena commands the

Night to hold back the dawn as husband and wife mingle in love.

The *Odyssey* climaxes with the mutual recognition of Odysseus and Penelope. The long separation and period of forgetfulness are over. The sweet song the couple sings that night in their great bed rooted to the grain-giving earth recounts their heartfelt struggles and fondest desires. Their dream of "blessed peace" for themselves, their island, and their descendants is the common dream of all humanity and the seed of a new Golden Age.

Afterword
Gently Down the Stream

While writing this book, I listened to Bill Moyers' acclaimed interviews with Joseph Campbell on the power of mythology. The exchange took place on PBS-TV in the two years leading up to Campbell's death in 1988. It was the first time I heard him speak in more than thirty-five years, and Campbell sounded just as inspired, wise, and compelling as the *upanishad* (forest teaching) he gave in Montana.

For modern society, Campbell was—and remains—a sage like figure, illuminating the path of the hero and heroine. He explored how modern society has severed its mythic and artistic roots with heaven and earth. He inspired his readers and listeners to discover and follow their own bliss. In working on this book, I discovered several Homeric parallels in my life that I had not previously recognized. As I mentioned in the introduction, I have enjoyed several beatific visions and dreams. However, unlike Odysseus, Orpheus, Virgil, Dante, and other spiritual seekers, I had not visited Hades. (See Appendix C for an update.) Yet, I realized that Thich Tri Quang, the Zen master in Vietnam, played the role of Tiresias in my life. We met against the horrific, bloodstained landscape of Southeast Asia. Every day numerous soldiers from both sides and countless farmers, mothers, and children were dying and crowding the Underworld like the ancient Achaeans and Trojans.

Tri Quang's penetrating insights and wisdom on how food governs destiny led me to devote my life to a healthy, peaceful, natural way of eating. For the last generation, I have been shouldering my oar as a writer, teacher, and counselor on diet, health, and the environment. In 2000, colleagues and I started Amberwaves, a grassroots network that took its name from *America the Beautiful*, the national hymn that begins "O beautiful for spacious skies, for amber waves of grain." Our mission has been to keep America and the planet beautiful and preserve and protect rice, wheat, barley, and other grains from genetic engineering, climate change, and other threats. This book, published by Amber Waves Press, is part of that mission.

Serendipitously, rowing kept turning up as a metaphor the deeper I got into this project. I learned that ancient Egyptian hieroglyphs were deciphered from a passage on rowing on the Rosetta Stone. A decree by Ptolemaus Epiphanes in 196 BCE stipulated that no one should be seized as crew for the galleys. In his praise, the edict notes that the young pharaoh donated grain and money in abundance to the temples of Egypt and patronized the vineyards and gardens. Ptolemaus sounds like one of the few virtuous rulers predicted by Hesiod in the dawning Iron Age.

In the *New York Review of Books*, I found out that Lewis Carroll, who wrote *Alice in Wonderland*, first read his book to the real-life Alice on an outing in a rowboat. A quick search turned up tributes to rowing by Walt Whitman, Emily Dickinson, D.H. Lawrence, Anne Sexton, and other noted poets and novelists.

A consistent theme in my writing and teaching, inspired by Tri Quang and greatly augmented by Michio Kushi, has been passing safely through the Spiral of History and the Vega Cycle that are now climaxing. On all sides, we are faced with destruction by fire: nuclear war and terrorism, global warming, and new viral epidemics. The spread of oil, plastics, and other petrochemicals pollutes land and sea. Genetic engineering destroys the integrity of species, and artificial electromagnetic fields and energy from satellites and cell phones cause bees, birds, and humans to lose their internal compasses and natural sense of direction. If by some miracle we can weather these fire-like challenges, we may still destroy ourselves from the foolish, unwise choices we make every day in our selection of low-quality, high-energy foods and abuse of cooking.

From ancient times, fire has been considered sacred. We are misusing this energy today like Prometheus (the strong-willed brother of Calypso) who nobly stole fire from the gods to to give to humanity. But in the myth, it was unfortunately used to cook meat, not make porridge, bake bread, or sauté veggies. A wrathful Zeus chained Prometheus to a mountain where he was condemned to have his liver perpetually devoured by an eagle—an appropriate punishment for abusing heavy animal food.

From an energetic perspective, the Four Ages can be correlated with the following ways of eating:

Diet and the Four Ages
Golden Age Awned wild cereal grains + other wild plant foods
Silver Age Domesticated plant foods + up to one half fish, seafood, and other animal food

Bronze Age Cultivated, awnless grains primarily in the form of bread, and other plant foods + up to three-quarters meat, dairy, and other animal food + wine

Iron Age Three-quarters animal food, processed food, and highly chemicalized food + one quarter plant food, including highly processed and GMO grains + alcohol, tobacco, and drugs

Since the Bronze Age, we have aspired to eat animal food as the center of the meal rather than as an occasional complement or festive dish as in the preceding eras. Gradually, awnless grains replaced awned grains, and consciousness dimmed as the streaming energy from the cosmos decreased. Until recently, modern civilization was built on consuming beef, pork, poultry, or other heavy animal food. Slaughtering was mechanized and no thought was paid to nature or the spirits of the slain animals. Today, to help balance this strong yang intake, we are eating refined sugar, high fructose corn syrup, GMO sugar beets, and ingesting a pharmacopeia of extreme yin drugs that would put the Lotus-Eaters to shame. They are sapping our will and causing us to forget our dreams. We are using electric, microwave, and other chaotic fuels instead of wood, gas, or other natural flame that gives steady, peaceful energy. We are seduced by high-octane fare like Odysseus's crew who could not resist the rich, tempting food and drink of the Cyclops, Circe, or the island of the Sun. We are as oblivious to our environment as Penelope's suitors and are recklessly feasting and eating the planetary family out of house and home.

Cooking is the highest art and involves all the elements. By mastering fire and water and the other pairs of opposites—like *moly*, the healing knowledge bestowed upon Odysseus by Hermes—we can break the enchantment of modern-day Sirens, Cyclops, Scyllas, and Charybdises. These include Monsanto, Cargill, Nabisco, McDonald's, and other multinational corporations that are turning us into swine, cattle, and sheep.

To cook whole, natural foods in a spirit of gratitude to heaven and earth is to remember our origin and destiny. Awned grains are particularly beneficial. Awns are the long bristles on the ends of growing barley, wheat, or other cereal grasses that serve as antennae to gather the higher waves and vibrations of the cosmos. Though the awns are discarded when processed, the kernels absorb the highly charged energy, and consuming awned grains gives heightened consciousness and energy. This realm of awareness is alluded to in Greek mythology as well as the world of Ideas in Platonic philosophy, the Kingdom of Heaven in Jesus's teachings, and other spiritual traditions. Barley, spelt, and wheat have particularly long awns and contribute to universal consciousness. In Crete, the awns were traditionally baked into the bread, a practice that continues today and which medical researchers have linked to the country's exceptional health and low rates of heart disease and cancer.

Observing a whole-grain based diet contributes to discovering our dream in life, to aligning or realigning ourselves with the North Star overhead, and joining in the circle of the dance of life. It is to bear Achilles's Shield that brings wonder to all beings, to hoist Odysseus's Oar that leads to blessed peace, and wield Calypso's Butterfly Axe that creates harmony among the sexes.

The Homeric epics point to a hopeful, peaceful future for our planet. All three major symbols in the poems—shield, oar, and axe—start out as weapons of war and suffering. But as the story unfolds, they are transformed into tools of peace and harmony. While many people believe human beings are innately aggressive and violent, recent archaeological discoveries suggest otherwise. In addition to the ancient Minoan civilization, excavations of the Indus River Valley Civilization in modern day Pakistan and India and of the Niger River Valley Civilization in Mali and other regions of West Africa show evidence of harmonious societies that prospered for a millennium or more (actually about 1500 years in all three cases) without violence and bloodshed, offensive weapons, armies, and war. In all three civilizations, there is no evidence of monarchy, central organization, or coersive authority of any kind. In these early Bronze and Iron Age societies, metals were used to fashion farming implements, tools, and jewelry. We don't have to go back to a mythical Golden Age in the dimly remembered Paleolithic or megalithic past to find evidence that human beings can live together peacefully. Our birthright and legacy—a world of enduring health and peace—is right beneath our feet in the soil and under the stars, if only we have ears to hear and eyes to see.

Voyage of Discovery

Sherman Goldman, my original editor at *East West Journal* and longtime mentor and friend, was an avid student of Homer and the classics. In the magazine, he wrote long, mesmerizing essays about his own journey, including his visit to Greece. Thirty-five years later, Maria Milland, a young woman from Copenhagen, tracked him down and revealed to Sherman that he was her father! She had been conceived in Athens by a young woman—a nymph—he met briefly on his odyssey. But the mother had never told Sherman and forgot his name until many years later when a film with a character of similar name jogged her memory. Like Telemachus, Maria was a spitting image of her father. She was a healer—a medical doctor—and had been to Tibet and other remote regions favored by her father. It was a miraculous reunion.

After several companionable years with Maria, Sherman entered the world of spirit. In the way that Odysseus fashioned a mound for his fallen comrade and planted his oar, I would like to honor Sherman at the close of this book. Of course, he was more like Calchas, the seer who foretold the outcome of the Trojan War and told the Achaeans they must return Chyrseis to her father, than Elpenor, the youngest crewman who fell off Circe's roof. Sherman composed a statement of purpose for the *East West Journal* that ran in each issue for many years. With a nod to Penelope's loom, it beautifully summarizes the theme of the *Iliad* and *Odyssey* and other great literature and art, and I would like to leave it as the epitaph for this book:

> We explore the dynamic equilibrium that unifies apparently opposite values: Oriental and Occidental, traditional and modern religious and technological, communal and individual, visionary and practical.
>
> We feel that the most exciting event on the stage of history today is the meeting of these two protagonists on a global scale affecting every individual. We investigate the play of balance in all fields—from ecology, agriculture, and nutrition through personal relationships, science and the arts, to economics, politics, and spirituality. We view reality as a magic carpet woven on the loom of complementary forces.
>
> We believe that people's freedom to chart the course of their lives as a boundless adventure springs from the most basic factors of physical vitality. Our theoretical articles on the frontiers of thought are inseparable from our how to departments. Regular columns about healthy diet, vigorous activity, and continual self-reflection construct a solid tripod holding the canvas on which we design our image of One Peaceful World.
>
> We see humanity as a foreground figure set in a larger background of nature and the infinite universe. The environment is our nourishment, and we are what we eat. By creating our bodies and minds from natural foods in a spirit of thankfulness, we can remember our organic relationship to the surrounding world, as parts within a common whole.
>
> We invite you to join in this voyage of discovery, whose point of origin is everywhere and whose goal is endless. The staple fare we offer is macrobiotic; the compass we follow is yin and yang; the future toward which we steer is all humanity's.

Appendices

A. The Spiral of History

Time moves in a spiral. Culture and civilization on our planet are governed by an inward, contracting spiral of history that like a clock has 12 hours or sections. The present spiral, extending back thousands of years, will reach a climax in the mid twenty-first century. In the future, it will reverse course and spiral in an outward, expanding direction.

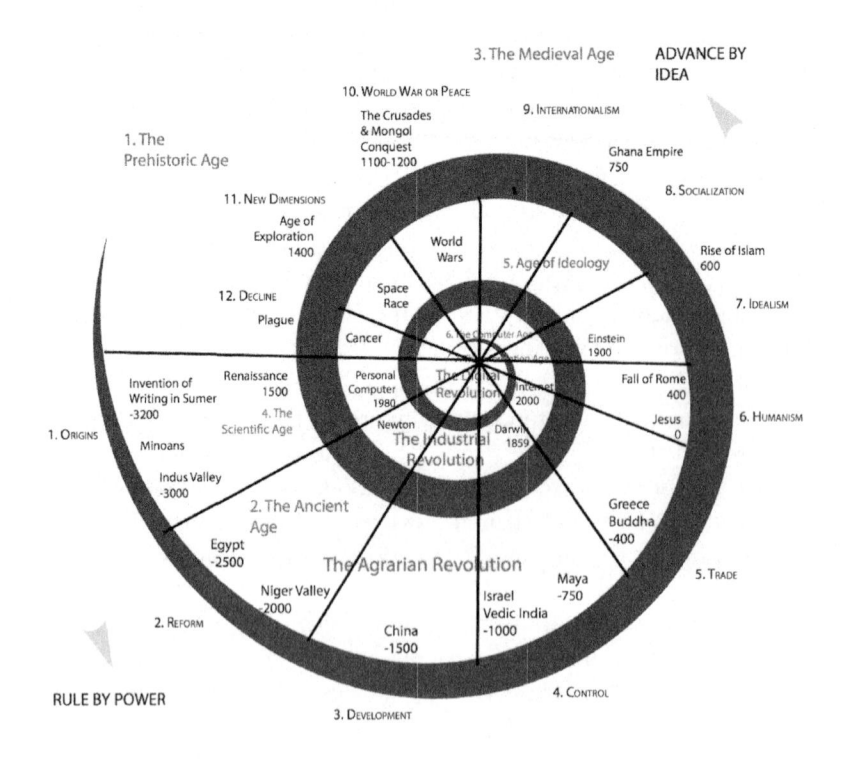

B. Homeric Recipes

These recipes are based on traditional foods eaten in the ancient Aegean and Mediterranean worlds. They serve about four or more.

Odysseus's Chewy Barley

Barley was the main staple in the Aegean and Mediterranean worlds. It was eaten as a whole grain, combined with other grains, beans, and vegetables, made into barley cakes and flat bread, concentrated into a natural sweetener, and steeped into a tea. Whole barley is stronger, chewier, and more nutritious than pearled or lightly refined modern barley. As a rule, barley is also awned, collecting and absorbing more cosmic energy than awnless grains, and contributes to higher consciousness.

1 cup whole barley
3 cups water
pinch of sea salt

Rinse and soak the barley in cold water for 4 hours or preferably overnight. Place in a heavy pot with a heavy lid with fresh cold water (or soaking water, if clean). Add a pinch of sea salt. Bring to a boil, reduce flame, and simmer for 50 to 60 minutes until done. Garnish with parsley and sesame seeds.

Variation: For morning porridge, rewarm the barley from the day before for 5 to 10 minutes, adding more liquid to the consistency you desire, and top with seeds, nuts, or berries.

Hephaestus's Golden Barley with Bulgur

Whole barley by itself is very chewy. For a lighter, more relaxing dish, add bulgur, a form of whole wheat that has been cracked and pre-cooked. This delicious combination, made from the grains depicted on Hephaestus's Great Shield, can protect you from most ills.

1/2 cup whole barley
1/2 cup bulgur
3 cups water
pinch sea salt

Rinse and soak barley 4 hours or overnight. Place in a pot, add water and salt, and bring to a boil. Reduce flame and simmer for 40 minutes. Add the bulgur when the barley is about half cooked since it is much lighter and takes only about 15 to 20 minutes to cook. Garnish with parsley and sesame seeds.

Variation: Substitute couscous, another light form of wheat that is steamed and cooks up fluffy.

Achaean Barleymeal

Barley gives light, upward energy and is especially good for nourishing the liver. This dish could have soothed Agamemnon and Achilles's wrath and possibly averted the quarrel between them.

1 cup barley flakes or barleymeal
3 cups water
pinch sea salt
1/2 cup grapes, melon slices, or berries
1 tbsp honey or barley malt

Place water and salt in a saucepan. Bring to a boil, add the barley flakes or meal, reduce flame, and simmer for 15 to 20 minutes or until done. Serve with fresh fruit and a little honey or barley malt.

Achilles's Spelt Cakes

Spelt cakes are tasty, delicious and satisfying. They can be made with speltmeal or flakes made from milling whole spelt and flavored with olives, nuts, seeds, and other ingredients. They give stamina and quickness and no doubt helped Achilles's maintain his endurance as the swiftest of the Achaeans. Pine nuts traditionally are eaten for longevity, a blessing denied to the tragically short-lived Achilles and one he later regretted in Hades when he met Odysseus and rued dying as a warrior rather than living as a farmer.

1 cup spelt flour
1 tbsp olive oil for mixing
water for the batter
1/4 cup pine nuts
honey to taste (optional)
pinch sea salt
2-3 tbsp olive oil for cooking

Combine barley flour and salt into a batter. Add pine nuts and honey, if desired. Ladle onto an oiled and heated skillet. Fry on each side for several minutes.

Variation: Combine all ingredients into a batter. Ladle into a baking dish, and bake in an oven for 30 minutes at 350 F. Let cool and slice into squares.

Andromache's Grape Leaves Stuffed with Bulgur

Grape leaves are a classic Greek specialty, but in Homeric times they were made with bulgur. Rice didn't come to the Mediterranean and Aegean worlds for another millennia from the Far East. These tasty morsels will satisfy even the strongest warrior and enhance any meal or Olympian banquet.

Half pound of grape leaves
2 cups onions, diced
1 fennel bulb, diced
4 scallions, finely sliced
1/4 tsp sea slat
1 cup bulgur
1/4 cup fresh dill, chopped
1/4 cup fresh mint, chopped
2/3 cup olive oil
1 cup water
1/3 cup lemon juice, freshly squeezed
2 lemons, cut into wedges

Blanch grape leaves individually in boiling water for about 1 minute. Rinse with cold water and drain.

Combine diced veggies and salt in a bowl and mix with your hands. Add the bulgur, mint, dill, oil, and other herbs or spices, if desired.

Place a large grape leaf with the vein side up on a table or cutting board. Take off the stem. Place 1 tbsp of the mixture near the stem. Fold both sides of the leaf over the filling. Then fold up the bottom and roll up the leaf in a cylinder. Place with the seam side in the pot. Prepare remaining stuffed grape leaves known as *dolmades* in a pot. Add a second layer. Pour water, 1/4 cup of olive oil, and lemon juice over the grape leaves to almost cover. Place a heatproof plate over the *domades* to prevent from coming apart while cooking. Bring wet ingredients to a boil, lower heat, and simmer for 30 minutes. After allowing them to cool, place in refrigerator overnight. Serve at room temperature with lemon wedges.

Hippocratic Stew

Hippocrates, the Father of Medicine, who flourished several centuries after Homer, recommended barley as principal food and used it in his practice. His favorite home remedy was Barley Soup or Stew made with soft barley by itself or prepared with beans and vegetables. This hardy stew is sure to cure what ails you.

1 cup whole barley, cooked
1/2 cup chickpeas, cooked
1 carrot, sliced thinly
1/2 onion, diced
3 cups water
1/4 tsp sea salt
scallions to garnish

Boil water. Add previously cooked barley and chickpeas with veggies and sea salt, reduce flame to low, and simmer for about 15 to 20 minutes. Garnish with freshly sliced scallions and serve hot.

Variation: Season with barley miso, a delicious fermented soybean paste. Though not native to Greece, miso was known in the East in antiquity and may have been brought to Asia Minor by Minoan merchant fleets.

Penelope's Loaf

When she wasn't weeping for her husband, weaving, or unweaving on her loom, Penelope oversaw her household, including the baking of barley bread, a major staple in her household and others throughout the ancient Mediterranean world. This is one traditional recipe.

2 cups barley flour, finely milled
1 tbsp olive oil
1/4 tsp sea salt
water for making the batter

Add oil and salt to the flour, form a ball of dough, and knead for 15 to 20 minutes. Set aside in a warm place to ferment with wild yeast from the air. Place is an oiled baking dish and bake in a preheated oven at 350 F. for 45 minutes or until done.

Variation: For variety, add olives, seeds, nut, or dried fruit to the batter. For a sweeter bread, add a little honey or barley malt.

Recipes

Hector's Wheat Rolls

Wheat is stronger than barley and was a principal grain in Troy and wealthier cities and regions. Unlike barley, it was customarily milled to make it lighter and more digestible. Hence, it cost more, and for ordinary people was reserved for special occasions. Wheaten rolls were undoubtedly eaten by the Trojan warriors, as well as ordinary citizens, throughout the war.

2 cups wheat flour, finely milled
1 tbsp olive oil
1/4 tsp sea salt
water for making the batter

Prepare similar to Penelope's Loaf but knead the dough into small rolls.

Paris's Waffles with Strawberries and Honey Glaze

Paris was ridiculed by soldiers on both sides for being more accomplished in the bedroom than on the battlefield. In keeping with his domestic skills, he may have also excelled in the kitchen. These waffles would be just the thing for Helios Day (Sunday) brunch with Helen.

2 cups white barley flour
1 tbsp olive oil
2 tbsp barley malt
1/8 tsp sea salt
water for making the batter

Combine ingredients and make a batter. Pour onto a waffle iron and toast on each side for about 5 minutes. Serve with warm honey and strawberries or other fruit.

Helios's Chickpea and Lentil Burgers

The life-giving rays of the Sun nurture the crops growing in the field and can be used to sun-dry foods as well as a source of energy for cooking. Unfortunately, Helios did not provide sufficient wild or domesticated plants on his island for stranded sailors. If Odysseus's crew had fields of chickpeas, lentils, and other nutritious crops to harvest, they may not have been tempted to slay the cattle of the Sun and lose their homecoming. These patties are known as *Revithokeftedes* and are a favorite on Chios, Homer's native island.

1 cup chickpeas, soaked overnight in water
1 cup lentils
3 cups water
1 cup barley or wheat flour
1/2 cup celery, thinly sliced
1 cup onion, thinly sliced
1/2 cup fresh mint, chopped
1/4 tsp of sea salt
1/2 cup olive oil, plus more for frying

Place the chickpeas and lentils in a pot, add water to cover by 2 inches, and add salt. Bring to a boil, skim off the foam, reduce heat, and simmer for 1 to 1 1/2 hours or until tender.

Sauté the onions and celery in an oiled skillet for about 5 minutes, add scallions and sauté for several more minutes until tender.

Combine half the beans and all of the veggies in a blender or food processor with 1/2 cup of the cooking liquid and purée. In a bowl, mash the remaining half of the beans and add to the purée, along with mint and other herbs or spices, if desired.

Refrigerate for 1 hour or a day or more to improve the taste and texture. Fashion into patties and deep-fry in olive oil or olive oil combined with safflower oil for 2 to 5 minutes on each side. Drain and serve with Barley Rolls above.

Variation: For a richer taste, serve with a tahini-lemon sauce.

Telemachus's Wild Oats and Lentil Loaf

In search of his father, Telemachus visited Peloponnese and admired the bounty of nature. Helen may have prepared this dish to shape him up for the trials ahead back home in Ithaca.

1 cup whole oats
1/2 cup lentils
1/2 cup onions, diced
1/2 cup celery, diced
2-3 red radishes, thinly sliced
4-5 cups water
pinch of sea salt per cup of ingredients

Soak oats overnight and cook with about 3 to 4 cups of water in a heavy pot with sea salt. After 30 minutes, when about half done, add the lentils and vegetables, and remaining water, and cook for another half hour or until done.

Circe's Spiked Veggies
This is just the ticket for a swinish crew or for porkies who need to slim down. It goes especially well with freshly baked bread or grains and beans.

1 cup onions, sliced in large pieces
1 fennel bulb, thinly sliced
1 cup green peas
1 cup carrots, thinly sliced
1/2 cup olive oil
2 cups water
1 teaspoon fennel seeds
1/2 cup lemon juice, freshly squeezed
1/2 cup dill, freshly chopped
sea salt to taste

Sauté the onions over medium heat for several minutes. Add the fennel bulb and sauté or 5 more minutes or until tender. Add the peas, the carrots, fennel seeds, and seasoning to taste. Add water, bring to a boil, reduce heat to low, and simmer covered for 15 minutes. Add remaining water, lemon juice, oil, and dill. Stir ingredients and cook for 10 minutes or until soft and ender. Top with remaining dill and serve warm or at room temperature.

Variation: You can replace the peas with fresh fava beans, green beans, or artichokes.

Calypso's Wild Bitter Greens
Wild greens grow throughout the Mediterranean and are a traditional delicacy known as *horta* in Greece. While this tender dish may not be enough to win Odysseus's eternal love, Calypso's delectable cuisine kept him well nourished, if not completely satisfied, for seven years.

1 pound mixed sweet greens (amaranth, beet, spinach, Swiss chard, pea
    shoots, escarole, romaine, orache)
1/3 pound mixed bitter greens (chicory, endive, mustard greens, water-
    cress, turnip greens)
1/2 pound zucchini
1 tomato, diced

1/2 garlic clove, minced
1/2 teaspoon oregano
1/8 cup olive oil
1-2 tbsp lemon juice, freshly squeezed
sea salt
pepper

Combine oil, lemon juice, and garlic in a small bowl and whisk. Add salt, pepper, or other seasoning and set aside.

Wash the greens and place wet in a large skillet. Over high heat, steam covered for several minutes. Turn greens over and steam covered for a couple more minutes or until wilted.

Steam zucchini in a small volume of water for 5 minutes and slice into 1/2 –inch-thick slices.

Drain the greens and chop broadly. Arrange on a platter surrounded by sliced zucchini. Add the diced tomato to the dressing, whisk, and serve over the greens and zucchini. Top with oregano and serve.

Phaeacian Seaweed Medley
As master mariners, the Phaeacians hosted a fleet that needed no maps or compass. Could it have been all the iron in the sea vegetables they ate that intuitively steered them in the right direction? Try this tasty dish made from native Aegean and Mediterranean seaweed, and see where your inner compass takes you.

1 ounce alaria or wakame
1 large cucumber, quartered lengthwise and sliced
1/2 cup red radish, thinly sliced
1 tbsp apple cider vinegar
1/8 to 1/4 teaspoon sea salt

Rinse seaweed, soak for 10 minutes, drain, and cut into small pieces. Place 1/2 inch of water in a saucepan and bring to a boil. Simmer radishes for 1 minute and remove. Simmer seaweed for 1-3 minutes and remove. Mix sea salt with vinegar and add to mixture. Put in a pickled press for 1-3 hours. Remove, rinse off excess salt, and erve.

Nausicaa's Tahini Custard with Apples and Raisins
Lovely Nausicaa was as fair as a goddess, and Odysseus was tempted to remain with her in Scheria. Perhaps he would have if she had given this delectable dish when he washed up on shore.

3 apples
1/2 cup raisins
2 cups apple juice
2 cups water
2 to 3 tablespoons tahini
pinch sea salt
5 tablespoons agar-agar flakes or 1 bar

Wash apples, core, and slice. Place the apples and raisins in a pot with the liquids, tahini, sea salt, and agar-agar. Mix well, bring to a boil, reduce heat to low, and simmer for 2 to 3 minutes. Chill in a shallow bowl until almost hardened. Place cooled mixture in a blender and blend until smooth and creamy. Place custard back in serving bowl and chill once more before serving.

Laertes's Pear Crunch

Laertes loved the pear trees, grape vineyard, olive grove, and other fruits of his orchard. Better to crunch this scrumptious dish with the townsfolk when they come calling than butt heads after the massacre.

4 pears, sliced
1/3 cup hazelnuts or other nuts
1 cup rolled oats
1 tbsp olive oil
pinch sea salt
1/2 cup water
2 tablespoons arrowroot flour or kuzu
1/2 cup honey
1/2 cup barley malt

Peel, core, and slice pears. Roast hazel nuts and rolled oats separately in skillet. Lightly sauté the sliced pears in olive oil with a pinch of sea salt. Put in baking dish. Mix arrowroot flour in cold water and pour over ingredients. Mix honey and barley malt with rolled oats and nuts. Sprinkle over pears. Bake 20 to 25 minutes in pre-heated 375-degree oven. Remove cover for the last 4 minutes to make the top crunchier.

Demeter Tea

Demeter is the Greek goddess of grain. Her name comes from *de* meaning "barley" and *mater* or "mother." Barley tea is light, soothing, and relaxing. Medicinally, it helps melt away excess fat and reduce fever. It is suitable for children and adults alike.

1-2 ounces of barley

Dry-roast unhulled barley in a skillet over medium flame for 5 to 10 minutes or until a fragrant aroma is released. Stir and shake pan occasionally to prevent burning. Add 2 to 3 tablespoons of roasted barley to 1 1/2 quarters of water. Bring to a boil, lower heat, and simmer for 5 to 15 minutes, depending on how mild or strong you like it. Serve hot or let cool and drink chilled in hot weather.

Zeus & Athena's Nectar of the Gods: A Father-Daughter Punch
Ambrosia and nectar were reserved for the gods—or their favorites. This divine concoction dedicated to Zeus and Athena packs the punch of an Olympian thunderbolt and the flick of the aegis. It is a memorable beginning or ending to any banquet.

1/2 cup lime juice
3 cups of Pramnian wine
2 cups of apple wine
1 cup Hymetus honey or barley malt
gingerroot, small handful grated

Mix all the ingredients and serve chilled or at room temperature.

Ariadne's Minoan Meze
Dakos is a Cretan *meze* (side dish) consisting of a slice of soaked dried bread or *rusk* (double-baked crust) with chopped veggies, a dip, or other topping. If you run out of thread, you can leave a trail of *dakos'* crumbs for your sweetheart to find her or his way home.

Loaf of bread
1/4 cup extra virgin olive oil
1/2 cup humus or other topping
Greek olives
oregano, salt, and other seasonings to taste

Slice a loaf of hearty barley, whole wheat, or spelt bread into *dakos*, or small 1 1/2-inch square pieces. Drizzle with olive oil and salt. Bake in a 350-degree oven for 10–15 minutes. Saturate with olive oil and sprinkle with fresh oregano. Garnish with an olive, let bread soften, and enjoy.

C Journey to Atlantis

This spring I dreamed I was counseling an old woman in the hospital. She was in bed with an oxygen mask, feeding tubes, and on other life-support. To recover, I told her she needed to observe a plant-based diet centered on whole grains, preferably awned. On a table near her bed was a clipboard with her medical chart. I picked it up and read her name at the top: MRS. ASKA. Recognizing whom my patient was, I awoke immediately.

In his classes, educator Michio Kushi taught that the ancient spiritual and scientific world community was called Aska. About 20,000 years ago, he related, long before the flood, a partial axis shift, and the emergence of civilization in Mesopotamia, Egypt, and other regions, the world was healthy, peaceful, and unified under the name Aska. Traces remain in old place names such as Alaska, Nebraska, Damascus, Glasgow, and Moscow.

Mrs. Aska, the patient in my dream, was clearly Mother Earth. The message of the dream was that a return to a sane food and agriculture system, based on whole cereal grains, is essential to the future of the planet.

While Michio's tale of a lost golden age was absorbing, it remains largely a vision and, in the view of most scientists, a fantasy. Was there any historical evidence that human beings lived together peacefully for long periods of time? This past year I learned about several such societies while researching a new book on the Spiral of History. The first, the ancient Niger River civilization in West Africa, was the subject of a presentation on the *Miso Happy Show*, a new online learning and variety program that Bettina Zumdick and I launched earlier this spring. The second was the Minoan civilization in the Aegean, and a third was the Indus Valley civilization in northwest Pakistan and India.

Each civilization last 1500 years or more and was characterized by an era of peace, prosperity, and elegant artistry and craftsmanship. There is no evidence of a central government, organized religion, military or warfare in any of the civilizations. All three had a sophisticated metallurgy, and bronze, iron, and other useful metals were used only for farm implements, cookware, and jewelry, not for weaponry.

1. Visit to England

In mid-May, the opportunity arose to visit one of these sites—the Minoan in Greece—after giving a seminar in the UK with Bettina and visiting her mother in Germany. After arriving in London, our first stop was Westminster Abbey, which Bettina had not seen before. The cathedral was dark and sepulcher, largely a monument to British royalty and colonialism. On one corridor, I found myself walking across the grave of Charles Darwin. I showed Bettina the Poets Corner and pointed out the tantalizing inscription "Christopher Marlowe 1564–1593?" on a stained glass window. It suggested his death was staged, and he went on to write the works of Shakespeare—the theme of several of my books. Ironically, as in Deptford, where he reputedly was murdered on the eve of a trial for heresy, he was the only one commemorated in the Abbey who was not actually buried there.

Next stop was the British Museum and the Egyptian Room. As avid students of Egyptian culture and mythology, we practiced visual diagnosis and observed how strong the constitutions of the ancient Nile dwellers were, with their large ears, small mouths, and flat noses. In another exhibit, Bettina was particularly fascinated with the Crystal Skull, a life-size quartz carving from Mexico. She marveled at the sophisticated technology, now lost, used to fashion it, and its anatomical depiction of subtle energy channels. Avoiding the Egyptian mummy room, whose energy was almost as foreboding as Westminster Abbey, we enjoyed the African exhibit. I was delighted to find a mask of Tjiwara, the ancient antelope culture bearer who introduced brown rice cultivation to humanity. The overall *nyama*, or life energy, of the sub-Saharan African room was joyful and life-affirming.

In Sussex, about an hour's train ride south of London, we gave a 9 Star Ki seminar organized by David and Nicola McCarthy, colleagues and directors of the Kushi School of the UK. We had only a handful of students, but they were eager to learn, and several more joined us online. David and Nicola are marvelous cooks and prepared a sumptuous repast for the program, including rice porridge with apricots and pumpkin seeds, sushi, veggie tempura, somen in broth with tofu and nori, kanten cake, cookies, and twig tea. The wedding with Prince Harry and Megan Markle took place over the weekend. The Royals and their guests should dine so well!

One evening in England, we had a psychic reading in which relatives and guides from the spirit world offered encouragement. My father, Homer, a Unitarian minister and social activist, and Bettina's dad, Josef, an artist and musician, appeared and blessed our projects and travels. On a more somber note, a spirit guide came with an image of an empty clay cup, warning that the earth was running out of clean water, and the planet faced an existential crisis. I felt like Odysseus at the mouth of the Underworld seeing his departed relatives and receiving the prophecy of Tiresias, the wisest seer in antiquity.

In America, over the weekend, there had been another terrible school shooting. On the way to Gatwick airport, our cab driver, a thoughtful immigrant from Pakistan, brought up a solution to terrorism and violence popular in his home country. Don't control the number of guns people can own, but limit the number of bullets. If each household were allowed only six bullets, it would be enough for self-defense, alert the neighbors and local authorities, and protect against mass slaughter. It was a practical solution akin to how Odysseus outwitted the Cyclops and safely led his men out of a murderous situation.

2. Visit to Germany

From the UK, we flew to Hamburg and were met by Lotte, Bettina's mother, and her sister Eva. A small, vivacious woman, Lotte reminded me of my own late mother, Esther. Lotte was also very literary, and named each of her three daughters after notable poets. Over the next several days, at Lotte's home in the countryside, I enjoyed her hearty bean soup, creamy millet porridge, savory tofu scramble, and other nourishing dishes. We ate our meals outdoors, following the sun, with breakfast on the bright rising eastern side of the house and dinner on the vivid setting western side.

Other highlights included a visit to the castle at Schwerin, a medieval fortress, with high fairytale turrets, a moat, spiral staircases, and murals of Parzival's quest for the Holy Grail. The palace is now a museum and site of the state parliament. In one room, Bettina pointed out to me a small, elegant sculpture of Paris presenting the Golden Apple to Aphrodite, the Greek goddess of love, which precipitated the Trojan War. I also enjoyed the sculpture of Heracles taming the Cretan Bull on the terrace overlooking the placid Schweriner Sea, the city's main lake. For lunch, we ate at a charming vegan restaurant, after which I duly accompanied the women who went shopping for essentials—shoes and natural foods.

The next day, Bettina made a delicious apple-couscous cake for an outdoor garden party with several of Lotte's lady friends and neighbors. On a bright, sunny afternoon, it was a relaxed gathering, with several children playing peacefully while the adults chatted. There was a high degree of environmental awareness in the group, and conversation touched on ways to protect the sea from plastic waste and other ecological challenges.

In the evenings, Lotte, Bettina, Eva, and I played Sand, a dice game (whose name reminds you that winning and losing are as fleeting as the sands of time). We also sat around the wood-burning fire and reminisced as the mercury started to drop. Everyone received a hot water bottle to sleep with in cozy featherbeds. One evening, Maya, the youngest sister, and her husband and two daughters arrived to join in the festivities. The rustic surroundings and the love and harmony among three generations of the Zumdick clan reminded me of visiting my grandparents on Lake Erie. Every summer, my parents, sister, and I would visit their remote cottage, and the family dinners, games, and sojourns into town for groceries constituted the happiest days of my childhood. During the psychic session in Britain, my grandmother's spirit appeared in the frilly shirt and apron she customarily wore preparing meals without electricity or running water. She was smiling and in good humor.

One night, Michio came in a dream and explained that everyone was born with five character traits or qualities. Bettina and I interpreted it as a reflection of the 5 transformations and the natural energy cycle. One's first impression of people is often negative, mirroring one of the two adverse relationships in the control cycle. If we give them a chance, we will usually discover three positive, or nourishing, aspects of their character that accord with our own.

Since there was no Wi-Fi or Internet in the farmhouse, the last morning of my stay we walked to a neighbor's (who had several alpacas lolling in the yard) to print out a boarding pass for my flight. At the local train station, I bid farewell to Bettina and Lotte and, accompanied by Eva, left for Berlin. Eva, an animated conversationalist, just accepted a new post as a museum curator in Oslo, and we talked about history and culture. She kindly saw me off at the airport on the next stage of my odyssey.

3. Visit to Athens

Arriving late at night in Athens, I took a cab to my hotel, the Ambrosia (named after the food of the gods), and discovered that the elevator had just stopped working. I was forced to take my heavy bags to my room seven flights up. After the paradisical sojourn in Germany, I felt I had arrived in purgatory, ascending a steep seven-story mountain. Then I remembered I had flown south from Berlin to Athens away from 5 Soil (in the north this year). Traveling in an ominous direction, known as *An Ken Satsu* ("Dark Killing Sword") in 9 Star Ki, courts unexpected difficulties. Trudging up the spiral staircase, it was a relief, knowing I was just going in a "bad" direction, not suffering a spiritual relapse.

The next morning, the Temple of Zeus took my breath away as I joined a mythology tour. By the imposing pillars, a small calico cat came and rubbed itself against me. This was a good omen, as cats traditionally guarded the granaries (the forerunner of temples), and it made me think of my own orange tabby Mischa back home, whose favorite foods are brown rice and salmon.

On the way climbing the Acropolis, the ancient citadel on a rocky outcrop above the city, I offered a silent prayer before the ruined temple of Asclepius. He was the son of Apollo, the god of medicine, and a healer whose symbol was the staff with the entwined snake. Apollo, Asclepius, Hygieia and Panacea (two goddesses) are invoked at the beginning of the Hippocratic Oath, which I administer to almost all my students. The central tenet states, "I will apply dietetic measures for the benefit of the sick according to my ability and judgment." The main staple in ancient Greece, original home of the Mediterranean Diet, was barley, and Hippocrates recommended eating barley porridge for 10 days to relieve illness. The shrine brought to mind my uncle Bill, an osteopath, who also appeared in spirit in England.

The Parthenon, dedicated to Athena, was dazzling in the bright, midday sun. I considered the Greek goddess of wisdom to be a spiritual guide, and for many years "Athena" was the PIN code for my bank account. According to legend, she and Poseidon, the sea god, vied to become patrons of the city. A contest was held, and Athena offered the citizens the olive tree, the source of health, peace and prosperity. Poseidon shook his trident and promised the people mastery of the sea and victory in war. A plebiscite was held. All the women voted for Athena, the men for Poseidon. Since women outnumbered men, the goddess of wisdom won the laurels, and the city was named for her. However, subsequent attacks by neighboring city-states proved disastrous, and the men of Athens blamed the women and took away their franchise. In the later Periclean age of democracy, the suffrage was limited to men.

On the other side of the Acropolis, I visited the temple of Hephaestus, the god of metallurgy. In the *Iliad*, he fashions a divine shield for Achilles that plays a pivotal role in the Greeks' victory over the Trojans. It depicts the four ages of humanity and is a central theme in *The Circle of the Dance*, a book I am completing on the Homeric epics. At his shrine, I offered a silent prayer to the god of fire for deliverance during the current 81-year Fire cycle. For lunch, I stopped at Vegan Nation, a café a few minutes from the Agora, the ancient marketplace, and enjoyed long-grain brown rice with tofu, sliced avocado and tomato, and a cool leafy greens drink.

4. Voyage to Phaeacia

The next morning, I caught a ferry from Piraeus, the port of Athens, to Santorini, one of the Greek isles. On the enormous boat, which carried several thousand passengers, I made friends with a young couple from North Carolina. Aisha, an art teacher, was recovering from a stroke, and I gave her some dietary advice. Her husband, Keith, in law enforcement, was writing a book, and we talked about publishing. In late afternoon, we arrived at our destination, site of an ancient Minoan outpost and one of Greece's top tourist attractions.

Minoan culture revered nature, reveled in song and dance, and controlled the trade of copper, olive oil, and other staples across the Aegean and Mediterranean. Santorini (aka Thera), a small archipelago shaped like a crescent moon, is best known as the site of the largest volcanic explosion in human history. In the early 1600s BCE, a volcano erupted, devastated the island, and sent a series of tsunamis, up to several hundred feet in height, toward Crete, home of the Minoan civilization. The peaceful, harmonious Aegean culture that had endured for nearly two thousand years was virtually wiped out. An aggressive, warlike Mycenaean Greek society soon replaced it. Except in myth and legend (King Minos and the Minotaur), Minoa was forgotten until archaeological excavation of Knossos in the early 20th century.

In the *Odyssey,* composed about the 8th century BCE (or 800 years after the explosion), a trace of Minoan cultural values remained in the portrait of the Phaeacians, the peaceful, golden-age society on whose shore Odysseus washes up and is befriended by the princess Nausicaa and her royal parents. Homer portrays a harmonious, semi-matrilineal society devoted to horticulture, navigation, music, dance, and other arts. After ferrying the Greek warrior home to Ithaca, the Phaeacian ships are destroyed by Poseidon who buries the island under a mountain—a clear echo of the Thera explosion.

At Messaria, a village on Santorini, I stayed at the Kalma, a delightful hotel with luxuriant palms, a peach tree, and picturesque views of the surrounding mountains and sea. The following day I visited Akrotiri, the site of an ancient Minoan city in which an estimated ten thousand people once lived. The remarkably well-preserved site was covered for millennia by volcanic ash and only excavated in the last few decades.

Walking through the narrow streets of the 3500-year-old settlement transported me back to Phaeacia as described by Homer. Vestiges remained of the paved streets, indoor plumbing, and other sophisticated technology. In the House of Ladies, a large three-story structure with ten rooms on each floor, frescoes were uncovered depicting women in elegant robes with kilts and jackets. Other houses displayed colorful murals of swallows, crocuses, and other flora and fauna, as well as a gala procession of ships. The naturalistic themes and design reminded me of the wildflower paintings my grandfather Alex composed that line the walls of my home in the Berkshires. He was an artist and died before I was born, but also came to me in the séance in England. I recognized him by the spiral walking staff he carved. In one Akrotiri kitchen, bowls for barley, olive jars, and other cooking implements remained in situ, as the inhabitants are believed to have all fled to safety before the final eruption.

Akrotiri was probably the inspiration for Plato's story of Atlantis, the fabled lost civilization that sank beneath the waves. Michio Kushi told me that in a previous lifetime he helped organize the evacuation from Atlantis in a fleet of small boats. I tried to envision him supervising the exodus and handing out rice balls, as he described, to the local macrobiotic community.

Despite a veneer of modernity, including graded mountain roads with hairpin turns, blue-domed Greek Orthodox churches, luxury villas, and trendy boutiques, Santorini has not changed all that much over the last several millennia. The tiny villages, with their cobblestone streets, are festooned with whitewashed houses, artsy shops, and seafood restaurants. I enjoyed three small red mullets, cooked whole and fried to perfection—my only animal food during two weeks abroad. After lunch, strolling on the beach, I dipped my hand in the wine-dark Aegean, and it felt like a homecoming.

A water shortage is one of Santorini's greatest challenges. Most of the fresh water arrives daily on large tankers. The small amount of well water and rainwater collected in cisterns on the island is insufficient to meet the needs of the millions of tourists who visit each year. Global warming and climate change are a latter day Scylla and Charybdis that could have a devastating impact on the local wine industry, and rising sea levels could drown the villages on the island.

5. Visit to Delphi

On the ferry back to Piraeus, I met an old Greek mariner. He had sailed the seven seas for most of his life, and the place he liked best was Portland, Oregon because of its tall forests that supplied timber for the cargo ships. He reminded me of Odysseus, the archetypal sailor, who lost all his men and ships and ended up stranded on Calypso's island for seven years. The beautiful goddess offered him immortality and eternal youth to stay and be her consort. But pining for his mortal wife Penelope, Odysseus declined. Calypso then gave him a double axe—the Minoan symbol of yin and yang and gender equality—to fell some trees and construct a raft. Though Poseidon sent a storm to capsize his little boat, Odysseus washed up on Phaeacia, the Minoan-like outpost.

Back on the mainland, I visited Delphi, the site of the ancient Oracle of Apollo and was enchanted with Mount Parnassus and the Castilian Spring. They are among the most sacred sites in Greek mythology and permeate the works of Marlowe, Shakespeare, Shelley, Byron, and other romantic poets. At a local restaurant, with a dazzling view of the mountain where Odysseus received a scar from a wild boar, I dined with several Indians surprised that I also ordered a vegetarian lunch of spaghetti neapolitan, grape leaves stuffed with rice and tomato, fresh bread, and tea.

The day's news reported the highest rates of childhood obesity in Europe were among children in Greece, home of the Mediterranean Diet. Like a modern day Circe serving up a toxic brew of fat and dairy, the food industry has turned kids (and adults) into swine. Except for peach juice, dry toast, and tea, there was little I could eat at the Ambrosia or Kalma for breakfast. As a rule, Greek restaurants had few whole grains, beans, or greens. Once in Santorini, I ordered a large side of sautéed spinach and put it in a "to go" box for several more meals.

6. Visit to Aska

On the plane and ferry, I read several books on ancient Egypt that I brought along as well as stored on my Kindle. Michio had introduced the notion of Aska, but did not explain what the name meant. It has been a koan, or Zen riddle, to interpret. In hieroglyphs, *As* refers to both Isis and Osiris, the mythical first pharaoh and queen of Egypt, who are identified with the constellation Orion and the star Sirius. These asterisms were believed to be the portal in the Milky Way (the celestial Nile) between this world and the next. *Ka* in ancient Egyptian has many meanings, including temple and sanctuary. Aska, I concluded, meant Heaven on Earth, a society or planet in perfect harmony with nature.

On my last day in Athens, I Skyped with my daughter Mariya, who is living in Russia with her family. She has been trying, so far unsuccessfully, to get a US passport for her newborn son. Because of deteriorating US-Russian relations, embassies in both countries are short-staffed and in chaos. After reassuring her that everything would work out eventually, I visited the National Archaeological Museum, a half hour's walk from the Ambrosia, and was delighted to find a display of the original frescoes from Akrotiri. The colorful mural of twin antelopes was particularly thrilling because I had given a presentation on "The Antelope Who Loves Brown Rice" for the *Miso Happy Show* earlier in the month. There is no evidence that the Minoans, like the West Africans, recognized the antelope and gazelle as agricultural culture-bearers. But barley, spelt, emmer, einkorn, and millet—grains enjoyed by antelopes as well as humans—were grown in the Aegean and Mediterranean worlds.

The exhibit of graceful Minoan and Theran bowls and cookware, fabrics and artwork, and other peaceful implements of daily life contrasted sharply with the rest of the museum. For the most part, the displays of Mycenaean and Greek art celebrated physical strength, state power, and military victory. Depictions of animal sacrifice, slavery, capital punishment, and other cruel and unjust practices were the norm.

At nearby Mama Tierra (Mother Earth) restaurant, I ordered the Macrobiotic Salad for lunch, consisting of organic quinoa, grilled tofu, baked sweet potatoes, kale, and tamarind dressing. In the afternoon, I took the metro downtown and visited the Acropolis Museum. Like the National Archaeological Museum, it largely commemorated a pageant of famous battles, the subjugation of women and girls, and endless rivalries and vendettas among the Greek gods, *polis* (states), leaders, and citizenry.

Like the Minoan display uptown, the Acropolis Museum had a small peaceful exhibit devoted to the Eleusinian mysteries. These centered on Demeter, the grain or barley goddess (*dea* = barley, *meter* = mother); Persephone or Kora, her daughter, who was abducted by Hades and spent part of the year in the Underworld; and Triptolemus, a young man raised by Demeter, to whom she taught agriculture. In turn, he introduced farming to humankind. On one statue were inscribed Triptolemus's three tenets: 1) honor thy parents, 2) honor the gods with grain, and 3) spare the animals.

According to Greek myth, Athena was born from the head of Zeus, after he swallowed her pregnant mother Metis. The supreme god feared a son would displace him (as he dethroned his father Cronus). Hephaestus, the smithy of the gods, then delivered the baby by Caesarean section by splitting open Zeus's head with an axe. This is usually interpreted to mean that Athena, the goddess of wisdom, was born fully grown, the offspring of thought or pure reason. However, she was also a war goddess and represents a middle way between the peaceful mother goddess of ancient Crete, Anatolia, and other regions and the warlike father gods of the Indo-Aryan migrants and invaders that displaced them. Historians speculate that the volcanic destruction of Thera and the subsequent collapse of Minoan civilization marked the end of matrilineal society. Mother Earth was no longer able to protect her subjects, and the male sky and thunder gods, ranging from Zeus and Poseidon to Indra and Yahweh, gradually overthrew Rhea, Asherah, Isis, and other mother goddesses, and the era of modern patriarchy began. Caught in the middle, Athena remained virginal and had no husband, consort, or romantic conquests. Tellingly, the axe used in her birth was the Minoan double-bladed axe. In muted or altered form, she carried forward the traditional Cretan and Theran arts of peace, weaving, and other crafts.

7. Return to Albion

Bidding Greece farewell, I flew back to the UK and for lunch enjoyed a plant burger made from oats, quinoa, sweet potatoes, and guacamole that I took out from Mama Tierra's. At Heathrow, Bettina returned from Hamburg, and we went to an Air BnB in Shoreditch, the original theater district in Elizabethan London. The next morning, we wove our way toward London's finance hub, enjoyed breakfast at Organic Planet, and went over the script for the evening's live broadcast of the *Miso Happy Show*. At Mushi Mushi, a macrobiotic oriented Japanese restaurant in Liverpool Station, we enjoyed a delicious lunch of miso soup, organic brown rice, tempura, pickles, eggplant, and seaweed salad.

The show was broadcast at the nearby apartment of Simon Brown, author of *Modern Day Macrobiotics* and *Macrobiotics for Life*. He described a recent project in which he coached nurses in India on how to treat diabetes with diet. Marlene Watson-Tara, another leading UK teacher and counselor, spoke about her work with autism, depression, and other chronic conditions. Bettina gave 9 Star Ki advice for summer travel, and I delivered a slide show on "Animals Who Cook," a lighthearted look at mammals, birds, mollusks, and insects who warm up, ferment, or otherwise process their food. Celtic music from the Morning Star Consort accompanied the talks. Afterward, we went out for a late dinner with Simon at Redemption, a vegan-friendly restaurant, and talked about the future of macrobiotics.

The following morning, we stored our luggage in Leicester Square and had a surprisingly tasty breakfast of oatmeal, topped with fresh berries and lightly sweetened with honey, at the National Gallery Café. After a quick tour of the National Portrait Galley to sharpen our diagnosis of the Tudors, Stuarts, and Victorians, we made a quick stop around the corner at the National Gallery and peeked at some gorgeous Monets, Renoirs, Cézannes, and other Impressionist canvasses. I was delighted to behold the original of Van Gogh's *Wheat Field with Cypresses* that graces my bedroom wall. In front of a theatre hosting a new play about Harry Potter, Bettina asked me to take a photo for her son, Sennin, to whom she used to read the magical tales as a child. Shrines to Harry's escapades at Platform 9 3/4 at King's Cross, Leadenhall Market, and Tower Bridge have replaced Chaucer's old landmarks on the contemporary London pilgrimage circuit.

At Heathrow, Bettina bought a book on Norse mythology and realized that Asgard, the ancient realm of the gods in Scandinavian and Teutonic lore, was a variant of Aska! The flight back to Boston and drive to the Berkshires went smoothly. On the plane, I read an article in *China Daily* reporting that rice had been grown in the desert for the first time. In Quindao, scientists announced the development of a type of salt-resistant rice that was planted in desert regions of Dubai and produced high yields. Such innovative, non-GMO strains could help alleviate future food crises in arid regions and mitigate the coming water shortage.

Like the suitors who ate Penelope and her son Telemechus out of house and home, the network of agribusiness and biotech companies are making our planet uninhabitable. Resolving the multiple challenges facing our species, including depleted soil, poisoned air, polluted water, and harmful electromagnetic fields, will require the will, focus, and vitality of Odysseus reclaiming the hand of Penelope—the patient and long suffering Mother Earth. At the end of the epic, Odysseus strings the great bow and sends an arrow through the lined up axe heads, proclaiming his return. The 12 double axe heads, the Minoan symbol of peace and harmony, represent the Zodiac and mastery of yin and yang.

My European odyssey brought me closer to Mother Earth and Father Sky and to the meeting of ancient and future worlds. In a contemporary House of Ladies, Lotte and her circle of daughters and neighbors, primarily female, represented a direct link with Rhea, the ancient Minoan mother goddess, and the peaceful, grain-based matrilineal cultures of the past.

By the time I came home, I realized that the legacy of Aska lay not in a mythical Atlantis, a legendary Phaeacia, or even the sacred ruins of Akrotiri, Athens, and Delphi. Aska dwells in the day-to-day love and care, joys and sorrows, and hopes and dreams, of ordinary people striving to live in harmony with nature. It exists in the hearts and mindfulness of everyone seeking to make a difference and create beauty in their lives.

Left: **Ladies in Blue Minoan fresco.** *Right*: **Bettina, Eva & Lotte Zumdick**

Glossary

Achaeans The Greek warriors in the Trojan War; also known as the Argives and Danaans

Achilles Hero of the *Iliad*; king of Pythia, son of the nymph Thetis and king Peleus; "best of the Achaeans" destined to die gloriously in battle or lead a quiet, peaceful life

Achilles' Shield The divine armor fashioned for Achilles by Hephaestus, the god of fire, featuring the cosmos and cycles of history

Aegis Divine object, conceived variously as a shield, cloth, or animal skin, carried by Zeus and Athena, used in battle, and occasionally lent to the other deities to inspire awe and terror

Aeneas Trojan hero and founder of Rome in Virgil's *Aeneid*

Aeolus The lord of the island Aeolia who gives Odysseus a bag of winds to carry him home

Agamemnon King of Mycenae and commander of the Achaeans during the Trojan War whose arrogance alienates Achilles; slain by his wife Clytemnestra and her lover Aegisthus upon his return

Ages of Humanity Eras of decreasing virtue spanning the Golden Age, Silver Age, Bronze Age, Heroic Age, and Iron Age

Ajax Son of Telamon, Achaean hero, and spirit Odysseus encounters in Hades

Alcinous Benevolent king of the Phaeacians who offers Odysseus hospitality on Scheria

Ambrosia food of the gods

Andromache Kindly wife of Hector and mother of baby Astyanax who begs her husband not to go into battle

Antikleia Odysseus's grief-stricken mother whose spirit he encounters in Hades

Antinous Arrogant leader of the suitors wooing Penelope

Aphrodite Goddess of love who sides with Paris, Aeneas, and the Trojans

Apollo The archer god who presides over the Muses, music, and healing; he protects the Trojans during the war; brings plague to the Achaeans when they abuse his priest; and is prayed to by Odysseus on his return

Ares Brawney and brutal god of war who supports the Trojans

Arete Noble queen of the Phaeacians who offers hospitality to Odysseus

Aska ancient scientific and spiritual world community, ca. 15,000 BCE, traces of which remain in geographical place names such as "Alaska," "Nebraska," and "Basque."

Athena Daughter of Zeus and clever goddess of wisdom, weaving, and war; she aids Achilles and Odysseus in their trials and tribulations

Barley Principal grain in the Mediterranean and Aegean worlds; consumed as por-

Glossary

ridge, bread, flat cakes, soup, stew, and beverages

Blessed Isles afterlife paradise for the dead favored by the gods

Breseis Beautiful captive "wife" of Achilles whom Agamemnon demands when his own abducted female war prize is returned to her father

Calypso Beautiful goddess who offers Odysseus immortality and eternal youth in return for staying with her forever on her island paradise

Cassandra Trojan princess who can forsee the future but is not believed

Charybdis The maelstrom that sucks entire ships to the bottom of the sea

Circe Sorceress who turns men into swine, but when her spell is broken serves Odysseus and gives him the knowledge he needs to return home

Cronos Ruler of the Golden Age, overthrown by his son Zeus

Cryseis Young woman claimed by Agamemnon but returned following the plague sent by Apollo

Cryses Priest of Apollo and father of Cryseis whose prayers to Apollo bring plague to the Achaeans until she is returned

Cyclops A cannibalistic race of giants, such as Polyphemus, who holds Odysseus and his men captive in his cave until tricked to release them

Demeter Goddess of grain whose name means Barley Mother

Demodocus Blind poet in the court of King Alcinous and Queen Arete who sings about the Trojan Horse and Odysseus's role in the war

Dreams of Horn and Ivory Penelope's classification of dreams into honest ones that come true or compell action (horn) or false, illusory ones (ivory)

Elpenor Youngest of Odysseus's crew who dies on Circe's island and in Hades asks Odysseus to bury his body and erect an oar on his mound

Erin Goddess of discord who threw the apple marked "To the Fairest" into the wedding of Thetis and Peleus, setting off a competition among Hera, Athena, and Aphrodite for the title

Eumaios The loyal swineherd in whose hut Odysseus stays upon his return to Ithaca

Eurykleia The old serving woman who recognizes Odysseus's scar when she bathes him on his return

Eurylokhos Odysseus's brother-in-law who leads the mutiny against him

Eurymakhos A leading suitor for Penelope and son of Eurylokhos

Gaia Primal goddess of the earth and mother of the Titans, giants, and many immortals

Hades The Underworld where the souls of the dead go after death; also the god of death; in Hades, Odysseus meets the spirits of Achilles, Tiresias, and others

Hebe Daughter of Zeus and Hera, cupbearer of the gods, and wife of Hercules

Hector The towering, seemingly invincible leader of the Trojans who takes the battle to the Achaean ships but ultimately is slain by Achilles

Hecuba Queen of Troy, wife of Priam, and mother of Hector

Helen Queen of Sparta and wife of Menelaus whose abduction or elopement with Paris precipitates the Trojan War; host to Telemachus in the *Odyssey*

Helios The sun god whose sacred cattle are eaten by Odysseus's men

Hephaestus God of metallurgy who fashions Achilles's Shield

Hera Principal wife of Zeus, goddess of marriage and fertility, and implacable foe of the Trojans because Paris selected Aphrodite over her in the beauty pageant

Hercules Earlier epic hero whose twelve labors compare with Odysseus's and who conveys an image of himself to the Ithacan in Hades

Hermes Messenger of the gods who also presides over esoteric wisdom and con-

ducts souls to Hades
Hesiod Poet and author of *Theogony* and *Works and Days* who lived about the same time as Homer
Honey Principal sweetener in the ancient world; used especially in wines
Homer The blind poet and author of the *Iliad* and *Odyssey* who lived about the 8th century BCE
Ichor Ethereal golden fluid or blood of the gods
Ino A Nereid, or sea nymph, who gives her veil to Odysseus when his raft capsizes
Iris Goddess of the rainbow and messenger of the gods
Ismarus City sacked by Odysseus upon leaving Troy
Ithaca Island homeland of Odysseus on the western side of the Greek mainland; also known as Thaki
Kleos The glory of a warrior immortalized in bardic song
Labyrns The double axe with a butterfly shape sacred to the Minoans
Laertes Odysseus's aging father who has retired to tend his orchard
Laestrygonians Cannibalistic race that destroys eleven of Odysseus's twelve returning ships
Lotus-Eaters Islanders who offer Odysseus's crew the flower of forgetfulness
Menelaus King of Sparta and husband of Helen; he hosts Telemachus in the *Odyssey*
Menis Cosmic anger of the gods and demigods such as Achilles that arises when social and universal harmony are endangered
Metis Practical wisdom, cunning, and craft, especially associated with Zeus, Athena, Odysseus, and Penelope
Minoan ancient Cretan civilization associated with King Minos and the tale of Theseus, Adriane, and the Minotaur
Moly The black and white magical herb Hermes gives Odysseus to counter Circe's enchantment
Nausicaa Kindly princess of Scheria who befriends Odysseus when he washes up naked and famished on the beach
Nectar Liquid refreshment of the gods
Nestor King of Pylos and elder statesman of the Achaeans noted for his long-winded speeches
Nostros Homecoming; the object of Odysseus's return voyage
Odysseus A leading Achaean warrior, diplomat, and strategist who designed the Wooden Horse and whose ten-year voyage home to his wife Penelope is the subject of the *Odyssey*
Ogygia The island of Calypso, the navel of the earth
Oikes Household, environment, root word for "ecology"
Paris Prince of Troy who selects Aphrodite as the fairest goddess and wins the love of Helen, the world's most beautiful woman, setting in motion the Trojan War; also known as Alexander
Patroclus Loyal friend of Achilles whose death in battle prompts him to reenter the fray and slay Hector
Penelope Long-suffering wife of Odysseus who deceives the suitors by weaving a burial shroud for Laertes by day and unraveling it at night
Persephone Daughter of Demeter abducted by Hades who made her queen of the Underworld
Phaeacians The utopian inhabitants of Scheria who welcome Odysseus when he is stranded on their island and convey him home to Ithaca

Glossary

Poseidon Tempestuous god of the sea and earth-shaker who thwarts Odysseus's homecoming because he blinded his son Polyphemus

Priam Aged king of Troy who pleads with Achilles for Hector's body

Prometheus Titan who gave fire to human beings for cooking meat and was punished by Zeus with an eagle pecking his liver

Scamandros Principal river of Troy personified as a god; Simoeis is the secondary tributary

Scheria The island of the Phaeacians where Odysseus washes up after capsizing

Scylla The loathsome six-headed monster that devours several of Odysseus's crew on their voyage

Sema Oracle or sign

Sirens The seductive harpies whose beautiful songs lure sailors to their deaths; Odysseus has himself tied to his mast to avoid their enchantment

Telemachus Son of Odysseus and Penelope who comes of age and sets off to learn of his missing father's destiny

Themis Goddess of cosmic order who upholds universal law and justice

Theogony Geneology of the gods by Hesiod

Thetis Immortal nymph and mother of Achilles who asks Hephaestus to make divine armor for her son

Thrinakia Island of the Sun whose cattle are sacred, but when consumed by Odysseus's crew brings doom on their ship

Tiresias Spirit of the wisest man in antiquity who foretells Odysseus's destiny on his visit to Hades ending with a journey inland carrying an oar on his shoulder

Titans Race of giants prior to the Olympian gods

Troy City in Asia Minor east of the Greek mainland where the Trojan War takes place over ten years

Winnowing shovel A farming tool to separate the grain from the chaff; a subject of Tiresias's prophecy

Zeus Ruler of the gods who presides over the immortals on Mount Olympus, who combines *menis* (anger) and *metis* (practical wisdom), and wields the thunderbolt and aegis

Bibliography

Athanassakis, Apostolos N., translator, *The Homeric Hymns*, Johns Hopkins UP, 2004.
Auden, W. H., *Achilles' Shield*, Random House, 1951.
Barnes, Craig S., *In Search of the Lost Feminine*, Fulcrum, 2006.
Benardete, Seth, *The Bow and the Lyre: A Platonic Reading of the Odyssey*, Rowman & Littlefield, 1997.
Blondell, Ruby, *Helen of Troy: Beauty, Myth, Devastation*, Oxford UP, 2013.
Bobbitt, Philip, *Achilles' Shield: War, Peace, and the Course of History*, Anchor, 2003.
Brann, Eva, *Homeric Moments: Clues to Delight in Reading the Odyssey and the Iliad*, Paul Dry Books, 2002.
Butler, Alan, *The Dawn of Genius: The Minoan Super-Civilization and the Truth about Atlantis*, Watkins, 2014.
Butler, Samuel, *The Authoress of the Odyssey*, 1897.
Connelly, Joan B., *The Parthenon Enigma*, Knopf, 2014.
Dalby, Andrew, *Rediscovering Homer: Inside the Origin of the Epics*, Norton, 2006
Dalby, Andrew and Sally Grainger, *The Classical Cookbook*, British Museum Press, 2000
Detienne, Marcel and Jean-Pierre Vernant, *The Cuisine of Sacrifice Among the Greeks*, U of Chicago P, 1989.
Edmunds, Lowell, editor, *Approaches to Greek Myth*, Johns Hopkins UP, 2014.
Felson, Nancy, *Regarding Penelope: From Character to Poetics*, U of Oklahoma P, 1994.
Finkelberg, Margalit, editor, *The Homer Encyclopedia*, 3 volumes, Wiley-Blackwell, 2011.
Fischer, Norman, *Sailing Home: Using the Wisdom of Homer's Odyssey to Navigate Life's Perils and Pitfalls*, North Atlantic Books, 2011
Goldberg, Michael J., *Travels with Odysseus: Uncommon Wisdom from

Homer's Odyssey, Circe's Island Press, 2005.

Hall, Edith, *The Return of Ulysses: A Cultural History of Homer's Odyssey*, Johns Hopkins UP, 2008.

Haller, Benjamin, *The Gates of Horn and Ivory in Odyssey 19: Penelope's Call for Deeds, Not Words, Classical Philology*, 104(4) 2009:397-417_.

Haywood, John, *Historical Atlas of Ancient Civilizations*, Penguin, 2005.

Hesiod and Apostolos N. Athanassakis, translator, *Theogony, Works and Days*, Johns Hopkins UP, 2004.

Homer and Peter Green, translator, *The Iliad*, U of California P, 2015.

Homer and Robert Fitzgerald, translator, *The Odyssey*, Farrar, Strauss, & Giroux, 1961, 1998.

Homer and Emily Wilson, translator, *The Odyssey*, Norton, 2018.

Knox, Bernard, *The World of Odysseus*, New York Review Books, 2002.

Kremezi, Aglaia, *The Foods of the Greek Islands*, Houghton-Mifflin, 2015.

Latacz, Joachim, *Homer: His Art and His World*, U of Michigan P, 1998

Lord, Alfred B., *The Singer of Tales*, Stephen Mitchell and Gregory Nagy, editors, 2nd edition, Harvard UP, 2000.

Loudon, Bruce. *The Iliad: Structure, Myth, and Meaning*, Johns Hopkins UP, 2006.

Loudon, Bruce, *Homer's Odyssey and the Near East,* Cambridge UP, 2011.

Loudon, Bruce, *The Odyssey: Structure, Narrative, and Meaning*, Johns Hopkins UP, 1999.

Marinatos, Nanno, *Minoan Kingship and the Solar Goddess*, U of Illinois P, 2010.

Muellner, Leonard, *The Anger of Achilles: Menis in Greek Epic*, Cornell UP, 1996.

Nagy, Gregory, *Homeric Questions*, U of Texas P, 1996.

Oesterley, W.O.E., *Sacred Dance in the Ancient World*, Dover, 2002

Perry, Laura, *Ariadne's Thread: Awakening to the Wonders of the Ancient Minoans in Our Modern Lives*, Moon Books, 2013.

Purves, Alex, *Unmarked Space: Odysseus and the Inland Journey, Arethusa_39_(2006)_1–20_*

Sabin, Frances E. and Ralph V.D. Magoffin, *Classical Myths That Live Today,* Silver urdett Co, 1958.

Schein, Seth L., Editor, *Reading the Odyssey: Selected Interpretive Essays*, Princeton UP, 1996

Segan, Francene, *The Philosopher's Kitchen: Recipes from Ancient Greek and Roman for the Modern Cook*, Random House, 2004

Straus, Barry, *The Trojan War: A New History*, Simon & Schuster, 2006.

Vinci, Felice, *The Baltic Origins of Homer's Epic Tales*, Inner Traditions, 2006.

Acknowledgments

I am grateful to my parents, partners, daughter, sister, and other relatives for their love and inspiration over the years, as well as friends, colleagues, and students with whom I have engaged in fruitful discussions on the themes and insights in this book. I am especially thankful to Bettina Zumdick, Edward and Naomi Ichikawa Esko, Sachi Kato, Anne Teresa De Keersmaeker, David and Nicola McCarthy, and Elizabeth Karaman for their friendship and encouragement over the last several years as this project was completed.

Quotations from the *Iliad* are from Peter Green's recent edition and those from the *Odyssey* are from Robert Fitzgerald's classic translation.

The cover illustration is from *The Iliad and Odyssey: A Giant Golden Book*, a children's classic illustrated by Alice and Martin Provensen.

The illustration of Achilles' Shield on the title page is from *The Homer Encyclopedia*, edited by Margalit Finkelberg.

Resources

Planetary Health, Inc.
A nonprofit educational organization that sponsors Amberwaves, a grassroots network to protect rice, wheat, and other grains from genetic engineering and climate change and to keep America and the planet beautiful. PHI also sponsors the Macrobiotic Summer Conference, Online Macrobiotic Winter Conference, and other activities. Contact: Alex Jack, president, Box, 487, Becket MA 01223 | 413-623-0012

Websites: www.amberwavesofgrain.com | www.macrobioticsummerconference.com | www.makropedia.com

Culinary Medicine School
A center for healing, awareness, and transformation, founded and directed by Bettina Zumdick, Lee, MA 01238, 413-429-5610. CMS is sponsor of the *Miso Happy Show*, an online learning and variety program hosted by Alex and Bettina.

Websites: www.culinarymedicineschool.com | www.misohappyshow.com

Alex Jack
Alex offers macrobiotic dietary and health consultations, 9 Star Ki readings, and other personal services, as well as lectures and seminars on a wide variety of subjects. Contact: Alex Jack, Becket MA 01223 | 413-623-0012 | shenwa26@yahoo.com

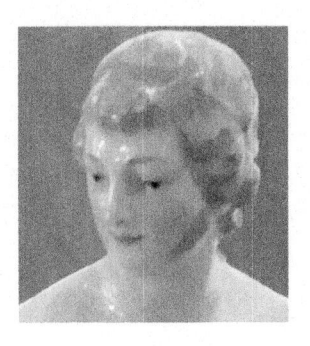

Index

Achaeans, Achilles best of, 189; Achilles' Shield, glanced at on, 54; Achilles' leadership of, 57, 153, 189; Achilles swiftest of, 204; Achilles' wrath and effect on, 36, 50; Aeolus' befriending of, 87; Aeolus's defriending of, 94; Agamemnon's leadership of, 119; Age of Heroes and, 191; Ajax mourning over, 100; allegorical interpretation of, 61; Apollo sacrificed to by, 74; Athena's support of, 55, 187; Athena's withdrawal of support for, 123, 187; battle of with the Trojans, 73; Calchas's prophecy concerning, 210; Chyrses' visit to, 32; cosmic order violated by, 62; Cyclops' question to, 93; death of in fighting, 8; Demodokos' song of, 188; destiny sown by, 95; diet of, 75, 204; encampment of, 55, 78, 126; fate of after the war, 66, 71; feast of, 76; fleet of, 33, 77, 134; fortifications of, 60; gods turn against, 64, 66, 71; grain compared to fallen soldiers among, 148; in Hades, 197; Helen idolized by, 63, 182; Helen's tapestry depicting, 178; Helios dishonored by, 123; indifferent to the outcome of the war, 29; Ismarus plundered by, 91; Laistrygons' torment of, 95; long hair of, 75; oar a war symbol of, 145; Odysseus introduces his crew as, 92; Odysseus' leadership of, 74; other names for, 31; plague visited on, 32, 74, 184, 187; patriarch of, 42; Penelope's deception of, 178; regression of, 63; ships of attacked and set afire, 127, 189; song of woe about, 177; survival of after the war, 53, 66, 71, 123; as a symbol of humanity, 66; Trojans implore return of Hector's body from, 33; victory of, 46, 184; warlike mentality of, 91; women abused, raped, and enslaved by, 168; Wooden Horse and, 188; Zeus's favor over, 42, 71

Achilles, aegis of, 57; Aeneas and, 127; Agamemnon's quarrel with, 32, 36, 37, 42, 58; Ajax and 55; Apollo slayer of, 45, 55; Arjuna compared to, 8; armor of, 98-99, 100, 108; ash spear of, 58; Athena's protection of, 14, 43, 57, 58, 59; Breseis and, 32; as cook, 78, 161; death of, 29, 30, 45, 47, 58, 100, 150, 167, 184; as a demi-god, 36; diet of, 74, 76, 77, 78; draft avoided by, 11, 29; embassy to, 32, 50, 55, 127, 150; as Everyman, 60; heart of iron of, 77; Hector's battle with, 33, 37, 39-40, 45, 59-60, 61, 77, 168, 185; Hector's corpse mutilated by, 33, 43, 60, 80, 150, 188; Hera's protection of 59, 82; horses of, 58, 73, 127; in Hades, 30, 87, 90, 98, 100, 111, 122, 153, 174, 183, 189; regret of in Hades, 98, 111, 153, 183; hut on beach of, 60; Iphigeneia and, 171; level of consciousness of, 42, 62; as Linos, 55; as a lion 173; Lykaon begs for life from, 68, 148; lyre played by, 47, 55, 138, 170, 189; gods' *menis* against, 61; Neoptolemus, son of, 183; Odysseus compared to, 89, 90, 99, 125, 189; Paris slayer of, 45; Patroclus, love for, 29, 43, 131; Patroclus funeral for, 61, 75-76; Priam meeting with, 33, 44, 46, 60, 78-79; Phoinix and, 41; Poseidon's protection of, 58; prophecy at birth of, 49-50; River, battle with, 42, 46, 66, 58; shield of, 47-66, 100, 124; sports competition of, 168, 185; sulking in tent by, 32, 127; *themis* violated by, 36; Thetis's protection of, 29, 40, 47, 58, 66, 79, 98; Trojan youths slain by, 58, 61, 65, 76, 105; as a warrior, 34, 35, 55, 58, 59, 69, 84; refusal of to fight, 30, 32; return of to battle, 32, 36, 58, 66, 75; women, attitude toward, 168; wrath of, 36, 42-43, 44, 58, 61, 77, 82, 90, 161, 188, 190; Zeus and, 40, 43, 45, 55, 58

Achilles' Shield, 47-66; Ages of Humanity depicted on, 124, 173; cosmos portrayed on, 149; grain-eating focus of, 83; Minoan civilization and, 173; music and dance on, 190-191; vertical orientation of, 150; fate of after Achilles' death, Hades, 99-100
Achilles Shield (Auden), 51
Acrobats, 173
Acropolis, 217
Acropolis Museum, 221
Adriane, 56, 157, 176, 191
Aeaea, 159, 177
Aega, 159
Aegean, 159; cultures and civilizations of, 64; diet of, 67, 69-70, 110, 149, 159, 203-212, 221; folklore of, 140; goddesses of, 158-159; Golden Age in, 173; hospitality in, 95-96; islands of, 184; matrilineal society of, 160; Minoans and, 166, 213; music and dance in, 193; ; origin of name of, 159; piracy in, 91; peaceful cultures in 218; recipes of, 203-212; sacrificial customs of, 80-81; seafaring in, 61, 125, 127, 129, 138, 145, 154, 166, 173; sports competition in, 158; trade in, 60, 145, 218; visit to, 219; utopian culture of, 112; violence and war in, 147; volcanoes of, 159
Aegeus, 159
Aegis, 57, 124
Aegisthus, 86, 119 183
Aeneas, 32, 34 58, 127, 169
Aeneid, 32
Aeolia, 94, 119, 130, 139
Aeolus, 87, 94, 95, 119, 121, 122, 130, 134,
Africa, 200, 214, 221
Agamemnon, and Achilles, 36, 58; arrogance of, 37, 55, 61, 74, 176, 187; Artemis and, 171-172; battle deaths by, 34; Briseis claimed by, 30, 32, 42, 189; Calchas and, 32, 171; Chryseis and, 30, 32, 42, 74, 127, 176, 187; Clytemnestra and, 64, 86; chastising of his men, 75, 168; diet of, 74, 75; drinking habits of, 194; dream of, 41; expedition to Troy led by, 31, 161; god's *menis* against, 62; level of consciousness of, 42; Menelaus compared to, 64, 76; sacrifice of daughter by, 83, 171; shield of, 49; slaying of, 64, 119, 162, 171; in the Underworld, 88, 98, 99, 122, 174, 183, 189; as a warrior, 34, 171, 189; women, attitude toward, 162; yielding of to priest of Apollo, 74, 127

Age of Heroes, 191
Age of Pisces, 180
Age of Taurus, 180
Agea, 161
Agenor, 59
Ages of Humanity, 24, 49-54, 56, 60, 63, 84, 178, 179-182; and diet, 70-73, 198-199
Agora, 217
Aiaia, 96, 192
Ajax, 55, 57, 67, 127, 150, 187, 189-190; shade of in Hades, 99, 100
Akrotiri, 218-219, 223
Alcinous, Arete wife of, 174; court of, 104, 105, 170; festivities presided over, 104, 105, 154, 186; lineage of, 103; Nausicaa offered in marriage to Odysseus by, 105; Odysseus recounts adventures to, 110, 138, 166, 186; Odysseus welcomed by, 102; palace of, 104; Phaeacians ruled by, 86, 104; prophecy recalled by, 134, 155; sacrifices of, 120; seafaring explained by, 129, 154; ship placed at Odysseus's disposal by, 133. *See also Phaeacians*
Alcohol, 75, 110-111, 189
Alexander, Carolyn, 28, 50
Altair, 179
Amaltheia, 161
Amazons, 159
Amberwaves, 196-197
Ambrosia, 79, 122, 180
Amphinomos, 115, 117,122, 151
Anatolia, 31, 121
Andromache, 77, 176, 204
Anger, 192. See Menis.
Animal food, 110, 116, 191-192. *See Meat, Cheese, Milk*
Antelope, 220-221
Anticleia, 87, 98, 169, 186
Antikythera mechanism, 178
Antinous, 88, 114, 115, 116, 117, 177-178
Antiphates, 95
Aphrodite, as Aeneas' mother, 32; Ares' affair with, 105; Golden Apple given to, 7, 17, 31, 32, 64, 215; Paris assisted by, 31, 45, 189; Diomedes' wounding of, 80; level of consciousness of, 41; Hector and, 43, 80; Hera begs favor of, 148; as an Olympian goddess, 172; Trojans support for, 55
Apollo, aegis wielded by, 58; Achilles slain by, 45, 55, 58, 62; Agamemnon's anger toward, 32; as archer, 57, 112, 184; art and, 45, 62; birth of, 61; brings death in old age to, 112; feast day of on the massacre, 187; level of consciousness of, 41; as

god of medicine, 20, 32, 45, 187, 217; as god of music, 20, 32, 187; as god of the sun, 45; Hector ministered to by, 80, 82; as son of Leto, 45; Hippocratic Oath and 217; Linos slain by, 49, 55, 191; lyre of, 79; *menis* of, 36, 187; Odysseus befriended by, 187; Oracle of, 220; plague brought by, 32, 74, 184; Poseidon fought by, 45; priest of, 32, 74, 111, 176, 187; Silver Age and, 61; singing of, 189; Troy's earlier destruction of, 64; as warrior, 59; as wolf-born, 76; Zeus's favor of, 82

Aquarian Age, 180
Aquarius, 180
Aquila, 179
Arcturus, 166
Ares, 41, 45, 55, 105
Arete, 84, 86, 102, 110, 169, 174, 176, 186
Argo, 126-127, 129
Argonauts, 155
Argonautica, 126
Argos, 138, 165
Aristotle, 44
Arlington Street Church, 13
Art, 170, 171
Artemis, 45, 112, 164, 171-172
As You Like It (Marlowe), 23
Asclepius, 217
Asgard, 223
Ash trees, 52, 57
Asherah, 221
Asia, 182
Aska, 213, 220, 223
Assembly of elders, 54-55
Assyria, 156
Astrological Ages, 180-181
Astyanax, 77
Athena, Achilles assisted by, 43, 55, 59; aegis wielded by, 57, 107, 108, 124; as Odysseus' anima, 167-168; Ares and, 41; attributes of, 18, 89, 108, 186; birth of, 89, 162, 221-222; Dawn held back by, 137, 196; Enyalios' battle with, 45; Alex Jack helped by, 217; Jason aided by, 126; as judge in the contest for Achilles' arms, 98-99, 100; in disguise, 16, 110,118, 124; Hector deceived by, 31-32, 45, 59; golden sandals and wand of, 123; as goddess of craftsmanship, 24, 108; as goddess of wisdom, 41, 45 Ithacan conflict ended by, 89, 117, 194; Jason aided by, 126; Judgment of Paris and, 17, 31, 32; level of consciousness of, 41, 94; as Mentor in disguise, 110,118, 124 menis of, 36; metis of, 124; as a Minoan goddess, 162, 175; mythological origins of, 162; Night held back by, 89, 137, 195-196; Odysseus assisted by, 33, 45, 86, 88, 89, 93, 94, 99, 100, 102, 105, 106, 108, 123, 124, 128, 152, 166, 167, 181, 190, 195; old man disguised as, 14; olives sacred to, 68, 117, 195, 217; Orestes favored by, 162; owl symbol of, 6; Palladium statue of, 169; Parthenon dedicated to, 171; Patroclus tricked by, 33; Penelope assisted by, 88, 122; Poseidon's conflict with, 140, 217; sacrifice proposed by, 118; as shepherd boy in disguise, 14, 105-106, 112; Telemachus assisted by, 86, 88, 106, 118, 128, 146, 183-184; Trojans, hated by 32; temple of in Troy, 11, 74-75, 187; *themis* and, 55; as a warrior, 34, 45, 48, 175; as weaving goddess, 176, 178; Wooden Horse dedicated to, 33; wrath of, 36; vengeance wreaked on Greeks by, 123, 187; Zeus confers with, 86, 89, 117, 124, 194

Athens, 64, 171, 194, 200, 216-217, 223
Atlantis, 65, 213, 219, 223
Atlas, 151, 165
Auden, W.H., 51
Aurai, 172
Autolykos, 185, 192
Awns, 199, 203
Axe heads, 88, 123, 128, 184. *See* Double Axe
Aztecs, 170

Babylon, 156
Baking, 113
Balios, 58
Ball playing, 103, 105, 170
Bard, 173
Barley, on Achilles' Shield, 49, 52, 55, 203; as Aegean principal food, 67, 110, 159, 203, 206, 217, 221; Ages of Humanity and, 70-71; Amberwaves and, 197; Amphinomous and, 115; Athena instructs Telemachus to pack, 110; awned, 199-200, 203; in the Bible, 67; in the Blessed Isles, 53, 71; bread, 68; bread offered by Nausicaa, 110; chewiness of, 203; Circe's preparation of, 96, 111; Cretan cooking and, 160, 200-201; Demeter and, 67, 148, 211, 221; decline of in future ages, 70-71; eaten of as porridge, soup, stew, bread, cakes, meal, 67; in Egypt, 67; in Elusinian Mysteries, 67; energy of, 204; Eumaios service of, 120; fallen soldiers compared to,

73, 74; in Greek diet, 70; in the Golden Age, 70, 190; hallmark of being human, 68; Hesiod on, 70; Hippocrates' use of, 206, 217; history of, 67; in the Iliad, 67, 69; inlanders' main food, 145; in the Book of Isaiah, 147; as life force, 73, 204; Mediterranean Diet and, 159, 203, 217, 221; in Minoan civilization, 67, 219; oar symbolizing threshing of, 149, 195; Odysseus' praise of, 115, 122, 152; Odysseus' scattering of in Hades, 119; in the Odyssey, 67, 110-113; ordinary soldiers and, 194; as key to peace, 71; Phaeacians grinding of, 103, 112; plowshare used to till, 147; servant women grinding of, 116; in Silver Age, 71; in Sparta, 110; on Thrinakia, 111; Telemachus sets sail with, 110; sacrificial use of, 67, 74, 82-83, 112, 118-119, 190; types of, 203; verticality of, 150; wheat compared to, 68, 70; wild, 67, 111; winnowing shovel used to thresh, 147; word for corn and, 148

Barnes, Craig S., 159, 161
Beans, 68, 128, 143, 159
Great Bear (constellation), 48, 51, 54, 102, 166
Beauty pageant, 30, 31
Beeswax, 88, 100, 132, 169
Beith, Gale, 21
Bergren, Ann, 167, 168
Bhagavad Gita, 10, 27
Bible, 67
Birds, 182
Black Elk, 20
Ewe, 119, 174
Blake, William, 27
Blessed Immortals, 81
Blessed Isles, 53, 71, 224
Blood, 111
Blood price, 54
Blood sausage, 114-115, 116, 117
Boar, Odysseus scarred by, 185, 193; as symbol of ignorance, 152; sacrifice of, 120, 131
Bootes, 166
Boston University School of Theology, 13-14, 15
Bow, of Artemis and Apollo, 57; of Cheiron, 58; contest of, 86, 106-107, 116, 151, 186-187; integrating feminine energy and, 186; of Heracles, 184; in the *Iliad*, 185; iron blades of, 123; musical instrument compared to, 186, 187; of Odysseus, 138, 184-188; of Paris, 184; symbol of, 187; as weapon of cowards, 40

Bread, Achilles' praise of in Hades, 153; Achilles' preparation of, 73; Ajax's eating of 142; Amphinomos' offering of to Odysseus, 115; baking of, 192, 198, 200, 206; barley, 68; in Bronze Age, 14, 71, 199; in the breadbasket of Aegean, 149; Cretan, 200; in Crusades, 67; dakos, 212; decline of, 84; Demeter's, 142; in Egypt, 14, 67; Elijah feeding of by ravens, 14; Elpenor's praise of, 111; Eumaios' offers of to Odysseus, 112; flat, 14, 203; in Greek diet, 70, 159; in Homer, 67; Hesiod on, 73, 84; inlanders' eating of, 142; on the island of the Sun, 111; leavened, 160; Lykaon's praise of, 148; music accompanies baking of, 192; Nausicaa's offer of to Odysseus, 110; Odysseus' baking of, 113; Odysseus' praise of, 165; Phaeacians' offer of to Odysseus, 112; rusk, 212; in sacrificial meals, 79; suitors and, 116, 117; as symbol of culture and civilization, 73, 142; in Troy, 81; unleavened, 14; wheaten, 68, 110
Breseis, 30, 32, 91
Britain, 44
British Museum, 214
Bronze, 60, 181
Bronze Age, 39, 52, 53, 54, 56, 60-61; archery of, 184; axes of, 181; cosmos as feminine in, 172; diet of, 71, 73, 74, 160, 194, 199; echoes of, 123; end of, 65; epics during 191; metals of, 200; Minoans in, 173; in the Near East, 147; ships of, 125-127; trade, 155; sacrifice during, 81, 180; violence of, 194; role of women in, 168; worship of bulls in, 120-121
Brown, Simon, 222
Bryon, 220
Buddhism, 182
Bull, in astrology, 180; leaping of, 158; in Minoan culture, 158, 160; sacred, 120-121; sacrifice of, 120, 131; as symbol of power, 152; Zeus changes into, 172
Butler, Samuel, 174, 175
Butter, 160

Calchas, 32, 171
Calliope, 188
Calypso, astronomical knowledge of, 102, 165-166, 180; Athena intervenes against, 128; as daughter of Atlas, 165; attributes of, 175, 186; Circe compared to, 163; cloak of, 167; concealment of, 163-165, 167; double axe of, 128, 154, 156, 165, 173, 174, 185, 186, 195, 200; feminine and, 17; food made by, 121, 163; Hermes'

visit to, 122, 123, 148; island as center of the world, 165; island as womb, 163; as mastermind, 174; as midwife, 166, 167; origin of name of, 163; Odysseus desired by, 86, 88, 102, 148, 163, 181, 183, 185; Odysseus offered immortality by, 101, 151; rejected by Odysseus, 163, 166, 168, 183; Odysseus helped to build raft by, 86, 102, 128, 137, 151, 154, 156, 174, 195; Odysseus welcomed by, 17, 86, 88, 92, 101, 181-182; as sister of Prometheus, 198; Telemachus hears news of, 86; weaving of, 123, 176, 177; lament of for treatment of women, 148, 163-164

Campbell, Joseph, on circle dances, 170; on the feminine in the Odyssey, 146, 175, 185; interview of with Moyers, 196; on myth and dream, 27; on the mythic quest, 191; on solar and lunar symbolism, 178, 179; studying with, 17-20; on the *Odyssey*, 19

Canaanites, 127
Cannibalism, 111, 192
Cassandra, 33, 187
Castilian Spring, 220
Catalog of Ships, 126, 170
Catreus, 172
Cattle of the Sun, 56, 88, 101, 109, 119, 123, 132, 144, 151, 174, 190; grotesque movements of, 101, 112 119-120; global warming and, 194
Cave of the Nymphs, 166
Ceres, 148
Charis, 47
Charities, 172
Charybdis, 88, 90, 101, 111, 132, 133, 169, 186
Cheese, 92, 110
Cheiron, 58
Chickpeas, 68, 128, 143, 159, 207
Children, 98-100
China, 148
Chios, 207
Chomskey, Noam, 12
Christianity, 68, 150, 156
Chryseis, 30, 32, 42, 74, 91, 187, 201
Chryses, 32, 74, 127, 150, 176, 201
Chthonia, 171
Cicones, 91
Circe, attributes of, 186; beauty and charms of, 97; Calypso compared to, 122, 163; drugs given by, 97, 121, 171, 186, 192; food of, 111, 119, 122, 163, 183, 190, 199; golden bowl of, 123; as daughter of Helios, 101; feminism of, 174; modern day, 26; Odysseus desired by, 96, 99, 102,

151, 183; Odysseus fights with and submits to, 96, 97, 111, 142, 163; Odysseus's indifference to, 168; Odysseus directed to visit Tiresias and Hades by, 97, 98, 125; Odysseus's visits to, 17, 87, 88, 96, 97, 100-101, 102, 111, 119, 130, 131, 132, 151, 185, 192; olive oil used by, 190; roof of, 98, 130, 201; song of, 96, 189; men turned into swine by, 17, 96, 111, 119, 151, 163, 180, 192; Scylla and Charybdis warned against, 101, 132; Sirens warned against, 132; cattle of the Sun warned against, 88, 101; weaving by, 96, 176, 177. *See also Ogygia*

Circle of Agricultural Peace and Plenty, 48-49, 51-52, 53, 55, 73, 173
Circle of the City of Peace and War, 48, 50, 53, 54, 73; as Troy and Achaean encampment, 60, 64; in Hades, 100
Circle of the Dance, 49, 51-52, 53, 56, 73, 173, 188-191; Phaeacians and, 102-103; Minoan civilization and, 173
City of Vintage and Pasturage, 49, 51-52, 53, 73, 173, 190
Climate change, 196-197
Clytemnestra, 64, 86, 162 173, 183
Coffin, William Sloane, 13
Cooking, 83-84, 113, 161, 199
Corn god, 170-172
Cowherd, 179
Crete, 56, 60; art and music of, 170; cuisine of, 160; excavation of 170; health and sickness of, 160; abduction of Helen and, 172; human sacrifice on, 170; as home of Minoan civilization, 155-156; Odysseus pretends to be from, 112, 115, 155, 173; Thera proximity to, 157; women of, 158; Zeus's childhood on, 161
Crew, appetite of, 121, 122, 168, 183, 190, 199; bag of winds opened by, 87, 95, 122-123, 151; ears of plugged with beeswax, 88, 132, 169; cattle of the Sun eaten by, 84, 101, 112, 123, 125, 132, 180, 190; compared to chaff, 143-144; Cicones attacked by, 91; unsanctified food eaten by, 122; Chryseis ferried home by, 127; fish compared to, 152; Jason's, 126; Lotus Eaters succumbed to by, 91-92, 110; nymphs on Goat Island's assistance by, 166; Odysseus's loss of, 26, 95, 98, 101, 123, 128, 130, 131, 140, 143, 165; Odysseus' rebellion against, 56; Odysseus warned by to leave Circe, 96-97; Odysseus lashed to mast by, 132, 147; of the Phaeacians, 129-130, 154; pirate raid of, 87; Polyphmus devours, 87, 92-93, 111;

sacrifice by to the gods, 119-120; Scylla seizes and devours, 101, 165; suitors compared to, 120, 122; swine turned into by Circe, 26, 87, 111, 151, 163, 180, 192; restored from swine to humans by Circe, 96, 119; of Telemachus, 128, 146; visit of to the Underworld, 98, 130;
Crocus, 171, 172
Cronus, 44, 52, 55, 75, 84, 161, 162
Crusades, 68
Cyclops, 89; as a cannibal, 92, 95, 157, 192; diet of, 92, 100, 199; fellow Cyclopses come to the rescue of, 87, 93; level of consciousness of, 93; modern day 199, 215; Odysseus' blinding of, 86, 87, 93, 157, 180, 192; Odysseus's visit to, 92, 107, 110, 129, 142, 169; Odysseus' outwitting of, 89, 90, 93, 165; Odysseus' clinging to ram of, 93, 165, 180; Odysseus' taunts of with his real name, 87, 93; Phaeacians and, 103, 157; as son of Poseidon, 93, 98; Tiresias's warning of, 98; as volcano, 157; Zeus not obeyed by, 92; gift to Zeus of the thunderbolt, 161

Daedalus, 56, 158, 173, 191
Dairy, 69, 120
Dakos, 212
Dance, on Achilles' Shield, 49, 56, 66, 190-191; Ajax comment on, 189; Apollo and, 41; in *As You Like It*, 21; circle, 15, 16, 23, 170, 191, 194; in the Golden Age, 191; Golden Ratio in, 21; healing power of, 25; Homeric epic performance of, 30, 44, 188; Alex Jack and, 12-14, 20-22; labyrinth and, 56, 173, 191, 193; levels of consciousness and, 38; of life, 200; matrilineal society and, 218; of the Minoans, 171, 173, 218; of the Muses, 170, 190; of the nymphs, 166; Orpheus and, 62; Paris off to, 189; Phaeacians' love of, 103, 105, 108, 154; servants' hanging likened to, 107; of the sexes, 168-170; spiral, 21, 170, 195. *See Circle of the Dance*
Dante, 99
Darby, Andrew, 175
David, A. P., 170
Dawn, of the Aquarian Age, 180; Athena holding back of, 89, 137, 195; golden 135; of new Golden Age, 57, 105, 108, 180; of the Iron Age, 198; radiant, 164; rosy-fingered, 12, 105, 123, 129
Death-Spirit, 48, 54
Declaration of Independence, 194
Delphi, 219, 223
Delusion, 41

Demeter, 67, 68, 81, 148, 161; origin of name, 211, 221
Democracy, 194, 217
Demodocus, 33, 86-87, 105, 188
Detienne, Marcel, 73, 83
Diet, and Ages of Humanity, 70-73; in the Odyssey 109-124; of ordinary soldiers, 194; and spirituality, 122. *See Barley, Food, Grains, Recipes, Wheat*
Diomedes, 29, 32, 34, 57, 58, 80, 168, 169, 173,
Dionysis, 68, 81
Divine, Achilles' Shield, 47, 57, 60, 66, 124, 150, 194, 217; aegis, 108; archer, 187; armor, 33, 36, 57, 58, 68, 125; assembly, 80; assistance, 64, 81, 87, 97; beauty, 76; beverage, 80; brothers, 172; cattle, 119; craftsman, 49, 56, 105; decree, 148; demonstration, 195; destiny, 122; energy, 80; gift, 55; intervention, 59; madness, 189; music, 189; Odysseus' respect for, 192; omen, 141; origin, 57, 122; physician, 187; prerogatives, 36; protection, 58, 59, 74, 76; race, 52; retribution, 56; sanction, 61; scripture, 7; semi, 79; song, 49, 191; themis, or order, 11; veil, 182; weapons, 43, 46; wrath, 90, 108. *See Heaven*
Divine Comedy (Dante), 25
Dolon, 55
Double axe, 12, 156; in the slaying of Agamemnon, 162; and the birth of Athena, 162, 222; Calypso's, 128, 156, 173, 185, 195; in the *Iliad*, 185; as a Minoan tool and symbol, 156-157; 165; 219-220; Odysseus's bowshot through, 181, 223; in the sacrifice, 118; Theseus slays Minotaur with, 176
Dream; American, 16; of blessed peace, 196; Calypso's recognition of man and woman's, 165; Joseph Campbell on, 25; city constructed of, 15; diet and memory and realization of, 200; endless, 39; humanity's common, 196; of Alex Jack, 13, 18, 20, 197, 213, 216; modern loss of, 199; myth as a collective, 25; Odysseus's crew's forgetfulness of, 92, 97; Odysseus' realization of, 99, 169; as a personal myth, 25; of One Peaceful World, 22; of Penelope's, 106, 115, 152, 181, 185; sea as realm of, 149; Sirens' song about, 147; two types of: horn and ivory, 181,185; Zeus sending of to Agamemnon, 41;
Drugs, 91-92; of Circe, 183; energetic effects of, 192; of Helen, 183; Lotus-flower, 87, 91, 92, 97, 101, 110, 121, 171,

183, 190, 192, 199; modern, 192, 199
Dumuzi, 170

Earth, on Achilles' Shield, 48, 100; alignment of with Milky Way, 23, 179; animal messengers and, 16; Atlas holding up, 165; Axis mundi connecting heaven with, 165; barley-giving, 52, 70; becoming one with, 143; between heaven and underworld, 150-151; blood soaked, 35; bounteous, 69, 71, 112; charred, 83; creation of, 54, 65; cultivation of, 116; dearest place on, 139; destruction of, 65; divine energy of, 80; dream of, 16, 20, 213; electromagnetic energy reaching, 23, 179; fate of, 194, 215; as father, 168; fertility of, 115; food for mortals from, 79, 81; fruits of, 71, 173; furrowed, 116; Gaia goddess of, 84, 162, 165; geological changes on, 23, 63, 72; glory covers entire, 142; Golden Race covered by, 52; grain-giving, 67, 111, 114, 122, 190, 196; gratitude to, 199; Hera as goddess of, 162; horizontal energy and, 149, 150; inhabitants of, 103; life on, 39, 147; marriage bed rooted to, 135, 141, 152, 196; Minoan goddess of, 156, 158, 159; mother, 213, 221, 223; nourishing, 67; oar planted in, 153; Odysseus' kiss of, 102, 128; Ogygia as center of, 163; paradise on, 66, 72, 94, 220; peace on, 63; rooted in the, 117; roots in heaven and, 197; shaking of, 182; sharing of by Zeus, Poseidon, and Hades, 44, 161; silent, 82; spiraling, 105, 170; sun-warmed, 123; Tartarus deep within, 44; wobble of on its axis, 180; Zodiac journey through, 180
Earthquakes, on Crete, 157; Phaeacians threatened with, 134, 155; Poseidon stirs up, 118, 134, 144, 155, 159; in the Younger Dryas, 63; Zeus, lord of, 102
Eagle, 106, 115-116, 180
East West Journal, 14, 16-17, 20-21, 200-201
Egypt, 67, 81, 155, 156, 213, 214
Elders, 194
Eleusian mysteries, 67, 221
Elijah, 16
Elpenor, 97, 98, 100, 111, 130, 131, 137, 153, 200, 201; meaning of name, 152; mound for, 150; oar planted for, 130-131, 141, 151, 152, 153
EMFs, 198, 223
Empedocles, 158, 160
England, 222-223
Enyalios, 45

Epic Cycle, 30
Erechteus, 171
Erewhon, 174
Esko, Edward, 24
Ethiopians, 79
Eumaios, 88, 106, 112, 113, 120, 135, 166, 189
Europa, 121, 172
Europe, 162
Eurydice, 62-63, 182
Eurykleia, 88, 117, 168, 180, 185, 186, 190,
Eurylokhus, 96, 132
Eurymakhos, 114, 117
Eurynome, 47
Eurytos, 184
Evans, Arthur, 170
Eve, 172

Fagles, Robert, 188
Falstaff, 28
Farming, Achilles and quiet life of, 153; on Achilles' Shield, 66; death and destruction compared to, 50; Demeter's teaching of, 221; factory, 8, 84; initiation rites and, 170; Odysseus' inland journey and, 139, 147, 148; organic, 24, 194, 195, 213; theme of in the Odyssey, 121; Tjiwara's introduction of, 214; tools made of metal for, 200; Triptolemus' introduction of, 221; water for, 65. See *Winnowing Shovel*
Fates, 176, 179
Fawcett, Ann, 14-21
Feminine, arts of, 45; Athena as Odysseus' anima, 167; in the Bronze Age, 172; Campbell, Joseph on, 17, 18, 185; extreme manifestation of, 169, 171; foods, 110; in Greek and Minoan myth, 159, 161; in the Iron Age, 172; male fear of, 171; Odysseus's encounters with, 146, 164, 165, 173, 185, 186; sea as, 167; orientation of the *Odyssey*, 174; Trojans and, 62
Fig tree, 69, 88, 101, 133, 151
Fire, Achilles' use of, 61; artificial forms of, 192, 199; cooking with, 83, 113, 199; Cyclops' camp, 92; dance of with water, 66; funeral use of, 83, 130; global destruction by, 24, 62, 63-64, 65, 66, 123, 181, 187, 193, 198, 217; Hector sets Achaean ships on, 32, 66, 127, 189; Hephaestus god of, 46, 47, 48, 59, 66, 217; on the shore of Ithaca, 94; New Testament prophecy of, 65; Plato's prophecy of, 65; stolen by Prometheus, 81, 83-84, 198; purification with after massacre of suitors, 124, 187; sacred, 198; sitting around, 216; Troy's camp, 54, 189; Troy set on, 62, 66;

Zeus's use of, 57, 66, 124, 181
Fish, 69-70, 111, 112, 115, 160, 180
Fitzgerald, Robert, 188
Five Transformations, 216
Flood, 83
Food, of the gods, 79-80, 122; in the *Iliad*, 67-84; in the *Odyssey*, 109-124; masculine vs. feminine, 110; modern processing of, 65; raw vs. cooked, 121; lack of in Underworld, 111. *See also Barley, Diet, Grains, Recipes, Wheat*
Forgetfulness, 190, 192
Fowl, 112, 160
Fruit, 68, 104, 110, 120
Funeral, grains served at, 83; of Achilles, 189; of Catreus, 172; of Elpenor, 131, of Hector, 79; of Patroclus, 75, 76; sacrifice during, 81. 83
Furies, 58, 62, 66
Fury, 37

Gaia 54, 84, 162, 165
Ganymede, 180
Geese, 106,115
Genesis, 83
Genetic engineering, 196, 197
Gilgamesh, 18, 65, 97
Ginsberg, Alan, 20
Glaucus, 57
Global warming, 165, 194
GMO, 192, 199, 223
Goat Island, 166
Goddesses, 158-159
Gold, 94, 95, 104, 133, 181
Golden Age, 52, 53, 122-124; on Achilles' Shield, 190; construction of, 52, 53, 73, 124, 191; Cronos and, 55, 84; diet of, 70, 71, 73, 198; end of, 63; Eurydice and, 63; Helen and, 61, 178, 182; Hesiod on, 155; Minoans and, 157, 170, 172; New, 53, 56, 73, 124, 176-196, 191, 196; Phaeacians and, 104, 108, 129, 133, 154, 218; Tiresias's prophecy and, 180
Golden Apple, 7, 31, 32, 215
Golden Calf, 101
Golden cup, 96
Golden Fleece, 126-127
Golden Race, 52, 112-113
Goldman, Sherman, 200-201
Gorgon, 57
Gottshall, Jonathan, 146
Graces, 66
Grain, in the Ages of Humanity, 52, 198-199; on Achilles' Shield, 148; Achilles' praise of in Hades, 111; in the Aegean, 112, 203; Ajax and, 68; amber waves of, 197; antelopes' eating of, 221; awned, 199-200, 203; in the Bronze Age, 14, 52, 71, 73, 199; in the Blessed Isles, 53, 71; Ceres and, 148; decline of, 70-71, 72, 84, 220; Demeter and, 67, 68, 148, 211, 221; Diomedes and, 68; domestication of, 72, 109, 153; double axe used for growing of, 156; dream of, 213; on Dulikhion, 115, 122; Elpenor on, 111; in the Elusinian Mysteries, 67, 73, 221; energetic effects of, 79, 207; English, Latin and Greek words for, 148; Far Eastern word for, 148; genetic engineering of, 26, 197, 198; in the Golden Age, 55, 70, 72, 73, 83. 84, 190, 198; in the Greek diet, 70; grinding of, 116; and health, 121; Hesiod on, 70, 73, 77, 83; as true human food, 25, 68, 195; in Iron Age, 71, 73, 84, 199; as key to peace, 71, 147, 148, 153; on Ithaca, 112; Lykaon and, 68; matrilineal cultures and, 223; Menelaus and, 68; among Minoans, 67, 155, 159, 223; Moses and, 14; music accompaniment to growing of, 193; in the Near East, 67; oar as symbol of, 149; Odysseus compared to, 112, 167; Odysseus' emphasis on, 110, 111, 115, 120, 122; Odysseus' kissing of the grain-giving earth, 190; Odysseus' scything of, 114; in the *Odyssey*, 109-124; and peace, 148, 194; Penelope's dream of, 115; Penelope's praise of, 116; Phaeacian women milling of, 177; as principal food, 110, 120, 148-149; in purification, 83; return of in new Golden Age, 72, 200, 213; use of in the sacrifice of animals, 82, 118; in a sacrificial meal, 78-79; of sand, 25; on Scheria, 120; in the Silver Age, 52, 73, 198; social judgment and, 122; on Sparta, 110; storage of, 126; seeds planted for the first time, 52; suitor linked to, 115; surplus of and rise of civilization, 72, 139; as symbol in Penelope's dream, 115-116; in Syrie, 112; in Thessaly, 139; Triptolemus' tenets regarding, 221; types of, 67, 159; Vega Cycle, and, 73; verticality of, 152; warriors, slain compared to, 73; wild, 72, 73; winnowing shovel and, 143-145. *See Barley, Wheat*
Grapes, 68
Grape leaves, 204
Great Bear, 102, 179
Great hall, 106, 107, 165, 174, 187
Greece, diet of, 70, 160; as a maritime society, 138
Green, Peter, 175

Hades (god), 62, 87; birth of, 161; as one of 3 brothers, 43, 159, 161; as lord of bulls, 120-121; Odysseus sacrifices to, 119; as ruler of the Underworld, 44

Hades (Underworld), Achilles in, 30, 90, 111, 153, 183; Agamemnon in, 183, 187-188; Ajax in, 99, 100, 150; Antikleia in, 98, 169; brides and bachelors in, 174; Circe guides Odysseus to, 125; Dante's visit to, 99; Elpenor in, 130, 153; Heracles' visit to, 99; Hermes as guide to, 150; Alex Jack's visit to, 197, 214-215; levels of consciousness in, 99; Muses and, 189; Odysseus's visit to, 11, 43, 87, 89, 98-100, 111, 119, 128, 130, 183; Odysseus and Achilles' meeting in, 30, 111, 183; Persephone queen of, 99, 119, 221; Tiresias's encounter in, 89, 98, 119, 128, 130, 137, 142, 153, 169, 188; Orpheus' visit to 62; Patroclus in, 35; sacrifice in, 119; suitors in, 117, 122; Virgil's visit to, 99

Hamlet, 60

Hansen, William, 139-140

Health, 121

Heart chakra, 191

Hearth, 81

Heaven, above, 150; on Achilles' Shield, 48, 100; accord between earth and, 16; Aska and, 220; Athena descending from, 117; axis mundi connects earth to, 165; bedchamber of, 44; beverage of, 79; broad, 136; burnt offerings to, 101; constellations of, 48; contest of bow as symbol of, 180; creation of, 65; cursed by, 94; daughter of, 64; father of, 88; fire from, 81; gifts of, 104; gods of, 170; gratitude to, 199; in a wild flower, 25; kingdom of, 39, 199; lords of, 131; moving through, 109, 144, 180; peace of, 63; Penelope's name goes up to, 152; power of, 85; present, 65; queen of, 44, 59; roots in, 197; shift in, 179; stars in, 59; taught by, 189; *themis*, mandate of, 36; under, 115; vertical energy of, 149; weapons of, 47; Zeus ruler of, 13, 30, 44, 162

Hebe, 80, 99

Hecatomb, 118, 136, 160-161, 166

Hector, Achilles battle with, 33, 39-40, 45, 59-60, 61, 77, 100, 168; Achilles's death foretold by, 62; Ajax battle with, 57, 100, 189-190; Andromache, wife of, 47, 77, 176; ambrosia given to, 80; Aphrodite's favor of, 80; Apollo's favor of, 58, 80, 82; Athena's deception of, 59; diet of, 74; battle deaths by, 34; body of claimed by Priam, 33, 45, 90; death of, 8, 30, 33, 45, 60, 75, 77, 82, 176, 184, 185, 188; funeral pyre of, 79; in battle, 32, 34, 35, 127; Hera's opposition to, 82; last words, 61, 77; level of consciousness of, 42, 45; Hecuba, mother of, 78; mutilation of body of, 33, 43, 60, 80, 82, 150, 188; Paris hectored by, 43, 184; Patroclus slain by, 33, 47, 56, 58; as son of Priam, 32; prayers of to gods, 81-82; as shepherd, 55; ships set fire by, 32, 58, 65-66, 75, 189; strength of, 45; Troy protected by, 54; skin of wolf worn by, 76; views of women of, 168; Zeus' favor of, 40, 44, 82; Zeus' disfavor of, 81

Hecuba, 74, 78

Helen, as an artist, 64, 178; beauty of, 7, 31, 53, 64, 97, 172, 178; Aphrodite's favor of, 31, 64, 189; armada launched for return of, 31, 62; berates herself, 183; Clytemnetra, sister of, 64, 162; level of consciousness of, 42, 64, 182; Diomedes assisted by, 169; drug of, 121, 171, 183; elopement or abduction of by Paris, 7, 30, 31, 43, 96, 161, 163, 172; Eurydice and, 62; Golden Apple and, 7, 61; as Golden Age, 61, 63, 64, 123, 178, 182; Helena, Montana and, 15; in Marlowe's play, 20; meaning of name of, 64, 182; Menelaus reunion with, 64, 162, 183; Minoan influence on, 161; Minotaur and, 172; mother goddess and, 170; Odysseus's relationship with, 169; patriarchal views of marriage regarding, 161; Troy and Sparta discuss return of, 31, 62, 96; robe of, 64; suitors swear an oath to, 31; Telemachus' visit to, 86, 110, 119, 122-123, 177, 181, 183; weaving and, 64, 176, 178, 179; Wooden Horse and, 33, 169, 174; as daughter of Zeus and Leda, 64

Helen (Euripedes), 64

Helena, Montana 17-18

Helenus, 184

Helios, 88, 101, 109, 119, 123, 132, 144, 174, 184

Henriad, 28

Hephaestus, Achilles protected by, 59; Achilles' Shield forged by, 33, 36, 47, 48-50, 57, 59, 100, 102, 105, 124, 150, 190-191, 194;Aphrodite and Ares outwitted by, 105; Athena delivered by from Zeus's head, 162, 221; as craftsman, 24, 42, 47, 56, 57, 58, 66, 103, 104, 181; as god of fire, 76; Hera's favor of, 59; Hera's rejection of, 47; level of consciousness of, 41; quarrel among gods ended by, 79; River

defeated by, 46, 59, 66; Thetis' visit to, 33, 43, 47, 66, 68
Hera, Achilles' protection of, 59; Agamemnon's denunciation of, 37; Aphrodite begs favor of, 148; ambrosia used by, 80; Artemis opposed by, 45; birth of, 161; chamber of, 58; golden apple and, 17, 31; Hector rejected by, 82; as mother of Hephaestus, 47, 66; Hermes employed by, 45; Leto jealous of, 45, 61; level of consciousness of, 40-41; use of ointment by, 69; River surrenders to, 59; Thetis' anger toward, 79; hatred of Trojans, 32, 44; Zeus enraged at, 44, 61; Zeus makes deal with to swap cities with, 44, 64; Zeus hanging of from the sky, 162; Zeus seduced by, 41, 42, 68, 148
Heracles, 25, 72; bow of, 184; Hades visit to, 99, 100; Iphitos slain by, 184; Labors of, 180, Troy destroyed by, 63-64;
Herbs, 68
Hermes, Calpyso, visit to, 86, 122, 123, 163-164; Circe, visit to, 96; level of consciousness of, 41; as guide to Hades, 150; Heracles' advice to Odysseus concerning, 99, 100; moly given by to Odysseus, 87, 111; Priam assisted by, 22; sacrifice to 120; as god of transitions and boundaries, 192
Hermione, 183
Herodotus, 79
Heroic Age, 53, 54, 73
Herzeloyde, 163
Hesiod, 25, 52, 53, 81, 172, 198; Ages of Humanity and, 57; on the Golden Age, 155; importance of grain in, 73, 83, 84; muses and, 188; shield of, 49;
Hesperides, 172
Hestia, 161
Hinduism, 10, 182
Hippocrates, 14, 70, 206; Oath, 187, 218
Hisarlik, 31
Hittites, 31
Hokusai, 66
Holy Grail, 163
Homer, Achilles' Shield glances at, 56; allegory in, 37-38; deaths personalized in *Iliad*, 34-36; on diet, 84; era of, 157; view of the gods, 46; Isaiah and, 147-148; muses and, 188; performance of his works 170; as a woman, 173-175
Homeric Hymn to Demeter, 67
Honey, 69, 84, 96, 97 113, 119, 160, 166
Horizontal vs. vertical, 149-150
Horn, 185
Horses, 54, 57, 73, 80, 112

Horta, 68, 209
Hospitality, 62, 92, 96, 121
House of Ladies, 218-219
Husband and wife, 169
Hygieia, 217
Hypereia, 103, 176

Iasion, 148
Ichor, 80
Iliad, allegory in, 45; levels of consciousness in, 39-40; food in, 67-84, 69; music and drama in, 44; comparisons of to the *Odyssey*, 85, 90; images of peace in, 50; violence in, 34, 47, 126
India, 61
Indo-European, 148, 165
Indra, 221
Indus Valley Civilization, 155, 200, 213
Industrial Revolution 72
Innana, 170
Ino, 102, 128, 166, 182, 186
Ionian Sea, 138
Iphigeneia, 64, 83, 162, 171
Iphitos, 184, 187
Iris, 80
Iron, 57, 61, 65, 76, 77, 78, 123, 181; Cronus castrated with sickle made of, 84; Odysseus made of, 123, 132, 181; Odysseus's bow of, 123; axe-heads of, 123, 185; Odysseus as Cretan merchant dealing in, 181; Penelope made of, 181; for forming tools and jewelry with, 200; transmutation of carbon into, 22-23;
Iron Age, Achilles, as warrior of, 61; anger and liver troubles in, 192; arrival of, 61, 74; 191, 192, 198; astrology and, 180; decline of virtue in, 71, 84; decline of Greece and, 183; diet of, 71, 73, 84, 199; end of, 191; role of the feminine in, 172; in Greek mythology 53-54, 56, 61; in Indian mythology, 61, 181, 123; as the age of ideology, 65; use of metals in, 200; modern, 23, 65, 66; precessional cycle and, 63; sacrifice and, 180; transition to, 181, 184, 198; Troy's sack and, 66; as an era of violence and war, 56, 91; worship of sacred bull during, 120-121; Zeus and, 84
Isaiah, 147
Isis, 220, 221
Islam, 68
Ismarus, 87, 91, 111
Israelites, 101-102
Ithaca, Achilles' Shield glances at, 194; Apollo assists Odysseus in returning to, 187; city in New York, 8; Cyclops' curses men of, 93; geography of, 110, 138-139,

190; rich in grain, 112; nymphs of, 177; as Odysseus' homeland, 6, 33, 85-86, 100, 190; Odysseus' departure from, 147; Odysseus's return to 88, 98, 105-106, 107, 112, 119, 123, 129, 134, 135, 137, 151, 173, 175, 181, 183, 185, 186, 190; Odysseus in sight of, 94, 149, 151; Circe's release of crew from, 97; Phaeacians drop Odysseus off on, 105, 112, 120, 134, 151, 177, 166, 195; Poseidon thwarts crew's return to, 94; recruiters come to, 29; Telemachus' return to, 106, 183; Tiresias prophesizes safe return to, 87, 98; townsfolk of, 123-124; Scheria compared to, 108, 168; Athena's arrival at, 117; Telemachus' future happiness in, 123; peace restored on, 124, 137, 180; suitors and, 187;
Ivanov, Mariya, 220
Ivory, 181, 185

Jack, Alex, childhood of, 8-9; visit to Delphi, 219; dreams, mystical experiences, and prophecies, 15-16, 18, 20, 22, 214-215, 216; visit to Germany by, 214-215; visit to Greece by, 213-223; study in India by, 10; Michio Kushi, study with, 12; peace work of, 12; visit to Phaeacia by, 218-219; visit to the Underworld by, 214-215; visit to UK by, 213-214; reporting by in Vietnam, 11-12
Jack, Alexander (grandfather), 219
Jack, Esther 9, 22, 27, 215
Jack, Homer, 8-9, 21, 214
Jack, Lucy, 6
Japan, 148, 182
Jason, 126, 155, 164
Jesus 83, 143, 199
Judah, 147
Judaism, 101
Judgment of Paris, 31, 64
Jung, Carl, 121

Kalchas 200
Kali Yuga, 53, 61
Karma, 96
Keersmacher, Anne Teresa de, 22-23
King James Bible, 143
King, Jr., Martin Luther, 8, 46
Kingdom of Heaven, 39, 199
Kleos, 30, 50, 90, 137, 169
Knees, 68, 79, 94, 169
Knossos, 56, 155 158, 166, 170, 191, 218
Kouroukan Fouga, 194
Ktesippos, 114
Kushi Institute, 21

Kushi Insitute of Europe, 23
Kushi, Aveline, 21
Kushi, Michio, Alex Jack's study and work with, 14, 20-21; on Aska; 220; on Atlantis 219; dream of, 216; on the seven levels of consciousness, 37; spiral of history and, 26; teachings of, 14, 26, 37, 97, 198, 213; transmutation and, 24
Kykeon, 67

Labryns, 156, 162, 173
Labyrinth, 56, 156-157, 173
Ladies in Blue, 223
Laertes, as father of Odysseus, 7; as member of Jason's crew, 126-127; reunion of with Odysseus, 33, 89, 90, 117, 195; Eumaios in service of, 113; Eurykleia in service of, 168; orchard of, 152, 190, 195, 211; shroud of, 86, 177-178; townsfolk confronted by, 124, 194
Laestrygonians, 87, 95, 130, 152, 192
Lamb, 74, 86, 115, 119
Lamos, 95
Lampetie, 174
Lattimore, Richard, 188
Leda, 64
Lemnos, 161
Lesbos, 161
Leto, 45-46, 61
Linear A, 158
Linos song, 55, 190-191
Lion, 34, 49, 56, 76, 96, 117, 152, 173
Lion Gate, 173
Little Dipper, 54
Little Iliad, 184
Liver, 81, 117
Livestock's Long Shadow, 194
London, 222
Loom, 152, 176-179; of cosmos, 179; of history, 176; of the nymphs, 166; of Penelope, 200
Lost Feminine, 159
Lost Paradise, 63
Lot's wife, 63
Lotus-Eaters, 87, 89, 91-92, 110, 121, 171
Lotus flower, 87, 91, 92, 97, 101, 110, 121, 171, 183, 190, 192, 199
Lykoan, 58, 68, 105, 148
Lyre, of Achilles, 47, 55, 138, 170, 189; on Achilles' Shield, 49, 55, 56, 105, 190; of Apollo, 79; 105; comparison of to a bow, 187; Cretan, 170; of Demodokos 173; Homeric performance with 170; of Orpheus, 62
Macrobioi, 79
Macrobios, 70

Macrobiotics, 14-15, 70, 74
Magna Carta, 194
Mali, 200
Marlowe, Christopher, 21-22, 27, 31, 56-57, 214, 220
Maron, 111
Marriage, on Achilles' Shield, 48, 105, 190; bed of Odysseus and Penelope, 89, 117, 135, 152, 195; of Helen and Menelaus, 161, 183; Hera, goddess of, 26, 45; of Hera and Zeus, 162; matriarchal rites and, 161; musical accompaniment to, 193; Nausicaa offered in, 105, 166; Odysseus unfit for, 146, 185; patriarchal rites of, 62, 159, 161; Penelope's prospective, 114, 116, 152, 166; Odysseus's homily on ,169; sacrificial rites at, 81; of Thetis and Peleus, 30-31; 161; of Weaving Maiden and Cowherd, 179
Masculinity, 161, 165
Matriarchy, 171
Matrilinear civilization, 160-161, 221
Matthew, 143
McCarthy, David and Nicola, 214
Meat 72-79, Achilles and Patroclus's cooking of, 161; balancing of with alcohol, 84; in the Bronze Age, 73-74, 120, 194, 199; Circe's preparation of, 163; crew's desire for, 120; Cyclops' raw diet of, 95, 101; derivation of the term for, 145; energetic effects of, 84, 152, 161; consumption of after the Flood, 83; eating of suspended during funerals, 83; lack of in Golden Age, 133; Greeks' gluttonous desire for, 75, 76; reserved for Greek officers, 194; Hector's challenge regarding, 168; lack of among inland dwellers, 145; in the Iron Age, 73, 192, 199; liver problems and, 83, 117, 161; in the Minoan diet, 160; in the modern diet, 10, 192, 199; Odysseus's love for, 165; Prometheus' theft of fire for cooking of, 81, 83, 198; Pythagoras and Orpheus's rejection of, 195; salted, 145; unsalted, 131, 136, 144, 145; sanctified, 119, 122; unsanctified, 84; suitors desire for, 113, 116, 117, 120; in Trojan diet, 74; warrior's diet high in, 192
Mediterranean Diet, 67-70, 160, 218, 220
Medon, 113, 193
Melissa, 161
Memory, 190; goddess of, 22
Menalaus, battle deaths by, 34; level of consciousness of, 42; Creten visit of, 172; father of, 172; as a lion, 76, 173; as man of iron, 181; marriage of to Helen, 161; Paris fighting with, 127-128; Paris's visit to, 31; Helen's reunion with, 162 183; Telemachus's visit to, 110, 119, 122-123; Trojans, sympathy for, 64; women, attitude toward, 168;
Menis (cosmic anger), 36; 89-90; of Apollo, 187; of the gods, 62, 101; of Poseidon, 94, 120; of Zeus, 36, 43, 84, 90, 124, 194
Mentor, 110, 118, 123-124
Meriones, 185
Mesoamerica, 53-54
Mesopotamia, 81, 155, 170, 213
Messeis, 176
Metals, 181
Metamorphoses (Ovid), 62
Mctis (Goddess), 89
Metis (cunning), 89; of Athena, 124; of Odysseus, 193, 168-169, 188; of Penelope, 108, 188;
Middle East, 14, 21, 158
Milk, 110, 119
Milky Way, 23, 63, 179, 220
Milland Maria, 200-201
Minoan civilization, Achilles' Shield glances at, 173-191; Adriana and, 157; Akrotiri and, 218-219; architecture of, 155; art of, 155-156, 162, 173, 218-219, 221, 223; Athena and, 162, 175, 222; Atlantis and, 27; bull leaping in, 158; collapse of, 157, 158-159, 171, 173, 191, 218, 221; cookware of, 221; crocuses and, 172; culture of, 218-219; dates of, 27, 157; diet of, 67, 148, 158-163, 221; derivation of the name of, 155; double-axe symbol of, 156, 162, 165, 185, 195, 219, 220, 222, 223; geographical scope of, 155; goddesses of, 148, 156, 158, 159, 175, 223; Golden Age and, 157, 170; Greek mythology and, 172; influence on Helen of, 162-163; Knossos, capital of, 56, 155; labyrinth and, 56; metallurgy in, 60-61; lack of military and war in, 156; Minos and, 155, 218; Minotaur and, 157, 159; Mycenaean destruction of, 27, 157, 159, 173, 218; mythology of compared to Greek, 172; exhibit of in National Archaeological Museum, 220-221; Odysseus as a native of, 173; peaceful culture of, 27, 158, 191, 200, 213; Phaeacians and, 155-156, 158, 169, 173, 182, 218; lack of sacrifice in, 158; Santorini and, 27, 218, 221; script of, 148, 158; sky lore of, 166, 175; women's role in, 156, 158, 159, 150, 161, 162, 171, 218, 221; volcanic destruction of, 27, 191
Minos, King, 56, 155, 156-157, 172, 218; as an office not a ruler, 158

Minotaur, 56, 157, 159, 172, 173, 218
Miso Happy Show, 220, 220
Misogyny, 172
Mnemosyne, 190
Moly, 87, 96, 97, 111, 142, 163, 192, 199
Monsanto 199
Moon, on Achilles' Shield, 48, 54, 66; agrarian rhythms and, 159; Athena as goddess of, 175; bulls associated with, 158; conjunction of with the Sun, 17; cycle of, 178; month, 179; Penelope as, 17, 178,179; Hera as goddess of, 162; Helen, as goddess of, 64; Minoan goddess of, 156, 159; Santorini shaped like, 218
Moses, 101-102
Mother Earth, 165, 213, 221, 223
Mother goddess, 170, 223
Mount Ida, 161
Mount Neritos, 138
Mount Olympus, ambrosia brought to by doves, 80; Athena and Zeus discuss on, 86, 117, 124; Hephaestus cast out of, 47; Hermes descends from to Calypso's, 163; immortals dwell on, 55; Hebe hosts feast on, 99; Hera rules from, 162; as symbol of spiritual ascent, 46, 150; location of in Thessaly, 139; Thetis darts down from, 77; Zeus brings Ganymede to, 180;
Mount Parnassus, 193, 220
Mount Pelion, 127
Mountain lion, 152
Moyers, Bill, 197
Mozart, 22
Mu, 65
Muellner, Leonard, 50, 54
Muses, Achilles' death mourned by, 188; Apollo and, 32, 55, 79, 188; as goddesses of art and music, 20, 79, 172; dance of, 170; Homer's channeling of, 56, 144; mother of, 20, 19; in the opening of the *Iliad* and *Odyssey*, 109, 144, 188; singing of on Olympus 79; Thamyris and, 189;
Music, of Achilles, 189; on Achilles' Shield, 49, 55, 173, 190-191; in the ancient world, 193; Apollo, god of, 20, 32, 41, 55, 188; Celtic, 27, 222; of Circe, 189; healing power of, 25, 63; in the Homeric epics, 188-191; Alex Jack and, 20, 21; levels of consciousness and, 38; Labyrinth and, 56, 158; Linos song, 49, 191; Marlowe and, 20; matrilineal society and, 218; Minoans and, 173, 191; origin of term, 20; Orpheus and, 62; Phaeacians' love of, 103, 105, 107; of the Sirens, 189; stringing of the bow compared to, 106-107, 186-187
Myceaneans, 157, 173; human sacrifice and, 170-171; metallurgy and, 60; Minoans displaced by, 27, 157, 159, 173, 191, 218
Myrmidons, 32
Myth, American, 15; ancient, 13, 14; as archetypes, 17; of Athena's birth from Zeus's head, 221; of Athens' founding, 171, 217; of atomic era, 25; awakening to, 6, Aztec, 170; biblical, 7; Big Bang as, 25; Joseph Campbell on, 16-17, 25, 146, 185, 191, 197; Chinese, 179; as a collective dream, 25; creation, 83; Cretan, 176; of Dionysis, 81, 189; double axe in, 156; Egyptian, 214, 220; feminine, 159-160, 172; of the four winds, 94; of Ganymede's abduction, 180; glory and, 90; Golden Age, 18, 157, 200; of the Golden Fleece, 129; Greek, 7, 15, 20, 30, 46, 51, 94, 171, 189, 199, 216; heraldic devices in, 49; of the Holy Grail, 163; of Inna and Dumuzi, 170; Iron Age in, 61; landscape of, 90; of Leda and the Swan, 64; Minoan, 158-160, 172; of Minos, 155, 216; of the Minotaur, 159, 172, 176, 216; mountains in, 151; Navaho, 16; Norse, 223; of Odysseus' son with Circe, 97; of Orpheus and Eurydice, 62-63; of Osiris and Isis, 170, 220; in Ovid, 62; precession of the equinoxes and, 56, 63, 65; of Prometheus stealing fire, 83-84, 198; patriarchal, 159-160, 172; of the rape of Europa, 172; 176; rituals and, 170; sacred sites in, 220; Sumerian, 16; swords in, 97; unconscious and, 149; weaving in, 179; of the Weaving Maiden and Cowherd, 179; of Zeus castrating Cronus, 84

Nagy, Gregory, 50
National Archaeological Museum (Athens), 220
National Portrait Gallery, 222
Nausicaa, Artemis likened to, 166; attributes of, 169, 186; as authoress of *Odyssey*, 174-175; Odysseus encountered by, 17, 86, 102, 103, 110, 112,185, 218; possible marriage of to Odysseus, 105, 151, 154, 166. 169; Odysseus' homily on marriage to, 169; olive oil and, 180, 195;
Naxos, 157
Nectar, 79, 180
Neolithic, 155
Neoptolemus, 183
Nereides, 172
Nestor, 42, 69, 86, 118
New Testament, 44, 65, 143
Niger River Civilization, 200, 223

Night, 89, 196
Nike, 126
Nine Star Ki, 216, 222
Noah, 65
Nobody, 93, 107, 142
North Star, 51, 54, 61, 72, 83, 200
Nostos, 90
Nuclear, 65
Nymph, 149; Calypso and, 163, 166; as a goddess and engaged woman, 166; on Goat Island, 166; on Ithaca, 166, 177; of the Sun, 166, 174; types of, 172; wood, 120

Oar, 125-153; Achilles' Shield compared to, 125; consciousness and, 192; of Elpenor, 98, 100 130-131, 141, 151, 152; in folklore, 140; Great Bear and, 179-180; in the *Iliad*, 127-128; horizontal and vertical orientation of, 150; inland journey and, 140-141; in the *Odyssey*, 128-137; Phaeacians and 103; propitiation of Poseidon with, 152; as a symbol of diet, 72, 145; as a symbol of memory, 149; as a symbol of the sea, 140; as a symbol of war, 72, 145-146, 195; winnowing shovel and, 147, 195; Tiresias's prophecy about, 87, 135-136, 147
Oats, 68
Ocean, 48, 79, 149
Oceanides, 172
Octopus, 152, 167
Odysseus

PERSONALITY & CHARACTER
Anger of, 89-90, 93, 188; bardic gifts of, 189; character of, 40, 43, 62, 89, 193; diet of, 77, 114, 115, 117; feminine side of, 167-168; heart of iron of, 181; indifference of to Circe and Calypso, 168-169; level of consciousness of, 43, 90, 94, 97, 101, 107, 122, 195; *kleos* of, 137-138; longing of for Penelope, 101, 151, 163; masculine prowess of, 168-170; meaning of the name of, 192; *metis* of, 40, 43, 100, 168, 188, 193; resourcefulness of, 40; relations wof ith women, 14, 18, 97, 110, 124, 146, 163-165, 168-170, 185-186; strength and virility of, 97; view of on supreme joy in life, 164-165; tears of, 164; vertical and horizontal positions assumed by, 151-153; wiles of, 90, 108, 138, 165; wine, view of, 189; journey of to wisdom, 90

ROLES, COMPARISONS, AND PROPS
Achilles' armor, contest for, 100, 124, 150;

Achilles' Shield, possession of, 56, 99-100, 124; as Aquarius, 180; astrological conjunctions symbolic of, 17, 178, 179, 182, 186, 223; as an athlete, 104, 138, 154, 186; axe given to, 128, 156, 185, 219; bath prepared for, 88, 135, 174; beggar disguised as, 88, 106, 114, 121, 165, 186; boar's injury of, 76, 185, 193, 220; bow of, 88, 106-107, 125, 138, 184-185, 186, 187, 188; as captain and rower, 125, 127, 130, 137, 145, 166, 179; as a cook, 113; as Cowherd, 179; as a creeping thing, 95; as a Cretan merchant, 88, 106, 115, 155, 173; as a diplomat, 138; dog, 88, 138, 190; as a dream interpreter, 106, 115; as a dullard, 175-175; kissing the earth by, 190; as Everyman, 60; evolutionary stages of, 152-153; flocks and cattle of, 110; golden bowl given to, 122; golden brooch given to 122; as master of concealment, 165; hall of, 113, 116; helmet of, 76; Heracles compared to, 180; Homer A. Jack compared to, 6; marriage bed of, 89, 108, 122, 141, 152, 181, 195; as a Minoan wayfarer, 173; moly given to, 18, 96, 111, 163, 192, 199; Mount Parnassus visit to, 193; as Nobody, 93, 107, 141; oar hoisted and planted by, 98, 125-153; as an octopus, 176; as an ox, 117; raft made by, 128, 152, 167, 182, 185, 220; as sacker of cities, 93, 109, 138; sacrifice made by, 74, 119, 180; scar on thigh of, 88, 185, 220; as a seed, 167; as a shepherd, 179; sword given to, 105, 154, 156; as a warrior, 34, 55, 117, 145-146, 175; winnowing shovel planted by, 143-144; Wooden Horse planned by, 33, 165, 169, 184; Yudhisthira compared to, 8

ADVENTURES, TRAVELS & ENCOUNTERS
Achilles recruited by 29; Achilles, embassy to, 32, 58, 77, 127; Achilles's shade, visit to, 30, 98, 99, 111, 153, 183; Aeolus, 87, 94, 95, 122, 130; Agamemnon, embassy to, 187; Agamemnon's shade, visit to, 98; Ajax, 98-99, 100, 150; Alcinous, 110, 120, 129, 133, 138, 154; Amphinomos, 115, 117; Anticleia, 98, 168, 186; Antinous, 114, 116; Apollo's favor of, 111, 187; Arete, 84, 110, 154, 169, 174, 186; Argive council, 58; Athena, 14, 33, 45, 86, 88, 89, 100, 102, 105, 117, 123, 124, 128, 136, 167-168, 178, 186, 190, 194, 195; Autolykos, 185, 192; banquet hall of, 113-114; death of foretold, 90, 136, 153; contest of the bow, 88, 106-107, 116, 151, 184-188, 223; Calypso, 86, 88, 101, 128,

137, 151, 163, 168, 177, 181, 183, 219; cattle of the Sun, 56, 101,112, 123, 132, 144, 163, 174-175, 186; Circe, 87, 88, 96-97, 100, 119, 123, 125, 130, 131, 168, 177, 186; crew, 26, 33, 56, 84, 87, 88, 94, 95, 96, 97, 100-101, 112, 120, 122, 123, 125, 129, 130, 132, 147, 180, 199; Cyclops, 87, 92-94, 95, 111, 129, 165, 195; Demodokos, 188; avoiding of the draft by, 11, 29; Elpenor, 100, 131, 137, 153; Eumaios, 88, 106, 112-113, 120, 135, 189; Eurykleia, 117, 185; falling asleep by, 94, 95, 134, 149, 151, 190; fig tree grabbed by, 151; Hades (god), 119; Helen, 169-170; Helenus, 184; Heracles, 99; Hermes 86, 87, 100; homecoming of, 11, 33, 66, 85; Ino, 102, 128-129, 166, 182; Iphitos, 184-185, 187; Ismarus, 87, 89-90, 91, 111; Ithaca, 55, 134, 135, 138-139, 154, 177, 186, 190; Laestr-ygonians, 87, 95, 111, 130; Laertes, 89, 117, 124, 190, 195; mast clung to, 151, 185; mast lashed to, 100-101; Medon, 193; Menaleus reports on fate of, 86; Meri-ones, 185; Nausicaa, 86, 102-103, 105, 110, 112, 152, 154, 166, 169, 174, 186, 195, 218; nymphs, 166; oar, 135-136, 182, 195; Penelope, 86, 88, 89, 90, 106, 108, 113, 115, 117, 122, 135, 135-136, 139, 144, 151-152, 163, 175, 181, 182, 195, 196, 219-220, 223; Persephone, 99, 119; Phaeacians, 14, 84, 86, 88, 102, 105, 112, 120, 129, 133, 154, 157, 173, 177, 218; Phemios, 193; Philoctetes, 184; Poseidon, 102, 118, 120, 121, 128, 134, 136, 140, 141, 144, 152, 220; Scheria, visit to, 102-105, 110, 112, 120, 122, 152, 168; Scylla and Charybdis, 88, 90, 101, 111, 132, 133, 168, 186; servant women, 124, 135; ship of capsizes, 101, 181-182; Sirens, 88, 100-101, 132, 146-147, 169, 186; suit-ors, 88, 106, 108, 113, 114, 116-117, 120, 122, 193; Telemachus, 88, 89, 117, 124, 135, 144, 177; Tiresias, 87, 89, 98, 99, 119, 125, 132, 136, 138, 139, 142, 144; townsfolk, 123-124, 193, 194; Trojan War, 86-87, 146; Underworld, visit to, 30, 87, 89, 98-100, 119, 130, 169, 183; wild boar, 180; Zeus' favor of, 66, 86, 101, 102, 132-133, 194; Zeus' disfavor of, 94, 101, 116, 119, 132-133, 181-182

Odyssey, Achilles' Shield foreshadowing of, 55; compared with, 47, 85, 90; composi-tion of, 174-175, 218; as homecoming, 33; recap of, 85-89; as a romance, 85; as a spiritual journey, 17

Ogygia 88, 101, 151, 154, 163, 164

Ohsawa, George, 24, 37, 97

Oike, 90

Olive, as sacred to Athena, 68; Calypso's axe handle made of, 68-69, 195; Cyclops blinded with stake made of, 93, 195; as a fruit in Greek diet, 70; marriage bed carved from, 89, 152, 195-196; on Ithaca, 195; oil from, 180, 195; on Scheria, 102, 104, 195

Olson, S. Douglas, 143-144

Olympians, 165

Olympic games, 161

One Peaceful World, 201

One Peaceful World (Kushi and Jack), 51

Orestes, 64, 162

Orion, 48, 164, 220

Orpheus, 62-63, 182, 195

Osiris, 158, 170, 220

Ouranos, 54

Ovid, 62

Paleolithic era, 160, 200

Palladium, 169

Panacea, 218

Pandora, 172

Panic Rut, 42

Paradise, 52, 61, 53, 73

Paradise Lost, 61

Paris, Achilles slain by, 45, 58, 62, 98; aka Alexandros, 7, 31; Aphrodite's protection of 32, 189; Apollo's protection of, 187; beauty enamored of, 148, 189; bow of, 184; as the constellation of the Cowherd, 179; death of, 45, 62, 184; elopement with or abduction of Helen, 96, 161, 163, 178; Hector 's humiliation of, 184; judg-ment of, 17, 31, 61, 64, 215; level of con-sciousness of, 40, 43; Menelaus, combat with, 76, 127-128, 189; sculpture of, 215; as a shepherd, 31; visit of to Sparta, 31, 172; as a symbol of humanity, 64; as a sym-bol of love, 62; as a warrior, 34, 127

Parker, Theodore, 46

Parthenon, 217

Parzival, 18, 163

Pasiphae, 172

Patriarchy, 158-159, 170-171, 221

Patroclus, Achilles' love for, 29, 32, 42, 43, 58, 76; Achilles' armor and, 47, 58; Achilles' Shield, glances at, 54-55, 56; as cook, 161; death of, 44, 47, 58, 75, 76, 188; desecration of corpse of, 33, 43, 55, 188; funeral pyre of, 61, 76; Hades, goes down to, 35; Hector, slaying of, 33, 58; level of consciousness of, 43; as a sacrificial animal, 83; shade of, 131, Thetis anoints body of with ambrosia, 58, 80; as a warrior, 32-33, 34, 56, 70

Peace, Achilles' choice of peace or war, 29, 50; Achilles' Shield and, 47-56, 58, 60, 66, 200; between Achilles and Agamemnon, 42; Amphinomos tries to make, 115, 121; arts of, 104, 154, 222; Athena's counsel of, 117, 124, 194; Athens and, 217; Axe, as symbol of, 200, 222; birthright and, 200; blessed, 131, 149, 153, 180, 196, 200; civilizations of, 213; clasping knees and, 68; cooking flame and, 199; Far Eastern word for, 148; fruits of 103; games of, 104; gifts of, 115; Golden Age and, 23, 24, 63, 70, 173, 191, 200; grains and, 71, 72, 79, 115, 121, 147, 148; in Hades, 122; Homeric epics point to, 200; Iron Age and, 71; Isaiah's prophecy of, 147-148; Ithacans agree to, 89, 117, 124, 194; Homer A. Jack's work for, 7; in macrobiotics, 19, 21-22, 24, 197; in *Mahabhara-ta*, 8; Minoan civilization and 27, 159-160, 171, 173, 191, 213, 218, 221; mission of, 187; modern threats to, 65; mother goddess and, 221; movement for, 7, 8, 10, 11; music and, 104; new era of, 23, 62, 72, 108, 123, 179, 200; oar as symbol of, 125, 147-148, 149, 200; Odysseus' bow and, 184, 187; between Odysseus and Poseidon, 140, 144; Odysseus changes into a person of, 153, 195; in *Odyssey* compared to *Iliad*, 85; offering of, 100; olive, symbol of, 195; Phaeacians and, 154, 218; prayer for 21; rhythms of, 159; sleeping in, 132; social judgment and, 38, 121; song of, 21, 56; Tiresias's prophecy and, 153; treaties, 81; trials end in, 136, 152; trade and, 129, 154; Troy, city of, 32, 62, 64; Troy, rejection of entreaties for, 161; Trojan War and desire for 28, 61, 62; Vega cycle and, 73. *See Circle of the Cities of Peace and War. Circle of Agricultural Peace and Plenty. One Peaceful World*

Peace (Goddess), 41

Peleus, 29, 31, 58

Peloponnese, 208

Peloponnesus, 139

Penelope, Amphinomos pleased with, 115, 122; Athena's favor of, 88, 122; attributes of, 178, 186; contest of the bow proposed by, 88, 106, 116, 181, 186, 187; Calypso's view of, 164; Clytemnestra and, 183; dreams of, 106, 115, 152, 181, 185; Eumaios and, 189; Eurykleia and, 185; golden brooch given by, 122; Hebe as model for, 99; horn and ivory dream of, 181, 185; iron heart of, 181; level of consciousness of, 108; as long-suffering, 86; loom of, 152, 201; maids of, 88, 90, 135, 185; lunar symbolism and, 17, 178, 179; marriage to suitors consented to, 88; false marriage rites for, 193; marriage bed of, 89, 136, 141, 152, 181, 195, 196; Odysseus meeting with, 88, 106, 115-116, 135, 152, 155, 169, 173; *metis* of 188; mingling in love of with Odysseus, 137, 196; as Mother Earth, 223; as a nymph, 166, Odysseus pining for, 17, 86, 101, 151, 163, 175, 219; Odysseus reveals himself to, 89, 195; Odysseus, recognition of, 185, 190, 196; Odysseus, reunion with, 33, 90, 113, 117, 144, 188, 223; pressure on to remarry, 86; suitors and, 151, 176-177, 199, 223; Telemachus and, 177, 183; thoughtful nature of, 108; Tiresias's prophecy told to, 89, 128, 135, 136-137, 139, 144, 152, 182; verticality of, 151-152; weaving and, 176-177, 178; Weaving Maiden and, 179

Pentekonter, 126

Periodic table of elements, 24, 26

Persephone, 62, 99, 119, 221

Phaeacians; arts of, 103, 193; Athena's visit to, 106; as Atlantis, 223; bard of, 33, 129, 188; court of, 33, 154, 157, 166, 177; Cyclopses plunder of, 157; dance of, 33, 104, 154, 170; diet of, 120, 121, 177; Golden Age and, 104, 108, 122, 154, 223; hot-tempered youth of, 104; as fatherland, 168; matrilineal culture and, 169, 218; meaning of the name of 157; as a Minoan colony, 158, 169, 173, 218, 220; music of, 103, 173, 193; oar-loving, 103; Odysseus' visit to, 84, 86, 102-105, 110, 129, 133, 154-155, 169, 195; Odysseus ferried home by, 88, 105, 112, 120, 133-134, 142, 154, 166, 195; Odysseus's tale to, 88, 93, 102, 164-165, 166; origin of, 103, 157; sacrifice of, 120; ships of, 129, 154, 210; ship of turned to stone, 120, 134, 151, 154, 157, 218; sports contest among, 154, 173, 186; weaving by, 177

Phaethusa, 174

Phemios, 193

Philoctetes, 184

Philoctetes (Sophocles), 184

Phoinix, 41

Pigs, in Aegean diet, 160, 192; Circe's sty, 99; corporations and modern food industry turning us into, 199, 220; Eumaios as herder of, 88, 106, 107, 112, 113, 120, 155, 181, 189; harvests ravaged by, 81; men turned to, 17, 26, 87, 96, 111, 151, 163, 171, 180, 192; turning of back to men, 119; suitors' slaughter of, 113, 120;
Pine nuts, 204
Piracy, 145
Pisces, 180
Plant-centered diet, 192
Plato, 199, 219
Platonic Year, 25, 60-62, 181
Pleiades, 48, 102, 172
Polaris, 51, 54, 61, 72
Polis, 50
Pollux, 64
Polyphemus, 87, 92, 93, 129, 142, 174, 195
Poppy, 171
Poseidon, Achilles assisted by, 43, 59; Apollo fights with, 45; Athena vies with, 140, 21; birth of, 161; as lord of bulls, 120-121; daughters of, 122; as earth-shaker, 162; level of awareness of, 45; *menis* of, 86, 94, 120, 121, 157; oar symbol of, 140; Odysseus' raft destroyed, 86, 102, 123-124, 128, 137, 151, 166, 220; Odysseus' ships capsized by, 86, 128, 140, 151; Odysseus thwarted by, 33, 94, 102, 140, 167; oceans ruled by, 44, 98, 140, 149; as patriarchal god, 221; Phaeacian ship turned to stone by, 120, 134, 155, 157, 218; son of, 86, 87, 93, 98, 102, 140, 157; sacrifice to, 98, 118, 131, 136, 137, 140, 144, 150, 152, 160-161; Tiresias prophecy about, 89, 98, 136; Troy leveled by, 63-64; trident of, 57, 144, 182, 217; unconscious, as symbol of, 45, 121, 149, 152, 195; world divided by 3 brothers, 44, 86, 159, 161-162
Potter, Harry, 222
Prayers of Repentance, 41
Precession of the Equinoxes, 51, 54, 64-65, 105, 179, 180-181, 184
Priam, Achilles, visit to, 33, 44, 46, 60, 77, 78-79; asylum sought by, 11; as king of Troy, 11, 32; death of, 33; as father, 34, 184; as heartbroken, 78; Hector's body claimed by, 77, 78, 90; Hermes' guiding of, 33; level of consciousness of, 43; rejection of by the gods, 81-82; sacrifices of to Zeus by, 44; Troy, return to, 79; Zeus's favor of, 45
Prometheus, 81, 83, 99, 198
Prowling Rocks, 101
Psukhe (life's breath), 50
Purification; astrological cycles and, 124; grains and, 83; of Odysseus's hall after the massacre, 117, 124, 187
Purves, Alex, 140-141
Pylos, 86, 118, 160
Pythagoras, 195

Quantum Rabbit, LLC, 24, 26-27

Ram, 76, 119, 131, 152, 180
Recipes, 203-213; Achaean Barleymeal, 204; Achilles' Spelt Cakes, 204-205; Adriane's Minoan Meze, 212; Andromache's Grape Leaves Stuffed with Bulgur, 205; Athena's Nectar of the Gods; A Father-Daughter Punch, 212-213; Calypso's Wild Bitter Greens, 209-210; Circe's Spiked Veggies, 208; Demeter Tea, 211-212; Hector's Wheat Rolls, 207; Helios's Chickpea and Lentil Burgers, 207-208; Hephaestus's Golden Barley with Bulgur, 203-204; Hippocratic Stew, 206; Laertes's Pear Crunch, 211; Nausicaa's Tahini Custard with Apples and Raisins, 210-211; Odysseus's Chewy Barley, 203; Paris's Waffles with Strawberries and Honey Glaze, 207; Penelope's Loaf, 206; Phaeacian Sea-weed Medley, 210; Zeus & Tele-machus's Wild Oats and Lentil Loaf, 208-209
Red Sea, 14
Remembrance, 183
Rhea, 158, 161, 221, 223
Rheus, 55
Rice, 223
Rituals, 170
River, 42, 59, 66
Rome, 32, 44, 139, 169, 194
Rome, David, 20
Rosetta Stone, 197
Rowing, 197
Rye, 68
Rylance, Mark, 22

Sacrifice, by Achilles, 79, 127, 160; in the Aegean world, 80-81, 160; on Aeolia, 119; by Alcinous 120; in Anatolia, 121; in ancient world, 191-192; animal covenant regarding, 82, 84, 199; animals' consent to, 82-84; animals used in, 81; to Apollo, 74; to Artemis, 171-172; to Athena, 75, 117-118; in Athens, 171; barley sprinkled on during, 67, 83, 112; in the Bronze Age, 120, 181; Circe gives Odysseus animals for, 119; in Crete, 170-171; in the Cyclops' cave, 119; to daughters of

Zeus, 166; decline of, 71; dietary excess tempered by, 191-192; double axe and, 156, 162; by Eumaios, 120; fragrance of, 111; to the gods, 43, 101, 121; in Greek art, 221; Greek tradition of, 160, 221; in Hades, 119; human, 83, 170-171; of Iphigeneia, 64, 82, 162, 171; on the island of the Sun, 101, 112, 119; Jesus and, 82; large public displays of, 160-161; levels of consciousness and, 122; Minoans and, 160; Minotaur's demand of human, 56, 156, 158; in the modern world, 192; music and, 193; by Nestor, 117; to the nymphs, 166; oar as symbol of, 143; by Odysseus, 115, 119, 140, 141, 180; in the *Odyssey*, 118-121; Orpheus and Pythagoras's rejection of, 195; in the Paleolithic era, 160; Patroclus' death and, 83; to Poseidon, 98, 117, 131, 137, 140, 150, 160; prayers and chants along with, 190; by Priam, 44, 79, 82; by Prometheus, 81; to Scylla, 101, 165, 186; in Silver Age, 71; suitors, lack of, 120; by Telemachus, 117, 131; for Tiresias, 119, 142; by the Trojans, 74, 75, 82; of Trojan princes by Achilles, 58; Tudor executions and, 119; voluntary nature of, 82-83; to Zeus, 40, 102, 117, 127, 161. *See Hecatomb*
Saffron, 171
Salt, 145
Santorini, 218-220
Scamandros, 59
Scheria, 86, 102, 133, 152, 154, 182
Schliemann, Heinrich, 31
School shooting, 215
Schwerin, 215
Scylla, 88, 90, 101, 111, 132, 133, 152, 169, 186, 192
Sea, Achaeans perish in, 71; as angry, 33; bass, 160; cave, 166; charybdis sucks clouds covering, 167; creatures of, 16, 168; everything down into, 101; depths of, 165; evolution and, 152, 168; far from, 143; fishing in, 70, 71; as flawless, brimming, 109; fowl, 112; goat, 159; god of, 118, 134, 140, 157, 167, 217; hauling ships down to, 127; land and, 150; line of, 135; mastery of, 124, 217; night, 134; nymphs of, 86, 96, 172; oar as symbol of, 149; as open, 134; order of, 141; people unfamiliar with, 138; Phaeacians migrate across, 103; as nourishing and terrifying, 166-167; pollution, 215; power, 173; as primordial, 195; as purple, 177; as rising, 65, 219; rovers, 146; rowing in, 93, 130; salt, 145; set out to, 132; snails, 160; space of, 141; survivors flung into, 133; swell, 131; as a symbol of humanity's origin and destiny, 149; as a symbol of the unconscious, 121, 149, 195; vegetables, 210; voyage, 137; ways, 194
Seareach, 104, 156
Second Epistle of Peter, 65
Sema, 153
Servant women, 88, 107, 117, 185, 189
Seven Levels of Consciousness, 27, 36, 37-41, 90, 93-94, 124, 142, 144, 151; on Odysseus's journey, 91-108
Seven levels of food, 121-122
Shakespeare, 21-22, 27
Shang Dynasty, 72
Sheep, on Achilles' Shield, 48, 49, 56; in diet of Astyanax, 77; on Crete, 160; of Cyclops, 92, 129; in Greek diet, 160, 192; Greek herding of, 69; in the Iron Age, 71; on island of the Sun, 56, 174; Odysseus conceals under, 87, 93, 111, 165; on Odysseus' estate, 179; slaughter of, 76, 78, 81, 91, 119, 120;
Shelley, 220
Shield, 48-49, 55-56, 57, 66, 125. *See Achilles' Shield*
Silver, 94, 95, 104, 122, 181
Silver Age, 52, 53, 55, 61, 63, 70-71, 73, 122, 173, 198
Silver Race, 52
Simoeis, 42, 59, 80
Sirens, 88, 89, 100-101, 132, 146-147, 189
Sirius, 220
Sisyphus, 99
Skamandros, 42
Sky, becoming one with, 143; between earth and, 150, 165; as brazen, 109; creation of, 54; as father, 223; fixed oar against, 131; as giant, 16; gods of, 165; Hera hung from, 162; lore of Calypso, 166; male gods of, 221; night, 158; Northern, 180; Odysseus drops out of in a dream, 106; pivoting in, 102; Zeus ruler of, 161, 172
Snyder, Gary, 90
Sparta, 62, 63, 64, 68, 110, 119, 120, 162-163, 177
Spear, 150
Spelt, 68, 204
Spiral of History, 26, 182, 198, 202, 213
Spiral, 163, 170
Spock, Benjamin, 13
Sports, 168, 186
St. Elias, 139
Strauss, Barry, 194
Strife, 48, 54, 190
Sugar, 69

Suitors, agribusiness and, 223; Athena and, 106, 107, 108, 110, 178, 184, 190, 195; Crew compared to, 120, 122; feasting of, 84, 109-110, 113-117, 120, 189, 223; Hades entered by, 117, 122; of Helen, 31; lack of sacrifice by, 120, 122; massacre of, 33, 85, 88, 98, 107, 109, 113, 116-117, 123, 124, 125, 131, 151, 152, 174, 184, 187, 193; number of, 106, 182; Odysseus mistreated by, 88, 106, 108, 114, 116; failure of to string Odysseus's bow, 88, 106, 187; omen about, 116; Penelope and, 86, 88, 108, 122, 151, 152, 177-178, 181; Penelope's dream of, 106, 115-116; relatives of, 55, 89, 117, 124, 193-194; servant women and, 88, 90, 107, 195; Telemachus and, 86, 88, 107, 110, 117; Tiresias's prophecy of, 131. *See Amphinomos, Antinous*

Sumer, 156

Sun, on Achilles's Shield, 48, 54, 66; agrarian rhythms and, 159; Apollo, god of, 45; cattle of, 56, 84, 98, 101, 109, 125, 131, 143, 144, 151, 180, 190, 194, 207; conjunction of with the moon, 17; foods cooked by, 83, 207; gold and, 15; Helen's name and, 64; Helios as god of, 88, 96, 101, 109, 144; Helios threatens to withhold rays of, 123; as Hyperion, 58; Knossos palace and orientation to, 166; land of the burning, 182; land of perpetual, 95; land of rising, 118; Lamos' lack of, 95; as masculine, 174; nymphs of, 172, 174; Odysseus as symbol of, 17, 178, 179; Island of, 88, 111, 119, 123, 166, 199; Minoan goddess of, 156; sacrifice to 112; Tartarus' lack of, 44; as rising, 109

Suns (Mesoamerican), 54

Syrie, 112-113

Tantalus, 99

Taplin, Oliver, 50, 66

Tartarus, 44

Telemachus; Athena and, 86, 88, 106, 110, 128, 146, 183, 184; childhood and adolescence of, 29, 107, 111, 183, 190; Eurykleia and, 168, 174; future marriage of, 123; herald and caretaker of, 193; hanging of servant women by, 107; Helen and, 86, 110, 119, 177, 181, 183; Ithaca, return to, 88, 106, 120; massacre of suitors and, 107, 116, 117; Menelaus and, 86, 110, 119, 123, 181, 183; Nestor and, 86, 118; Odysseus and, 88, 106, 114, 116, 124, 135, 177; Penelope and, 120, 177; sacrifice and, 118, 120, 159-161; suitors and, 86, 114, 177-178; townsfolk and, 89, 123-124

Telemachy 86, 160

Terror, Panic, and Strife, 42

Tezcatlipoca, 170

Thaki, 138

Themis (goddess), 36, 41, 79

Themis (divine order), 11, 36, 41, 55, 64, 120

Theogony, 25, 54, 80-81, 89, 172

Thera, 157, 191, 218, 221

Theseus, 56, 157 159, 176

Thessaly 139

Thetis, 29, 31, 47-48, 55, 66, 76, 79, 80, 98-99

Thrinakia, 98, 101, 119, 131, 144, 151

Thuban, 72

Tibet, 200

Tiresias, blood offering to, 102, 119, 142; cattle of the Sun warns against, 88, 98, 101, 131, 132, 135-136, 144; Circe directs Odysseus to, 87, 97; gold scepter of, 123; long, happy life prophesied by, 89, 125, 136, 153, 180, 188; interpretations of the prophecies of, 99, 137, 138, 145; Alex Jack and, 27, 197, 215; massacre of the suitors foreseen by, 131; oar mentioned by, 87, 89, 98, 100, 125, 128, 130, 131, 137, 138, 144, 145, 153, 188; Odysseus' visit to, 98, 99, 130, 137, 169, 182; peace with Poseidon advised by, 98, 125, 140; prophecies of, 131, 132, 152, 153, 180; safe return to Ithaca foreseen by, 87; use by of word for winnowing shovel, 143

Titans, 44, 45, 81, 83, 151, 159, 165

Titanesses, 172

Tityos, 99

Tjiwara, 214

Totem pole, 150

Transmutation, 24

Trees, 69

Tri Quang, Thich, 10-12, 196, 197

Triptolemus, 221

Trojan, children, 98; elders, 96; feasting, 75, 81; gates, 56; horses, 54, 58, 178, 182-183; music, 189; peace efforts, 161; plain, 59, 150; princes, 12, 58, 61, 76, 105; sacrifice, 74, 81; shepherds, 7, 180; shore, 66, 75, 126, 127; spy, 55; soldiers in Hades, 122; warriors, 32, 33, 57, 58, 60, 125; women, 47, 75, 77, 146

Trojan War, Achilles' Shield and, 54-55, 62, 150, 217; as an allegory, 61; bow's use during, 184; casualties in, 8, 29; end of, 20, 162, 177; Epic Cycle, 30-31; futility of, 29, 73; gods take sides during, 32-33, 40-41, 42, 54, 55, 57-58, 59, 80; historicity of, 30-31, 101, 148; hospitality violated during, 96; inlanders' unfamiliar with, 142; oars used during, 141; participants in, 28; prophecy concerning, 201; songs of, 86-87; start of, 17, 97, 161, 171, 215; survivors of, 53, 86. *See also Wooden Horse*

Troy, allies, 31, 32; as city of peace and war, 64; feminine culture of, 61-62, 161, 184-188; final assault on, 90; other names for, 31; Menelaus's sympathy with, 42; sack of, 66, 123, 146, 187; siege of, 31-32, 54; Silver Age and, 63; in Turkey, 161; wheat main food in, 68, 207

Tumult, 48, 54, 190

UN Declaration of Human Rights, 194
Unconscious, 45, 121, 149, 195
Underworld, 44, 62, 87, 97, 98-100, 111, 121, 153. See also Hades.
Unifying Principle, 97, 163, 191, 192
US Constitution, 194

Van Gogh, 222
Vedic India, 53, 72, 81
Vega, 72, 83, 179
Vega Cycle, 25-26, 51-52, 53, 60-65, 72-73, 178, 181, 187
Vegetables, 68, 83, 120, 159
Vegetarianism, 195
Vegetation diety, 170-171
Veil, 182
Verticality, 149-150, 187
Vietnam, 196
Virgil, 49, 99
Volcano, 157, 191, 218,

Wa, 148
Water, Achilles seizes Trojan princes in, 58; on Achilles' Shield, 48; Andromache's fetching of, 176; celestial, 180; Charybdis' maelstrom of, 132; clear, 119; in cooking, 199; crew stocks up on, 91; cup, 194-195, 215; dance of with fire, 66; daughters of Danaus leave their jugs of, 62; destruction by, 24, 62-66, 123, 181, 187; in a dream, 18; earth formed from 65; energy of, 65; as feminine symbol, 17; Hera's fight against, 59-60; Laistrygon girl's fetching of, 95; Minoans' indoor system of, 155; modern crisis of, 65, 219, 223; of mythic life, 16; nymphs of, 149, 172, 182; oars control flow of, 126, 127, 132, 136, 149, 150, 164; Scheria's piping of, 104; Poseidon's dominion over, 102, 161; prophecy regarding, 215; purification with after massacre, 124; River, personification of, 46, 66; sacrificial use of, 82, 118, 119; sailing on open, 102, 134; sailing on troubled, 26; springs on Ogygia, 163; storage of, 110, 126, 216; suitors' waste of, 110; Tantalus reaches for, 62, 99; Troy, rivers of, 59; Zeus, combines energy of, 66. *See Ocean, River, Sea*

Watson-Tara, Marlene, 222
Weapons, 52, 133, 147, 156
Weaving, 96, 104, 176-179
Weaving Maiden, 179
Westminster Abbey, 224
Wheat, 68, 110, 207
Wilderness, 52, 53, 61, 65, 72, 73
Williams, David "Bill," 218
Williams, David Rhys, 21
Wilson, Emily, 175
Wind, Hera's raising of, 59; Aeolus, god of, 87, 94, 130, 134, 137, 151; Agamemnon sacrifices daughter for favorable, 64, 83, 162, 171; Athena's influence over, 123, 128; bag of, 87, 94, 122-123, 130; Calypso's influence over, 164; favorable, 95, 126, 131, 160, 164; unfavorable, 95, 143, 144, 164, 171; four winds, 94; gods provision of, 127; on Mount Neion, 139; Odysseus's ship blown by, 87, 94, 99, 164, 167; Phaeacians' influence over, 133, 134; Poseidon's stirring up of, 102, 128; sailing and mastery of, 126, 130, 142, 149; smell of sacrifice to the gods wafted by, 81; symbol of for spirit and thought, 94; symbol of for karma, 95; West, 87, 94, 104; Zeus' influence over, 133, 164

Wine, Achaean use of, 75, 161, 194-195; on Achilles' Shield, 48, 55, 73; in the Aegean diet, 70, 84, 160; Agamemnon chastises excessive drinking of, 75; bowl, 123, 181, 194; in the Bronze Age, 120, 155, 199; Circe offers spiked, 96, 97, 111; cup, 116, 122, 165, 194; Cyclops gets drunk on, 93; Crew's imbibing of, 111; -dark sea, 90, 120, 155, 164, 173, 181, 219; Dionysus and, 189; Elpenor's indulgence of, 153; energetic effects of, 84, 145, 192; Eumaios' offer of, 113, 117; as a feminine food, 110, 174; on Hector's funeral pyre, 79; Helen's spiking of, 183; honey sweetened, 69; on the island of the Sun, 111; plundering of from Ismarus, 91, 111; Minoan trade in,

153; Nausicaa's offers of to Odysseus, 110, 112, 180; nectar compared to, 80; Odysseus's use of in moderation, 77, 87, 115, 117, 165; Odysseus as target of a pitcher of, 114; Phaeacians's offer of, 133; sacrificial use of, 69, 74, 75, 81, 118, 119, 120, 122, 129; use of in Sedar, 14; song and, 189; spilling of during massacre, 117; storage of, 110, 126; leading of to tall tales, 189; suitors' excessive drinking of, 110, 114, 116, 120; suitors offer of to Odysseus, 114, 117; Telemachus sets sail with, 110; Trojans' use of, 74, 75, 81; as yin to meat's yang, 84

Winnowing shovel, 131, 143-145, 147, 148-149

Woman/women, Achilles disguised as, 29; on Achilles's Shield, 49, 54-56, 191; Agamemnon's misogyny, 42, 168; animal sacrifice and, 119; Amazons, 159; Athenian, 217, 218; authorship of the *Odyssey* by, 173-175; in the Bronze Age, 168, 172; as casualties of war, 8, 50, 64, 91; as booty, 17, 146, 168; Calypso's lament for, 165; dancing of, 170; dream vs. man's, 165; Eurykleia's enslavement, 168; grinding of corn by, 104; Hector's misogyny, 168; House of Ladies on Akrotiri, 218; in the Iron Age, 71; Menelaus's misogyny, 168; Minoan, 156-158, 171, 215, 221; Odysseus and, 17, 91, 110, 124, 146, 168, 193; Phaeacian, 104; rituals of, 171; sacrifice and, 190; servants, 107, 117, 124, 151, 189, 193; Trojan, 17, 32, 47, 48, 54, 168; unique gifts and talents, 170; Zeus's rape, affairs, and seductions of, 44

Wooden Horse, 33, 87, 89, 141, 165, 169, 174, 184, 188

Works and Days, 25, 52

World tree, 165

Wrath, 7, 42-43, 77

Wycliffe Bible, 143

Xanthos (horse), 58
Xanthos (river), 46

Yahweh, 15, 44, 102, 221
Yin and yang; on Achilles' Shield, 191; in Chinese philosophy, 150; Circe and Odysseus, 97; Circe and Calypso, 163; as complementary opposites, 25; compass of, 201; double axe symbol of, 185; love and strife, 46; massacre of suitors and, 195; *metis* and *menis*, 90; in rowing, 150; in macrobiotics, 26, 201; in Ohsawa and Kushi, 97; in moly's root and flower, 192; Odysseus and, 146, 223; in peace and war, 45; Scylla and Charybdis, 169; in sound and music, 20; two tumblers on Scheria, 191; water jugs on Scheria, 180; qualities of Zeus, 90

Younger, John, 171
Yugas, 53

Zen, 220
Zephyr, 94
Zeus, Achilles disfavored by, 43; Achilles prays to, 43, 59, 127; Achilles laments mercilessness of, 45; aegis of, 58; Agamemnon questions, 36-37; Alcinous sacrifices to, 120; in assembly on Olympus, 45, 55; Ajax's death blamed on, 100; Apollo favored by, 58, 82; Ares disfavored by, 41; Athena, birth of, 89, 162, 221; Athena meets with, 86, 89, 117, 123, 124, 128, 194; Blessed Isles and, 71; Bronze Age presided over by, 84; Calypso ordered to free Odysseus by, 86, 101, 122, 128, 137, 164; and cosmic order, 45, 140; Cretan childhood of, 161, 162; Cronus tricked by, 44, 84, 161, 162; Cyclops' wrath toward, 92; Cyclopes give thunderbolt to, 161; diet of, 162; Delusion fathered by, 37. 41; dominion over world shared with brothers by, 44, 159, 161; double axe and, 156, 221; Dream sent by, 41; eagle sacred to, 83, 180; Europa raped by, 122, 172; fire and watery destruction meted out by, 123; Ganymede abducted by, 180; as heavenly ruler, 13, 44, 45; gods encouraged to take sides in war by, 45, 80; Hebe fathered by, 80; Hector admired by, 44; Helen fathered by, 31, 64; Hera bargains with, 44, 64; Hera hung upside down by, 162; Hera's seduction of, 41, 42, 69, 80, 148; Hera as wife of, 26; Hermes dispatched by, 86; Heroic Age and, 52; Hephasteus son of, 162; Iasion stricken down by, 148; Iron Age presided over by, 71, 84; Ithacan rancor ended by, 89, 194; judgment of Paris and, 31; level of consciousness of, 40; Leda seduced by, 64; Leto seduced by, 46, 61; as lord of bulls, 120-121; love affairs of, 162; marriage of Thetis and Peleus and, 30-31; *menis* of, 36, 43, 84, 90, 124, 194; *metis* and *menis* combined in, 90; Metis wife of, 89; Minos fathered by, 155; on mortals' failings, 45; Muses fathered by, 20, 188; Nike missiles named after, 9; nymphs, daughters of, 166; Ocean vis-

ited by, 79; Odysseus equal to in counsel, 138; Odysseus favored by, 66, 86, 122, 128; Odysseus's homecoming ordained by, 66, 88, 101; Odysseus disfavored by, 94, 119, 181; as patriarchal god, 159, 221; Odysseus's crew prays to, 92; Odysseus' praise of, 104, 120; Patroclus' body ordained to be returned by, 45; role of in the epic, 44; Poseidon in conflict with, 102, 140, 167; Polythemus' rejection of, 92; Priam's sacrifices to, 44; prisoners from Underworld released by, 161; Prometheus chained by, 81, 83, 99, 198; Rhea mother of, 161; sacrifice to, 118, 120, 160; sacrifice during Olympics to, 161; sacrificial smoke regales, 118; ship on Thrinakia smitten by, 112. 123, 125, 181; Silver Age presided over by, 52, 84; Sleep's beguilement of, 42; stone porticos of, 55, 58; storm sent by after raid on Ismarus, 91; strangers protected by, 92; Strife dispatched by, 42; Sun god complains to, 88; swallow- 88; swallowing of by Cronus, 162; Telemachus proposes sacrifice to, 120; tempest raised by after eating of the cattle, 88; temple of, 11, 216; Themis wife of, 41, 79; Thetis clasps knees of, 68, 79; thunderbolt wielded by, 57, 101, 107, 116, 123, 124, 133, 157, 101, 107, 116, 133, 164, 181, 188; Titans war with, 83; Trojan War, and origin of, 30; Trojan War survivors and, 53, 71; Trojans plotted against by, 75; will of, 164; women mistreated by, 30, 44, 162-164; Yahweh compared to, 102

Zinn, Howard, 12

Zodiac, Odysseus's 12 ships symbolic of, 17, 179; Heracles' 12 labors symbolic of, 180; Odysseus's encounter with 12 women symbolic of, 186; Odysseus' shooting of bow through 12 double axe heads symbolic of, 223; signs of, 17; 12 Trojan youths symbolic of, 65

Zumdick, Bettina, 213-216, 222, 223

Zumdick, Eva, 216, 222

Zumdick, Josef, 214

Zumdick, Lotte, 215, 216, 222, 223

About the Author

Alex Homer Jack is an author, teacher, and macrobiotic dietary counselor based in the Berkshires. He studied philosophy, religion, and the classics at Oberlin College, Benares Hindu University, and Boston University School of Theology. His mentors include philosopher philosopher Krishnamurti, Zen master Thich Tri Quang, educator Michio Kushi, mythologist Joseph Campbell, and nutritionist T. Colin Campbell.

Alex is founder and president of Planetary Health, Inc., a nonprofit educational organization that sponsors Amberwaves, the Macrobiotic Summer Conference, the Online Winter Macrobiotic Conference, and other activities. He served as a correspondent in Southeast Asia during the Vietnam War, editor-in-chief of *East West Journal*, director of the One Peaceful World Society, and executive director of Kushi Institute. He serves on the guest faculty of Rosas Contemporary Dance Company in Brussels, the Kushi Institute of Europe, and the Ohsawa Center in Tokyo. He has also presented at the Zen Temple in Beijing, the Cardiology Institute of St. Petersburg, and Shakespeare's New Globe Theatre in London. With Bettina Zumdick, he is the host of the *Miso Happy Show*, a monthly online learning and variety program.

With Michio Kushi, Alex co-authored *The Cancer-Prevention Diet* (St. Martin's, 3rd edition, 2010), *The Macrobiotic Path to Total Health* (Ballantine, 2002), *The Gospel of Peace: Jesus's Teachings of Eternal Truth* (Japan Publications, 1994), and *One Peaceful World* (2nd edition, Square One Publications, 2017). He also wrote the international bestselling *The Mozart Effect* for Don Campbell (Avon, 1997), *A Visit to the Land of the Gods* (One Peaceful World Press, 1999), and annotated editions of *Hamlet* (Amber Waves, 2005) and *As You Like It* (Amber Waves 2013). His most recent books are *The One Peaceful World Cookbook* with Sachi Kato (BenBella, 2017) and *Awned Is the New Organic* with Bettina Zumdick and Edward Esko (Amber Waves, 2018).